Soliloquy of a Farmer's Wife

The Diary of Annie Elliott Perrin

17 December 1917–31 December 1918

Edited by Dale B. J. Randall

OHIO UNIVERSITY PRESS

ATHENS

Ohio University Press, Athens, Ohio 45701
© 1999 by Dale B. J. Randall
Printed in the United States of America
All rights reserved

Ohio University Press books are printed on acid-free paper ∞™

03 02 01 00 99   5 4 3 2 1

Library of Congress Cataloging-in-Publication Data
Perrin, Annie Elliott, 1866–1938.
    Soliloquy of a farmer's wife : the diary of Annie Elliott Perrin
(17 December 1917–31 December 1918) / edited by Dale B. J. Randall.
        p. cm.
    ISBN 0-8214-1266-3 (cloth : alk. paper). —
ISBN 0-8214-1267-1 (paper : alk. paper)
    1. Perrin, Annie Elliott, 1866–1938—Diaries. 2. Farm life—Ohio—
Geneva Region. 3. Farmers' spouses—Ohio—Geneva Region—
Diaries. 4. Geneva Region (Ohio)—Social life and customs.
5. Geneva Region (Ohio)—Biography. 6. Pine Castle (Orlando,
Fla.)—Biography.
I. Randall, Dale B. J. II. Title.
F499.G44P47 1999
977.1'34—dc21
    [B]   98-49756

The Gospel says there is no us and them.
Science says there is no moral lesson.
The photo album says, who are these people?

Ellen Bryant Voight, *Kyrie* (1995)

She washed and baked
On the rainy day
To be ready to hoe
In the sun's bright ray.

"Soliloquy of a Farmer's Wife,"
Geneva Free Press-Times, 6 June 1918

From the outward world about us
    From the hurry and the din,
Oh, how little do we gather
    Of the other world within!

Alice Cary (1820–1871), "Secret Writing"

She hath done what she could.

Mark 14:8. Text of funeral sermon chosen for
herself by Harriet Stone, mother of E. C. Stone,
Geneva Free Press-Times, 16 October 1918

Contents

Illustrations

Frontispiece: Bert and Annie (Mr. and Mrs. B. H. Perrin) in their work clothes

1. *"Our Trip to Florida"*

2. From Early Spring to Early Summer

3. From Henry's Furlough to Harvest Time

4. *From First Frost to Year's End*

Postscript

Appendix A

Appendix B

Preface

> The diaries of American farm women are . . . usually . . .
> bare-bones records. . . . They deserve careful reading, be-
> cause they can tell us very much indeed about how people
> lived in earlier times. They give us a sense of seasons and
> how time was used. They tell us about a place. . . .
>
> Jane DuPree Begos, *A Women's Diaries Miscellany*

THE BARE-BONES DIARY of Annie Perrin records events
in the life of a Midwestern farm wife at the time of
World War I. Far from an effort to demonstrate any
ladylike accomplishment, and far from an attempt at
introspection, it scrappily records the events in Annie's
life—and events in the life of her family—as they scroll
by her, day by day.

The year and two weeks that Annie records are both
commonplace and extraordinary. They are commonplace in that most of the time Annie and her family
carry on all their long-familiar daily and seasonal work
in the fields, the orchards, and the house. And they are
extraordinary in that as the diary begins, the family is
leaving Geneva, Ohio, in order to search for a new home
in the countryside around Orlando, Florida. The trip is
potentially a major turning point in all of their lives.
After investigating and pondering for many weeks, however, they decide not to settle in Florida, and the diary

moves on to record the family's return home, their labors on the farm, their sending of a son to war, and the onslaught of the deadly Spanish flu pandemic.

Despite the momentousness of the times, both personal and national, the wonder is that Annie kept a diary at all. Hard-working, busy, and basically shy, and with no special sense of self-worth, she was not very likely ever to have thought of recording the events of her workaday life. Nevertheless, she received as a gift a little blank-paged diary book in which to write about the family's trip to Florida, and afterwards she continued to write in it until the end of the year. Then, having completed one final entry for the last day of December 1918, she seems never again to have kept any further record of her life.

Since Annie's diary-keeping began with her effort to write about "Our" trip, the question of the book's readership might at first appear to be partly answered. For a while in the beginning the diary seems somewhat akin to a shareable album of snapshots. Very quickly, however, its essentially private nature becomes clear. Annie's occasional reticences, her fleeting intimations, and her use of an occasional "+" to mark a day do, indeed, keep alive the ongoing possibility of readers besides herself. Even while they do so, however, they convey still more strongly a sense that these are private gestures within a private space. In the highly unlikely event that another member of the family ever took up the diary to read in it, about the worst her husband, Bert, would have found is that on such and such a day he was "peeved." Lettie, their daughter, Annie's closest confidante, would have found nothing worse than that she had been set down as "cross." Then again, neither Bert nor Lettie nor anyone else is likely to have picked up the book at all. The chances are good that the diary remained for the rest of her life a book with a readership of one. In fact, no one now can say for sure whether even Annie herself ever read straight through what she had written. That she never forgot it is nonetheless clear: at its back she kept (and kept updated) the addresses of her correspondents.

Though Annie sometimes wrote letters to relatives and friends, and though she had cordial relationships with a number of women on nearby farms, she would have been puzzled by the latter-day notion of a "support group." Her own closest affinities with other women were with her twin sister, Fannie (after the Perrins returned from Florida, their first visit was to Fannie and her husband), and with Lettie. In 1918 Lettie was in her seventh year of working as a teacher to make a life of her own, but at the same time she continued to be Annie's main helper at home.

Twenty years later, when Annie died, it was Lettie who inherited Annie's diary. At that point it became a family memento, something to dip into and then put away for safekeeping. Lettie did both of these things. Then sixteen years later, when she herself died, the book was passed down to her younger son, the editor of this volume. Caught up with building a family of my own and a career several hundred miles from Annie's Ohio,

I, too, put the diary in a safe place and did not take the time to read in it for nearly forty years. In short, the provenance of the eighty-year-old book on which this edition is based is clear and direct.

Despite the essential plainness of Annie's prose—bare-bones, indeed—it is also at the same time both elliptical and allusive. Annie's unexplained allusions are sufficiently numerous, in fact, to render the diary virtually incomprehensible to a casual reader—or, in fact, without considerable investigation, even to a trained historian. Hence the unusual fullness of documentation in this edition. Rather than pursuing a strategy of occasional supplementation (a relatively easy row to hoe), I have chosen to offer instead what is virtually a dual text or, better perhaps, a complementary pair of texts, each dependent on the other. Although a skeptical eye might view my explanatory notes as approaching the Scriblerian, the fact is that that same eye would soon find itself puzzled into hazy incomprehension without them. I have taken the title of this book from an anonymous poem written by an Ohio farm wife in 1918,[1] and I have done so in order to acknowledge that the originating and guiding element here is Annie's voice. Nevertheless (to indulge in a bit of academic jargon), the book as a whole is not univocal but antiphonal. The reason is that with my own responsive words I hope to make Annie's words as fully intelligible as possible, and perhaps in some instances supply a resonance such as they might have had for Annie herself.

Moreover, I make use of extensive footnotes in order

[1] See Appendix D.

to convey also a fuller sense of Annie's milieu, a sense of the farm where she lived and worked, of the nearby village, and—especially toward the end—of the war-obsessed and flu-afflicted larger world that enveloped her.

No matter how complete the annotations, of course, it is impossible to convey a complete sense of the past. One who has not drawn water from a kitchen pump can only imagine what that sensation might be like. One who has not tried to read or write by the light of a kerosene lamp will never know the nature of such an experience. As it turns out, I still have a reasonably clear recollection of the slight resistance and metallic sound of Annie's kitchen pump, and of the penetrating, sharp smell of her Rayo lamp—by the light of which one autumn I drew my diagrams for plane geometry. Fortunately, too, I can still call to mind parts of Annie's house, though I have not been in it for over half a century. At the time Annie wrote her diary, to be sure, I was not yet born, but for an otherwise puzzled reader, a reader who might question how I can possibly know this or that detail, the point may be worth making that I know many things about the Perrin family, their farm, and their village because as a child I often visited there. As a young man, in fact, I lived for a while in Geneva.

Some of my recollections of the old terrain were bound to prove useful for this project, but in order to attempt a reasonably serious edition of Annie's diary I have had to turn to a good many exterior sources, such as the U.S. census (for both Floridians and Ohioans), contemporary runs of the Geneva and Ashtabula news-papers, and a generous handful of family records. One gratifying discovery along the way has been that so many of the people named in the diary can still be identified. But a few have eluded me. Who, for instance, was May, the woman who telephoned Annie and then came to the farm to visit her one Thursday in July? Whoever she was, she has become, like Mrs. Fasler and Marvin, a salutary reminder that however hard one tries, one can never really recapture the past.

Identifiable or not, all of these people, these one-time warm living beings who have preceded us, are, when viewed by the world's usual yardsticks, profoundly unimportant. They published no novels, discovered no vaccines. Instead, they merely lived earlier-twentieth-century quotidian lives, and their human worth now lies in the eye of the beholder. That last fact is central to the purpose and significance of this book. The most widely known person encountered by Annie in 1918 was a clergyman she heard down in Florida: Dr. Kerr Boyce Tupper. Although Dr. Tupper was a scholar and a spellbinding preacher to thousands in his day, even he now survives only marginally in a few widely scat-tered documents.

This book is no lament for things lost, however, nor a sentimental remembrance of things past. On the con-trary, by means of an extended introduction, a post-script, and four appendices, I have attempted to "place" Annie's present. If a certain nostalgia creeps in here or there, I should think it most likely to be strongest among the illustrations. Nostalgia can be one of the most potent elements in photography's appeal. With its unequivocal recording of past times, photography is sometimes capable of arousing a fundamental sadness that things can never again be as they were. And true it is that no matter how lively these people look, almost all of them have now departed.

Though I cannot deny that the historical excavating necessary for this project has had a genealogical appeal for me, my enthusiasm for it comes in part from the fact that so many aspects of the research have been a pleasure. In pursuing Annie's family and friends, I have read that ninety-three tramps stole a train in San Bernardino, California, in 1914; that Jack London's widow wrote an Hawaiian opera; and that in Geauga County, Ohio, early in 1919, the former Miss Stocking sued her husband, Mr. Garter, for non-support.[2] I have learned that the hole in American macaroni was abolished for a while in order to save "cubic miles of room" on transport ships, and that in 1918 a spider living in Martins Ferry was found to have on its back a picture of the Kaiser.[3] Even more hapless than the spider, perhaps, were those worker bees conscripted by the Allies to carry secret military messages.[4]

Less risible but more thought-provoking is the information from 1914 that the U.S. Surgeon General was worried about pollution in the Great Lakes. And coming from 1915 is the sobering news that for the preced-

[2] *Geneva Free Press-Times [FPT]*, 16 November 1914, p. 4; 4 January 1918, p. 2; and 7 January 1919, p. 2.

[3] *FPT*, 22 November 1918, p. 4; and 14 November 1918, p. 2.

[4] *FPT*, 1 July 1918, p. 3.

ing three years the U.S. Department of Agriculture had been experimenting with reducing the amount of nicotine in tobacco.[5]

[5] *FPT*, 19 December 1914, p. 1; 10 September 1915, p. 4.

Still closer to the specific realities of the Perrin family are the countless references in the newspapers of the day to Geneva names that I heard spoken by my elders in my own early days. Unnamed in Annie's diary, to be sure, but in various ways and to varying degrees part of her world were such Genevans as Jimmy Simmons, Vern Atkins, Byron Sprague, Will Prentice, and Jimmy Zito, and the Burkholders, Woodworths, Shands, Kildays, and Cosgroves.

Toward the end of writing previous prefaces I have generally felt the need to admit a feeling of guilt. So it is again. In editing Annie's diary I have encountered errors in death certificates, census records, city directories, college certificates, newspaper accounts, and family papers. Still, I would feel remiss if I did not express regret here for my own errors of both commission and omission. I am mindful of Bret Harte, who was hugely successful in the 1870s for his writings about the Far West, but in later years lived in London long enough to think that the wild poppies of California were crimson. At this point I know not what my particular errors may be, but *mea culpa*. I am sorry.

Fortunately, as I commence putting the whole project to bed now, I have the compensatory pleasure of thanking those who have helped me. Most notable among these are Raymond and Eileen Perrin of Hendersonville, North Carolina, and Carol Jensen of Parma, Ohio.

Further specific and heartfelt thanks go to J. Samuel Hammond (Rare Book Librarian and Carillonneur at Duke University) for his efforts to produce an index that a variety of readers might find useful. Notably helpful, too, was Rima Selius of The Ashtabula County District Library, who parceled out to me some of the microfilm rolls of the *Geneva Free Press-Times* and the *Ashtabula Star and Beacon* (all of which were produced by The Ohio Historical Society). Also very helpful at different times and in different ways have been Jean B. Anderson, John O. Blackburn, Sean M. Breit, John Carlson, Timothy J. Floreth, Steve Follett, Edward W. Jensen, James L. Jensen, Jason S. Karam, Richard B. Keyse, Doris E. Weston, and (last but never least) Phyllis R. Randall.

In a more general sort of way, I would like to thank the helpful volunteers at The Family History Center in Chapel Hill, who have made available some of the resources of the Salt Lake Family History Library. Further multiple thanks go to the skillful and patient members of the Division of Audiovisual Education in the Duke University School of Medicine, where most of the photographs in this volume have been processed. As for librarians close to home, I am immeasurably indebted to the staffs of several of the libraries at Duke University —particularly those at the Reference, Interlibrary, Special Collections, Documents, and Newspapers and Microfilm desks in The William R. Perkins Library. Though they are too numerous to name individually here, they know who they are, and I would like them to know also that I count them as colleagues, co-conspirators, and friends. Finally, I would like to thank the Duke University Council on Research, whose grant in the spring of 1997 enabled me to include some additional illustrations.

Both now and throughout my time of working on this project I have had to face the realization that rescuing Annie's diary is a little like picking up and taking home a Lake Erie periwinkle or an iridescent purple shard of freshwater clamshell just a moment before the waves of that great lake draw it back into themselves to keep forever. The diary presented in this volume is both unique and representative, and it has come perilously close to disappearing from view. I would like to think, therefore, that enabling Annie Perrin to be heard here may in some degree occasion curiosity and interest in others like her and, at the same time, serve as a belated and partial kind of thanks for all her years of painful effort, fruitful work, and selfless love.

A Note on the Text

THE DIARY IN WHICH Annie Perrin made daily entries for some of December 1917 and all of 1918 is a small (3¾-by-4¾-inch), silver-colored, cloth-bound volume with gilt-edged pages (Fig. 1). Now faded and frail, with a binding that is frayed and loose, it bears the publisher's title "Lest We Forget" not only on its cover but also on every page inside that is labeled with a day of the year. Borrowed from the refrain of Rudyard Kipling's "Recessional," the words "Lest We Forget" are soberly apt for both a personal diary and the times in general.[1]

Lest the further potential of this made-to-be-filled volume be overlooked, the publisher has included some printing on the title page that identifies it also as "a Book for Ladies' use, in which to record Memoranda, Engagements, etc." On the verso of this same page, Annie's daughter Lettie has written "A Merry Xmas to Mother. From Lettie and Henry." And beneath this inscription Annie herself has written "Our Trip to Florida."

Three members of the Perrin family—Annie, her husband Bert, and their younger son, Raymond—departed from Ohio for Florida on 17 December 1917, so Annie actually began her record of their "Trip to

[1] Kipling's poem opens thus:
God of our fathers, known of old—
Lord of our far-flung battle line—
Beneath whose awful Hand we hold
Dominion over palm and pine—
Lord God of Hosts, be with us yet,
Lest we forget—lest we forget!

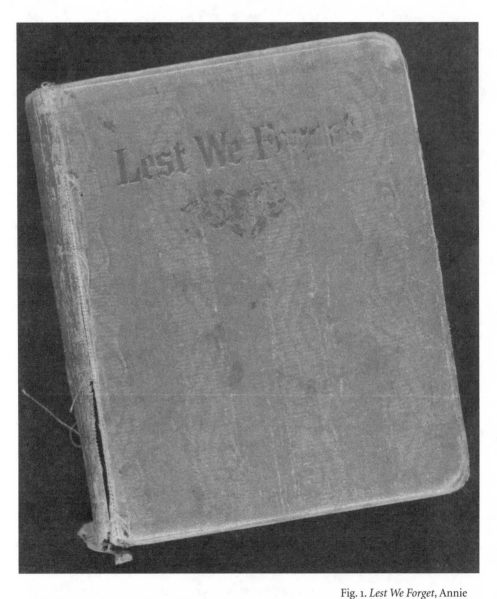

Fig. 1. *Lest We Forget*, Annie Perrin's diary, actual size.

Florida" in a back section of the book where the man-
ufacturer intended a lady to write her "Memoranda,"
"Church Notes," "Club Notes," "Dinners and Invitations," and "Record of Guests." Still farther toward the
back of the book are some pages variously labeled

"Physician's Services," "Inventory of Silver," "Inventory of China," "Inventory of Linen," and finally "Addresses." Here Annie has listed the names and addresses of a few of her relatives and friends.[2]

With the sole exception of this address list, and so far as Annie's sometimes faded penciling is discernible, all of her words are reproduced in this edition. All of her spellings are preserved, even though they sometimes vary from entry to entry. Preserved also are her inner-sentence capitalizations, whether or not they were ever significant even to Annie herself. The only regular exception to this policy is the normalization of Annie's use of interior "s's," which vary unsystematically between capital and lower case letters. Furthermore, whereas Annie often designates people by an initial (occasionally by two), their names are expanded here within brackets whenever such additions have not seemed overly conjectural. For easier reading, even Annie's most frequently used initials are expanded: "B" for both Bert and Bernice, "L" for Lettie, "R" for Raymond, and "V" for Vere. Furthermore, the occasional letters or words that have been editorially inserted in any entry for the sake of clarity are likewise made visually obvious by their enclosure within square brackets.

There also has been a more significant kind of change. In order to enhance the readability and hence the accessibility of the diary, the editor has occasionally formed sentences—always with Annie's own words— in passages where Annie herself has done little more

[2] Promising though such a list might seem at first, there is unfortunately little overlap between it and the names in the diary.

than jot a series of phrases. To suggest the nature of these changes, here is a randomly chosen entry just as Annie wrote it for 25 July 1918:

> *Still looking for rain. The boys are hoeing corn. Pa went to town for Flour. Lettie is ironing Laura working on the little dress. picked my first cucumber today.*
>
> *After dinner work was done up <u>we</u> <u>all</u> went up to Fannies had a very pleasant time stayed to supper had a cool ride home, stopped & got our pictures. they were all good.*[3]

[3] For the edited version, see the diary entry for 25 July.

Because Annie has used a pencil throughout and because she has made few erasures or cross-outs, the actual physical pages of her diary generally give the impression that she has worked rapidly. In fact, her text itself implies that while she has begun some entries in the morning, she has written others at the end of a busy day, with little time or energy left for jotting more than a few of her thoughts and feelings. An overall fringe benefit of her frequent haste and casualness is that the words of the diary seem close to Annie's speech. Along with some colloquial grammatical structures typical of many Americans of the day ("Done up the morning work," she writes on 3 February), she also includes unconsciously a rare hint or so of her English background. For example, she writes "Rained so we eat in Auto" (22 February) and "Done chores, eat & up about an hour" (5 May). In both of these instances, where most Americans would write "ate," Annie's "eat" stands for "et" (that is, "ĕt").

Also included in this edition are four appendices.

The first includes the only two pieces of Annie's correspondence that the editor knows to exist (one to her brother Gilbert's wife, Pearl, and a much shorter one to her mother, Louisa Parfitt Elliott), both dating from 1897. The second appendix consists of four letters written by Annie's older son, Henry, to his sister Lettie in 1918—the year of the diary. Whatever other kinds of insight they may provide, both of these first two appendices (and both in very different ways) confirm the central importance of the concept of family as it is revealed in Annie's diary. The third appendix is a partial family tree of the Elliotts and the Perrins, in effect a systematic ordering of some of the cast of characters in Annie's familial world. Finally, there is a fourth appendix consisting of an anonymous and decidedly homespun poem from the local village newspaper concerning what is, after all, the major subject of this book: the lot of a farm wife in 1918.

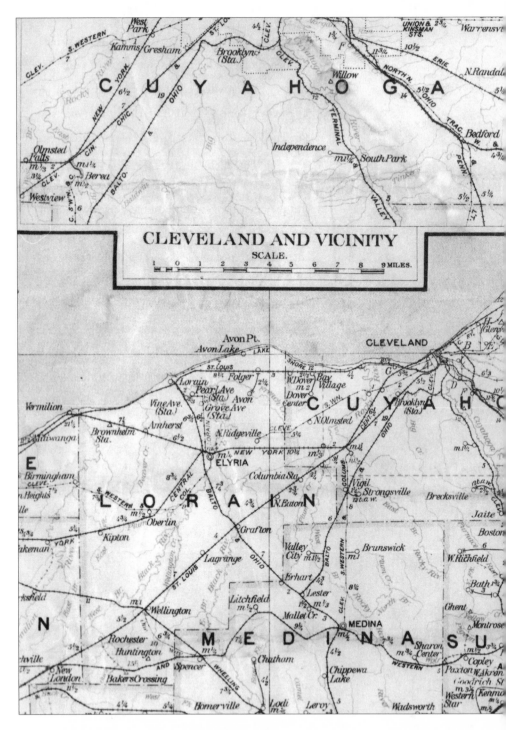

Detail of *Post Route Map of the State of Ohio . . . 1918*

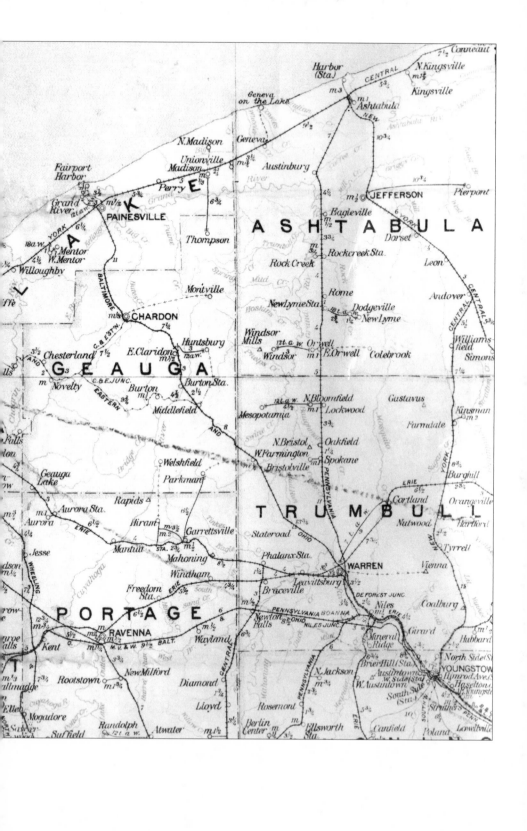

Introduction

IN MID-DECEMBER of 1917 Annie Elliott Perrin, an Ohio farm woman, received from her daughter, Lettie, and her older son, Henry, an early Christmas present—a diary in which to record the events of a trip she was about to take to Florida.[1] During the worst of the winter cold, Annie, her husband Bert, and their younger son, Raymond, were preparing for a significant and, as it turned out, a long-remembered leave from their labors at home on the outskirts of Geneva, a village in the northeastern-most county of the state (see map, p. xxxi).

Annie for years had worked hard to keep the family going. After finishing her daily chores (after she "Done up the work," as she put it), she generally turned to such other tasks as baking, washing, ironing, sewing, scrubbing, and churning. Often enough, too, she had to intersperse these chores with others such as setting a hen, fixing a fence, planting tomatoes, or sorting peaches.

After she arrived in far-off Florida, things changed drastically. She still had to cook and do a bit of cleaning, of course, but there were fewer people to "do" for, smaller quarters to care for, and no constant press of farm chores. As soon as they left home, in fact, life for all of the travelers was suddenly far different from any-

[1] Born Annie Luella Elliott on 21 February 1866, Annie married Bertrand Henry Perrin on 20 October 1887. For a comment on her English heritage, see pp. 7–15, and for her later years, see Postscript. Some basic background concerning Bert is given in notes 6 and 34. For a partial family tree of both Annie and Bert, see Appendix C.

1

thing any of them had ever experienced previously. For one thing, they had many new sights to see, and they took the time to see them—sights like the old fort in St. Augustine, the alligator farm on Anastasia Island, and the aviation field at Daytona.

They also spent a good deal of time viewing real estate. Clearly the Perrins were weighing the reasons both for and against buying property in the Deep South. "The . . . boys," Annie wrote on 28 December, "have gone for a walk to look at more land," and the next day all three of the Perrins "Walked about a mile to look at an orange grove."[2] Back home in Geneva the peach orchard was about played out. The previous winter had destroyed many peach trees in the area, and as early as August, about four months before they left, Ohio officials were estimating that the state's peach crop for the current year would be only about twenty-six percent of the normal yield.[3] A month or so earlier than that, in fact, the *Geneva Free Press-Times* ran a short front-page item headed "Peach Crop Not a 'Howling Success'" and noted specifically that "B. H. Perrin . . . will have scarcely none" (21 July 1917).

A month after this news appeared, the fabric of the family's lives was shaken even more badly: with potatoes to be dug and tomatoes to be picked, Raymond was totally incapacitated. As an item in the newspaper put it, "Raymond Perrin is critically ill with typhoid

[2] The evidence mounts: on 21 February the family "walked out to see vacant houses"—hardly a tourist activity. On 12 March Mrs. Newell hoped that Bert and Annie would buy an orange grove she owned. And so on.

[3] *FPT*, 13 August 1917, p. 3.

[4] *FPT*, 28 August 1917, p. 3.

fever."[4] His condition became so alarming, in fact, that he had to be signed into Ashtabula General Hospital.

Florida, meanwhile, was doing its chamber-of-commerce best to lure Northerners southward. A number of Genevans had already bought land there, drawn at least in part by pamphlets such as *A Happy Message to Northerners from the Land of Year-long Spring* (1918). On the title page of this particular publication a postman is pictured in the midst of a blizzard, gamely tucking Florida's *Message* into a rural free delivery mailbox. Inside the pamphlet, a northern farmer might read that in Florida "We have from three to four crops each year. We are near good markets. Our shipping facilities are good." Furthermore, "We do not use our time and energy to put away provisions for ourselves and farm animals, to last through the winter. We do not split wood or shovel snow. We find growing good big crops more profitable."[5]

[5] *Happy Message*, p. 3. One of the most lyrical statements on the subject was produced a few years later by L. M. Rhodes:

Florida is the playground of the western continent, the garden of the United States, where babbling brooks, rippling lakes, silver rivers and crystal seas blend in eternal melody with stately palms, gorgeous magnolias, flaming poinsettias and myriad song birds. . . . (p. 69)

Florida's various kinds of blandishment certainly did no harm. The population of Orange County—where the Perrins settled for a while—rose from 19,107 to 38,000 between 1910 and 1925, and, still more remarkably, the population of Orlando climbed from 3,900 to 22,000 (Dovell, pp. 92–93).

Still another factor playing its part in the Perrins' thinking was the death of Bert's father earlier this year.[6] Though he left no will, Henry Perrin had over the years risen from farm laborer to farm owner. In fact, he had become what one might call a man of property, and his numerous descendants now became various kinds of beneficiaries.[7] If ever Bert and Annie were to consider a major change of life, this winter was the time for it.

Fig. 2. In this picture from 1915, Henry Perrin (center) stands on the south side of the South Ridge road in front of the Perrin farmhouse. He is flanked by his two sons, Bertrand (with his tie tucked in) and Frederick. Clearly discernible a few feet behind the three is the roadside footpath that links farm to farm on the Ridge, and beyond the path are two of the large sugar maples that shade the front of the house.

[6] Henry Perrin (25 February 1834–19 March 1917) was the son of Thomas Perrin (d. ante 1851) and Mary Bowley Perrin (ca. 1816–ca. 1883) of Wiltshire, in the southwestern part of England. More specifically, the Perrins were from Malmesbury, on the northwestern edge of the shire. Their family church was the twelfth-century abbey church that survived from Malmesbury Abbey, and fortunately the local parish, thanks to a long-established tax for poor relief, was able to care for the local poor. In the census of 1841 Mary Perrin (age twenty-five) is listed as an agricultural laborer living in the Union Workhouse with Henry (then seven) and Sarah (three).

At the time Henry was growing up, boys were often "put out" to work at the age of seven or eight, and even those lucky enough not to have to go out until they were ten or twelve had to work during certain seasons— for example, during hay-making and potato-planting (*Reports of Special Assistant Poor Law Commissioners* [1843], pp. 29–30). In most agricultural parishes there were day-schools which were attended by a good many children of the laboring class, and sometimes the boys attended—always with time off for farm work— until they were twelve or so. At school they were taught the rudiments of reading, writing, and arithmetic. An observer of the time, however, writes that "Boys taken from school to be put out to farm-labour . . . cannot often write with sufficient ease for useful purposes" (*Reports*, p. 37).

In the census of 1851, when Henry was seventeen, he was listed as a "farm servant" attached to the household of David Godwin, a farmer in Crudwell, a village some four miles northeast of Malmesbury. (His mother was by this time earning her keep as a lace-maker.)

Formerly a major occupation in Malmesbury, lace-making in 1851 was maintaining only "a languid existence" [Crittall, pp. 180–81; Caird, p. 75]). Possibly Henry was one of the many boys who were apprenticed to a nearby farmer—in effect, taken off the hands of both family and parish —until the age of twenty-one. Whether or not he was apprenticed, however, northern Wiltshire was mainly a grazing district where the demand for farm laborers was not heavy, the land had to "bear the burden of a population not required for its cultivation" (Caird, p. 75), and the average wages were about 37 percent lower than in northern counties (Caird, "Outline Map" following title page).

Poor and apparently fatherless, in any case, Henry was twenty-one when he left for America in 1855. Like a good many other emigrants from Wiltshire (Gilmore, pp. 20, 27), including his future wife, he settled on the west side of Cleveland, Ohio.

Henry's wife (and Bert's mother) was Jane G[ertrude?] Perrin (14 July 1839/40[?]–29 July 1914). Jane was the daughter of John Ody (1796–ca. 1843–50), a laborer, and Anne Worville (or Warvill) Ody (ca. 1800–ca. 1882), who had been married on 23 August 1819. Anne Ody signed herself with an "X," and in the census for 1851 listed herself as having been born in the village of Lea. At that time she was a widow and living in nearby Malmesbury, where she, like Henry's mother, engaged in lace-making.

The marriage of Henry Perrin and Jane Ody took place on 27 November 1855—the year of Henry's arrival in America. He was twenty-one and she was about sixteen. Bert was the fourth of their seven children. (This note is based in part on miscellaneous letters and notes shared with the editor at various times by Carol Jensen and Eileen Perrin.)

Bert's seriousness about the possibility of leaving the farm is clearly discernible between the lines of a series of advertisements he placed in Geneva's *Free Press-Times* in the last half and especially in the final three months of 1917. No one of the ads tells the tale, but cumulatively they convey the impression of a man lightening his load. Bert put up for sale two double harnesses, an "eligible" seventeen-month-old Holstein bull, six ten-gallon milk cans, a pair of "kind and gentle" mules, quantities of fine white potatoes (not less than five bushels per buyer), ear corn, corn stalks, six tons of clover, a Tornado stalk shredder (with table and belt), ten tons of baled timothy, fifty crates of corn, fifty bushels of seed oats, twenty bushels of White Cap seed corn, and ten bushels of White Giant seed potatoes.[8] No other man or family in the township of Geneva set forth anywhere near so extensive and, it would appear, so telling a list of items for sale. And leave the Perrins did, on 17 December.

Apparently they had in mind a particular destination in Florida. Having traveled down by train from the North, they soon made their way to Pine Castle, a rural community about five miles south of Orlando. (The place had acquired its somewhat odd name back in the 1870s when an early settler built a striking house there with vertical pine siding and little wooden turrets made of pine.)[9] A good deal smaller even than the Perrins' own village back home, Pine Castle in 1918 had a population of about three hundred and fifty people—some of whom still maintained residences back north. Unincorporated and unequipped with electric lights or a water system, the area was at least in these ways not unlike the Ohio countryside that the Perrins knew best. However, Pine Castle also had its own post office (managed by the local grocer), a grade school, a couple of churches, and even a recreational park.[10]

Once they had established something of a base in Pine Castle, the Perrins found themselves not only welcoming their old friends the Seymours from Ashtabula County but also meeting a good many new people. Besides taking time to examine real estate, in other words, they had—and took advantage of—plenty of time for visiting. And still there was time to spare. Probably this was especially true for Annie. Without the demands of the farm, she eventually found that in Florida "The days seem 36^{hrs} long" (13 March). Nevertheless, the days were often enlivened with callers and pleasant automobile drives. Annie attended a party and musical program at the local parish, a good play at the grade school, and even a moonlight fishing expedition in a sailboat on nearby Lake Conway. Toward the end of March, when the Perrins finally left for home, some thirty new and old friends gathered to bid them goodbye.

Florida, it turned out, was not for them. Annie observed early in their stay that "we can look out of the windows here and see Oranges in all of the door yards. But I would rather be in Ohio" (26 December). By the middle of the next month she was writing that "every day makes one less to be here" (15 January). She was

[7] On 29 March 1917 the Probate Court of Cuyahoga County, Ohio, filed an "Application for Letters of Administration" which indicates that Henry died intestate. His son Frederick (usually "Fred"), who figures significantly in Annie's diary, is said to have been everyone's choice to serve as administrator of the estate. Fred himself, born after Bert (19 February 1870), died over ten years before him (2 May 1933).

[8] These items appear in advertisements of 2 August 1917, p. 2; 7 August, p. 2; 2 October, p. 4; 16 October, p. 2; 7 November, p. 4; 3 December, p. 2; 10 December, p. 4; and 13 December, p. 2. The ads are useful also for conveying a sense of the scale and nature of the Perrins' farming.

[9] Will Wallace Harvey (1832–1912), the builder, subsequently dated his writings from "Pine Castle" or "My Castle of Pines." Most of the structure burned in 1912 (Linton, pp. 12, 15).

[10] Orlando *Directory* for 1921, p. 302; 1922, p. 368; and 1923, foldout between pp. 358 and 359.

inclined to think that "the natives are rather distant" (28 January). She did not like the meat (9 February). And overall she concluded, "Guess I am a Northiner all right" (23 January). Furthermore, "I think Pa & R[aym]. wish they were at Geneva" (11 January). Though at the front of her diary she has written the title "Our Trip to Florida," and the purpose of the gift-book from Lettie and Henry was obviously to encourage her to record what promised to be the biggest adventure of her life, Annie, Bert, and Raymond were all back home in Ohio by 23 March.

Most of Annie's diary therefore proves to be the day-by-day record of a woman living on a farm about fifty miles east of Cleveland. The sixty-three acres of Perrin land lay a little over a mile southeast of the village of Geneva, and about five miles south of the gray and pebbly beaches of Lake Erie. Had Bert decided it would be advantageous for the family to leave this base for a new one in Florida, doubtless Annie would have returned to Geneva to pack. However, she had spent all of her life up to this time on an Ohio farm—in fact close to the beaches of Lake Erie—and northern Ohio would always be the place she knew and liked best.

About seventy years earlier Annie's father, William Elliott (16 December 1824–7 November 1897), arrived in northern Ohio from Batcombe, England, a considerable village tucked away in the rural southeastern part of Somersetshire. William's father, Jacob Elliott (1800–1862), was a farm laborer there, and his mother, Susanna Maidment Elliott (ca. 1802–after 1862), a tollgate keeper.[11] As one of seven children in the family of a farmer, William necessarily learned about farming. Moved to action by his ambition for a better life, however, he somehow managed to learn also about woodworking, and so came to be not only a fine carpenter and coffin-maker but also a contractor and builder.[12] Many years later Annie's twin, Fannie, would remember "the pretty little box he made for mother in which to keep her stationery, pen and ink and such things. It was inlaid with [mother-of-]pearl, lined with velvet, and was a very fine piece of work."[13] Some of the Elliotts, it turned out, had an artistic strain.

Like William himself, the young woman he married seems to have strived for a better way of life. A twenty-three-year-old redhead, Louisa Parfitt Elliott (5 May 1824–4 June 1900), who likewise was one of seven children, came from Westcombe, one of several hamlets contained within Batcombe.[14] Her father, James Parfitt (1775–7 December 1842), came originally from Bruton, some three miles to the south, and in his final twelve years was employed as head gardener for a wealthy Westcombe landowner, Thomas Henry Ernst (1774–1855). "Esquire Ernst," as he was called, was a Justice of the Peace in Westcombe, and the husband of Elizabeth Strachey Ernst, whose father had served as Archdeacon

[11] At the time of the 1851 census, Jacob and Susanna had separate households in Batcombe, she at the Toll Gate (with their children Louisa, John, and Eliza), and he at No. 19 Seat Hill (folio 170[b]). Because both were originally from East Knoyle in Wiltshire, it may be said that the parents of both Annie and Bert had Wiltshire roots.

[12] In the 1851 census his brother John, age eighteen, is listed as an apprentice to a carpenter (Batcombe, folio 170[b]).

[13] Fannie Elliott Keyse, "A Brief History," p. 1.

[14] Greenwood, pp. 10–11.

[15] *Burke's Genealogical and Heraldic History,* p. 705.

While still in his teens, Ernst had gone out to India with his best friend, (Sir) Henry Strachey, a cousin of his future wife. For the next twenty years or so he served as a civil servant in Bengal, where at first he was Head Assistant in the Office of Secretary to the Board of Revenue (1 May 1793). Later that same year (5 December) he became Commissioner of the Court of Requests, and thence he proceeded through a series of appointments, serving finally as Third Judge of the Provincial Court of Appeal at Benares (12 May 1809) and then at Patna (16 March 1811; Dodwell and Miles, pp. 166–67).

In his later thirties Ernst resigned from the civil service (19 December 1811), returned to England, and then did some traveling both within the country and on the Continent. In one of his several journals he recorded that while touring through Switzerland, he had had breakfast one morning with Madame de Staël and Schlegel—and thus heard them argue on "the grand question of peace or war" (Ernst, DD/SWD/4).

In 1817 the property at Westcombe came on the market, and in 1818 or 1819, shortly before his marriage to Elizabeth Strachey, Ernst purchased it. Originally consisting of only fifty acres, the estate grew to five hundred acres by 1842, and at the time of its sale in 1927 it sprawled over some eight hundred and twenty-one acres (Ernst, DD/SWD, introductory note, p. 1).

[16] Fannie Elliott Keyse, "A Brief History," p. 1. Fannie adds that Louisa's brother Henry was a bookkeeper, and her Uncle Joseph a lawyer.

[17] ALS, James J. Elliott to Dale Randall, 13 June 1948.

of Suffolk and Chaplain to George III.[15] It was in the garden of the Ernsts, therefore, a notable but not noble family, that Louisa as a girl first went to work with her father. Many years later she would recall that one of her tasks at Westcombe House had been to weed the violets and the pinks. Another was to train the rambling branches of the rosebushes on the gray stone garden walls.

When Louisa was fourteen, however, her mother— "whose family had more schooling than many of the middle class in those days"—told her she must learn about something besides "pulling weeds and growing posies."[16] Sporadic though her education had been until that point, she began to attend school regularly. Perhaps partly because of her father's post in the Ernst household, and certainly because of her own native ability, Louisa managed to acquire sufficient education to serve for a while as governess to the Ernsts' children, Henry and Harriet Ann. In later years she would be remembered by her own family not only with affection but also with admiration as a woman who "did some splendid original writing."[17]

From Westcombe and the Ernst estate Louisa moved on to teach school on the Channel island of Guernsey. She cannot have been there long, however, for when her widowed mother died in 1846, Louisa returned to Westcombe and moved into what had been her parents' little stone cottage. Four years earlier, when her father, age sixty-seven, had died of consumption, he was remembered by those who knew him as a man who had been "remarkable for strict, faithful discharge of all his duties." Never a man of means, at least he "left a bright example of Christian patience and contentment."[18] Now after the death of her mother, Louisa apparently remained in her parents' home until her marriage to William in Batcombe on 16 September 1847. William was twenty-two years and nine months old, and Louisa about seven and a half months older. Following a wedding breakfast of fried liver, the bridal couple is said to have taken a coach to William's home.

A year and a half later, on 28 March 1849, William left for America. He boarded the *Cosmo,* a three-masted sailing ship, in Bristol, and after a voyage of five weeks arrived in New York.[19] Probably having his destination in mind from the beginning, he immediately set out for the Western Reserve in Ohio, traveling partly by water and partly by stagecoach.[20] Only a week or so later he reached Cleveland, a city of about seventeen thousand, where the people were "all alive with business and confident of future greatness."[21]

The day after he arrived, William signed on as a carpenter with a man named Thomas Earle. In subsequent days he proceeded to work on a number of houses— four whole weeks, he reported, on a house for Mr. J. Bramley.[22] There is no way of knowing the extent of the savings William brought from England, but he had sufficient funds in July to look for a house. The one he

[18] Quoted from "To the Memory of James Parfitt," a roughly transcribed and unattributed scrap of photocopied typescript.

[19] Built at Bideford, Devonshire, in 1825, the *Cosmo* was owned mainly by William Cross, a Bristol merchant, and sailed with William Outerbridge as master. It was 113'9" long, 28'4½" wide (below deck), and had ornamental galleries on each side at the stern as well as a male bust as a finial on its stem-post. Noted as a swift vessel in earlier years, capable of making the Bristol–New York voyage in twenty-five days, the *Cosmo* was extensively damaged in a gale in the fall of 1843. After being virtually rebuilt, it continued to sail— and make Bristol–New York runs —until 1859 (Farr, *Records of Bristol Ships*, pp. 6, 116–18).

[20] Griffiths gives a detailed account of his own similar trip in *Two Years' Residence in the New Settlements of Ohio, . . . with Directions to Emigrants* (1835). Having sailed steerage class from Liverpool to New York, Griffiths bought a ticket on a "Steam-

Packet" going some hundred and fifty miles up "the noble Hudson" to Albany. In Albany he transferred to a canal boat and traveled mostly via the Erie Canal (and partly by stagecoach) to Buffalo, a trip of some three hundred and sixty miles. From there he traveled about a hundred and eighty miles more, completing the final leg of his journey on a Lake Erie steamboat to Cleveland (pp. 21–27).

21 Johnson, p. 77.

22 Though an unattributed but family-made transcription of a note by William from 1849 clearly gives this last name as "J. Bramley," one should also consider as possibly corrective the fact that a man named J. M. *Bradley* was serving that year as a trustee and officer of Dover Township (Ellis and Wobbecke, pt. 1, ch. 7, p. [3]). A photocopy of the transcription was kindly provided to the editor by Richard Keyse in a letter of 27 January 1997.

23 Dover Township is said to have been "America's second-largest grape-producing region in the late 19th century" (Van Tassel and Grabowski, p. 1081).

24 Previously the congregation had met in "barns and cabins and houses" (Ellis and Wobbecke, pt. 1, ch. 8, p. 2). William's church,

found and bought (from Mr. Benjamin Reed) was in the five-mile-square rural township called Dover (much later renamed Westlake), some twelve miles west of Cleveland's center and immediately south of Lake Erie. A small place, the house stood on the east side of Dover Center Road—which itself led straight north to the lake.

Now William could send for Louisa to join him. By this time she had borne their first child, Frank Riddle Elliott (6 November 1848), so in the fall of 1849 it was not one but two more Elliotts who set sail from Bristol for New York. This second voyage took seven weeks, and Louisa would later recall that "the last two seemed as long as the first five." Once landed, she and her infant —not yet a year old—headed westward. Their trip to Cleveland took twice as long as William's had, and adding to the stress of the journey itself there was a good deal of trouble with the baggage: through some mistake, Louisa's belongings were sent to Milwaukee, so William had to go fetch them.

William had previously made sure, of course, that the area around Dover was good for farming, and the Elliotts, despite a difficult beginning, soon became a farm family.[23] William was never merely a farmer, however. He had his skills as a carpenter to draw on, and in time he became a contractor and builder. In the summer of 1853, it was he who built the Dover Methodist Episcopal Church on Center Ridge Road (Fig. 3).[24] Both he and Louisa would become lifelong members of

Fig. 3. Annie as a girl attended the Dover Methodist Episcopal Church, seen at the distant left here in an early photograph taken from the corner of Center Ridge Road and Dover Road. The large building just right of center is the Phillips Hotel (once a stage stop), and the awning-shaded building at the far right is Dover's general store. (From Robishaw, Fig. 1, courtesy of The Westlake Historical Society.)

constructed of timber from the nearby forests, its boards hewed and planed by hand, still stands (Robishaw, p. 359, and Coe, n.p.). In fact, it continued in use as a church as late as 28 October 1956, after which time it became an Odd Fellows lodge.

its congregation, and all the Elliott children would be reared there.

Being a great reader of the Bible as well as a craftsman, William built for himself a little stand so the Good Book might always lie open on the family's kitchen table. Louisa, too, had a special interest in the Bible—in fact, taught a Bible class in Sunday School for many years. As Fannie recalled, she "was in her element when she could teach or pray in public."

After the birth of Frank, William and Louisa had nine more children, of whom Annie and Fannie were the seventh and eighth (see Figs. 4 and 5). An incompletely informed posterity will be left to wonder what the Elliotts' friend "Mrs. Martin" may have meant when she said she hoped that by the time she came again, the little pair "wuld be dade and burried."[25] Perhaps it is enough to know that twins are generally much more likely to be underweight and premature than are children born singly, and that with or without the good wishes of neighbors, rates of early deaths for them tend to be high.[26]

[25] Fannie Elliott Keyse, "Brief History," p. 2.

[26] In keeping with numerous other writers, Peter Mittler observes that twins' "embryonic and foetal development is fraught with considerable risks, some of them of a general nature . . . [and] others specific to twin pregnancy, such as foetal crowding, or unequal distribution of blood supply due to the 'placental transfusion syndrome'" (p. 38). Peter Watson summarizes: "Life, for both identical and fraternal twins, is more complicated than for singletons. . . . More than half the twins born in the United States weigh less than 5½ lb at birth and are classified as premature" (p. 78).
Magnifying the fact that, as Ainslie puts it, "twinship must be considered an at-risk developmental situation" are the mother's difficulties in simultaneously caring for two infants. Mothers of twins typically feel overwhelmed and exhausted (pp. 163–64). Furthermore, their problems are often exacerbated because, as in the case of Annie and Fannie, twins "tend to be born to older mothers, who may already have a large family, making it more difficult for her to spend as much time with them" (Mittler, p. 37).

Fig. 4. In what appears to be the earliest surviving picture of the "dear little twins," a formal portrait made by J. F. Ryder (of 171 and 173 Superior Street in Cleveland), Annie and Fannie look out on the world with a wariness that is, after all, reasonable enough.

Fig. 5. Annie *(back row, left)* and Fannie *(back row, second from right)*. Both members of the church their father built, the twins pose here with other girls of their Sunday School class. For an occasion such as this, both have donned big hair ribbons and brought their long ringlets forward over their left shoulders. Though at first glance Annie might seem to place one hand rather pertly on her hip, more probably she is simply leaning slightly on an upper knob of the chair's back.

At long last, when Walter, the tenth and last child, arrived in 1868—twenty years after Frank—Louisa was forty-four years old. In a picture of her from about that time, she wears a trim, practical, and unpretentious dress, and has pulled her wavy hair back taut, the way William is said to have liked it. All in all, and even granting the customary constraints of nineteenth-century photography, she appears warily self-controlled, a woman of strength, but a woman whose life has not been easy.[27]

[27] Much of the information in this section derives from Doris Weston (ALS to Eileen Perrin, 10 February 1974; and ALS to the editor, 24 February 1997), Eileen Perrin (miscellaneous notes), and Richard Keyse (ALS, 27 January 1997).

Fig. 6. Louisa Parfitt Elliott, mother of Annie Elliott Perrin. Her unassuming dress, severe hairstyle, and serious expression serve to mute Louisa's femininity as well as to suggest her strength of character.

Fig. 7. Like her mother, Annie generally had both an air of seriousness and a down-to-earth quality. This picture from about 1915 captures also the nurturing strain in her nature. Though she was not especially devoted to cats (which are generally just useful mousers in the barn), she has gathered these two in her arms and holds them kindly and comfortably.

Annie's unpretentiousness was perhaps even more pronounced than that of her mother (Fig. 7). In the scattered snapshots of her that survive from about 1918—when she turned fifty-two—she appears to be a pleasant, hard-working, heavy-set, and decidedly matronly woman. However, she was also rather small-boned and not especially strong. Her finespun and totally white hair, her delicate skin, and her hesitant smile somehow suggested that there was something not merely sensitive but also fragile about her. Like many another twin, she probably had a somewhat fragile sense of herself.[28]

Had Annie's children not given her a diary to fill, it is unlikely she would have attempted to record her daily doings in 1918 or any other year. The family's trip to Florida was obviously major, however, and whatever else it did or did not achieve, it took her farther from home than she would ever go again. Probably she accepted the chore of recording the family's adventures with a feeling of alert and quickened interest. It is harder to say why, though, busy as she was, she continued the diary for nine more months after the family had returned home and the realities of the farm had again become pressing. Possibly she wrote on all of the remaining blank pages partly out of a sense of duty to the gift-givers—they had spent money for the book—and partly out of a sense that one really should carry through the things that one sets out to do. In any case, Annie filled its pages faithfully and never forgot it afterward. As late as 1938, the final year of her life, she took it up to

[28] As Ainslie writes, "The idea that twins encounter undue difficulties in identity formation is pervasive" (p. 52). While the presence of a twin helps to dilute "anxieties inherent in early development" and binds the twins psychologically, "the consolidation of a cohesive sense of [individual] identity is made more difficult by the context of twinship" (pp. 73, 79).

Annie and Fannie, having been given rhyming names and dressed alike as children, almost certainly constituted in their earlier years a human entity that could not be carried forward into adulthood. Among other writers who comment on such matters, Hagedorn and Kizziar report that some twins who have been "reared very closely expressed underlying feelings of 'being somehow incomplete' without their twins" (p. 121).

make one final entry at the back, where she kept her list of addresses.[29]

Inevitably, Annie's diary entries are brief and fragmentary. For one thing, the book in which she wrote is very small (see Figs. 1 and 36). For another, though sometimes she made entries early in the day and sometimes at midday, she often made them when she was nearly exhausted from a day of hard work. Certainly she was capable of writing more neatly, even more accurately,[30] but here within this private space she simply tried to set down quickly and plainly a few of the facts and recordable feelings that came to her mind on any

[29] Annie's last dateable entry, made with a shaky hand, records the address of the new home to which her daughter Lettie and her family moved in the spring of 1938.

[30] A transcript of her more careful but still informal writing, a letter to her sister-in-law Pearl, is included here as Appendix A.

Fig. 8. Here, from about the turn of the century, is Dover Center South, one of the several schools in Dover Township. Behind the flagpole at the top of the picture is the belfry, accessible only by a ladder from the second story; on one occasion some of the boys are said to have pushed and pulled a goat up here (Weston, p. 11). To the left is the woodshed, and at the bottom, running off to the right, a bit of the long flagstone path leading from the double front doors. All of Annie's formal education took place here in the 1870s and early 1880s. (From Hadsell and Rutherford, Fig. 268, courtesy of Pearl Malle Gollin.)

given day. Though punctuation was something she neither knew nor cared about, she had many long years
ago learned to read and write well enough for her needs
when she attended Dover Center South, one of the local
ungraded schools back in Dover (see Fig. 8).[31] Clearly
her parents were not unmindful of learning. Louisa had
been a governess, after all, and William, though a carpenter and farmer, is said to have deeded part of his farm
to Dover Township in order that his younger children
might attend school.[32] At that time, however, schooling
there extended only through the eighth grade.[33] A lucky
handful of neighbor children were able to leave home
and continue their studies elsewhere, but the first class
to graduate from Dover High School was that of 1901.[34]

At any rate, Annie's brief and totally unpretentious
words convey a great deal not only about herself but
also about the personalities and interrelationships of
the various members of the Perrin family. Having married when she was twenty-one and Bert was twenty
(Figs. 9 and 10), Annie had been a wife for some thirty-
one years at the time of her diary, and naturally Bert
plays a major role in it.[35] Taking major parts also are
her daughter and oldest surviving child, Lettie Jane, age
twenty-six; her oldest surviving son, Henry Bertrand,
twenty-four; and Raymond Austin, the last of the children, twenty-two.[36]

When it came to the farmwork recorded in the diary,
Raymond (or Raym, as his mother calls him) did most.
Several years earlier, after completing the eighth grade,
he dropped out of school in order to keep the farm

[31] The Dover schools remained ungraded until 1896 or
1897 (Weston, p. 18).

[32] Noted in the reminiscences
of Glenn A. Tanner in Robishaw,
p. 334.

[33] Despite the early cutoff, at
least one of Annie's schoolmates
became famous. Jack Miner
(1865–1944), who later referred to
what he termed his A-B-C education (*Jack Miner and the Birds*,
Introd., n.p.), took a particular
shine to Fannie—and she to
him. When he was stumped by a
question, Fannie would sometimes hold up her slate so he
could see the answer on it (recollected by June Haskin, 18 October
1997). Thanks to Miner's kindly
observations much later in
life, the name of the children's
teacher, Miss Minnie Chubb,
is also preserved in print (Coe,
p. 11).
  Like Annie and Fannie, Jack
was the child of first-generation
English parents. While he was
still a boy, however, the Miners
moved to Canada, where Jack
later established a bird sanctuary
at Kingsville, Ontario (1904), and
eventually won worldwide recognition as a naturalist, conserva-
tionist, and author (Wallace,
p. 580).
  The opening chapter of his
autobiography is called "Sweet
Childhood Days in Ohio" (*Jack
Miner: His Life and Religion*, pp.
1–12). Among other things, he
would long recall how in Dover
in the early 1870s the passenger
pigeons—extinct in 1914—used

to migrate over the countryside in "countless numbers, I might say in clouds" (*Jack Miner and the Birds*, p. 170).

[34] Hadsell and Rutherford, p. 100; Robishaw, p. 329.

[35] Bert—that is, Bertrand Henry Perrin—was born a little more than a year after Annie, on 10 September 1867, apparently in Brooklyn, west of Cleveland. Married in 1887, the couple celebrated their fiftieth wedding anniversary in 1937.

On 19 August 1939, somewhat less than a year after Annie's death, Bert married Agnes Mumaw, a local woman some twenty-eight years younger than he. Agnes proved to be more a chauffeur and nurse than a wife —or even a housekeeper. For one short but memorable period she kept a bushel basket of piglets in a corner of the dining room.

When Bert died on 24 July 1944, at the age of seventy-seven, Agnes inherited his Packard sedan and a third of his holdings aside from real estate (the farm had been Raym's for a number of years). After briefly protesting the amount allotted for her first year of support, she vanished from the scene (Bertrand H. Perrin, "Last Will and Testament," 16 September 1942, and No. 26298, Probate Court, Ashtabula County: "Exceptions by the Widow to the Inventory," 13 October 1944, and "Exceptions Overruled," 20 March 1945).

[36] See Fig. 11. Lettie lived to be sixty-two (26 May 1892–20 September 1954); Henry to seventy (28 June 1894–7 February 1964); and Raymond to seventy-one (19 March 1896–8 June 1967).

Fig. 9. A recently married young woman, wide-eyed and somber, Annie here rests her left hand lightly on a davenport arm—thus unobtrusively displaying her wedding ring. In the late 1880s she was still young enough to let some of her fair hair fall down her back, but before long she wound it all on the top of her head.

Fig. 10. Bertrand Henry Perrin as a young man. Though this photograph is undated, it probably was taken about the same time as that of Annie in Fig. 9.

Fig. 11. Here, wearing their Sunday best and grouped at the back of the Perrin house in the clear, cool air of 21 March 1920, are *(left to right)* Henry, Lettie, and Raymond. On this particular weekend Lettie has returned home from Warren to tell Roy Andrews—off-camera but very much present—that from now on the two of them are to be no more than friends.

going. In other words, Raym proceeded into adulthood with about the same amount of education that Annie had had. In 1918, no matter how he may have viewed this earlier educational sacrifice, he was acutely aware that other men his age were going to war. With a few exceptions, in fact, every man born between 6 June 1896 and 5 June 1897 was supposed to register for the draft on Wednesday, 5 June 1918.[37] Everyone realized, nevertheless, that farmwork was essential to the nation, and despite an ominous and persistent pain in his side (before many months passed he had to have an appendectomy), Raym continued to farm. A bright, strong, curly-headed young man, stubborn yet good-natured, sometimes stern-faced but also quick to grin, he is in the diary forever "fitting out" the ground, dragging, plowing, hoeing, and doing anything and everything else that needs to be done on the farm. Built into his character, furthermore, for better or worse, was a drive to do everything as well as possible.

37 *Ashtabula Star and Beacon* [*S&B*], 29 May 1918, p. 2.

As the old proverb has it, though, "Fruit ripens not well in the shade." The fact is that Raym felt a nagging urge to be his own man, to cut loose from the demands of both his father and the farm. Hence the trips he took to find work down in Warren and Akron. The results of these forays are a little unclear within the confines of his mother's diary, but soon afterwards he did, indeed, escape to a job at The Firestone Tire and Rubber Company in Akron. Then before long, at the urging of his parents, he returned to Geneva. A hard-working, thoughtful, practical, earnest young man with a look-you-straight-in-the-eye kind of integrity, Raym settled down to farming there for about twenty-five more years.

Henry, at the time Annie wrote, had been gone from the farm for about four years. Doubtless a few Genevans would have remembered him as the bright-eyed twenty-year-old who recited "Jim Bludsoe" with comic fervor at the North Star Grange.[38] However, the first of what would finally prove to be a lifelong series of jobs took him to Collinwood in Cleveland, where he worked as a shipping clerk for the New York Central Railroad storehouse. More recently, for about the last two years and continuing into the early months of Annie's diary, he had been working at Firestone and living in Akron at 101 Archwood Avenue. He had also signed on with the local Naval Reserve Corps there, and thus committed himself to drilling on Monday and Wednesday evenings and Sunday afternoons.[39] Quite soon afterward, moreover, and without the slightest sign of regret, he would travel still much farther from home and begin training at the Great Lakes Naval Training Station in Illinois. Life at Great Lakes turned out to be both tough and exhilarating. As the local newspaper had it, "Each day bugles are blowing, awkward squads drilling, patriotic pulses beating and the air is filled with the thrill of preparation for war."[40] It was one of the best times of his life.

No longer living at home during the period of Annie's diary, Henry figures in it mainly as the writer of frequent letters and postcards from various camps,

[38] *FPT*, 18 February 1914, p. 2. John Hay's poem tells of a steamboat engineer ("He warn't no saint") who saves the passengers of the *Prairie Belle* but goes down with his ship (Rice, *Poems of Worth*, pp. 80–81).

[39] ALS, Henry to Lettie, 1 April 1918.

[40] *FPT*, 19 April 1917, p. 1.

and as the delighted recipient of boxes (cookies, apples, a sweater) from home. At Great Lakes, his alert intelligence, personal responsiveness, and somewhat thin-faced good looks, together at this stage with a sort of country-boy eagerness and naiveté, were not only quickly winning him friends in the service but also catching the eye of officers who thought him promising.[41] When Henry returned to Geneva for a summer furlough, the official justification was that he was needed to help out with the farmwork at home—and he did, indeed, pitch in. Like Lettie, nevertheless, Henry had aspirations that had little to do with farming.

Lettie herself had long since taken steps to protect herself from falling into a life as difficult as her mother's.[42] To the end of her days she recalled growing dizzy while weeding onions at the age of six. Though at the time of Annie's diary she continued to help at home as much as possible, Lettie had been teaching school since 1911. After graduating from Geneva High School in 1909, she took summer courses at Kent State Normal School (1914) and the College of Wooster (1916), and in an effort to create a career for herself, she even joined the Northeastern Ohio Teachers Association. Having begun to teach in a one-room schoolhouse in Thompson, about seventeen miles south and west of Geneva, she at first progressed merely to a one-room schoolhouse closer to home. Up on the Padanarum Road in the rural, northwestern outskirts of Geneva, she was more or less within walking distance of the farm. In fact, one day when she failed to make it to school was actually news-

[41] In an undated letter to Lettie sent some time in April 1918, he writes: "Yesterday P.M. an officer came to see me. I believe I told you about taking the Psychiatric Test. Well there were 6 from our Co. that stood a high percentage & I was one out of the 150. He wanted to know if I would accept a transfer to the Public Work Stores Dept."

[42] When Lettie Jane was a child, her father called her "Sunshine Jane" (the name "Jane" coming from Bert's mother, Jane Ody Perrin), and Henry in his letters of 1918 tends to call her "Sis" and occasionally "Tish," as if her given name were "Letitia." To Annie, however, who named her daughter after one of her older sisters, she was invariably "Lettie."

worthy: on 2 March 1914 the *Geneva Free Press-Times* ran a little second-page item noting that "School was not held today in the Padanarum district" because "Miss Lettie Perrin . . . was unable to reach the school-house on account of the drifted snow in the roads."[43] In the summer of 1915, however, another brief item in the paper announced that "Miss Lettie Perrin, who has very efficiently taught in this school for the past three years has accepted a position in the grammar grades of North Geneva."[44] At the three-room centralized school on the lake road near Maple Avenue she was not only closer to the farm but also sharing the building with the young

[43] Though the newspaper does not note the fact, the weather that kept Lettie from coming to work was so severe that Raym could not take her even by cutter (see Fig. 12).

[44] *FPT*, 20 July 1915, p. 3.

Fig. 12. Early on a winter morning, Raym pauses at the head of the Perrin drive with a harnessed horse and cutter (or sleigh). To the left is the front of the farmhouse. At the center and running diagonally off to the right is the snow-covered South Ridge road. To the right also and a little downhill, a few bare branches of some orchard trees rise above the level of the road.

woman—Vere Smith—who eventually would become her best friend. Clearly the two worked well together. No other teachers in town received public praise that year, as Lettie and Vere did, for their students' "excellent Christmas program."[45]

[45] *FPT*, 24 December 1915, p. 2; 28 December, p. 3.

At the time of Annie's diary Lettie had moved yet again, this time to Geneva's so-called graded school building. Here she was in charge of the sixth grade.[46] In the spring of 1919, though, immediately after the close of the diary, she was in charge simultaneously not only of part of the sixth grade but also of the eighth—which assignment probably figured in her decision to leave Geneva and begin teaching elsewhere in the fall of 1919.[47]

[46] Information such as this is for the most part impossibly scattered, but the *Free Press-Times* of 21 August 1918 gives both Lettie's name and position and also those of her fellow teachers (p. 1).

A variety of supplemental personal details about growing up and going to grade school in Geneva in these earlier years of the century may be found in Sutliff's *The Loveliness of Love* (1995).

[47] *FPT*, 12 May 1919, p. 1.

Wherever Lettie had been teaching thus far, her life had been split between school and farm. And not without considerable strain. In 1918 Henry wrote to say "You ought not to work so hard. Some day you may see your mistake" (21 April). Annie made frequent tell-tale notes in her diary such as "Lettie was all in tonight" (24 April). Sometimes she was "cross."

The fact is that Lettie not only worked hard to make life on the farm—especially Annie's life—easier, but all the while she yearned for a life for herself that had room for plays and picture shows, music and books. She had long been an avid reader. One of her earliest memories was of lying under a big shade tree on a grassy hillside and reading fairytales. And another related memory was of her Grandmother Perrin, who found her there one day and went grumbling to others about the child reading "of all them demmed books."[48] Adept with language and a born mimic, Lettie in 1914 recited "Aunt Dinah on Matrimony" so well that those assembled at the meeting of the North Star Grange demanded an encore —which she was able to provide.[49]

In January of 1917, at the relatively ripe age of twenty-four, she ventured to join the Park Street Church of Christ down in the village. Whatever else such a move might suggest, it demonstrated fortitude: since the church had no baptistry at the time, the newly baptized were all plunged into icy water outdoors—some in Grand River, some in Lake Erie.[50] Never with much cash at her disposal, Lettie demonstrated a similar strength of purpose and sense of daring in 1918 when at one point she worked hard to turn an old brown overcoat into a wearable dress and at another she splurged on a handsome hat.

Bert (sometimes called "Pa" in the diary) was a solidly built, outgoing, likeable man's man. At fifty-one, his hair was thinning and his waist expanding, but when occasion demanded he could still muster up a good deal of physical strength. During his earlier years in Cleveland he had worked as a guard in an asylum, as a mover (with his lifelong friend Will Harvey), and as a butcher (in his father's grocery store).[51] Just how a young city man had come to be a farmer is a little difficult to explain, but his own earliest years were spent in rural surroundings, and his father before him came from a farming background in England. Indeed, it was Bert's father who in 1904 bought the Geneva farm. And it was

[48] These recollections slightly antedate the Perrins' move to the farm. When the family first settled in the countryside near Geneva, they lived for a time at Eagle Hill, South Ridge west.

To recognize that family attitudes may have been complicated, one should note also that Lettie's Grandfather Perrin served for a while on the Board of Education for Brooklyn Township, west and south of Cleveland (Johnson, p. 421).

[49] *FPT*, 18 February, p. 2. Other items in Lettie's repertoire included James Whitcomb Riley's "The Raggedy Man" and "Little Orphant Annie" (Rice, pp. 178–79,180–81). Besides her natural flair for such things, she had, in keeping with the taste of the times, studied dramatic reading at Wooster. In her copy of Eaton's *Dramatic Studies from the Bible* she wrote neat notes on such subjects as Queen Esther pleading for her people and Moses' farewell.

[50] Many documents of the church were destroyed in a fire of 1926, but Dr. Larry Wade, the pastor of the church (now known as Park Street Christian Church), has kindly retrieved and conveyed the preceding facts from the surviving membership rolls (21 October 1997).

Situated at the corner of Park and Eagle Streets, and by denomination belonging to The Disciples of Christ, the church was thriving in 1917–18 under the Reverend W. A. Myers. Among the numerous people Lettie knew there were her cousin Allen Foster and his wife, Nina (see the extended notation for Annie's diary entry of 19 May).

[51] Bert's father is classified in the U.S. census of 1900 as a grocer, his son Fred as a grocer's salesman, and Bert himself as a clerk. Annie, Bert, and their children were then living at 221 Birch Street. During this Cleveland period they also lived for a while at 220 Vanek. An old family story relates how little Henry (age five

in 1899) broke some eggs in the store, thereby covering himself with messy evidence but assuring his parents solemnly (his tone of voice was long imitated), "*Lettie did it.*"

[52] *Ashtabula County Records,* vol. 172, p. 303 (9 May 1904), and vol. 296, p. 350 (13 July 1910).

Possibly pertinent also is the fact that there had been other Perrins living in the area at least since 1804, when John Perrin(e?), a native of New York, emigrated and settled on land near Saybrook. A farmer who worked and served as both a surveyor and a local magistrate, he lived only a short distance east of what would become Bert's and Annie's farm (Large, 1:158, 168). In fact, a William Perrin was a trustee of nearby Conneaut Township in 1807, and when Ashtabula County was formed on 22 January 1811, he was selected to serve as one of its first grand jurors (Williams, pp. 161, 148).

[53] When Geneva was incorporated in 1866—the year Annie was born—some of its houses were already about sixty years old.

from his parents, Henry and Jane Perrin, that Bert and Annie purchased the place in 1910.[52]

In 1918 Bert was often off to town. Usually this meant nearby Geneva, a village of about twenty-seven hundred that only two years before had celebrated its centennial (Fig. 13).[53] Sometimes, though, it meant Ashtabula, a city of over twenty-two thousand, some nine miles to the east and a relatively lively place—especially if the looser and rougher atmosphere of Ashtabula Harbor

Fig. 13. Seen here is the central crossroads in the village of Geneva. West Main Street runs to the left and East Main to the right. Heading toward the horizon (and eventually Lake Erie) is North Broadway, and veering off toward the lower right, South Broadway, where Annie and Bert moved in 1924. A few trees remain in this photograph taken about that year, but because of the traffic congestion it caused, the Civil War monument that once stood in the intersection has been moved to a nearby schoolyard. (From Large, vol. 1, plate facing p. 304.)

Fig. 14. Main Street, Ashtabula, with the Perrins' favorite movie theater, the Majestic, to the right. Off to the left are Candyland, one of the city's main "confectionaries," and the Colonial Restaurant, which featured lunches. (From Large, vol. 1, plate facing p. 55.)

was taken to be part of the scene (Fig. 14).[54] Sometimes Bert was simply away, leaving Annie to wonder where.[55]

Related to the family economy in a major sort of way was the fact that during the course of the diary Bert begins to make regular trips to Cleveland. A genuinely big and sprawling metropolis (Geneva's *Free Press-Times* often referred to it as "The Sixth City" because it was the sixth largest in the nation), Cleveland was a place Bert knew well. The Cleveland area had long been his home territory, after all, and after the death of his father, he acquired some rental property there.[56] Though

[54] In 1918 Ashtabula claimed to be "the greatest ore port on earth" (*S&B*, 26 February, p. 10). Whether or not this was chauvinistic exaggeration, Ashtabula truly was among the important iron ore receiving ports in the world. Ships had been built there ever since 1815 or thereabouts, and the ore that was arriving in great quantities in 1918 came into the harbor on a seemingly endless series of long and low-slung barges. Wherever one went on the southern shore of Lake Erie, the ore boats might be seen inching their way across the horizon —except, of course, in winter, when ice became a problem.

[55] On one occasion a couple of years after the close of Annie's

diary, Lettie's new husband, coming to the farm for a visit, remarked on the fact that Bert had put in an appearance (Myron Randall, Diary, 29 October 1920). A few days later, on what was presumably intended to be the occasion of the elder Perrins' first visit to the newlyweds, Myron observed in the slang of the day, "Mrs. Perrin . . . arrived by her lonely as expected" (5 November).

[56] Annie, who was always kept on the periphery of Bert's business life, says little of such matters —but see her entries for 1 April and 4 June.

Just as there are indications in the diary that the family's affairs have entered a new phase since the death of Bert's father, so are there hints that Fred, Bert's brother, had a helpful hand in them. A lifelong bachelor, Fred knew how to be generous. A number of years earlier, when his father declined to help, Fred offered to pay for the hospitalization and nursing of his and Bert's sister Mamie Foster (from notes of Carol Jensen, n.d.).

[57] As Holbrook writes, "Old farmers agree that hand milking probably drove more men off the farm than any other task" (p. 104). At the Perrin place, the probability that Raymond did much of the milking is enhanced by the frequently recited family story that when Raymond was getting ready to go out somewhere for the evening, Bert would generally observe significantly, "We milk at five." When the herd was bigger, as a matter of fact, the milkers arose at 4:30.

[58] Geneva was situated in the heart of Ohio's peach country. As the village newspaper observed early in 1918, "the peach belt, along the south shore of Lake Erie, . . . produces from 75 to 90 per cent of the total crop of the state" (*FPT*, 11 January, p. 1).

sometimes Bert was to be found slogging away alongside Raym back on the farm, the fact is that in the main he was more inclined to manage property than to work it. He was a smart and careful manager, and as he gradually acquired more real estate, the farm itself prospered.

Naturally Annie's diary yields many details about the Perrin farm. Though unfortunately it lacks some now-lost facts that were everyday knowledge to Annie and her family (for instance, who did the milking), a great deal may be inferred from what she includes.[57] Clearly the family was not heavily into dairying in 1918. When they first returned from Florida, they had but a single cow. Equally clearly the family had already invested a good deal of time and energy in fruit, especially peaches—Elbertas, Crosbys, and Salways.[58] In the first month after their return from Florida, Annie wrote that she hated to see the men take out some of their old peach trees (24 April). After the damage of a long and brutal winter, there were large quantities of brush to be burned in the orchard. Still, enough trees remained for a bountiful fall crop, and in time more were planted.

Another of the Perrins' major crops in 1918 was tomatoes. After working all morning and serving the usual noon-time family "dinner" on 28 May, Annie helped to "set 1000 tomato plants." Then a few days later, on 11 June, just as the young plants were beginning to harden, there was such "a terrible wind & thunder storm" that the family had to set out five hundred replacements.

And after that they still needed to find, buy, and plant another two hundred.

More typical of Ashtabula County farms in general, the Perrins' potato and corn crops were also fairly large.[59] Both play major parts in Annie's diary from May through November, with corn demanding the most attention in October, and potatoes—after the cold and rain began to worsen—in November. May, June, and July were all hard enough, with the need to prepare the fields and plant and cultivate, but the demands of threshing and harvesting, peaking first in August and then again in October and extending into November, stressed the family to its limits and finally contributed to Annie's breakdown late that month.

Bit by bit, Annie's diary yields glimpses not only of the farm and farming but also of the farmhouse. Whenever it was built, the Perrin house was certainly old in 1918. At some point, indeed, the family found tucked away in one of its walls an embroidered sampler bearing the date 1828.[60] What one sees in photographs taken about the time Annie wrote her diary is a thoroughly weathered clapboard dwelling, strong, low, partly one story, partly a story and a half. As glimpsed darkly here in Fig. 15, the house is vacant and partially boarded up for the winter of 1917–18. Though this bleak and somber image catches none of the normally busy life of the farm, it probably suggests the general layout of the place better than any other picture that survives. Clearly visible here are the two main front doors of the house. The one to the left, temporarily sealed off with wide planks

[59] The most recent figures available in 1918 indicate that the largest single crop in Ashtabula County, and the one raised most generally, was oats (981,856 bushels in 1910). Running second was corn (602,913 bushels) and, third, potatoes (498,066 bushels) (*Farm Journal . . . Directory of Ashtabula County*, p. xv).

[60] Though the sampler bears also the name of its maker, Elisabeth Mary Paisley, one cannot say how old it was when placed in the wall. Nevertheless, a recollection of Sophia Hawley, who settled on the South Ridge in 1834, provides a glimpse of the period. Hawley wrote that she passed "many a night spinning and weaving while hungry wolves howled at the door" (quoted by Ellsworth, p. 182; see also Harvey Rice, pp. 188–89). Furthermore, settlers had to deal with wildcats, elks, bears, and panthers (Ellsworth, p. 19). The recollections of the Reverend Rufus Clark (1819–1886), printed in his *Early History of the South Ridge*, are focused on Conneaut,

twenty-some miles east of Geneva, and are rich with similar information about pioneering days in the area.

A Revolutionary War veteran, Major Levi Gaylord, from New Cambridge, Connecticut, is said to have come to Ohio in 1804 and built a log cabin on the South Ridge near where the Perrin farm was later situated (Williams, pp. 116–17; Upton gives 1806 as the date of Gaylord's arrival [1:561]). Theobalt Bartholomew, likewise a soldier in the Revolution, from Charlotte, New York, settled on the Ridge close to the west bank of nearby Cowles Creek in 1805 (Williams, p. 173). When the frame schoolhouse slightly east of the Perrin place was erected in 1821, it was the successor to a still earlier log schoolhouse (*Ashtabula County History*, p. 79).

One of the most interesting details of this sort is that part of the Perrin farm bordered land settled originally by Elisha Wiard. After Theobalt Bartholomew, "The next settler was Elisha Wiard, who came from Connecticut, and located some quarter of a mile north of Bartholomew's. Wiard was a young, active, and industrious settler, and made considerable improvement. He died in the winter of 1812" (Williams, p. 173).

In fact, at least some property owned by the Wiard family came to constitute part of the Perrin farm. Though the latter was a patchwork that eventually grew to be slightly over a hundred acres, the land bought by Henry Perrin on 9 May 1904 from the heirs of Erastus and Beulah Carmer had been purchased on 29 April 1850 by Erastus Carmer from Lemuel and Anna Wiard (Deeds, vol. 172, p. 303, and vol. 37, p. 766). Ownership by the latter dated back to 7 March 1844, at which time Lemuel Wiard purchased the land from Truman Watkins, who in turn had acquired it on 4 March 1831 from Enoch Barnum (Deeds, vol. 30, p. 9 and vol. K, p. 240). The trail

Fig. 15. A melancholy image of absence, the Perrin farmhouse stands vacant during the winter of 1917–18.

nailed to the casing, was an entry into the dining room, and the one to the right, centered under the attic window, led to the sitting room. Also discernible in this picture are the two porches of the house: a fairly big, practical, square one at the back, off the kitchen, and a much smaller front one at the far right. This seldom-used second porch afforded the house yet a third front doorway—one that allowed winter's fine-grained snow to sift in on Lettie's bedroom floor.[61] Toward the left side of the picture are two windows, one looking out from Raym's bedroom (the room nearest the front), and the other from the pantry (toward the back, nearest the kitchen). In the distance, far beyond the house, are some low-lying fields, white with snow, and, farther yet, the wooded skyline to the south.

Seemingly merged with the mostly snow-covered grass of the front yard, and rising from the lower center and going off toward the right, is the snow-covered road. Deserted as it is here and showing few traces of traffic, this was actually one of Geneva's two main east and west thoroughfares. Sometimes called the Ridge Road, it runs along the crest of a long and fairly narrow rise known for miles in both directions as the South Ridge. (As such a name suggests, another rise a short distance north and running more or less parallel to it is known as the North Ridge.) Geologically speaking, the South Ridge marks the southernmost reach of Lake Erie's glacial predecessor in ages past. In other words, the Perrin house stood on the sandy edge of an ancient beach.[62] Whether snow-covered, muddy, or dry, the road that ran along it was always at least somewhat rutted. Little wonder: built in 1802 over an old Indian trail, it was the first and only, then later the main route through northern Ohio. It was the road traveled by both covered wagons and stagecoaches. (One of the stage stops, in fact, stood just a short distance west of the Perrin place.)[63]

Opposite the house, on the north side of the road, lay the Perrins' peach orchard. (The apple orchard, also across the road, lay farther to the east.) Because the temperature is less variable on this north side than on the south or even on level ground, the trees were just about ideally situated. Beyond the orchard lay the vineyard (eventually planted with row on row of blue Concords), and beyond that a fertile bottomland suited to nearly any kind of crop.

Farther yet toward the north and Lake Erie, but vis-

goes cold at this point, but it is significant that parts of the Perrin farm under discussion in the present volume extended on both the east and west sides of Barnum Road. (For most of the information in this paragraph the editor is indebted to Judith A. Barta, Ashtabula County Recorder.)

Though many details concerning the early period are lacking, it is safe to say that at the time Bert's father bought the house in 1904, the area had been settled for about a hundred years.

[61] Though different parts of the house were modified at various non-dateable times, the year "1906" is inscribed in the cement foundation of this two-room west wing. A couple of years after moving in, apparently, the Perrins decided that this part of the house needed shoring up. During another of its remodelings, the family discovered that some of the walls had been stuffed with newspapers from 1859 through 1862 (recollected by Raymond Perrin, Jr.—who has some of the papers).

[62] Moina Large makes the point that "the high bank overlooking the beach of Lake Erie" is itself a third "ridge" (1:82). "From this latter elevation," she writes, "there is a gradual rise to the North Ridge, and from that a continued incline to the South Ridge."

[63] Edward Campbell, p. 9; Williams, p. 27; and Weston, p. 6. In the year of Annie's diary the roads running along both South Ridge and North Ridge were sometimes virtually unusable. The *Free Press-Times* records on 8 March that "A truck loaded with brass, bound for an eastern city, broke two drive chains pulling through the mud on the South ridge one day recently" (p. 1). In later days, tamed and paved, it became Route 84.

ible from the front yard and looking something like a child's toys, the cars of the Nickel Plate Railroad occasionally passed back and forth on their east-and-west-running tracks. (The New York, Chicago, and St. Louis Railroad Company was known universally as the Nickel Plate.) In the daytime, muffled by all the normal sounds of day, the trains could barely be heard, but in the gathering dusk or the dark of night, their faint rattling and rumbling and their dim whistles provided a kind of distant, recurring reassurance.

A little farther still lay the tracks of the C.P. & A. (These initials stand for Cleveland-Painesville-Ashtabula Electric Interurban Traction Company, but no one ever used that name, either.) In the rural countryside of 1918 the C.P. & A. trolley was a precious link to other people and places.[64] Its big red cars with their overhead poles ran hourly (Stop 58 was the one nearest the Perrin house), and a passenger could ride either eastward or westward for two cents a mile—raised to three cents in October, 1918—with a minimum fare of ten cents.

Close and cheap as the trolley was, however, the country was still the country, and the placement of Stop 58 sometimes posed problems for anyone trying to ascend the Ridge to the Perrin farmhouse, especially with luggage or in bad weather or in the dark. On one memorable night in 1916, according to the *Free Press-Times*, a group of eleven "Girls Encounter[ed] Real Mud on Way to Perrin Farm."[65] Rather extraordinarily, Lettie had invited a group of friends for an evening party, and

[64] Hilton and Due record that "No state approached within a thousand miles of Ohio's interurban mileage of 2,798. No Ohio town of 10,000 was without interurban service, and the territories along the shore of Lake Erie . . . had highly developed networks" (p. 255).

The C.P. & A. was a subsidiary of the C.P. & E. (Cleveland, Painesville, and Eastern Railroad) designed to run from Painesville eastward to Ashtabula. Laid piecemeal over the years by different entrepreneurs, the tracks reached Geneva in 1903. At the time of Annie's diary the tracks entered Geneva on West Main Street, ran eastward to Centennial, then headed south to the Nickel Plate Railroad, turned eastward again, and ran along the north side of the tracks, heading toward Ashtabula (Ellsworth, p. 86).

Useful as the system was, the

their climb from the trolley stop to the house proved so daunting that the skittish lot of them were ready to abandon the whole venture when a kind "neighbor came to the rescue with a lantern."

Since the front of the Perrin house was situated on the crest of the South Ridge and parallel to its axis, its back side (where the slope of the land made possible some basement windows and doors) seemed much larger and more open. Behind the house and a little to the east was the weather-battered barn. And behind the barn was a pasture that sloped at first slowly and then fairly precipitously, with a few cow paths (later there would be more) that went sidling downward toward Cowles Creek. There at the southernmost base of the Ridge one could often see the stop-motion flight of a dragonfly or hear the clear *kong-queree* of a red-winged blackbird. There, too, with a summertime pole and a tin can of fresh worms from the chicken yard, nearly anyone might catch a fish—most likely a yellow-bellied sunfish or a bluegill, but sometimes a sizeable sucker.[66] Near the bottom of the slope there was also a sturdy little bridge that let north-and-south-running Barnum Road cross the creek on its way southward towards Clay Street. From up in the barnyard on a hot summer day, one could see the dust stirred up on the bridge when an occasional wagon or even an automobile clattered over its planks. Farther yet south and off to the east of Barnum Road there were more pasture and meadowland. To the west were still more pasture and, finally, an old wood made lively by colonies of chipmunks and red

company constantly lost money. When its last car ran in 1926, it had yet to pay its stockholders their first dividend (Edward Campbell, p. 41).

[65] 25 January, p. 2.

[66] Cowles Creek—generally pronounced "crick"—took its name from Noah Cowles, one of the earliest settlers to live near it, some time before 1808. It runs westerly for about a mile and a half and then, a little west of Mt. Pleasant Cemetery, where most of the Perrins are buried, it veers and runs northward and at last empties into Lake Erie at a point called Chestnut Grove (in later years transmuted into Geneva State Park).

squirrels. When fall came, the nuts there could be heard dropping from the trees.

More immediately in back of the house, the closest outbuilding was the milk house. This was a small, cylindrical, cement-block structure with a roof like an upside-down funnel. It stood on a patch of land just outside the north-facing lower entrance to the barn, handy to the cows. With troughs of water inside to keep the ten-gallon milk cans cool, the interior of the milk house always seemed either clammy cool or cold.[67]

However old the barn itself may have been, it seemed sturdy as a rock. Though later it would be painted white, in 1918 its siding was a weather-worn silvery gray. Inside, and especially when the haymow was yet to be filled, the rooftree seemed even higher than it was because the light in those upper regions was so dim. As a sort of natural counterbalance, though, shafts of sunlight or moonlight found their way through the cracks between the vertical siding boards. And always the place was fragrant—most of all in July when the hay was fresh, but even when everything was crackling hot in August and the breezes dropped and the cicadas droned.[68]

Like the basement of the house, the pungent lower level of the barn was tucked into the southern slope of the Ridge. Like the basement, too, therefore, its south side had some light-giving windows and doors from which one could look out over the barnyard and beyond to the pasture. This lower level of the barn had all the usual feeding troughs, the usual battered stalls and stanchions, and the harnesses, milking stools, and pitchforks

[67] The milk house may be glimpsed in the background of Fig. 101.

[68] Presenting some statistics to support its natural pride, the local village newspaper observed in the spring of 1918 that Ashtabula County "is the banner hay county of the state, as it is the banner dairy county. 47,530 acres of hay land produced 64,926 tons of timothy and 1,784 were cut for seed. . . . Hay stacked was 11,901 tons" (*FPT*, 5 April, p. 1).

—though in 1918, when the family first returned from Florida, the place was strangely quiet. As the farm began to prosper, this same space would be filled with workhorses (at the west end) and a sizeable herd of cows (mainly black-and-white Holsteins), shuffling and munching, flicking their tails and exhaling warmth. In the summer following the family's trip to Florida there were not yet many animals, but enough horses (at least three) and mules (two) to do the plowing, tilling, and planting, and to pull the wagons, the buggy, the cutter, and the stoneboat.[69] Early or late, however, the barn was mainly Bert's and Raym's world. Obviously it was in some measure Annie's, too, but everyone in the family assumed that neither barn nor barnyard was really a woman's territory.

Out of eyeshot from the road and huddled close to the east side of the barn, protected by it from the wind and suitably distant and downhill from the house, there was a little two-hole outhouse. This smallest of all the outbuildings marked another fact of life never mentioned by Annie in her diary. In 1918 a discreet advertisement in the village newspaper sometimes gave notice that someone was trying either to buy or sell an "outdoor closet,"[70] and in later but still pre-plumbing years when this Perrin "closet" was prettied up with white paint like the barn, a small grandson would name it the "birdhouse." At the time of the diary, though, it was simply a necessary little building where an old newspaper or an out-of-date Sears and Roebuck wishbook might

[69] The Perrin stoneboat, like everyone else's, was a sturdy sort of dry-season sled. It took its name from its major use—carrying stones from where one did not want them to where one did.

[70] For example, *FPT*, 21 September, p. 4.

be read again before being put to its final use. Or, if need be, a couple of people might talk there.

A small handful of other rough-and-ready structures —such as the chicken coop—were scattered out in back, but clearly none were so important as the house and the barn. Clearly, too, just as the outside of the house may in later years be glimpsed in random snapshots intended to record the look of something else, so some interesting hints about its interior may be glimpsed inside Annie's diary. Most of these occur after school let out and Lettie took charge of the spring cleaning.

She started with the low, slope-ceilinged attic (10 June), then proceeded room by room through the first floor, variously with the help of Annie and Raym, but never Bert.[71] She cleaned Henry's room next and even did a bit of painting there. Some of the woodwork in this wing and in certain other places in the house had been put together from odd pieces of lumber, but a good coat of paint helped to tie things together a bit. She next moved on to her own bedroom (the one with the door leading out to the little front porch), then her parents' bedroom, and then Raym's. Four bedrooms, at this point.

She next took on the sitting room, where Raym did a good job of cleaning the rug. This was the central and oldest part of the house: down in the basement, one could see that its floors were supported by thick, hand-hewn beams, some still with their bark. The family kept most of its better furniture here, including the

[71] Bert's abstinence from all housework was typical of the time. A newspaper advertisement this spring begins "House-cleaning is ripe, and the average man is staying away from home just as much as he can and as he says, 'Letting his wife have all the fun she likes'" (*S&B*, 27 April, p. 3).

upright piano, the little marble-topped walnut table from Annie's parents' home, and the deep red, cherry-wood platform rocker that was one of Annie's and Bert's wedding presents. Lettie then moved on to the dining room—which together with the sitting room stretched across most of the front of the house. As big as this room was, there was understandably a prominent scorch mark on the floor where (as Annie remarks in her diary entry of 16 September) a room stove stood during the winter months. Next on Lettie's cleaning agenda was the kitchen and, finally, on 27 June, Annie's notation "Now all the cleaning is done." In fact, Lettie still had to attack the pantry—a narrow and food-fragrant little place situated off the east end of the dining room, where the floor and sturdy shelves, stacked and packed full of tins and crocks and mason jars, were handy to the kitchen.

Spring cleaning aside, when Lettie helped her mother with the regular weekly cleaning, she usually did the house only "to the kitchen"—there being a well-worn step down from the dining room into what was, after all, Annie's major workplace. The downward step from one room to another was an indication that the kitchen, big though it was, may once have been a back porch. Situated on the south side of the house, in any case, this room collected a brighter daylight than any of the rooms across the front of the house. Here on the south wall was Annie's tall and massive iron cookstove. With a constantly replenished supply of wood from the big box at its side, it put forth a good deal of heat—heat more welcome in the cold months than in the hot ones. On the east wall was a sink with a cast iron hand pump, its water drawn from a shallow well in the basement. In the middle of the room was the family's old main dining table, surrounded by sturdy wooden chairs. And in one or another space left open on the floor, a big metal tub was sometimes brought out so that members of the family could bathe, even on a cold winter's night, in water that had been pumped from the pump and warmed by a fire in the cookstove.[72]

Not surprisingly, Annie's preparation of food plays a major role in her diary. At the outset, in Florida, the family had to buy nearly everything. In that exotic land to the south, fortunately, the countryside teemed with oranges. Annie served her guests orange pie (2 February), johnnycake with sliced oranges and tea (4 February), and cornmeal muffins with orange sauce (18 February).

Back home, she constantly baked bread (more than she ever troubled to mention) and sometimes cakes and pies. Beyond the johnnycakes, corn cakes, and cornmeal muffins she made in Florida, she baked an angel food cake (a special treat for Lettie's birthday), a crumb cake, caraway cupcakes, oatmeal cookies and sugar cookies, and, as Christmas came close, fruitcake and plum pudding—these last two being mild reminders that both Annie and Bert shared an English heritage. Because of the shortage of sugar, Annie made particular note of baking a "war cake" (28 March). Beginning on 15 July, Ashtabula County was placed on a "sugar

[72] June S. Pepin, owner of the house since 1945, has kindly provided a half dozen or so details for this and the preceding paragraphs on the interior of the house (ALS, 20 October 1997).

card" system, and August and September were expected to "see a far greater shortage than was at first anticipated."[73] When Annie made an apple pie on 9 August, therefore, it was "Sweetened with syrup," and on 20 August she managed to produce "a sugarless cake & frosting" with some "Corn syrup."[74] Her underlining marks the strangeness of such things.

Other images of both the farm and the family are suggested by the range of vegetables Annie mentions. The long, large, rectangular garden, west and south of the house, sloped down the back side of the Ridge toward the creek. Annie writes of the cucumbers that the Perrins raised there, and of the peppers, turnips, string beans, onions, cabbages, and squash.[75] On 5 July she picked the first of the season's beans. On 25 July she picked the first cucumber, and on 12 August a peck of tomatoes. In the fall (24 October) the cucumbers, peppers, and onions became makings for pickles, chili sauce, catsup, and chow-chow (three quarts of this last). On 30 October Annie was apprehensive about the possibility of rain because three other workers besides Raym and Bert had come to help dig the rest of the Perrin potato crop over in the field east of the house. Then, sadly, rain it did.

There are fewer kinds of fruit in evidence in the diary, but plenty of peaches, grapes, and apples. This was, after all, fruit country. There were apples—Rome Beauties and Baldwins—for making pies, for mailing to Henry in far-off Key West (7 October), and, of course, for canning (sixteen quarts on 30 October). Most espe-

[73] *S&B*, 15 July, p. 1; 26 July, p. 2.

[74] Hence the significance of Henry's later comment to Lettie that sugar was plentiful in the Navy (ALS, 9 December).

[75] A brief item in the Geneva newspaper once reported that "B. H. Perrin, of the South Ridge, has on exhibition in a window of King's hardware store, a mammoth squash, which weighs 178 pounds. From seven seeds of this variety of squash, Mr. Perrin raised one half ton of squashes. The mammoth is said to be finer in texture than the Hubbard squash" (*FPT*, 24 October 1914, p. 2).

cially, however, there were endless baskets of peaches—especially sweet Elbertas—to be sold or canned or dried.

In addition to this already lengthy array of home-grown edibles, Annie's chickens occasionally made good Sunday dinners. The government had tried to put a moratorium on killing chickens, but it was a weak and waffling gesture. In any case, many farmers and their wives raised chickens for their own tables, not for selling, and the Perrins were no exception. On 25 September, for instance, they dined on rooster—and Annie was moved to underline the word.[76] (Had this one been a tyrant in the chicken yard?) The family even sent some of their butchered pig to be smoked. On 21 December Annie notes that "Bert and I went to town for our smoked meat."

The hint here of Annie's pleasure in the family's degree of self-sufficiency may be found also when she tells of going out to pick wild berries. Untilled patches of the countryside yielded plentiful wild strawberries, small but sweet, and blackberries and elderberries. Wild cranberries, native to the area but rapidly disappearing, were still to be found at the moist southern base of the Nickel Plate trackbed. On a couple of occasions Annie tells of walking down to the back meadow to dig fresh "greens"—by which she means either dandelion or pigweed leaves. In the fall she gathered peck basketsful of mushrooms (and big, white puffballs, too, though she does not name them), for they sprang up quickly and handsomely in the sandy loam of the orchard. For the most part, all of the Perrins were too busy to go foraging for

[76] In 1944, shortly before signing himself into the General Hospital at Ashtabula for what proved to be a fatal prostatectomy, Bert promised his grandchildren that when he came home he would kill his old rooster for a celebration feast.

wild things, but Annie was not inclined to refuse any gifts that nature might bestow. At one point she notes tellingly, "Bert ought to be thankful we have enough to eat" (12 May).

Family finances affected both farm and family, of course, though Annie says little about them. Whatever the current state of the family's financial situation, her diary entries touching on the subject enhance an overall impression that she was instinctively abstemious on her own behalf. During the fifty-four weeks covered by the diary she reports buying for herself only "a new hat & a p[ai]r of white gloves" (30 January), a pair of slippers (16 March), and, when summer comes, "some garments" (3 August)—a modest way of referring to new underwear. Beyond these few pieces of apparel, there is also, late in the year, a $4.00 pair of glasses (16 December). But that is all. As for managing the household, obviously routine necessities—coal, salt, kerosene —had to be purchased to run even a frugal home of three or four people, but it is a rare event when Annie records buying a set of new curtains in Ashtabula so as to dress up the newly cleaned dining room (24 June).

When it comes to being careful with household money, Bert was at least an improvement over his father. Like the young hero of Henry Fielding's novel *Joseph Andrews*, Henry as a boy was charged with scaring crows out of a farmer's grain fields—and "when the season of crow keeping is over," wrote Hannah More of such boys, "then they glean or pick stones."[77] Never afterwards did Henry forget the early lessons he learned in Wiltshire

[77] More, p. 12.

[78] If this story is not literally true, it is at least true to the family stories told about Henry. Moreover, it jibes well enough with the recollection that Edward L. Foster offered Henry's daughter Mamie an engagement ring in 1880, but Henry did not allow her to accept it until 1884 —in which year the wedding finally took place in the two-story bay window of the big Perrin house on Pearl Road (recollected by Virginia Cappallo Larimore, 30 January 1988).

In fairness, a clue to Henry's character that points in a contrary direction is to be found in a letter he addressed to all of his children on 23 July 1883, when he and Jane were visiting in England. One passage reads:

Mamie and bessie you must kiss Nellie and our Fred such Big Popers for me about 100 apice[.] tell Fred I shall try and get him an acordian in London and Miss Nellie her Dol[.] Mother has already something for Mamie and Bessie[.] we dont hardly know what to buy Bert[.] watches cost more here than at home but we shall bring something[.]

(Henry's colloquial "Popers"— that is, "poppers"—derives from "pop," meaning "to pop with the mouth, to smack the lips" [Farmer and Henley, p. 347].)

[79] From manuscript notes recorded by Allen's niece, Carol A. Jensen, in the early 1990s. Though this anecdote, like that about Henry and the sack of potatoes, is probably accurate, its

both from his own hard father and from life. Living in the United States during the lean years after the Civil War, he continued to keep a tight rein on the money that came his way. As soon as he garnered a bit, he liked to put it in the bank. Even after he had begun to do rather well for himself, acquiring pieces of real estate here and there, it is said that he presented his daughter Mamie with a sack of potatoes as her wedding gift.[78]

It is more understandable, then, that Allen Foster, a nephew of Bert's who appears several times in Annie's diary, would in later years tell a comparable story about Bert. In the late summer of 1922, when Allen and some other visitors were calling at the Perrin farm, "Bert dragged us all out to the barn to see his latest wonder," which proved to be a new watering system for his cows. Allen afterwards enjoyed quoting himself as asking, "But Bert, isn't Annie still pumping water in the kitchen?" It was a question, Allen said, that Bert answered with a scowl.[79]

Whatever the financial constraints or capabilities of the Perrins in 1918, Annie's diary abounds with pleasant glimpses of friends and relatives, sudden afternoon and evening callers, and frequent overnight visitors. There were the Lowes, the Wetters, the Seymours, and the Penneys, the Seamans, the Slocums, the Hartners, and more.

It is all the more striking, then, that the only day Annie pronounces "perfect" is one when she and her family attended the Perrin family reunion on the Fourth of July. Because of the war, Ohio's Fire Marshall had decreed a fireworkless Fourth,[80] but, thankful to have her sailor son, Henry, home on a month-long furlough, Annie and all the rest of the Geneva Perrins climbed into their Overland Light Six—the one unmistakable sign that they really were not doing badly—and happily motored westward to the home of Bert's widowed sister, Bessie Dobson, in Brooklyn, just south of Cleveland's west side.[81]

Beyond the involvement of Raymond, Lettie, and Henry in these and other events concerning home and family, clearly all three, now in their twenties, maintained their own varied and complex personal ties with other young folks. Annie often reports that Raym has gone over to nearby Saybrook to be with "B."—that is,

Fig. 16. Bernice Michel (right) and Lettie Perrin on the Fourth of July, 1917. The two young women and their companions—who included Henry and Raym—were enjoying a triple date at Geneva-on-the-Lake.

main usefulness is as an indicator of Bert's reputation within the family.

The fact is that not too many years earlier it was something of an advance for farmers to have "the pump right in the kitchen," as Riley writes in "Griggsby's Station" (p. 83). Moreover, Myron Randall writes at about the same time as Allen's anecdote that Bert's workmen were putting together a system that would enable water to be "piped to barn *and* house" (Diary, 22–25 August 1922; italics added). Whatever phases of the operation came first or last, the project was both long-drawn-out and complicated. On one of the days when Myron happened to be visiting, the Perrins invited the "pump men" to dinner (Diary, 16 September), and late in December the diggers were still digging the well (17 December).

[80] S&B, 13 March 1918, p. 1.
[81] The Perrins began to hold annual family reunions in 1915—only two years before the death of their founder. "Bessie," as Carol Jensen remarks, "was the one who orchestrated the closeness of family" (ALS, 17 October 1991).

[82] Bernice Jane Michel (9 January 1898–28 March 1967) was the daughter of George Michel (1867–1953) and Rose Carter Michel (1871–1955).

Formerly a farmer on the North Ridge, Michel sold off his stock in the spring of 1913 and took a job as an engineer on the Nickel Plate (*FPT*, 10 April, p. 2). Never very successful at farming, he also had bad luck during his five years on the railroad. Early in 1914 the *Free Press-Times* reported his hospitalization at Dunkirk, New York (15 January, p. 2). Apparently his head had been badly cut "while he was on his engine," and he lay unconscious on the engine floor until a worried conductor came to find out why the train was not slowing down as it should.

In the year of Annie's diary, when he was still only about fifty years old, Mr. Michel returned to farming on the old home place —where Bernice, too, now lived.

[83] Information kindly supplied by Jerome R. Brockway, County Superintendent, Ashtabula County Schools (24 April 1996).

[84] The school where Bernice taught was constructed in 1883 on a foundation that originally supported a wooden building erected in 1838. In 1910 both the building and its site became part of Geneva Township Park, and during the year 1918, at the time of Annie's diary, it was supposed to be converted into a sort of combined caretaker's lodge and teashop (Ellsworth, pp. 180–81).

[85] The threat of Lake Erie waves has always been real, both here and elsewhere. A body of water somewhat larger than Vermont, Erie is "the most tempestuous and choppy of the Great Lakes," with a shore line that— despite some beautifully calm days—has always tended to be "restless and unstable" (Hatcher, pp. 15, 18, 21). In 1918 the cliff near Bernice's old school was

Bernice Michel, whom he married a couple of years later (see Fig. 16).[82] Bernice, a June 1916 graduate of Geneva High School, was a spirited, hard-working, and striking brunette and, like Lettie, a teacher. In order to make her own way she had taken courses at Ashtabula County Normal in Kingsville, and—like Lettie—Kent State Normal.[83] Now teaching in Saybrook, close to home, she was a good deal more agreeably situated than when she found herself teaching for a while in the little red brick schoolhouse at the end of Austin Road in Geneva-on-the-Lake.[84] There, near the edge of Lake Erie's steep cliff and beach, she was often depressed by the roar of the waves and the winter winds that blew in off the water.[85] Also making for a bleak atmosphere at the school was the fact that only a few years earlier "A large amount of the timber at the township park has been cut down . . . , giving the appearance of devastation."[86] Teaching in Saybrook, on the other hand, Bernice was inland, comfortably nearer home, and closer to Raym. Their wedding took place on Wednesday, 23 June 1920, at the Michel farm, in front of a bank of ferns and palms. Bernice wore a white satin gown with net trimmings and carried a large bouquet of roses.[87] Her sister Effie was the bridesmaid, and Raym's brother, Henry, best man.

Four years after the time of Annie's diary, on 7 November 1922, Henry himself married Vere Smith of Akron, Ashtabula, and Geneva.[88] Within the calendar year of 1918 and almost as if seeking a place to alight, Vere lived for a while in each of these towns.[89] Well

caving in so rapidly that Genevans already knew they would soon have to move the lakeshore road farther south.

[86] *FPT*, 23 April 1913, p. 2.

[87] *FPT*, 24 June 1920, p. 1.

[88] The daughter of Bert and Rose Fales Smith, Vere Stella Smith was born in Montville, Ohio, on 9 November 1892. She survived Henry by a number of years, dying in Geneva on 4 March 1975.

[89] A letter from Henry to Lettie reveals that Vere found brief summer employment at Firestone in Akron (29 June).

Fig. 17. Vere Stella Smith as she appeared in earlier days. Within Annie's diary she appears as Lettie's good friend, and later she became Henry's wife.

before that, however, she had been not only Lettie's fellow teacher in the North Geneva school, but also a familiar figure in the Perrin household. Earlier still, she had taught school in Rock Creek and Hartsgrove. Like both Bernice and Lettie, she had graduated from Geneva High School and attended Kent, and like Lettie she had attended Wooster.[90]

[90] Brockway (24 April 1996).

Fig. 18. Vere Smith and her future brother-in-law, Raymond, enjoy a moment at the southeast corner of the Perrins' side porch. Looming behind them to the left is the barn. In the background to the right are the snow-covered barnyard and pasture—for the moment, a blur of winter white. Unseen to the left of the photographer are a few steps, the family's cast-iron dinner bell (at the top of a sturdy post), and a short path leading to the driveway.

Fig. 19. Here Henry carries Vere (probably unnecessarily) across a little rivulet in the spring-wildflower-time of 1916 or 1917.

Pale and coal-black-haired in 1918, slight and fragile in appearance (she weighed only 115 pounds), Vere (see Figs. 17–19) was almost birdlike in her movements. Perhaps even more than Lettie, she was a reader. For that reason or some other, she had her own way of looking at things. For instance, as a hostess she made bold at one point to serve her young lady friends maple syrup, wafers, and pickles.[91] Possessed of a quick, gentle laugh that generally came with a slight lift of her head, she was ever and always an even-tempered, patient, good companion. In a letter of 13 October 1922, Lettie's hus-

[91] *FPT*, 14 March 1916, p. 2.

92 ALS, Myron W. Randall to Lettie.

93 The place of the wedding has been noted by May Colling, Ashtabula County Genealogical Society, 12 May 1997.

band calls her a "jewel."[92] Less than a full month later, and despite the medical treatment he was receiving in Kentucky at the time, she and Henry were married in the Seelbach Hotel in Louisville.[93] It was not a very good beginning and did not auger well.

Annie's diary records the names of several of Lettie's young women friends, but that of only one young man. Roy Andrews, who rather hovers in the background of

Fig. 20. Lettie and Roy Andrews about 1917, both serious enough about themselves and each other to pose together for a professional photographer.

Annie's account, was a blonde, strapping, self-confident, and promising young farmer from down in Thompson (Fig. 20). He and Lettie had been friends at least since 1911, when she was only nineteen. And the family certainly liked him. On Sunday, 28 July, during one of his visits, Annie reports that "The boys had a rough and tumble this morning." Though rambunctiousness usually set her nerves on edge, she at some level must have approved, for she writes simply that "Raym & Roy tore the bed to pieces," then follows that news matter-of-factly with a report that "The 3 boys[94] went to Lake [Erie] & had a bath." Nevertheless, and despite a subtle but strong bolstering by the friendship between Roy and Raym, the long-lasting relationship between Roy and Lettie was decidedly on the wane in 1918. In a letter to Lettie of 22 May 1919, Henry wrote of one of his own admirers, "Perhaps we can be just friends again like you and Roy." The fact is that Lettie had lived—indeed, was still living—too intimately with the hardships of farm life to settle down with even a promising farmer. In the fall of 1919 she took a new and better job down in Warren, Ohio,[95] and there, on 6 September 1919, she met Myron Welcome Randall, a fellow schoolteacher. Short, black-haired, bright-eyed, and a pretty good dancer, Myron was a recent graduate of Earlham College—and the opposite of Roy in nearly every way. About nine months later, on 29 May 1920, before a Justice of the Peace in Jefferson, Ohio, Lettie married him.[96]

∽

[94] Roy, Raym, and Henry.

[95] The term "better," of course, is comparative. Across the U.S., "Salaries paid teachers in 1918 [averaged] ... $606 for elementary teachers and $1031 for those teaching in high schools." Moreover, rural salaries generally "fell far below" these averages, bottoming at $150 and $200 per year (*FPT*, 13 March 1920, p. 1).

[96] See Figs. 21 and 22. Myron (23 June 1896–12 November 1983) was from far-off southwestern Ohio. Born in Somerville in Butler County, he was the son of

Jonas Pearl Randall (1870–1949) and Mary ("Matie") Smith Randall (1876–1964). In Warren, the seat of Trumbull County, forty-five miles or so south of Geneva, Lettie and Myron had both taken new jobs—she to teach at the Dickey Avenue School, and he to teach Spanish at two of the city's junior high schools (the East and the West).

Fig. 21. Mr. and Mrs. Myron W. Randall stand on the steps of the Dayton, Ohio, post office on 3 July 1921. Along with Myron's parents (Jonas and Mary Randall) and his grandmother (Sallie E. Randall), they have driven out from Richmond, Indiana, home of the elder Randalls, on a day that is—as the white clothes hint and as Myron writes in his diary—"Hot in its superlative!"

Fig. 22. The three younger Perrins and their "prospects" (as an uncle calls them), all soon to be spouses and in-laws. This sextet that converged on the farm for Sunday dinner on 9 May 1920 are *(left to right)* Myron Randall, Henry, Lettie, Vere Smith, Raym, and Bernice Michel. Lettie has here the "tired out" look she got when overstrained, but note also her comfortably companionable elbow on Henry's shoulder.

Inevitably and centrally, of course, the diary reveals most about Annie and consequently much about Bert. A constantly hardworking wife, Annie was also a devoted mother ("I am sick to hear from the children," she writes while in Florida [30 December 1917]), and despite Bert's quick temper and old-fashioned, Johnny Bull willfulness (she often did not know where he was), she was totally committed to him. Never does she really complain in the diary, and yet sometimes her simple record of how she has worked during the day seems almost an inverted comment on what Bert has done. "She always did do more than her share," Henry observes in a confidential letter to Lettie (1 June 1918). In fact, all three children were devoted to her and supported her as best they could. Even with their help and concern, though, and despite the frequent visitors who came to the farm, Annie often felt lonely. A sensitive woman herself, she was upset by insensitivity in others—as when, for example, Mr. Seymour pretended to have difficulty parking or when Mrs. Norris was cross with the children. After Annie saw the torture instruments at the old fort in St. Augustine, she reported that they had made her feel sick, and probably she meant it literally.

Beyond the obvious fact that Annie could not record more than a fraction of all that she did, saw, thought, and felt, she generally reined in what was on her mind. A self-controlled woman not only in the actions of her life but even in the privacy of her diary, she turned to implication whenever direct statement might be difficult. A reader must often infer what has "peeved" Bert or why a day has proved "unpleasant" or why Annie herself felt "punk" or "blue." In other words, a handful of mysteries lie scattered about in the diary. One of these is the series of +'s that occur sporadically throughout. Since these marks probably indicate some private matter of delicacy, and since they are by no means monthly, one might guess that they allude not only to herself but also to her relations with Bert. In any case, two-thirds of them occur during the three-month period when both were in Florida, certainly not relieved of worries but free for a while from the grinding routine of the farm. Possibly, therefore, the other third of the +'s, stretching over a little more than nine months, may be, at least in part, indirect reminders of how stressful a life on the farm really is.[97] At the very least, they stand as reminders to a reader that Annie's diary does not tell all.

The fact is that Bert was in many ways the opposite of Annie. As the old saying has it, he was wedded to his will. To be fair, however, he too had his "nerves" and his physical complaints. While they were down in Florida, Annie reports that he had to see Dr. Roney (18 February). Back in Ohio in early summer, she writes that he had "again" consulted Dr. Case, whose diagnosis was "nerves" (24 June). In the fall she writes that "Bert complains of his back all the time" (23 September). And like his father, as a result of his work he eventually developed a hernia.

Bert was a strong, spirited man, nonetheless, the sort who liked to tell jokes and who before long proved himself good at amusing grandchildren—at least for a while —with a stomping foot and a noisy nonsense song ("Georgie Morgan played the organ . . .").[98] He was the sort of man who liked chewing tobacco (there was a shiny black spittoon in the sitting room) and cigars (preferably White Owls).[99] He was averse to neither beer nor wine (though Annie mentions neither in her diary), and he especially enjoyed a good game of pool or billiards (likewise not mentioned) down in the village. Per-

[97] It has been suggested to the editor that Annie's +'s reflect the erratic and waning menses of a woman approaching menopause. However, their frequency during the period from early January through mid-March makes this interpretation extremely unlikely: no one has menses every week for a stretch of nine or so weeks (personal communication from Dr. Margaret Humphreys, M.D., Ph.D., Departments of Medicine and History, Duke University, 28 April 1998).

[98] Bert's ditty continues thus: *And his sister beat the drum. Sister Molly made hot tamales, And Jenny went dum-dum-dum!*
The song had a particular local coloring because Bernice Michel's Aunt Jenny (a sister of Bernice's mother) was the wife of George Morgan—and a South Ridge neighbor well known to the Perrins. As Raymond Perrin, Jr., recalls, "Jenny . . . was quite

deaf and had no teeth. As youngsters, we were fascinated when she would snuffle her nose, which would almost disappear into her chin" (ALS to Dale Randall, 18 December 1978).

Whatever spin Bert himself put on his jingle, either intentionally or because he had forgotten the original, the song has a specific English music hall background (Iona and Peter Opie, *Lore and Language,* p. 13).

[99] In 1918 these six-centers were an inch longer than the regular "Owls."

[100] The night of Saturday, 14 December, was therefore something of a landmark, for Annie and Bert played six games, and Bert won four of them.

haps it was just as well that eventually he installed a wine barrel and a pool table in the basement of the house. Though from Annie's standpoint these were a mixed blessing, some of the best evenings were those when Bert was willing to stay home, perhaps even play dominoes. A significant fact may be that sometimes he *was* willing. Dominoes is the only game ever mentioned in the diary, and Annie, tired though she usually was by day's end, often won.[100]

Besides being tired, Annie was sometimes also in pain. Doubtless her pain, work, and worry sometimes exacerbated one another. Whether the newspaper on a given day had World War I bursting into fresh flames or merely smouldering, as it had for several years, the war provided an important backlight to her diary. Annie, after all, had two sons in their twenties. Meanwhile the spectre of Spanish influenza loomed, then faded, then returned—an uncertain but real menace. For a time in the fall it mainly just shut down public gatherings, but at last it attacked the Perrin family itself. Also and inescapably Annie had to cope with large and small worries relating to the farm—including, as winter closed in, Raym's growing dissatisfaction with his life there and finally his decision to look for a job in some nearby city.

Ill health—both Annie's own and that of the other members of her immediate family—is one of the recurring themes in the diary. Annie was able to go back to work quickly after Dr. Kelley extracted an aching tooth (27 May), but more deeply troubling were her headaches and her literally dragging foot (26 October). Henry's reaction to this last symptom speaks volumes. From faroff Key West, he wrote to Lettie on 3 November: "Am very sorry to hear that ma isn't well. She must have worked too hard this fall. I hope her old troubles will never come back. It makes me feel awfully bad when I think how she has suffered with that trouble."

However "that trouble" was diagnosed professionally, it surely was related to "nerves" that had had to bear too much. There is reason to think that many years before, when the family was living in Cleveland, Annie suffered a nervous breakdown. At what surely was one of the lowest times of her life, she was actually taken to the asylum where Bert worked, and shown there to the doctors as an interesting case. "Nervous prostration" was a common term in the air at the time. So was "hysteria."[101] What did the Cleveland doctors have to say? Even without their conclusions to ponder now, it is safe to say at least that a patient's unconscious translation of emotional pain into a camouflaged and culturally acceptable language of bodily distress is no rare phenomenon. Even distanced by decades from the situation, it is possible to suggest that perhaps the degree of stress Annie experienced in the closing months of 1918 can be gauged in part by her similar symptoms at the time of her sister Fannie's death in 1932: Annie was then partially paralyzed, "unable to use one foot and leg."[102]

Whatever Bert's virtues, early or late, he was never an easy man to live with. The family seems never to have brought itself to talk much about the matter, but in two

[101] The umbrella term "hysteria" had already long survived the recognition of its etymological meaninglessness. In fact, investigators back at the turn of the century were increasingly willing to recognize that a variety of psychogenic symptoms may be triggered by shock, overwork, or emotion—or by some painful mix of these elements (Veith, pp. 254–55).

[102] Myron Randall, Diary, 9 July. One might ponder also the comparable facts that in 1861, following the death of her beloved Prince Albert, Queen Victoria temporarily lost the use of her legs, and that in 1883 the

same phenomenon occurred after the death of her devoted chief attendant, John Brown (Munich, pp. 108–9). In both instances the royal physicians considered the possibility of psychological causes.

letters from Lettie to Myron in 1922 she touched on the subject. In the first she says, "Perhaps you wonder why I didn't give dad any of the information you sent." Then she adds, "You know how he raves" (1 November). In the second letter (postmarked 6 December) she remarks, "Dad is still mulish." And this time she adds guardedly, "Will tell you more later. Makes mother about sick."

The final four words here speak volumes. In fact, Lettie's partial explanation to a new member of the family throws considerable light on the family's dynamics in general—and also, it is clear, on Annie's refraction of them in her diary. When Bert was faced with problems too big or too numerous, he could vent his feelings by raving. And for him there was always the village: he could and did leave. Years later, in fact, and once only, Lettie told her own younger son how in Bert's and Annie's earlier years—perhaps when they lived in Austinburg in the 1890s—Bert disappeared one winter for a number of weeks. Where he went and what he did the family never knew, but it involved a trip on a Lake Erie boat (ice played a part in the story) and a substantial amount of time away, possibly in Canada. In striking contrast, Annie was wholly focused on hearth and home. When faced with problems—new, old, or ongoing— she internalized them and continued to work, holding her peace and biding her time as best she could. She did so because it was her nature and because to her it seemed important above all else to keep the family together. When things were not going well, in short, Bert generally took it out on the family or left. Or perhaps did both. Annie, trying to hold their mutual world together, took it out on herself and stayed.[103]

Toward the end of the diary, whatever the complex of problems may have been, matters come to a head. Annie reports suffering a severe and lingering facial ache and a swollen eye (24 November). "Seems I cant stand it," she writes (25 November). Then finally she fell and hurt herself (26 November). Bert, to his credit, tried briefly to take care of her. Sometimes one of her eyes appeared to fly upwards, and when Dr. Childs was summoned from the village he ordered that Annie "must not try" her eyes (27 November).

An odd but telling detail suggests how badly the routine of life went awry for Annie in November. Throughout the rest of the year after the family returned from Florida, the chore of ironing was endlessly woven into the fabric of her life. Whatever else had to be done, Annie had ironing to do, sometimes only a little, but sometimes a whole afternoon's worth. Generally the household irons (two because they needed to be heated alternately) were brought out about nine days a month. During the blistering drought of August, in fact, they were heated and put into action no fewer than fourteen times. Lettie's occasional help with the chore was, of course, like her help with the cleaning, a significant contribution, but in November, with threshers coming and flu striking and Annie at her lowest, the ironing days shrank to an all-time and telling low of four.

Luckily, the epidemic of Spanish influenza spared

[103] Hard as Bert might be sometimes, he was very likely a significant improvement over his father, Henry, just as Henry, in turn, appears to have been an improvement over *his* father, Thomas.

Two incidents from Henry's early years in England cast light on the characters of all three men—and ultimately on Annie's situation. The first goes this way: once when Henry as a small boy asked for more egg at breakfast, his father responded by saying, "Here, boy, I'll give you more egg," and jammed some into his mouth. In later years, Bert's father could not recall a time in his boyhood when he had not been hungry.

The second incident occurred some years later when Henry and a handful of other Malmesbury boys gathered one day in late summer in the market square (at the intersection of Oxford and High Streets) and began picking up sacks of cowpeas to see who could carry the most. It turned out that Henry could. (Wiltshire sacks for wheat, beans, and cowpeas generally held four bushels [Davis, p. 245].) When he came home and related the feat, however, his father cursed and whipped him, saying, "If you get hurt, you won't be worth anything"— meaning, of course, that he would not be able to work. (Raymond Perrin, Jr., in 1995 remembered hearing both of these stories when he himself was young.)

As a boy, then, Bert's father was already hardened by work and toughened by determination. Much later in life, ironically or not, he would indeed injure himself permanently as a result of heavy lifting. At the age of fifty-nine, in a petition for a pension, he described how he had been disabled back in 1886 as a result of "changing a Wagon box to a hay rack" ("Claim for Pension," General Affidavit, 27 June 1894; document provided by Carol Jensen).

[104] Crosby, p. 21.

both Annie and Bert. (Bert's touch of "grip" while down in Florida was not Spanish flu.) For some reason that no one understands, the disease proved to be hardest on those in their twenties.[104] Then again, no one either within or outside the family was unaffected by the disease. In Geneva the epidemic crested in two major waves, causing the first closing of schools on 8 October. Thus it temporarily freed Lettie to work more at home. When she herself came down with flu, however (14 November), she immediately became an additional burden on her mother. Annie, after making dinner for nine hay-bailers on the first day of Lettie's illness, felt the need to be up and down every hour all the following night in order to give her spoonfuls of the medicine that Dr. Childs had prescribed. Not until 20 November did the doctor make his last house call for Lettie (she had had a week-long siege of it)—and then, only two days later, he had to return to diagnose and prescribe something to ease the pain in Annie's face. He "says it is nerves," she writes (22 November). Meanwhile the schools had reopened—only to close again on 12 December because of the renewed virulence of the flu.[105]

[105] Research now seems to suggest that influenza "killed many more of the world's total population during the fall, winter, and early spring of 1918–19 than the mere 21 million usually attributed to it. It was a demographic catastrophe, comparable in its destruction of human life in this century only with World War II" (Crosby, p. xiv).

Focused as Annie invariably was on the immediate demands of her own daily life, she has relatively little to say about the deadly disease of war. In fact, she does not mention it at all until 26 March, when she writes simply, "Wish the terrible war over." Her most striking statement on the subject is a simple "War is H. and makes H." (24 August)—which proves to be the strongest expression to occur in this diary of a woman who never swore. Although Annie was definitely no joiner, she did a little Red Cross work while down in Florida.[106] Back home again in Geneva, she even attended an occasional meeting of the local chapter of the Soldiers' Mothers' Club. Once, indeed, and surprisingly, a group of fourteen of these women met at the Perrin house (7 November). And like many another war mother, Annie placed a card with a blue star in a front window of the house to let passersby know that the Perrins had sent a son to war.

One notable mark of the war in the diary occurs in the entry for 18 July when Annie records that the "Yankies" have "captured thousands of prisoners." Down in Geneva the shop whistles tooted, bells rang, and bands played. "Every one [is] excited," wrote Annie—though her entry for this date closes with the observation that the Perrins "Mowed the last of [the] hay today." Then at last, about four months later, on 7 November, she recorded with relief that the Great War had ended. Bert and Raym went down to Geneva to witness firsthand the townspeople's unbridled expressions of joy and relief. Even up on the South Ridge, Annie and Lettie could hear the factory whistles. Both the news and the celebrating were premature, of course, but soon they were followed by the real Armistice on 11 November. Bert, Raym, and this time Lettie, too, all went down to the village to share in the excitement, but Annie, who always preferred quiet to confusion, decided again to stay at home.

World War I can be glimpsed most clearly in the diary

[106] Lettie, meanwhile, may be glimpsed working more frequently for the Red Cross. Like many women all across the country, she signed up for a surgical dressings class, which required that all participants work in Red Cross workrooms and wear white caps and long, sanitary white aprons. During 1917 and 1918, literally millions of surgical dressings, hospital supplies, and articles of clothing were shipped to Europe. See note to Annie's entry of 25 March.

when Annie comments on Henry. She tells of helping to pack away his civilian clothes and of going with the family to see him off at the train depot in Ashtabula (4 April). The next day he was to leave Cleveland for Camp Farragut, in Great Lakes, Illinois. Once enrolled there as a member of the Naval Hospital Corps, he quickly became a Hospital Apprentice, 2d Class. And almost at once he began to write home, addressing separate letters and cards to individual members of the family, by that means trying to keep them all abreast of how he was faring. (It was mainly the women, though, who replied.) He made memorable expeditions to Chicago—"The Queen of the North and the West."[107] Then about three months later, after considerable to-do, Annie reports on 3 July that she, Bert, and Lettie have all returned to Ashtabula in order to escort him home for an agricultural furlough. On the grounds that he was needed to help with the farm work, Henry had been granted nearly a whole month of leave.

On 31 August, a month after his return to duty in Great Lakes, Annie received word that Henry expected to be sent to Key West. By mid-September he was already settled there and liking the place, though it is clear that the influenza epidemic had by then become serious. In fact, though no one grasped the devastating dimensions of the problem at the time, the epidemic reached its first peak among navy men on shore duty in the States in the final week of September.[108] Not until 23 October did Annie realize that Henry himself had contracted the disease. Unfortunately he had a very bad

[107] Carleton, pp. 115–22.

[108] Crosby, p. 57. Official Navy records report 236 deaths for the week ending 21 September; 880 for the week ending 28 September; 651 for the week ending 5

time of it—perhaps because, as the doctors told him even before he left for service, his lungs were in some way "wrong." It was especially happy news, then, that he was able before too long to inform the folks back home that he was on the mend. On 12 November, in fact, Annie heard that he had already left Key West for Norfolk, Virginia. By this time his bout with the flu had separated him from his former buddies, but at least he had regained reasonably good health. And from Virginia, on Christmas Eve, as Annie's diary draws near its close, Henry finally sailed for France.

October; 515, 12 October; 332, 19 October, and so on. Crosby concludes that perhaps as many as 40 percent of Navy personnel had influenza in 1918. In all, the Navy lost "4,136 of its officers and men to the flu and pneumonia in the last third of 1918." Thus, "almost twice as many American sailors died of the pandemic than as the result of enemy action in 1918" (pp. 121–22).

Despite the worrisome uncertainties of the flu epidemic, the war, the demands of the farm, and her own health, Annie's words sometimes give glimpses of her wry and quiet sense of humor. She puns ironically on the name of Hotel Pine Castle, where the family landed in Florida: after some friends departed, she wrote that now "we have this Castle to ourselves" (10 January). Kept awake one hot southern night, she observed next day that "The roosters had a midnight concert" (27 February). And back home once again, she noted that "Raym and Pa built a bungalo for the pigs" (7 June) and that Raym had helped by "slicking up [the] hen park" (20 November).

Annie's diary, though, is far more a work of substance than of style. Whereas one must search for hints of her humor, Annie's words give more evidence than one might have anticipated concerning her pleasures, large and small. When she, Bert, and Raym were in Florida, she enjoyed sailing on Lake Conway and visiting with friends. So relaxed were things in Florida that there was time for a bit of religion. There was even time one Sunday to entertain a preacher and his family (6 January). Perhaps more strikingly still, on one blazing winter Wednesday (27 February), when the thermometer climbed to 94° in the shade, Annie attended a tent meeting that featured no fewer than five preachers. At another tent meeting she saw a woman go into a trance and "speak in the unknown tongue" (5 March), and a week after that she attended "an open air service to hear a woman preach" (13 March). Annie's verdict on the latter's performance is a simple "No good." Though as a girl she had attended the Methodist church in Dover, Ohio, at mid-life such religious gatherings were mainly something to do. Whatever spiritual stirrings she may have felt, none breaks through the matter-of-factness of her daily diary notes. Though both of her parents were committed Methodists, Annie's own life seems to have been grounded on moral and affective bases, not religious ones, and after she returned home from Florida, she did not attend church again.[109]

Sunday at home was welcome, to be sure, but as a day of respite, not worship. As often as might be, therefore, it was also a day for visiting—sometimes with a hint that a breezy auto ride through the countryside could be nearly as great a pleasure as the visit itself. A

[109] Following the Perrins' return, Lettie was apparently the only one in the family who went to church. Annie may have neglected to mention (or perhaps did not know about) other occasions when Lettie attended, but she does specify 29 September, 6 October, and 1 December. Few or many times though this may seem, they reflect Lettie's inten-

visit might involve a walk no farther than Pardon Allen's pond. Only a few doors down the South Ridge road to the east, the Allens had a wooden box of a boat to punt or row, as well as dozens of pink and white water lilies, warm and fragrant in the sunshine of a summer afternoon. Near or far, however, calling on people was frequent and generally spontaneous, and a visit of any distance would sometimes turn into an overnight stay.

When Bert sold the family automobile on 30 August, therefore, everyone's wings were suddenly clipped. There was no denying that the Overland had been a major source of pleasure for them all. Of course the family still had its buggy and wagon, even a cutter for snowy weather, and it still had access to those big red Interurban cars at Stop 58. Nevertheless, the sale of the automobile shrouded the Perrin household in gloom. Whatever Bert's motives may have been, Annie and Lettie, left alone at home on the evening after the sale, ate supper together in unprecedented silence, and many years later, Raym still occasionally reminisced solemnly about the loss of the Overland.[110]

As for pleasures other than visiting or simply going into town, there was the upright piano.[111] The Perrins were not an unusually musical family, but Lettie managed to teach herself to play popular sheet music, and she and her brothers—especially Raym—liked to sing. Singing was a good way of sharing. One Sunday afternoon in the fall (13 October), for instance, Lettie and the Lowe girls, Lulu and Grace, sang for everyone for

tion to go with some frequency. On 29 September Henry wrote to her, "Did you & Irine go to church to-Day? You want to stick to your word."

Later generations sometimes misperceive the churchgoing habits of their predecessors. At the time Annie wrote, about 53.7 percent of the people living in Ohio were without any church affiliation. Nationwide, the figure jumped to 56.1 percent (*FPT*, 11 May 1920, p. 4).

[110] The reasons for Bert's sale are probably not discoverable, but his irritation at Raym's making too free with the car may have exhausted such patience as he had. Then, too, it may be that Bert had had a serious scare of some sort. In his later years, when he owned another car, he never drove it himself.

[111] Advertisements of the day suggest that a piano may have been a lesser indulgence than it would later become. In Geneva, for instance, when Bernhard's Music Store offered for sale a number of "square" pianos,

"thoroughly overhauled, suitable for district schools, lodges, etc.," the advertised cost was a reasonable "$25.00 and up" (*FPT*, 11 October 1915, p. 4). More typical, though, was Bernhard's advertisement for new pianos from $250 to $350 (*FPT*, 10 December 1915, p. 2).

about an hour with Lettie at the piano. Annie names no particular songs in her diary (later on, her favorite would be "My Blue Heaven"), but Lettie bought and put her own name on a good many pieces of sheet music. Some became so worn that she finally fastened their loose pages together on Annie's sewing machine.

During the course of a good afternoon or evening the low-ceilinged old sitting room on the Ridge might resound with "When the Harvest Moon Is Shining," "By the Light of the Silvery Moon," "Garland of Old Fashioned Roses," "The Daring Young Man on the Flying Trapeze," and "There's Someone More Lonesome Than You." There was "Can't Yo' Heah Me Callin' Caroline," a solo that sold for sixty cents, and "Silver Bell," featuring on its cover a noble Indian warrior and a dusky Indian maid on a rocky peak against a moonlit sky. Carrie Jacobs-Bond was clearly a favorite composer, with "I Love You Truly," "Just Awearyin' for You," and "A Perfect Day" each promising on its cover to be "As unpretentious as the Wild Rose." (Pink wild roses flourished in the yellow clay countryside around Geneva.) Raym was especially fond of belting out the finales of "Road to Mandalay" and "A Little Bit of Heaven Shure They Call It Ireland." Judged by their tattered condition, however, the family's all-time favorites included "When You and I Were Young, Maggie" ("I wandered today to the hill, Maggie . . ."), "Down by the Old Mill Stream" ("where I first met you, / With your eyes of blue, / dressed in gingham too"), and "Beautiful Ohio," a paean to the Ohio River ("Beautiful Ohio, in dreams again I see / Visions of what used to be").[112] While a World War raged "Over There," and perhaps even as afternoon rain or pellets of evening sleet stung their windowpanes, the Perrins in their Geneva farmhouse continued to find respite and pleasure in visions of a kinder, gentler world than they themselves had ever known.

In December, as the year was ending, the family enjoyed a small musical breakthrough: they acquired a windup Victrola. Though Bert was not one to spend on

[112] See Figs. 23 and 24. Years later—in 1934—Lettie sent Annie an unlabeled clipping explaining that the original "creaking old mill" was not in the U.S. but on the bank of Twenty Mile Creek near Hamilton, Ontario. George Johnson wrote the lyric for his sweetheart, Maggie Clark, who later became his wife. In 1866, over a decade after her death, he had the poem set to music. Lettie and Myron both thought Annie would be interested in all this.

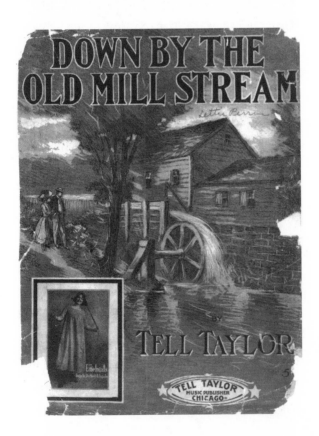

Fig. 23. "Down by the Old Mill Stream" (1910), first popularized in vaudeville, is a standard number for barbershop quartets. Sung at home as directed ("Andante espressivo"), it goes slowly enough for everyone to find the notes and help create a few moments of shared nostalgia. Although Lettie sewed together the tattered pages of her copy and they have subsequently had time to come loose again, her name beneath the title remains clear.

Fig. 24. "Beautiful Ohio," a waltz copyrighted in 1918 by Shapiro, Bernstein and Co. of New York City, was an "ASCAP top seller" that year (Cohen-Stratyner, p. 30). The fact that it is a good example of commercialized sentiment was no deterrent to the young folks gathered at the piano in the Perrin farmhouse. Besides, whether they thought about it or not, the Ohioan subject matter was likely appealing to them.

[113] On 8 November Henry wrote to Lettie, "I hope Dad will help you get the Vic!" See diary entry and note for 20 December 1918.

family luxuries, he agreed to help Lettie pay for it.[113] Like singing at the piano, playing phonograph records for oneself and others was a common home entertainment. Newspaper ads often told one so, and the Perrins themselves had been entertained with other folks' records while visiting in Pine Castle, Cleveland, and Ashtabula. Now up on the Ridge the new "Vic" provided pleasure for everyone. Raym thought the machine "fine" (21 December), and Bert became particularly fond of such records as Sir Harry Lauder's "Wee House 'Mang the Heather" and "I Think I'll Get Wed in the Summer-

time." Bert also grinned happily when listening to a little handful of comic monologues, most of all "Cohen at
the Telephone." (Cohen, in a thick stage Yiddish—"I
ain'd svearing atchoo"—tries to explain to his landlord
that the wind came and blew down a shutter—"No, I
didn' say shuddup.") Also available for a mere seventy-
five cents was "Will You Remember," the waltz from
Sigmund Romberg's *Maytime* ("For Dancing") and the
contralto Elsie Baker singing Carrie Jacobs-Bond's
"I Love You Truly." Vere liked best "My Isle of Golden
Dreams," played by Selvin's Novelty Orchestra. There
was even an inching toward the classical, thanks to
Lettie—Offenbach's "Barcarolle," for instance, as sung
by John McCormack accompanied by Fritz Kreisler.
Probably the young folks' generic favorites, though,
were the fox trots, especially the twelve-inchers because
they provided music for nearly five whole minutes of
dancing.

Back in early 1916 Lettie went so far as to join for a
while a group of young women who had formed what
they called the G.M.C. Club. Though their main aim
was simply to get together now and again and perhaps
do some embroidery, they soon talked themselves into
throwing a Valentine's Day party at which "Thirty cou-
ples danced to music provided by an Ashtabula orchestra."[114] In fact, "A great variety of the latest dances were
on the program among which the Moonlight and Kiss
Waltz, together with the 'spoon' dance, appeared to be
the favorites."

Partying was unusual for the Perrin family, however,

[114] *FPT*, 12 February 1916, p. 2.

and aside from neighborly visits, the most frequent out-of-the-house entertainment for the family was going to Geneva or Ashtabula to see a picture show. Between 21 December 1917 and 19 August 1918 Annie saw at least nineteen films, about one every twelve or thirteen days. After Bert sold the automobile, though, she saw no more.

Probably it is significant that even during the family's most lively movie-going phase this year—April through August—Annie does not always bother to mention what show she has seen, for the simple reason that going somewhere was as important as seeing a show. She does note that she and Bert saw Theda Bara's *Cleopatra* (27 April) and that she thinks it "Very good," but she offers no opinion on Mary Pickford as Rebecca Randall in the much-touted *Rebecca of Sunnybrook Farm* (17 May). On the first Saturday in June the entire Perrin household rode over to the Majestic in Ashtabula to see *Tarzan of the Apes,* with Gordon Griffith as Tarzan and assorted acrobats in skins as his ape friends. On the warm summer evening of 11 July, Annie and Bert saw Mae Marsh as the heroine of a Christmassy film called *The Cinderella Man,* and two days later they saw *My Four Years in Germany,* a sober ten-reeler based on Ambassador James W. Gerard's book of the same name. *My Four Years* was obviously propaganda, but presumably it was redeemed by its grounding in fact. Not surprisingly, Annie went to no such sensational shows as *To Hell with the Kaiser* or *The Claws of the Hun*—though the men, Bert and Raym, did take in *The Beast of Berlin.*

On 3 August Annie, Bert, and Lettie all watched Jack Pickford play the lead in *Tom Sawyer*—which had been offered to the public as a "clean, wholesome" entertainment that "will never grow old."[115] Then on 19 August Annie saw her last film of the summer and the year: George Beban played the role of an energetic "Canuck" in the north-woodsy *Jules of the Strong Heart*.

[115] *Variety's Film Reviews*, vol. 1, under 14 December 1917.

When at last Annie took up her diary to fill its final blank page for the year 1918, she was contemplating the work she had to do to prepare for family pleasure of an altogether different sort—celebrating New Year's Day. Always she was working toward a life that was somehow a little better than life. Of course she knew as well as anybody, probably better than most, that in 1919, when it came, life would flow on in its usual murky, frustration-filled way. It would bring to her and her family new problems, lots of hard work, and continuing bouts with pain, but it would also provide some scattered hours of pleasure.

Whatever stress or pleasure her diary encapsulates and preserves from late 1917 and the whole of 1918, however, Annie's simple words convey also an unflagging concern for the three of her children who survived into adulthood. Only a single entry on 18 August makes mention of her son named Vernon, who died of diphtheria in 1899 at the age of ten. Somehow factoring into the overall dynamics of the family, however, is the general perception that "Vernie" had been Bert's favorite among the children. Perhaps Bert had had too much hope for him to hope so much ever again.

In any case, and despite all, Annie's commitment to Bert, like that to her children, was firm. Bert was often difficult and always strong-minded. Like many another man, he tended to see things only from his own perspective. Despite his willful ways, however, despite his noise and his inability or disinclination to understand Annie, and despite his unsettling readiness to climb onto nearly any trolley or train if it led away from work, Bert was not a bad man. If when all is said and done he seems in some ways too much a man of his time, that was not altogether his fault.

However one reads and understands Annie Elliott Perrin's diary—informal, scattered, and scribbled as it is—it comes down to us packed with the random facts of life as she found them. It follows her first into an exotic world of alligators and oranges, a world that furnishes both a frame and a contrast for all that follows, and yet a world that is already, by the diary's ending, receding rapidly into the past. Though some things about it would remain in Annie's mind for the rest of her life, the whole Florida adventure was constantly being pushed farther into the background by an ongoing press of events. The fact is that her own everyday world was one of churns and curtain stretchers, tomatoes and peaches, wagons and cutters, windup Victrolas, kerosene lamps, and foot-pedaled sewing machines.

Above all else, however, and wherever she might be, Annie's world was one in which family was important. Family mattered constantly, sometimes painfully, and always deeply. Far better than many a more formal document, therefore, Annie's diary still vibrates with the life of a family.

1

"Our Trip to Florida"

17 December 1917–23 March 1918

Monday, 17 December 1917

Pa, Raym & I left home at 9 oclock to take the train at the N.Y.C[entral Depot]. For Florida.[1] We made good connections at Cleveland [and] went on the big four to Cincinnati.[2] Got there about 9.30. Went to the Grand Hotel.[3] Took our rooms[,] then went out and got lunch at the Manhatten.[4] Then home to bed. (Met Mr Norris & family[.][5] Are traveling with them[.])

Tuesday, 18 December

Got up at 6 oclock. Went out and got lunch[,] then went to Depot to take train[.] Found the train was late. Got on train[,] then waited four h[ou]rs, on track[.] This is night [and we are] having some trouble about getting a berth[.] Will reach Chat–[tanooga, Tennessee] tonight, but expect to be asleep.

Wednesday, 19 December

Had a pretty good night[.] Slept in upper birth so saw nothing of Tenn[essee]. Just had breakfast in the dining car. The buildings look queer to me. We see lots of Georgia pine.[6] We see some snow this morning but will soon be out of it.[7]

[1] Annie's simple opening words elide the fact that less than a week earlier, because of the worst blizzard in years, "Geneva has not only been shut off much of the time from the outside world on trolley service, but comparatively few trains have gone through on either railroad" (*Ashtabula Star and Beacon* [*S&B*], 11 December, p. 10).
　Only five days earlier, in fact, under the headline "Horse Drops Dead," one of the now-traveling Perrins became newsworthy:

> Mr. and Mrs. Bert Rose, South Ridge east, were coming home last evening with a wagon load of goods, including 450 lbs. of coal and some grain. Their horse dropped dead in East-wood street in front of [the] Hillsdale home, of heart trouble. Mrs. Rose went home on the [interurban] car. Raymond Perrin, who had just passed the couple before the horse fell, was summoned. The two men hitched Mr. Rose's wagon back of the Perrin rig and Mr. Perrin took it home. W[illiam]. S. Marshall removed the horse this morning. (*S&B*, 12 December 1917, p. 8)

Mrs. Rose was formerly Grace Williamson, daughter of Ellen Williamson, a widow who for a while in 1918 helped with the weekly wash in the Perrin household.
[2] "Big Four" was the nickname of the Cleveland, Cincinnati, Chicago, and St. Louis Railway, an affiliate of the New York Central that served the four cities specified in its corporate name (Hubbard, p. 186; Grant, p. 201). See Fig. 25.
[3] Standing opposite Union Central Station, at the southwest corner of West Fourth and Central Avenue, the Grand was certainly convenient. As Roe puts the matter, "The tired passenger . . .

has but to cross a narrow street and enter an elevator, where he is at once hoisted to the floor of the Grand's magnificent rotunda" (p. 232). With its "lofty ceiling of cut glass," its fluted columns, tessellated floors, and marble staircase (p. 233), the Grand was a surprisingly splendid first stop for the Geneva farm family. First opened in 1874, it boasted in the early 1930s that it was one of the city's hotels that had "stood the Test for Respectability" (*Williams' Cincinnati Directory . . . 1931–1932*, p. 2321).

⁴ Here and throughout, Annie's word "lunch" refers to any light meal.

The Manhattan Restaurant at 17 West Fifth Street was one block west of the Perrins' hotel (*Williams' Cincinnati Directory* for 1910, p. 2539). Most restaurants would have been closed at the time the Perrins "lunch" this evening, but the Manhattan was "one of the first restaurants in the country to remain open on a 24-hour basis" (*Cincinnati Enquirer*, 25 August 1929, Sec. 2, p. 2).

⁵ The Lee L. Norrises lived in Ashtabula, some nine miles or so east of Geneva, at 343 Main Street, near Tyler Avenue (*Farm Journal*, p. 66). Acquaintances rather than friends, the two families now drew together because of their mutual distance from home and their mutual destination. About a year and a half later, however (30 April 1919), Lee and Emma Norris purchased a seven-acre plot immediately adjacent to some of the Perrin orchards and fields (*Ashtabula Records of Deeds*, vol. 236, p. 15).

⁶ For the first time in her life, Annie was seeing longleaf pines —striking because of their soft, long, ten-to-sixteen-inch needles.

⁷ Back home that day, the roads in many places in the county were badly blocked by drifts, making it necessary for traffic to take to the fields (*Geneva Free Press-Times* [*FPT*], 20 December, p. 2).

Fig. 25. The "Winter Tourist" Perrins very likely saw "Big Four" advertisements such as this one from Ashtabula's *Star and Beacon* of 13 January 1917 (p. 8). Later that same year, as the wording here promises they could, the family took advantage of their "Stopover privileges"—which meant they took three days, not one, to reach Jacksonville.

Thursday, 20 December

Landed in Jacksonville about 8.30 last night. Went to the Atlantic Hotel[.][8] Got rooms[.] Then the Norris family and we went to get lunch. Then home and to bed. This morning is cloudy. Pa is up and out[.] I am resting.

Friday, 21 December

Here in St Augustine.[9] One of the most beautiful places I ever saw. Took an Auto out to Hastings this after noon.[10] Pa & Lee stayed out there. The rest came home. Had a fine supper[.] Met some new people here from Canada.

Tonight Mrs. N[orris].[,] Madge,[11] Raym & I went to a picture show[.] Saw Billy Burk.[12] It was good. Came home and went to our rooms.

Saturday, 22 December

This is a beautiful day[.] Mrs Norris[,] Madge, Raym & I went out to the old <u>fort</u>.[13] Went down into the dungeon. Saw all the horrible ways of punishment. We saw many of the old relicks[.] It made me sick to think of all the misery and suffering they went through[.][14] One never tires of seeing the grand & beautiful things of this place. Lee & Bert just came back from Federal Point.[15]

[8] The Atlantic, handily situated near the train station in downtown Jacksonville (136 West Bay), was a relatively new hotel in a fairly old building. Established about 1910, it was originally the Astor House, built in 1878, and would remain in operation until 1951—and then be demolished to make way for a parking lot (*Florida Times-Union*, 13 December 1951, p. 25).

[9] That is, the Ohioans had now traveled some thirty-six miles farther south on the Florida East Coast Railroad.

[10] Hastings, with a population of only nine hundred or so, was situated in the center of Florida's potato-growing region (Stockbridge and Perry, p. 205). Potatoes were probably of interest to the men. During the preceding winter Ashtabula's *Star and Beacon* had reported that in Ohio "the potato situation is conceded to be the worst ever experienced here" (22 February 1917, p. 1). In contrast the traveling Genevans could have read in their own hometown paper that "Florida Potato Growers Made Small Fortunes" (*FPT*, 21 August 1917, p. 1). Ralph Gray had recently returned to Geneva from Hastings with the report that one man there had planted 130 acres of potatoes and cleared $50,000 for his crop. A woman Gray knew cleared $40,000 from hers. In fact, "Many of the growers in that section have felt so flush, with their large returns, that they have abandoned Fords and the cheaper priced automobiles and are buying Hudson super-sixes, and the like."

[11] The Norrises' daughter.

[12] In her early twenties at this time, Billie Burke, the future good witch Glinda of *Wizard of*

Oz fame, was onscreen at the Jefferson in *The Land of Promise*. According to the *St. Augustine Evening Record*, "'Isn't she fine!' was heard all over the house in comment on her splendid work" (21 December 1917, p. 5).

Burke's character in the film has traveled to Canada ("The Land of Promise") and "married a rough farmer, loathing him all the while, but hoping to escape from the monotony of her life." Fortunately, she finally comes "to love him and appreciate his good qualities." Evening seats: 10¢ and 20¢.

[13] In 1565 Pedro Menéndez de Avilés built a wooden fort here called San Juan de Pinos. After Sir Francis Drake destroyed it in 1586, it was rebuilt and renamed San Marco. The English called it St. John for a while, then it was San Marco again, and at the time of Annie's visit it was called Fort Marion (after General Francis Marion, South Carolina's Revolutionary War hero known as "The Swamp Fox"). See Fig. 26.

[14] Though local tour guides traded in horrific suggestiveness, the facts of the matter are tame. Long before Annie's visit, some folks had observed that "Within the northeastern bastion is a chamber known as 'the dungeon,'" but "there is good reason for believing that it was originally intended as a magazine" (Norton, pp. 163–64). See Fig. 27.

[15] To the north, on the St. Johns River, Federal Point was a rural community with a population of about 350 (*Florida: The Playground*, p. 110). Potatoes may have been the attraction again. During the preceding spring (26 April 1917), C. W. Gray wrote from Federal Point to inform friends back in northeastern Ohio that he had recently harvested 495 barrels of potatoes. As the *Ashtabula Star and Beacon* commented, this "isn't bad for a half year's work" (1 May, p. 12). The travelers also could have read about Mr. and Mrs. Milton Hundertmark, fellow Genevans

Fig. 26. An aerial view of Fort Marion published on a 1912 postcard issued by the W. J. Harris Co. of St. Augustine, Florida. The caption reports that this "oldest fortification in the western continent . . . is in all respects a castle built after the plan of those of the middle ages in Europe."

Fig. 27. "The Famous Secret Dungeon" in the northeast bastion at Fort Marion. "In this dungeon were found crumbled human bones, a report of the finding of which is now on record in the War Department" (W. J. Harris Co., 1904).

Sunday, 23 December

Sunday[.]

We all took the St[reet] car and went to Anastasia Island. We put our hands in the water. I tasted it. We picked up some shells. Went into the Aligator farm.[16] Saw Native birds, squirrels, coons & snakes. The Island is 25 mi[les] long. The beach looks like a great bank of pure white snow. How I wish the children were here.

Monday, 24 December

+[17]

Took the train for Orlando at 10.10. A journey of about 100 miles. Was all day getting there. Tried to find a lunch room at Platki.[18] Walked over a mi[le] before we could find one a white person could eat in.[19] Got into Orlando about 7. oclock[,] tired & sick. Went to lunch[,] then to bed. The flees were thick in our room. The town is quite pretty. Just as we landed we saw a Auto burn up.[20]

who had actually established a winter home at Federal Point, where they "engaged in potato growing and other agricultural pursuits" (*FPT*, 6 October 1917, p. 2). Other Genevans buying land in Federal Point included Frank Gray, Arthur Gray, A. H. Parker, and Alex Stuart. In the words of the *Free Press-Times*, "The contiguity of these people makes it very pleasant" (13 October, p. 1).

Only the day before, in contrast, the Geneva paper ran a front-page piece on the situation back home: "Frost Ruins Potato, Corn Crop—Loss Is Big." To be sure, a more positive view of the situation in Geneva may be extracted from an advertisement submitted by Bert himself and first run a few days later: "For Sale—Fine white quality potatoes; delivered (not less than 5 bu.) for $1.50 per bu. B. H. Perrin, South Ridge, Phone 723" (*FPT*, 16 October, p. 2).

Still, as time passed, the bad news prevailed. On 1 November the same paper reported "Flood and Frost Damage to Crops" (p. 1). In particular, "Acres of potatoes are under water."

[16] The Alligator and Ostrich Farm and Museum of Marine Curiosities was for the Perrins a ten-minute trolley ride from St. Augustine. C. J. Sweet and L. C. Kelsey, two Geneva realtors who visited the alligator farm about a year later, wrote to the *Free Press-Times* that one might see there approximately "6,000 alligators ranging in size from six inches to twelve feet in length and up to 250 years of age" (29 January 1919, p. 3).

[17] See Introduction for a conjecture concerning this mark and other later ones like it.

[18] Having arrived in Palatka via the East Coast Railway, the Perrins were now twenty-eight miles from St. Augustine, fifty-six from Jacksonville.

[19] Finding a place to eat was complicated not because the Perrins were over-nice in choos-

ing but because restaurants were segregated. The 1917 Orlando *City Directory* printed widely separated—that is, alphabetically segregated—lists of what it termed "Eating Houses" for "colored" people (p. 300) and "Restaurants" for white people (p. 312).

20 The fact that it was Christmas Eve was displaced for the moment by the immediate events of the journey.

21 Orlando, the county seat of Orange County, had a population at this time of about 18,000 and was Florida's major shipping center for oranges, grapefruit, and tangerines. In the words of *The Standard Guide, Florida* (p. 81), "The streets extend from the business district into the residence sections, past well-kept parks, beautiful lakes, orange groves, rose gardens, truck gardens, patches of bananas, wonderful palms, and nearly all the time beneath the shade of mighty oaks, interspersed with camphor, maple and eucalyptus trees."

22 Pine Castle, five miles south of Orlando, was about one-seventh the size of Geneva. Though too small to have a bank, it did have a post office, a public school (white), and two churches (both white) (*Florida: The Playground*, pp. 48, 209).

Once arrived in Pine Castle, the Perrins registered at Hotel Pine Castle—which was located on Fairlane, a short distance from the railroad tracks. Later on, after they moved to a small house nearby, the hotel remained a social base for them.

23 That is, Raymond picked up the luggage that the family had not been able to carry with them.

Tuesday, 25 December

+

This is Xmas morning[.] I can not realise it. It is quite warm and no one seems to act as if xmas is here[.] Raym has gone to dinner[.] I had none. This afternoon an Auto took us out to a beautiful Orange grove[.][21] I picked my first orange & grape fruit. It is certainly grand. Came back to Pine Castle [and] took rooms for a few days.[22] Raym went to O[rlando]. Got suit cases.[23]

Fig. 28. Hotel Pine Castle, where Annie, Bert, and Raymond settled during the earlier part of their stay in Pine Castle, Florida, during the winter of 1917–18.

Wednesday, 26 December

+

This morning finds us all in our rooms at Pine Castle[.] Mrs Norris & I have cleaned up some, and washed
bedding so we can sleep clean. Our trunk came this
morning so Mrs N[orris]– & I have my house dresses
on and are keeping house.[24] L[ee]. & B[ert]. have gone
to Orlando. We can look out of the windows here and
see Oranges in all of the door yards. But I would rather
be in Ohio.[25]

Thursday, 27 December

Today was quite cloudy. But is brighter now. Mrs
N[orris] & I have done up the dinner work [and] now
are going out to see some of [the] sights near here. Mr
N[orris] & B[ert] just brought us each a pretty rose.[26]

Took a walk this afternoon. Saw two pretty lakes.[27]
Some wild ducks. Saw several small places for sale. All
have Grape fruit & oranges.

Tonight I made two Johnny cakes for supper.[28]

[24] The trunk, the suitcases
fetched the day before, and
whatever the Perrins managed to
take with them on the train all
suggest that from the beginning
they planned no short stay.

Note the hint of formality in
Annie's wording: she refers to
her friend as "Mrs" Norris, despite the fact that she knew her
well enough to loan her a "house
dress."

[25] Annie's last two sentences
here, set down early in her trip,
provide a preview that is something like the conclusion reached
by Sweet and Kelsey, fellow
Genevans who wrote of Florida
in 1919: "Altogether it is a fine
country, but after all is said and
done, Ohio still looks good to
us" (*FPT*, 29 January, p. 3).
Florida simply was not home.

[26] Up to the end of this paragraph, one has here an example
of a mid-day entry.

[27] At the time of the Perrin
visit, Orange County was dotted
with over fifteen hundred freshwater lakes, the two closest to
the hotel being Lake Conway, a
big lake to the east, and much
smaller Lake Mary to the west.
Though Pine Castle itself was
quite level, Stockbridge, a few
years later, described the region
as "hill country, with pines, oaks
and palmettos crowning the ele-
vations" (p. 240).

[28] With cornmeal as its basic
ingredient, johnnycake is a frugal
and quintessentially American
dish, its basic recipe (referring to
cornmeal as "indian meal") hav-

ing been set in print at least as early as 1796:

> Scald 1 pint of milk and put to 3 pints of indian meal, and half pint of flower—bake before the fire. Or scald with milk two thirds of the indian meal, or wet two thirds with boiling water, add salt, molasses and shortening, work up with cold water pretty stiff, and bake. . . . (Simmons, pp. 52–53)

Annie probably varied these ingredients by using bacon drippings (which she always saved in a tin with a lid) or adding one or two eggs or a little cream (*Mountain Makin's*, p. 15).

[29] A standard phrase of the day, as in "Adelbert Bartholomew, 84, . . . caught a hard cold and this resulted in pneumonia." (*FPT*, 6 December 1919, p. 3).

[30] That is, Bert, Raym, and Lee.

[31] Another entry made relatively early in the day.

Friday, 28 December

I have a hard cold.[29] B[ert]– is feeling better this morning[.] R[aym]. still coughs. Hope he will soon be better. The three boys[30] have gone for a walk to look at more land. Mrs N[orris] & I have done up the work. M[adge]– is still in bed. The sun is bright today[.] Hope it will warm up.[31]

Saturday, 29 December

We all went down to the lake this afternoon.[32] Walked about a mile to look at an orange grove. Came home. The nigger brought our first wash home[.][33] All came home tired and hungry.

Tonight just after supper the bell rang. There was Mr Seymore & family.[34] How glad we were to see them[!] They are going to spend a few days with us.

Sunday, 30 December

This is Sunday. Mrs S[eymour, Mrs.] N[orris], & I took a walk. This afternoon several friends called in. We have had a real pleasant day. Raym acts home sick and I am sick to hear from the children.

Two weeks today we left home and not a word from home yet. The children[35] are going to a neighbors.

[32] This is Annie's first reasonably specific reference to Lake Conway—by far the most consequential body of water near Pine Castle.

[33] Although Annie and Mrs. Norris previously managed to do at least a partial washing (26 December), Annie this time paid someone else do the job. The black washerwoman's equipment may be surmised from Packard's observation that "Every Southern backyard seems to hold the big, black, three-legged iron pot for boiling clothes" (p. 29). One should observe also that Annie's term "Nigger" here was a culturally standard one at the time and provides no indication one way or another as to her views on race.

[34] Fig. 29. Back in 1914 Fred and Rose Seymour of Ashtabula, Ohio, became neighbors of the Perrins on the South Ridge, living there at the old Lockwood place (*FPT*, 5 December 1914, p. 2). A couple of years later, however, they returned to Ashtabula, where they lived at 37 Kingsville Avenue (*FPT*, 28 September 1916, p. 2).

The Seymour family, which included a daughter (Vera) and two sons (Frank and David), was to spend considerable time with the Perrins in the coming weeks, visiting in the evenings, going fishing, and making trips to Orlando. Not surprisingly, the two families saw far more of one another in Florida than would be possible after their return to Ohio in the spring. See also the note to the entry for 6 April.

[35] Probably all five of the Ohio young folks.

Fig. 29. Annie and Bert with their friends the Fred J. Seymours outside Hotel Pine Castle. Standing, left to right, are Mrs. Rose Seymour, Frank (the older son), David (the younger), Mr. Seymour, Bert, Vera Seymour, and, nearest to the palmetto tree, Annie.

Monday, 31 December

Mr S[eymour]. took Mr & Mrs N[orris].[,] Pa & I to Orlando this fore noon. Came home[,] had dinner[,] then went to Kiss[immee]–. About 20^{mi}[.][36] Was too cold to ride[,] but it was a pretty little place. We are all hugging the stove today. Seymors are still here[.] How good it seems. I wish I could see Lettie & Henry[.][37]

Tuesday, 1 January

The pump froze so we couldent get water. Mr S[eymour]. built a fire [and] got water for us. Pa got milk & oats for breakfast[.][38] The three men left for Tampa[.][39] We [three women] all got the dinner[,] then Mrs S[eymour] & I went out to an orange grove and got grape fruit & oranges[.] The children all went for an Auto ride.

[36] Approximately thirteen miles to the south by rail, Kissimmee was fairly isolated, but the soil of the area was said to be "especially adapted to the cultivation of vegetables, which can be brought to perfection, in ordinary seasons, in January and February" (Norton, p. 71).

[37] Somehow Annie's pleasure was incomplete without her two older children. One might note also that no one made any fuss over the fact that it was New Year's Eve. (This entry is the final one at the back of the volume. Annie placed her next one at the front under the rubric "January 1.")

[38] Annie had been preparing meals ever since the Perrins arrived in Pine Castle, but this is her first reference to buying food. Throughout the course of their stay, the family's store-bought edibles came from the grocery of Mr. Epaminandus D. M. Perkins, next to the railroad tracks.

[39] Messrs. Perrin, Norris, and Seymour were exploring territory about ninety miles beyond their base near Orlando.

Wednesday, 2 January

Bright & cold[.] Mrs N[orris] & [Mrs.] S[eymour] have gone for a walk[.] I am getting dinner. The children have gone for a ride. Oh joy[!] I have my first letter from home from Lettie. Also one from Henry. Ray got letters and seems much brighter[.] An old lady called on us this after noon[.] Her home is in Ten[nessee]–.

Thursday, 3 January[40]

Nothing of much importance. Mrs S[eymour]. and I went out and got things for dinner. After dinner we had several callers[.] The people seem quite friendly here. Oh dear[,] the children are noisy and tonight got into a regular racket. Hope it will soon be quiet. Madge [Norris] & Vera [Seymour] crying. Did not sleep much[.] Mrs N[orris]. sure was mad. Talked terrible[.][41]

[40] By mistake, Annie put this entry on the page designated for Friday, 4 January.

[41] Clearly Annie recorded portions of this entry at different times. In fact, the last three sentences appear to have been written Friday morning.

Friday, 4 January[42]

This is a pretty bright morning. Mr. S[eymour] & family have gone home. Have been with us since Sat[urday] evening[.] It seems so quiet now they are gone. Raym feels pretty down. We are washing today.[43] Bert & M[adge]. Have gone to the store. I am getting dinner. Hope I will hear from home folks today[.][44] Tonight we went to a tocky party at the Parish.[45] There was a programme of music. Then [they] served sandwichs & sweet potatoes[,] Possom, [and] coffee.[46] The v[i]olin solo was the leading feature.

[42] This entry was made on the page intended for Thursday, 3 January.

[43] Whether or not Annie had to resort to the southern outdoor-kettle method of washing, she had a big job on her hands—this time and many times thereafter during the course of the year. One of the photographs in Raym's album shows the back porch of a house where the residents kept their long wooden laundry bench, and on it their big metal washtub—which on washday had to be filled with hot water. Items to be washed were most likely scrubbed on a washboard. Then the hand-cranked wringer (if one was available) would wring most of the water out of the clothes. And then, after being rinsed in fresh water and wrung again, all of the laundry, still wet and heavy, had to be carried out and hung on the clothesline.

Back home, though probably not here in Florida, additional niceties included adding a little blueing if the wash was all white. If there were things to be starched, the starch needed to be mixed with water and cooked and stirred a while on the stove before those items (or parts of them, most usually collars and cuffs) were dipped in it.

[44] Annie's hope for mail was linked to Bert's trip to the store because the proprietor of the grocery, Mr. Perkins, was also the postmaster, and the Perrins had to go to the store to pick up their mail.

[45] Annie had just heard for the first time the term "tacky party" —and faithfully recorded the Southern pronunciation of "tacky." In earlier days the word had referred to an inferior "jade of a horse" (Farmer, p. 526) and

then later, by extension, to Southern "po' whites" (*OED*). At least as early as 1890, however, and doubtless in Pine Castle in 1918, tacky parties had become "those in which the guests wear their old clothes" (Thornton, 2:883). Still later, and tellingly, a tacky party would become "a party to which the guests come dressed as hayseeds or hillbillies" (Mathews, 2:1698).

The particular tacky party attended by the Perrins was given by the local Methodists, who held their indoor social and community events in the parish house behind the Union Church building. Situated at the northeast corner of Orange Avenue and Wallace Street (Linton, p. 39), the house was only a short walk from Hotel Pine Castle.

[46] A possum (or, more properly, an opossum) is an omnivorous scavenger, one variety of which, the so-called Virginia opossum, is tied closely to southern culture. Back in 1608 Captain John Smith, leader of the Virginia colony, described it as being the size of a cat and having "a head like a Swine, and a taile like a Rat" (quoted by Wilson, p. 389).

In subsequent years poor southerners, white and black alike, became hunters of the animal for both its fur and its meat. The latter, besides being rather greasy, has been described as "sort of like dark meat of chicken, only stronger-tasting and loose on the bone, and stringy, like pork" (Roy Blount, Jr., quoted by Wilson, pp. 389–90).

The amazing durability of the possum is reflected in the old southern tale of one that was killed and put in a roasting pan to cook, but ate up all the sweet potatoes and gravy in the pan and then escaped when the oven door was opened (Wilson, p. 390).

[47] Throughout the year, Saturday was the normal day for room-to-room cleaning.

[48] Probably the man identified on 13 February as the "Proff." More specifically, since there

Saturday, 5 January

Bert and L[ee] have gone to Orlando. Mrs N[orris] & I are cleaning up the house[.][47] Looks quite homey. Raym looks lonesome. He has gone to the lake with a teacher across the street from us.[48] I baked pies today. This afternoon was warm enough to sit on the poarch[.] The men just came home so now we must get supper. Raym is home and going to the store for us.

———

was only one male teacher in town, Raym probably went to Lake Conway with Charles L. Durrance—who had come to town fairly recently and was currently serving as principal of the local grade school (Orlando *Directory*, 1919–1920, p. 281). Mrs. Delma Ford Green described him many years later as "my eighth and ninth grade teacher and a wonderful, strict teacher" (quoted by Linton, p. 46).

Lake Conway is not merely large; at the time it was also Pine Castle's main source of recreation, a place where people swam, fished, and sailed as well as took baths and washed their hair. Mr. Durrance, in fact, was to be remembered for wryly nicknaming Lake Conway "The Pine Castle Bathtub" (Linton, p. 79).

Sunday, 6 January

This is a beautiful day. L[ee] & B[ert]. have gone out about 20^{mi} to look at a Grove. Mrs N[orris] & M[adge] have gone to S[unday]. S[chool]. I am getting dinner. Noon and we are having a regular thunder storm. Evening. We have the Preacher and family here.[49] The men came home about 7 oclock [and] brought some nice oranges. [They] Had dinner with a man from Nova Scotia.

This has been a rather lonesome day. I miss being at home. Seems so hot here.

Monday, 7 January

This is the prettiest morning we have had[.] Seems like an Ohio May morning. This morning I done our washing, [and] baked pies. The men have gone to Orlando with a man to look at a grove. Mrs N[orris] & I are going to call on Mrs Fox this afternoon.[50]

This morning Raym brought me five letters & a card from Lettie. How glad I was to hear from the children[!] Mrs F[ox] seems real Nice.

+

[49] Since the preacher brought his family, he probably was from the local Methodist congregation. See the entry and note for 10 January.

[50] Mr. and Mrs. Fox were new acquaintances from Bicknell, Indiana (see 14 January).

Tuesday, 8 January

Pa, Raym & I went to Orlando to look at a place, a good house but think it would be very lonesome. R[aym] & I got home at noon. Had a punk dinner.[51] N[orrise]s are thinking of leaving. I have a terrible head ache today[.] This after noon walked to the P.O. with Mr Fox[.] Every one seems very friendly here.[52] But the natives are rather distant I think.

+

Wednesday, 9 January

Another fine day[.] Mrs N[orris]. is packing her trunk. I just made a pie. Got dinner [and] done the morning work.[53] Pa feels peeved about it.[54] Raym is down on the Lake.[55] [This] Afternoon, Pa, L[ee] & E[mma]. have gone for oranges. Things are a little pleasanter today.[56] But nothing to brag about.

[51] For Annie and her times, "punk" meant "poor."

[52] That is, at Hotel Pine Castle.

[53] "Doing" the morning work refers to routine chores. After breakfast was cooked and served, for instance, the dishes had to washed, dried, and put away. Then the kitchen needed a quick sweeping with a broom, and the beds needed to be made. If there was no indoor plumbing, the slop-jars under the beds were likely to need emptying and washing. Generally, too, there were various things to "straighten out."

[54] The "it" here is vague, but may refer to Bert's feeling that the Norrises were deserting.

[55] Once again, nearby Lake Conway.

[56] Though Bert was "peeved" today, things previously had been even more unpleasant.

Thursday, 10 January

Another beautiful day. Mr N[orris] & family left for St Petersburg this morning so we have this Castle to ourselves[.][57] We went to the train with them.[58] Tonight Pa & I went over to the Methodist ministers[.][59] They have a nice home. Met Mrs Dr Roney there.[60] They played a number of records for us[,] some good ones. That ended another day at Pine Castle.

Wonder how many more will come here. Hope some one we like.

Friday, 11 January

This morning a Mr Smith called on us from Jefferson O[hio].[61] Looking for Mr N[orris]– [but] they had left for St Petersburg. This evening a man & wife came from Medina O[hio]. Are staying at the Hotel. They seem like very nice people.[62] We are having a terrible thunder storm. I done a big washing, and cleaned up. I think Pa & R[aym]. wish they were at Geneva. Not much to write about today[.]

57 Exploring about 170 miles farther south and west, the Norrises planned to travel all the way to the coast.

58 Small as it was, Pine Castle was a stop on the Atlantic Coast Line Railroad.

59 The Methodist minister currently serving in Pine Castle under the Maitland Mission was G. W. Herndon. Appointed only the previous month, the Rev. Herndon was a supply pastor whose term had just begun (1 January) and was to extend through December 1918. (Information provided by Nell Thrift, Florida Conference Archives, United Methodist Church.)

60 Lydia Roney, the local physician's wife (and the first Floridian Annie names), was also calling on the minister and his wife. See the entry and note for 18 January.

61 Since Jefferson is the county seat of Ashtabula County, this Mr. Smith was practically from home. The Smiths up that way were nearly as plentiful as the wild blackberries, though, so he is hardly identifiable here.

62 This is Annie's first impression of A. D. and Ella Aylard, who now begin to appear frequently in the diary.

Saturday, 12 January

Just came back from renting a cottage. The people that came last evening hate to see us go. Well here we are in our new home[.] Some dirt I must say. We are right on the Dixie highway, so guess we wont be lonesome if Autos will be company.[63] Have five rooms. Two chambers,[64] & 3 rooms below. Dirt & bed bugs plenty. Will have to fight them.[65]

+

[63] "Orange county claims the distinction of having started the good roads movement in Florida, and it was the first to complete its system of hard roads from county line to county line. The central branch of the Dixie Highway traverses Orange county" (Reese, p. 34). Running northward from Pine Castle to Orlando, this road, earlier known as Black Bear Trail, eventually became Orange Avenue. Within Orlando, it was "the principal business street of the city and the dividing line for streets running e and w" (*Orlando, Florida City Directory . . . 1919–1920*, p. 350). See Figs. 30 and 31.

[64] That is, upstairs bedchambers. An instance of English English in Annie's diary.

[65] However well Annie fared with the dirt, her attack on the bloodsucking, foul-smelling *Cimex lectularius* was probably only partially successful. Gasoline was recommended as a bedbug deterrent by an expert writing in 1903, but the truth is that gasoline destroyed only the bugs themselves, not their eggs (Charles Campbell, p. 221). When gasoline was used, in fact, "a new and full-size crop of bugs" was likely to regain "possession of the bed within a few days."

In 1916 another knowledgeable writer, C. L. Marlatt, observed that "the most efficient remedy for bedbugs is to fumigate the infested house or rooms with hydrocyanic-acid gas"— which, the writer goes on to say, "is deadly poisonous" (p. 11). More practically, he observes

Fig. 30. Annie and Bert pose somewhat stiffly on the front steps of the cottage they rented during the second phase of their stay in Pine Castle (12 January–18 March).

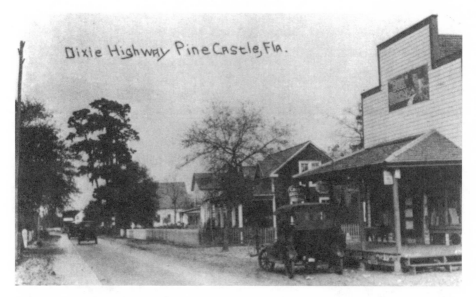

Dixie Highway Pine Castle, Fla.

Fig. 31. Pine Castle, looking northward up the Dixie High-way from its intersection with Waltham. At the right is the feed store, with benches on either side of the door and, above the porch, an advertisement for Bull Durham To-bacco. Toward the left rear, dripping with Spanish moss, are some of the remaining pines that once covered much of the region. Off to the left, beyond camera range and parallel to the road, are the railroad tracks leading to Orlando. (From Linton, p. 52.)

that among "simple methods of control perhaps the most effi-cient is in very liberal applica-tions of benzine or kerosene ... introduced with small brushes or feathers, or by injecting with syringes into all crevices of beds, furniture, or walls where the in-sects may have concealed them-selves" (p. 12). Most practical of all, however, is a "liberal use of hot water, wherever it may be employed without danger to fur-niture, etc." (p. 12).

Whatever method Annie tried (Ephraim Felt in 1917 wrote of still others), the chances are good that she did some serious clean-ing with hot water and soap.

Sunday, 13 January

This is a grand day. Bert & I both feel about sick. I just got a card from L[ettie]. Seems good to hear from her. Raym is out on the lake. I have been cleaning all the morning. This afternoon B[ert] & I walked out over a mile to a family by [the] name of Etty.[66] Seemed very friendly. But oh such a place to call home[!][67] Gave us a cabbage & some lettuce[.] Invited us to come and fish.

+

Monday, 14 January

Today is bright[.] Just got my work done up and Mrs Noel from Tenn[essee]– & Mrs Fox from Indianna called on me[.][68] Had been here about an h[ou]r when Mrs S—[69] & family came with all their furniture. Are going to stay at the Hotel. Also Mr S[eymour] and F[rank] from Ashta[bula]–. We spent the evening at the Hotel. Mr & Mrs Aylard are very nice people[.] They lost their only child last June. Got Henrys picture today[.] Is just like him.

[66] Born in England, Thomas Etty was a sixty-one-year-old general farmer on the outskirts of Pine Castle. He and his Georgia-born wife, Jane, who was some sixteen years younger, were having a hard time of it: besides their own Florida-born children, Horace (age fourteen) and Pearly (nine), they had taken in a Virginia-born orphan, Robert Ford (twelve). (From *Orlando, Florida City Directory, 1915–1916*, p. 257; *1922*, p. 368; and 1920 U.S. Census for Orange County.)

[67] Annie had not previously been inside a "cracker" home. As a native of Pine Castle has explained, "The cracker house usually consisted of four rooms—one for cooking, one for eating and gathering, and two bedrooms. Most bedrooms had two beds, depending on how large the family was" (Linton, p. 29).

[68] John Noel is listed as a winter resident in the section on Pine Castle in the Orlando *Directory* of 1919–20 (p. 281).

[69] Perhaps Seymour. See 18 January.

Tuesday, 15 January

This forenoon I got my work done up. V[era] & D[avid] were here about an h[ou]r. this afternoon[.] Mr & Mrs A[ylard]. [and] B[ert] & I went to a grove[,] got two baskets of oranges[.] Then went to the Newel Grove [and] got one basket.[70] Visited a while[.] Came home too tired to walk. Got supper. Raym went to a party [and] came home 11.30. Was about 40 at party[.] Another day gone. Every day makes one less to be here.

Wednesday, 16 January

Raining and it rained nearly all night. Mr S[eymour] took B[ert] & I to Orlando with him. I was sick all the way home. Dont feel much better now. I got a film for the Kodac. Raym is writing to Lettie[.] Frank S[eymour]– is here. Pa is over to the Hotel[.]

Raym & Frank went out and got five doz[en] oranges today.

Thursday, 17 January

Still raining[.] I dont feel good.

Raym is out somewhere[.] B[ert] & Mr A[ylard]. have walked out to a grove. Feel lonesome[.] I thought I would hear from Lettie today. B[ert] is complaining more than at home[.] I guess he has the Gripp[.][71] Mr A[ylard] & wife spent the evening here. Like them better all the time[.]

70 Although Lester C. Newell and his wife, Ellen, are both listed under Pine Castle in the *Orlando, Florida City Directory and Orange County Gazeteer* for 1917 (p. 275), Mrs. Newell is listed in 1918 as a widow, a winter resident of Florida who still maintains a home in Ashtabula, Ohio (*Ashtabula Directory*, 1918, p. 206; Orlando *Directory*, 1921, p. 301).

71 "Grippe" was at this time a term for influenza, but it was often used quite loosely.

Friday, 18 January

Today I washed & ironed.[72] Felt a little home sick today. Got a letter from Henry saying it is 16° below zero at Akron.[73]

Got a letter from Lettie this afternoon[.] Says it is very cold up there. Mrs Noel called on me this P.M.[,] also Mrs Seymour & Mrs Stowe. [This] Evening B[ert]. has gone to see Dr Roney.[74] Hope he will soon feel better.

Saturday, 19 January

Bert went to Orlando today. It is General Lee's birthday. So they were going to close the bank.[75] Bert is feeling some better. We got six letters today. They all tell how cold it is in Ohio.[76] We are having summer weather now. I must bake something for Sunday. Guess we will go to church tomorrow[.]

[72] Annie did far less ironing in Florida than after her return home, but the job was never easy. After the laundry had dried, the items to be ironed were separated out and sprinkled lightly with water shaken from the fingertips. It was then necessary to fold or roll these items so that the moisture would distribute itself more or less evenly throughout the fabric. The actual process of the ironing itself could then proceed, though it would be intermittently slowed by the need to keep reheating the iron (or irons) on the stove—where, of course, a fire had to be kept burning, no matter the temperature outside.

[73] At this point Henry was still in Akron (about seventy miles south and west of Geneva) working for Firestone Tire and Rubber. In Cleveland the ten-below-zero temperature on 13 January was the lowest on record for nearly half a century (Rose, p. 758).

[74] Dr. David C. Roney (b. Kittanning, Pennsylvania, 1855–d. Orlando, 1923) received his degree from The Hospital College of Medicine, Central University of Kentucky, in Louisville, and was first licensed to practice in Indiana (1897) and then, later, in Florida (1914). Subsequently practicing alternately in Orlando and Pine Castle, he was in one of his Pine Castle periods at the time Bert turned to him for help.

[75] Florida banks were generally open until noon on Saturday, but the birthday of General Robert E. Lee (19 January 1807–12 October 1870) was an official holiday (*Rand-McNally Bankers' Directory*, p. 1411).

[76] A headline in the *Geneva Free Press-Times* for 14 January more or less summarizes Ohio's winter: "Coldest Weather in 41 Years Was December Record" (p. 1).

Sunday, 20 January

This has been a beautiful day[.] Mr & Mrs Aylard, B[ert] & I went to the Baptist church [and] heard Dr Tupper speak.[77] It was fine[.] Met so many Pine Castle people. Were introduced to about a doz[en]. They all seem very friendly.[78] After servises we went over to Mr Reeds[.] Mrs R[eed]. plays in the church.[79]

Mr & Mrs S[eymour]. and Mrs B[80] spent the evening here.

Fig. 32. The Pine Castle Baptist Church, built about 1915 at the southeast corner of the Dixie Highway and Hoffner Avenue—only a few hundred feet north of the feed store seen in Fig. 31. (From Linton, p. 43.)

[77] Judged by their building and their preacher, the Baptists in Pine Castle were thriving. By about 1915, no longer dependent on sharing the Union Church building with the Methodists and the Missionary Alliance, the Baptists were already sufficiently strong to build a new church for themselves (see Fig. 32).

The preacher for this Sunday, moreover, Dr. Kerr Boyce Tupper, who had agreed to serve periodically as pastor of the Pine Castle Baptist Church, was primarily the pastor of First Baptist in Orlando. The Pine Castle congregation, with only eighty-seven members in 1918, was fortunate that Dr. Tupper was willing to come down from his home in Maitland (seven miles north of Orlando) on the first and third Sundays of each month—leaving the clerk of the Pine Castle church (J. W. Matchett) to provide at least some sort of local continuity (information from the Wekiwa Baptist Association *Annual* of 1918 and a letter of 30 October 1996, both provided by Bill Sumners, Director of The Southern Baptist Historical Library and Archives).

It is somewhat startling to realize that Dr. Tupper, originally from Georgia and now in his sixty-fourth year, was not only a world traveler and the owner of a choice private library of some four thousand volumes, but also a frequent contributor to literary and religious journals, a compelling speaker, and, in short, a famous preacher. During his earlier stint of preaching at the First Baptist Church of Denver (1890–96), his congregations are said to have ranged from 1,000 to 1,200 every Sunday, and over 500 people were added to the church roll (*National Cyclopaedia of American Biography*, 8:69).

78 Annie is thinking here of people from the town, not merely the hotel. This is a corrective to her observation of 8 January.

79 Though he was not above offering occasional advice to humans, Dr. Stanley W. Reed was actually a veterinary surgeon—and obviously finding enough farm animals nearby to keep his practice going. About fifty-four years of age, he was another native Ohioan—as was his wife, Florence (about fifty-eight). (Orlando *Directory* for 1915–16, p. 257; 1921, p. 302; and 1920 Census.)

80 Possibly Mrs. Bumby, whom Annie mentions on 31 January.

81 That is, the long walk was exhausting.

82 A real kindness, since Annie had a sensitive complexion.

83 Annie at this point was probably working on a yoke. Once home again, in any case, she refers to a yoke she crocheted for Fannie while down in Florida (see entry for 3 April).

Monday, 21 January

Today is hot[,] 84°[.] Mr & Mrs S[eymour]. Mr & Mrs A[ylard]. B[ert] & I just came from Newels grove[.] Almost done out[.][81] Took some pictures. Hope they will be good. Raym went to Orlando today. <u>Nothing</u> doing.

Mrs A[ylard]. gave me a sun hat[.][82] I am crocheting some.[83] Looks like rain. Got three letters & a card today.

Fig. 33. Sitting together at the edge of the front porch floor of Hotel Pine Castle on 21 January 1918 are *(left to right)* Mr. A. D. Aylard, Bert, Mrs. Ella Aylard, and Annie (still wearing her apron)—Ohioans all.

Tuesday, 22 January

It rained all night[.] This morning is bright & cold. About 66°. Raym is out on the lake. Bert has gone to Orlando. Mrs S[eymour]. and the ministers wife[84] were here about an h[ou]r this afternoon.

Bert and I spent the evening at the Castle.[85] [Mr.] S[eymour]. came just as we were coming home.

Wednesday, 23 January

Got letters from Henry today. Is very cold up there. Nothing but just ordinary things today. Gets warmer every day. Went to a Red Cross entertainment at school house[.] It was Punk.[86] Laughed at nothing. Not much like Geneva Entertainments[.] Guess I am a Northiner all right[.]

Thursday, 24 January

Got word today that Uncle Fred is coming.[87] He got here ahead of his letter. B[ert] & R[aym] met him in Orlando.[88] Fred D[obson]. came with him.[89]

Spent the evening over to Mr Brewers.[90] Such lovely bright nights here. But when the sun sets there is no Twilight. But beautiful moon light.

[84] Most likely the wife of the Reverend Herndon, the Methodist minister whom Annie and Bert visited on 10 January.
[85] That is, at Hotel Pine Castle.

[86] See note to 8 January.

[87] Bert's bachelor younger brother, Frederick W. Perrin (19 February 1870–2 May 1933), was a canny and successful business-man from Cleveland (see Fig. 34). His arrival suggests that he, too, was interested in Florida real estate.
[88] Then all three men took the short run down to Pine Castle on the Atlantic Coast Line Rail-road. Bert and Raym had a twelve-mile round trip from Pine Castle to Conway to Orlando and back (*Grant's Tourist Guide*, p. 17).
[89] Fred Dobson was Fred's and Bert's twenty-four-year-old nephew—the son of their wid-owed sister Bessie (see note to 4 June).

Friday, 25 January

The boys are all gone to the lake. I am busy now. Five in the family. Mrs S[eymour]. spent the afternoon here. In the evening Mr & Mrs S[eymour] were here until 9 oclock. The tree toads sing until I am lonesome hearing them. [Uncle] Fred bought Raym a boat today. $22.[91] Now he will have some amusement.

Saturday, 26 January

87°

Another grand day[.] They have all gone over to the grove to get some fruit to send home. I washed and ironed today[.] Cleaned clear through.[92] It is too hot to work. Was invited to go to Orlando tonight, but did not go.

Sunday, 27 January

This is a very hot day[,] 89°. B[ert] & F[red Perrin]. came home [from Orlando] about done out. After dinner we went to the lake. Raym took us out in the boat. We certainly had a fine ride. Took us across to the Island. We landed [and] went into a grove[.] Got about 1½ doz oranges. Came back[.] Just dark[,] got supper. Fred, B[ert], & I spent the evening on the poarch. Raym & Fred D[obson]. were out with girls.[93]

Monday, 28 January

Mr Seymour came over and invited us to go for a drive. He took us to Orlando & Winter Park[,] a very pretty place about 12^{mi} from Pine Castle, a home for the wealthy built by Northern men on lake Seminole.[94] We enjoyed our ride very much[.] Got back at noon. F[red]. P[errin]. & F[red]. D[obson]. sent fruit by mail today[.] Cost $1.28 for 19 lbs.

Tuesday, 29 January[95]

Fred[s] P[errin] & D[obson]. have just left for [St.] Petersburg. Took our pictures. Came home & Mrs M.[96] came in for a while[.] Then it was time to get dinner. After noon I help the Red Cross tie a comfortable.[97] In the evening we went to the Baptist church to hear two lady missionaries speak [and] it was very good.

[94] In 1881, Loring A. Chase of Chicago and Oliver E. Chapman of Canton, Massachusetts, received the first deed to the land on which Winter Park was built, and in 1889 F. B. Knowles of Worcester, Massachusetts, was identified as the "principal owner of Winter Park" (*The Seminole*, pp. 2, 21).

Situated four miles north of Orlando, the town was touted in 1926 as "one of the first communities in Florida to adopt a town plan," and altogether had become a pleasant, well-ordered place where "oak trees planted along its streets arch across the thoroughfares which wind in and out among beautiful lakes" (Stockbridge and Perry, pp. 240–41).

Annie may have been mistaken in her reference to "lake Seminole," however. Though the name "Seminole" itself occurs frequently in Florida (the land the town stood on had been held by Indians as recently as 1860 [*The Seminole*, p. 1]), and though Norton claimed that from the observatory of Winter Park's Hotel Seminole one could see some fourteen lakes (p. 276), the most notable bodies of water nearby were named Maitland (toward the north), Osceola and Virginia (east and southeast), and Killarney (west) (p. 277).

[95] On this same day a neighbor of the Perrins back in Geneva, Eugene C. Stone, testified in the *Free Press-Times* to the unusual severity of the winter on the South Ridge: "Mr. Stone says that the last day his sheep were out for pasture was October 29th. It snowed the night before.... Practically,

therefore, there has been no pasturage for three solid months"
(p. 2).

96 Possibly Mrs. Marden (see 2
February).

97 Annie means "comforter"
—that is, a sort of bed covering
consisting of two layers of cloth
with a filling (perhaps down) between them. Small, hand-tied
knots made of yarn drawn
through all the layers provided a
means of stabilizing the filling.

Fig. 34. Annie and Bert, together with their two Ohio guests,
Fred Perrin (far right) and Fred Dobson, pose outside the
"WHITE" door of the Pine Castle, Florida, depot. Annie's
summer hat contrasts nicely with her brother-in-law's winter coat, and her hand resting lightly on Bert's shoulder contrasts tellingly with Bert's own hand in his pocket.

Wednesday, 30 January

Today has been very warm. In the afternoon Mr &
Mrs S[eymour] came along and invited B[ert] & I to go
to Orlando with them[.] Mrs B——98 went with us.

I got a new hat & a p[ai]r of white gloves.99 Pa treated
all to ice cream. Came home with a head ache. Raym
went out and got fruit to send to Bernice[.]100

98 Perhaps Mrs. Bumby,
whom Annie and Rose Seymour
visited the next day.

99 The gloves, if not the hat,
sound like protective coloration.
Many years later some polite
southern women, no matter the
heat, still insisted on wearing
white gloves on Sunday.

100 This is Annie's first reference to Bernice Jane Michel,
Raym's "girl" back in Ohio.

Thursday, 31 January

This morning I did a big washing. So hot I could hardly stand it in the afternoon[.] [Mr.] S[eymour]– and B[ert] & I went to lake Jessimine to fish[.][101] Mrs S[eymour] & I visited with Mrs Bomby[.][102] The men fished. Got one Jack,[103] 3 Perch, 2 cat[fish], 1 trout. I picked some violets and a sprig of holly. Raym was out fishing with some boys.

Friday, 1 February

Another hot day[.] Got a letter from Henry telling of terrible cold and snow at home. I done my ironing this afternoon. Mrs S[eymour]– & Mrs A[ylard] were here this afternoon. In the evening we went to an ice cream social for the R[ed] cross[.] Raym wasent shaved so would not go.

Got a letter from Sister F[annie]. today[.][104]

[101] Lake Jessamine lies a little to the north and west of the Perrins' base.

[102] Mrs. Maxie V. Bumby, the Georgia-born wife of Jesse Bumby, a local general farmer, was about Lettie's age (twenty-six), but already the mother of a twelve-year-old son and a nine-year-old daughter (1920 U.S. Census).

[103] A "jack-salmon" was said to be one of some 657 kinds of fish found in Florida's freshwater lakes.

[104] Annie's twin sister was Fannie Idella Keyse (21 February 1866–3 July 1932), the wife of Walter R. Keyse (1864–1938). The Keyses were at this time living and farming in Madison, Ohio, about six miles west of Geneva. A few years earlier they had lived in Rocky River, a village west of Cleveland—not far from Annie's and Fannie's girlhood home in Dover—and Walter had run a general hardware store ("Farm and Garden Seeds a Specialty"). Eventually they returned to the area west of Cleveland and had a home in North Olmsted. (The quotation here is from a 1906 bill of sale provided by Richard Keyse, 13 May 1997).

Saturday, 2 February

89° at the Castle[.]

Not much to write about today. Done my Saturdays work[.] B[ert] & R[aym] were out all the morning [and] came home to dinner. In the evening Mr & Mrs Burer[105] & Mrs Marden spent the evening here [and] told snake stories[.][106]

Went to bed with a head ache. Treated them to orange pie.

[105] Possibly the Rev. Mr. Brewer and his wife, Frances.

[106] In the Orlando *Directory* of 1919–20 Melissa Marden is listed as a winter resident of Pine Castle and the widow of Frank L. Marden (p. 281). At other times of the year, she is said to live in Charleston, Illinois.

Sunday, 3 February

Done up the morning work. Then all got ready to go over to the Hotel and eat dinner with Aylards. Had a very nice dinner and a pleasant afternoon. Mrs Dr Roney & Mrs Sweet came so all had a pleasant time.[107]

Went home about 5.30 oclock. Got supper[.] I had neuralgia so did not feel like much. Went to bed but not to sleep.

[107] Anna Sweet of Pine Castle was the wife of Charles J. Sweet, a truck garden farmer (Orlando *Directory* for 1921, p. 302).

Monday, 4 February

Some cooler today. R[aym] & B[ert]. went to Orlando with Mr S[eymour]. Got back to dinner.

Done up my dinner work [and] went to call on Mrs Fox. Had a pleasant time.

Got home just in time to get supper. Mrs Fox said it was 80° on the shady side of poarch. I made Johny cake.[108] Had sliced oranges and tea.

[108] See note to entry of 27 December 1917.

Tuesday, 5 February

Mrs S[eymour] came over this morning before we were up[.] Wanted us to go to Daytona with them[,] a trip of 80^{mi}[.] We done some hustling [and] started about 9.15 oclock[.] Some parts of the drive was beautiful[,] some like a wild jungle. We crossed the St John[s] river on the ferry.[109] In Sanford we saw <u>acres</u> of lettuce, Cellery, & cabbage. Got into New Smyrna a little after noon[.][110] Had dinner[,] then went on to D[aytona] + [drove] across the Halifax river[111] over a toll bridge[,] 35^{cts} [and then on] to the ocean, [where we] took pictures[, and] gathered shells.[112] Put up at City Hotel for the night.[113]

[109] The sightseers headed just about due north.

[110] Though still heading northward, the travelers had now gone about 130 miles and veered more toward the east (*Grant's Tourist Guide*, p. 39). New Smyrna, in Volusia County, is about fifteen miles from Daytona.

[111] Annie here crossed out and wrote over "St. John river."

[112] After crossing the Halifax River (actually a salt water lagoon about three-quarters of a mile wide), the travelers had to cross the slim peninsula separating the Halifax from the Atlantic before they could at last gather shells.

[113] The City Hotel in Daytona, at 39–41 Orange Avenue, was conveniently situated on the same street as the toll bridge across the Halifax. Advertised as an "Old Landmark" in 1914, its

rates that year were "$1.00 and Up," and, as Annie's next entry suggests, it had a "Cafe in Connection." On the same page as the 1914 ad is the proud claim that Daytona is "The Prettiest Resort in the World / Summer and Winter" (Daytona *City Directory*, p. 32).

Back home in Geneva, meanwhile, the newspaper reported a temperature of 17° below zero at 8:30 A.M. (*FPT*, p. 3).

[114] Since no geographical name seems to fit here, perhaps Annie refers to a family named Stone—such as did live, in fact, in the rural outskirts of Orlando.

[115] Fig. 35. Seeing an airplane of any sort was something of an event, and the Perrins saw one of the Curtiss flying "Jennies" (specifically, a Curtiss JN4) such as were being used to train 90 percent of America's pilots for action in World War I (Bright and Higham, p. 309).

At the time America entered the war, the Air Service personnel consisted of only 65 officers and 1,120 men, but with extraordinary alacrity the U.S. managed to create "a network of flying fields and schools, a large instructional force, and a maze of equipment and curricula" (*War Department Annual Reports, 1918*, 1:1385). When the Armistice was signed in November 1918, the total strength of the Air Service was a little over 190,000 (1:56).

[116] The beach at low tide here was a hard and level stretch of sand several hundred feet in width.

[117] De Land, the county seat of Volusia County, is some twenty miles inland from Daytona Beach. The travelers were returning by a somewhat more northerly route than the one they took Tuesday.

Wednesday, 6 February

+

This morning we took breakfast at the Hotel then drove out to Stones.[114] Then back to Daytona and to the Av[i]ation field at Daytona beach to see a <u>bud</u> go up. It was a Curtis machine.[115] The school is right on D[aytona] beach.[116] He made 4 flights while we were there. We got more shells. Then went to dinner. Left soon after 1. for home [and] came back through Deyland, a much prettier drive[.][117] Got home soon after six tired out. Raym took some pictures. Both of us got sand from the ocean.

Fig. 35. The JN4 trainer pictured here on Daytona Beach (with Bert in the foreground) was a dual-control biplane with a speed of 43 to 72 miles per hour, climbing ability of 300 feet per minute, and 90 horsepower. When fully loaded, it weighed 1,890 pounds (Fales, p. 23).

Thursday, 7 February

It has been very warm all day. I havent felt very good today.

Mrs S[eymour]. came over [and] she is feeling bad about the Hotel people moving up stairs.

In the evening Aylards & S[eymours]– came over[,] left at 9.30[.] We went to bed.

A very quiet day.

Aylards took rooms up stairs.[118]

Friday, 8 February

Today I cleaned up clear through. When [we were] eating dinner Mr S[eymour]. came in to have B[ert] & I go fishing with them. I went over to the Peni—[119] for the first time, then over to Ettys lake[.] Got no fish. In the afternoon mail I got a letter from Lettie,[120] and one from Reba.[121] Burnt my corn cakes black while reading letters[.]

Below zero at home & above 70° here.

[118] That is, they now moved into part of the house the Perrins were renting. Possibly Mrs. Seymour was feeling bad yesterday because the hotel proprietors wanted to move into quarters that the Aylards had been occupying.

[119] Annie apparently refers here to one of the peninsulas that shape Lake Conway into sections.

[120] Doubtless Lettie mentioned the cold again. In Ashtabula County the thermometer plunged to twelve degrees below zero on the night of 1–2 February, and, on 4–5 February, to an amazing eighteen degrees below. All in all, the winter had now become the coldest one in many years—and produced a huge harvest for the area's ice merchants (*S&B*, 2 February, p. 10).

[121] Mentioned only this once in the diary, Reba was a young woman from back home. Inspired partly, perhaps, by a crush she had on Henry, she later professed to think as much of Annie as of her own mother. In 1919, after Henry had returned to the States and was lying in fairly dire condition in a Philadelphia hospital, she attempted to renew her botched negotiations with him by writing and sending him a

lavish assortment of flowers. Henry thought it "A poor time for sentimental letters" and gestures, however, and confided to Lettie his distress at having "buried things dug up" (ALS, 22 May 1919).

122 In her spare time, Annie crocheted yokes not only for her sister (21 February and 3 April) but also for her daughter.

Saturday, 9 February

Finished Letties yoke today.[122] Terrible warm here[.] Bert saw fresh straw berries in the store this morning. Raised near here[,] 75^{cts} a q[uar]t. Not any for supper today. But have plenty Grape fruit, and oranges[.] We get lettuce and cabbage from a garden near here. I do not like the native meat.

Sunday, 10 February

Another beautiful day[.] The thermo[meter] was 106° on the Hotel poarch this afternoon.

B[ert] & R[aym] went to Orlando to church with M[r]. S[eymour].[123] I wrote letters home. In the evening we went over to the Castle [hotel and] spent a very pleasant evening with Mr & Mrs Aylard. Mr S. V. [and] Mr & Mrs Tiner sang hymns.[124]

Came home at 9.30[.]

123 Since this was the second Sunday of the month and Dr. Tupper preached in Pine Castle only on the first and third Sundays, possibly the three men paid a visit to Tupper's home church, First Baptist, in Orlando.

A more striking possibility is that Bert and Raym attended the eleven o'clock service at the Christian Science church on Orange Avenue. Back home in Ashtabula, Mr. Seymour was a member of the Church of Christ, Scientist (S&B, 17 February 1919, p. 3).

124 James G. and Alice Tyner, both Florida-born and still in their thirties, were younger than the Perrins (in fact, had a daughter about two years old), but they were nonetheless interesting as another fruit-farm family (1920 U.S. Census).

Monday, 11 February

I did a big washing today. Bert went to see Dr Roney.[125] Is feeling better. This after noon Mr & Mrs Dovid[?], Mr & Mrs Aylard & I went over to Mrs Newels. Had a good visit. She gave us a basket of grape-fruit[.] B[ert]. went to Orlando with Mr S[eymour]. [and] got our pictures [that were] taken at Daytona. All good. Got a letter from Henry & a card from Lettie today.

[125] A second visit.

Tuesday, 12 February

Washed bed clothes [and] done about ½ of weeks ironing after dinner. Called on Mrs Sweet. Then went with Bert & Seymours to catch bait for fishing.

Got a letter from Aunt B[essie]– & Uncle Fred tonight.

Seymours spent the evening here. Bert feels cross and out of sorts[.] +

Wednesday, 13 February

Finished ironing this morning. Bert & Seymore have gone to catch shiners to fish with.[126] After dinner [I] called on Mrs Sheldon [and] then Mrs. S & I went to lake Conway[.][127] Met Mrs Smith & [Mr.] Smith. Mrs Fox & [Mrs.] Perkins were there and Mrs Black. She took Mrs Fox and I for a boat ride.[128]

Lots of children bathing. Also Raym & the Proff.[129]

[126] Shiners are small and generally silvery freshwater fish.

[127] Mrs. Diantha Sheldon was the widow of Homer Sheldon (Orlando *Directory* for 1917, p. 276). Apparently Annie went to the lake either with her or Mrs. Seymour.

[128] In this most socially complex of all her entries Annie mentions both Floridians and out-of-staters: besides Mrs. Sheldon, these include a couple named Smith (perhaps William T. and Emma Smith—the only Pine Castle Smiths listed in the 1917 Orlando *Directory* [p. 276]), Mrs. Fox from Indiana, Mrs. Della Perkins (wife of the Pine Castle postmaster and grocer), and Mrs. Mary J. Black, the young wife (about nineteen) of James A. Black (about twenty-six), a professional baseball player. Both of the Blacks lived in Pine Castle with her mother, Charity H. Matchett, a nurse (U.S. Census of 1920).

The size and miscellaneous character of the group suggest that Annie and the others have congregated at Pleasure Beach on Lake Conway. Though she nowhere uses the name, Pleasure Beach was the most popular recreational place on the lake, in fact the usual location for church and school picnics. Because it was situated at the east end of Wallace Road, the point on the lake nearest the Union Church, Pleasure Beach was also used regularly for baptisms. Its chief drawbacks were alligators and snakes.

[129] Probably Mr. Durrance (cf. 5 January). Although the designation "Prof" was used facetiously on some occasions, on others it was applied matter-of-factly to a grade school or high

school teacher. When Lettie and her new husband later came visiting in Geneva, the *Free Press-Times* reported that "Mr. Randall is professor of Spanish in the [Warren] city high schools" (15 June 1920, p. 2).

Whoever Raym's companion at the lake may have been, Raym himself wore a bathing suit with big white capital letters that spelled "GENEVA O" along its V-shaped neckline. His photograph album preserves images of him not only wearing the suit but also doing creditable handstands on the banks of Lake Conway.

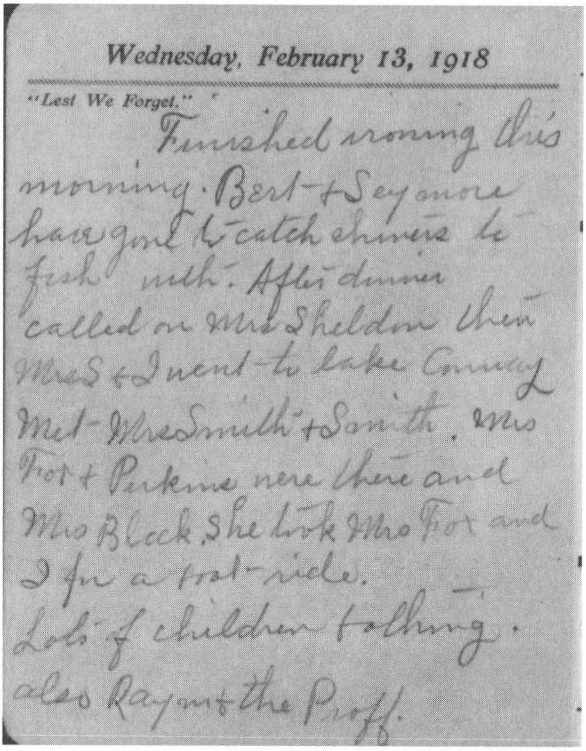

Fig. 36. Annie's diary, 13 and 14 February 1918. Actual size.

Wednesday, February 13, 1918

"Lest We Forget."

Finished ironing this morning. Bert + Seymore have gone to catch shiners to fish with. After dinner called on Mrs Sheldon then Mrs S + I went to lake Conway. Met Mrs Smith + Smith. Mrs Fox + Perkins were there and Mrs Black. She took Mrs Fox and I for a boat-ride. Lots of children bathing. also Raym + the Proff.

Thursday, 14 February

Got morning work done up. Then put up lunch to go to Orlando Fair. Bert[,] Raym & I went with Mr and Mrs Seymour & David. Saw the stock birds, chicken[s,] fine plymouth rocks.[130] The school exibets. Then to the auto & had lunch. Sat there and watched the races, all pretty good but not like Ohio. Got home about 5.30 tired hot & cross. Mr. S[eymour]. pretended he could not get out of parking space[.] It up set me.

[130] Annie's thoughts here move quickly from general to median to specific kinds of birds. The Plymouth "rocks," sometimes called Barred Rocks, were a favorite breed of the day, valued as good layers and meat birds.

Thursday, February 14, 1918

"Lest We Forget."

Got morning work done up. then put up lunch to go to Orlando Fair. Bert Raym & I went with Mr and Mrs Seymour & David. saw the stock, birds, chicken fine plymouth rocks. The school exibits, then to the auto & had lunch. eat there and watched the races, all pretty good but not like Ohio. got home about 5.30 tired hot & cross. Mr. S. pretended he could not get out of parking space it with set me.

Friday, 15 February

We both got a letter from Lettie today. I feel tired out from yesterday. Raym has gone over to work for Mrs Newel.[131] Mrs S[eymour]– came over a few minutes this afternoon. Then we went to lake Conway. Raym took B[ert] & I for a boat-ride.

Several there bathing[.] Seymours spent the evening here. The <u>hottest</u> day yet.

[131] As a widow with a grove of fruit trees, Ellen Newell had need of good help.

Saturday, 16 February

102° Another hot day. I went to P.O.[,] then to the Hotel. Mrs S[eymour] gave me a fresh pie for dinner. After noon we all went to the lake[,] chatted a while[, and] then came home to supper. Seymours spent the evening here.

Sunday, 17 February

Bert & Raym have gone to lake Conway[.] Got a card from L[ettie].[, and] a letter from Henry. He sent money for my birthday.[132] We spent the day at the lake[.] Raym took me for a ride but lake was pretty rough.

A valentine card from Lettie[,] the only one I have seen this year.

[132] Annie's birthday was 21 February.

Monday, 18 February

Got a birthday card from Henry & Mrs Smith today & a letter from Mrs Smith[.][133] H[enry]. has to be examined tomorrow.[134] This afternoon Bert & I went to the lake then got some oranges & <u>buds</u>[.][135] Came home [and] then went for violets. Mr & Mrs Aylard were here to supper[. We] had corn meal muffins and orange sauce[.]

[133] Rose Fales Smith was the mother of Lettie's friend, Vere.
[134] For the military draft.

[135] Annie's underlining indicates the strangeness of a tree that produces both fruit and buds simultaneously.

Tuesday, 19 February

This morning I sent a box of flowers to Henry.[136] Lettie will be there so both will have them. Bert went fishing, got a big Jock.[137] Mrs Dr Roney called in the afternoon. Then we both went to a food demonstration at the Parish [and] saw a bean loaf made. I called it punk.[138] They dont cook like we do.

Wednesday, 20 February

90° in the shade today. I washed. Raym worked in forenoon.[139] Bert went fishing. Nothing doing[.] It seemed a long lonesome day. Went over to the Hotel in the evening[.] It was a beautiful bright night. But every one complained of the heat. The natives dont mind it[.]

+

Thursday, 21 February

87° Much cooler this morning[.] Bert complains of his back. Mr & Mrs Aylard took dinner with us today[.] Mr A[ylard]. brought roses for me.[140] Had a good dinner. Then walked out to see some vacant houses, came home [and] had ice cream[.]

Raym was lying down when we came home. The end of my 52 birthday.

136 This somewhat unusual gift from a mother to her son is an indication of Henry's early interest in flowers. In later years, in the large yard of his cottage (later his home) at Palmetto Lake in Geneva-on-the-Lake, he created one of the most remarkable gardens in Ashtabula County.

137 That is, "jack." See 31 January.

138 Annie means that she *considered* it "punk." She would never be rude.

139 In the Newell grove (see 15 February).

140 Probably for Annie's birthday.

Fig. 37. Annie Perrin and Ella Aylard, two Ohio housewives, met each other and found warmly sympathetic companionship in faroff Florida. Here, in the early evening of Annie's birthday, they perch briefly on the porch rail of one of the vacant houses that they and their husbands have "walked out to see."

Friday, 22 February

A cool quiet day. Raym dident feel like work today. In the afternoon Mrs S[eymour] came over[, and] then we went to lake Conway. Rained so we sat in Auto till shower was over[,] then went home. Bert was out on the lake fishing. Mrs Black & Vera were swimming. Nothing doing so we went to bed about 8 oclock

Found some mistletoe today. 5 letters & 2 cards today.

Saturday, 23 February

Mr & Mrs Seymour, Mr & Mrs Tyner, Mr Aylard, Bert, Raym & I went fishing[.] Took our lunch and ate it in the boat by moon light. The lake was some rough. Pa & Mrs S[eymour] got out and went to shore[, and] Bert [was] waiting on the beach for us when we came in.

Sunday, 24 February

Bert has been miserable with back ache today. It is 90° in the shade. In the afternoon walked to the lake [and] met some people from Milan O[hio]. Mr & Mrs Mooney. They were neighbors of J. W. Brown in Milan O[hio].[141] Seem very nice people. Said they would call on us.

[141] Back home in Geneva, J. W. Brown was now a close neighbor of the Perrins. See note to entry of 2 May.

Monday, 25 February

Very nice day[.] The air is filled with perfume of orange blossoms[.] Bert & I walked to the lake[,] stopped in Reeds[142] on our way home. Met Mrs Finley[,] ate oranges[, and] had a pleasant chat.[143] Raym worked all day today. Four cards & a letter today[.]

[142] A couple from the local Baptist church. See note to 20 January.
[143] Blanche Finley was the wife of Lotan H. Finley, a self-employed painter who lived in Pine Castle but maintained a business address in Orlando with his partner, Louis T. Marks (Orlando *Directory* for 1921, p. 301; U.S. Census, 1920).

Tuesday, 26 February

Bert & I went to Orlando with Seymours [and] got home in time to cook dinner. Raym finished at Newels this noon.[144]

In the evening we went over to the Hotel.

A beautiful evening. Sent flowers to Lettie & Sister Fannie today[.][145] 89° in shade today[.]

Wednesday, 27 February

One of the The hottest days[.] 94° in the shade. Bert[,] Raym & I went & gathered oranges to send home. Was nearly sweltered. In the evening we went to a Tent meeting[,] 5 preachers. A little girl played the hymns on a small organ. B[ert]– put in a bad night. The night was perfect. The roosters had a midnight concert. We couldent sleep[.] +

Thursday, 28 February

Raym & I went up to Halls [and] got a box of grape fruit to send home.[146] Sent a box of oranges & grape fruit.

Mrs Newel and Mrs Fox were here this afternoon. Walked to P.O. with Mrs Fox[,] got a letter from Lettie & Florence Elliott.[147] Seems hotter than yesterday[.] Went over to the Hotel a while in the evening. Got a letter from Henry saying he is sick. I washed today.

[144] Annie's first notice of Raym's work for Mrs. Newell was on 15 February.

[145] Apparently struck by the fragrance and accessibility of the orange blossoms, Annie wanted to share something of her feelings about them with the two women who were most important to her.

[146] Though Clinton C. Hall, now about sixty, had retired from farming in Vermont, he was able to look after a certain number of fruit trees in Pine Castle. His wife, Sarah M. K. Hall, also originally from Vermont, was fourteen years older than her husband, but helping with the family finances by taking in a couple of women boarders (U.S. Census, 1920). In the Pine Castle section of the 1919–20 Orlando *Directory*, Mr. Hall appears as a Justice of Peace (p. 281).

The *Directory* of 1921, however, lists Sarah as a widow (p. 369).

147 Florence Elliott was the daughter of Annie's brother Thomas Henry Elliott and his wife Alberta ("Bertie") Coffman Elliott, of Chicago.

148 Perhaps because of their English genes, various members of the all-blue-eyed family reacted badly to excessive sun and heat. Although Annie is more explicit on the matter today, this may be what ailed Bert on the night of 27–28 February.

Friday, 1 March

Havent felt well today. Too hot for me[.][148] Raym took lunch[, then] went in an auto about 7 mi[les] from here fishing. Pa went to Lake conway with Mr Sey[mour]– [and] caught 4 trout. It has been a long lonesome day[.] In the evening Bert went to a tent meeting.

Too hot for me[.] Mr S[eymour] says it was 94° today.

Saturday, 2 March

Cleaned up clear through. Then ironed. Bert went to Orlando to get shaved. This afternoon Raym & Bert are at the lake [but] I did not feel well enough to go. Raym is going to take some pictures. Aylard returned this afternoon. Went to Eustice.[149] Lots of people from N[or]th there.

149 Eustis ("The Queen City of the Lakes") is in appropriately named Lake County, about forty miles northwest of Pine Castle.

Sunday, 3 March

+

Went to the lake after dinner. Saw Raym come in with his sail boat. A number of people bathing. A thunder shower came. So we went to the Hotel. I went up to see Mrs Aylard. She was quite ill.

Spent the evening at home[, and] went to bed about 8 oclock.

Took pictures at the Hotel[.]

Monday, 4 March

This morning Mr S[eymour] took a load of us out about a mile N.W. of here to see a big rattle snake they caught last week. It has 15 rattles[.][150] In the afternoon went to the lake [and] Raym took Mrs Fox[,] Marvin & I clear across the lake[,] put up the sail & came back flying. Lake got rough[.] Pa was nervous. All got in safe[.] Called to see Mrs Aylard [and] she is feeling some better[.]

[150] This snake was indeed big: the rattle of an adult "rattler" usually has from six to ten segments.

Tuesday, 5 March

Nothing doing today[.] Very quiet[.]

After dinner went over and called on Mrs Aylard[.] She was feeling better. From there went to Mrs Sheldons [and] sat until mail came in. Got none. Home again[.] In evening went to tent meeting. Heard a woman speak in the unknown tongue.[151] Went into a trance.

151 Despite Annie's apparent nonchalance, "Speaking in tongues" is supposed to be a guarantee of the Holy Spirit's presence (Acts 2:1–13).

Wednesday, 6 March

Been alone all the morning. Wrote two [letters to] Lettie & Henry. After dinner Mrs Noel & I went to lake Conway.[152] Raym took us for a boat-ride.

Mrs S[eymour] & Vera spent the evening here[.] Bert went to tent meeting.

152 Mrs. Noel was an acquaintance from Tennessee.

Thursday, 7 March

People here quite frightened. Saw Northern lights for the first time[.][153]

Good rain today. In the morning got all through cleaning[.] Mr & Mrs S[eymour] came in [for] about an h[ou]r.

Got dinner. Went over to the Hotel a while[,] then Mrs S[eymour] and I went to the lake. Raym spent the evening at Blacks. B[ert] & I went to bed at 8 oclock[.] A little cooler today. Mrs Aylard was able to go to Orlando.

Raym saw N[orthern] lights[.]

153 These opening words, written the next morning, are squeezed in at the top of the page.

Florida is so far south (technically in a "minauroral" region) that displays of Northern Lights (aurora borealis) are very infrequent. William Petrie observes, however, that "auroras at low . . . latitudes are likely to be spectacular and to attract considerable attention" (p. 56)—and understandably frighten people. Along with other literary passages, Petrie recalls W. E. Aytoun's "Edinburgh after Flodden":
All night long the northern streamers
Shot across the trembling sky:

Friday, 8 March

Cooler today. Went to P.O. in the morning[,] got a letter from Henry. Raym took pictures of double house[,] Perrins & Aylards. After noon went to Orlando with Mr & Mrs Seymour & Mrs Noel.

Came back[.] Bert went fishing[.] Mr A[ylard]. threw out his line [and] the hook went clear through Mr S[eymour's] ear, had to cut hook to get it out. In the evening went to tent meeting. Mrs Reed[154] called in the afternoon.

Saturday, 9 March

+

Cleaned up the house [and] got dinner.

Raym is at the lake

Bert[,] Mr Aylard, [Mr.] Fox & Raym went out to Bear head[155]—and got an aligator. Mr S[156] & R[aym]. both shot at [it.] It is about 4 f[ee]t long.

Raym dident come to supper tonight. Pa was very much peeved.[157]

Fearful lights that never beckon
Save when kings or heroes die.
(Aytoun, p. 16)

Large or small, such displays are "caused by high energy 'bullets' in the form of electrons and protons which enter the top of the atmosphere. As they proceed downward colliding with oxygen and nitrogen particles, a variety of reactions are induced which result in the production of auroral light" (p. 78). Different shapes tend to form at different heights: "draperies" at a height of about 68 miles, for instance, and certain kinds of red arcs at about 155 miles (p. 49). Yellow-green is the most common color for these sky-shows, but red, orange, yellow, blue, violet, and white may also be seen (p. 71).

Orlando's *Morning Sentinel* ran a front-page article on Saturday headed "Actual Aurora Borealis Seen." For some local people, as Annie suggests, "the conviction was strong that the world was coming to an end."

The *Sentinel* reported also that at about ten o'clock the citizens of Tampa saw the northern sky "lighted up with a strange red glow." Farther north, in Washington, D.C., "Brilliant lights in the sky over the capitol . . . brought a large part of the population into the streets to observe what was thought to be a big fire." So huge was the show, in fact, that in England the air-raid watchers on the Kentish coast saw "bands of red and white light which shone over the sea with far more powerful effect than the full moon."

[154] Mrs. Reed was the woman who played for the Baptist church.

[155] Bear Head Lake is a little south of Pine Castle.

[156] Though he did not make it into Annie's list of today's explorers, "S" is for "Seymour." For Mr. Aylard, see Fig. 38.

157 Judging from other evidence, it may be that Raymond picked up the habit of independence from Pa. Whether or not Bert ever thought of applying the old proverb to himself, he liked to observe that "The apples don't fall very far from the tree."

Fig. 38. Whoever fired the winning shot, a gratified Mr. Aylard holds here the alligator bagged on 9 March at Bear Head.

Sunday, 10 March

+[158]

A very lonely day[.] Raym is at the lake[.] In the afternoon Mr Mooney & family[159] came from Orlando. Here about an h[ou]r. Seymours were here to lunch.

Raym went to tent meeting[.]

Every body seems peeved today. Think it is time to leave Pine Castle.

Monday, 11 March

A terrible wind all day & quite chilly. Bert went to Orlando with Mr S[eymour]. Brought our codac pictures home. <u>All good</u>. [In the] Afternoon I took them over to the Hotel. Everyone delighted. Ordered 32 more[.] When I came home found a dish of mulberries on the poarch. Found out Mrs Newel brought them.

Tuesday, 12 March

Very quiet. Have been home all day. Bert got a q[uar]t of straw berries [for] 15^{cts}[,] pretty good ones.[160]

In the evening we went to a chicken supper given by the Baptist [church]. Good crowd[.] <u>Punk</u> supper. Seymours came home with us. Were here about an h[ou]r. We met Newels people on the way there[.][161] She wants us to buy the grove.

[158] This time the mark "+" is very heavily penciled, as though Annie intended the symbol to signify something special.

[159] From Milan, Ohio (cf. 24 February).

[160] Earlier, on 9 February, Bert refused to buy strawberries at seventy-five cents.

[161] Used as it is here, the phrase "Newels people" is likely to mean "business representatives."

Wednesday, 13 March

Lonesome hot & dry[.] The days seem 36^hrs long[.]
Went over to S—[162] in the afternoon[,] came home[,]
made short cake for supper.[163] After supper went to an
open air service to hear a woman preach. No good[.][164]
She took up a collection [and] got 20^cts.

[162] Probably "Seymours."

[163] Within the family, a light supper sometimes consisted entirely (or almost entirely) of berries with shortcake and cream. It is therefore impossible to say whether Annie refers here to a dessert or to a main dish.

[164] The likely subject of Annie's critical evaluation here was Mary Stafford. A woman of about sixty-six, originally from Illinois but now a resident of Pine Castle, she identified herself for the 1920 census as both a citrus grower and a minister.

[165] Did the Pine Castle Smiths, William T. and Emma, have a home elsewhere? This was about the time of year when winter residents began to think of heading north.

[166] If Annie's thoughts at this point shift back to William and Emma Smith, it is probably significant that in the Orlando *Directory* for 1919–20, Emma is listed as a widow (p. 281).

[167] The broad term "bottlebrush" refers to any of various shrubs and trees bearing dense spikes of flowers that look something like the kind of brush used to clean the insides of bottles.

[168] Nina K. Foster of Geneva was the wife of one of Bert's nephews, Allen H. Foster. See notes to 19 May and 21 July.

[169] Pine Castle's school, built in 1912, was a trim, white clapboard structure where three teachers taught nine grades. Downstairs there were three

Thursday, 14 March

Smiths left for home today.[165] Bert & I went over
to Ettys [and] found her very sick. Dr came while [we
were] there. Wanted me to help him. So I was there
about an h[ou]r. Came home. Had a letter from Lettie.
It was cold in Geneva when she wrote. Mr Smith will
not live long.[166]

Friday, 15 March

Mr & Mrs Aylard[,] Bert and I walked over to
Newels[.] Had a good visit. Got some mulberries. A
lady gave us a sprig of bottlebrush.[167] Got home [and]
found a letter from Fannie & Mrs N[orris]. In the afternoon got one from Lettie[,] Henry, & Nina Foster.[168]
In the evening went to the school house to see a play
given by the pupils.[169] Topsy Tirvy[,] very good.[170] 87°
in shade today.

Saturday, 16 March

Bert & I went to Orlando with Seymours. Got some slippers. Got home about noon[.] After dinner Bert & Raym took the boat over to Mrs Newels to keep for us.[171] We had a thunder storm. All were glad of the rain[.] In the evening Raym went out somewhere. Mr & Mrs S[eymour]. were here about an h[ou]r.

Went to bed. Still raining and Raymond not home yet.[172]

Sunday, 17 March

96°.

The Ohio people & the Fox family were invited to eat dinner at the Hotel. There were 18 of us to dinner.

In the afternoon we went to the Baptist church. Mrs Tyner invited us to go over and have lunch and spend the evening. A thunder storm cooled it off. Mr Aylard gave a toast[.]

Monday, 18 March

Left Pine Castle about 9.45[.] About 30 of the friends came to the Depot to wish us good bye.[173]

Mr & Mrs Aylard[,] Bert[,] Raym & I. We all had seats together [and] had a fine lunch on the train. Got into Jacksonville about 4.45. Went to the Flagler Hotel.[174] Then went out and had lunch. Home and to bed.

magnate and financier who was co-partner with John D. Rockefeller in the business that in 1870 became The Standard Oil Company (Johnson, p. 308). Down in the South, Flagler brought forth not only the Florida East Coast Railway but also the Overseas Railway that at this time and for a few more years stretched from Florida City to Key West (*Jacksonville . . . City Directory*, 1926, p. 588).

At the time of Flagler's death on 21 May 1913 Geneva's *Free Press-Times* ran a front-page article calling him the "builder of Florida."

175 Raymond turned twenty-two.

176 Each of these newly created camps had a population greater than that of Geneva. About twelve miles from Jacksonville, Camp Joseph E. Johnston was established in October 1917 on a 3,036-acre reservation that could accommodate some 27,000 men. It served as a Quartermaster Corps training and mobilization post for less than two years, however, closing in June 1919 (Roberts, p. 179).

Near Macon, Camp Wheeler sprawled over 3,909 acres (within a total reservation of 21,480 acres) and could accommodate some 43,000 men (*War Department Annual Reports, 1918*, vol. 1, no. 3, foldout following p. 1333).

177 Annie first wrote this sentence and the next in the space designated for 18 March, but then copied them verbatim here where they belong.

178 The Princeton, at 45–47 West Mitchell in the downtown area of Atlanta, was well within walking distance of the main passenger train stations.

Tuesday, 19 March

This is Raymonds birthday[.]175

Left Jacksonville for Atlanta at 7.10[.] Made good time [and] had a pleasant trip. Saw the Boys camps at Jacksonville Fl[orid]a[.] and at Macon[,] Georgia[.]176 We got into Atlanta about 5.20.177 Put up at the Princeton Hotel[.]178 Had lunch. Then took a walk around the City[.] Certainly a fine place. Back to Hotel & bed[.]

Wednesday, 20 March

We got up at 5 oclock this morning. Went to a restaurant [and] had a fine breakfast. Then took train for
Chattanooga. Got into Chattinooga about 1 oclock. Put
up at Glenn Hotel[,][179] then took a sight seeing trip
to battle fields.[180] There were 18 of us. Chichamauga &
Missionary ridge, 600 f[ee]t above the City.[181] Saw 3
different camps of soldiers. Saw where the most bloody
battle [of the Civil War] was fought[.][182]

Thursday, 21 March

Got up at six oclock. Went out to breakfast. Then
took a sight seeing trip to Mt Lookout.[183] There were 9
of us. We all had our pictures taken on top of the Mt.[184]
Picked up acorns [and] picked some flowers. It was a
grand trip. Got back[,] had dinner[, and] then took the
train for Cin-[cinnati.] Got there about 2 oclock in the
morning. Mrs A[ylard] & I put up at Hotel Charles[.][185]
The rest staid at the Emery[.][186] Slept very little[.]

[179] Apparently new in 1917, the
sixty-room Glenn (owned by the
Glenn estate and managed by
Mrs. N. L. Trollinger) stood at
1449 Market Street between 13th
and 14th Streets. This was close to
the railroad terminals but not
exactly a good neighborhood.
A rather large, three-story, and
mainly brick building in which
retail stores of various kinds oc-
cupied much of the ground floor,
the Glenn was spectacularly destroyed by fire on Christmas Eve
and Christmas morning in 1928.
(Information for this note has
been provided by Suzette Raney,
Chattanooga-Hamilton County
Bicentennial Library.)

[180] In the Civil War fighting at
Chattanooga, Ohio was heavily
represented. As a consequence,
according to an article in the
Geneva Free Press-Times,

> *Ohio has spent more money*
> *memorializing the battlefields*
> *of Chattanooga than any other*
> *state. This state has fifty-five*
> *monuments and fifty-three*
> *markers at Chickamauga and*
> *eleven monuments and seventy*
> *markers at other places around*
> *Chattanooga. The total cost of*
> *these memorials was $129,200.*
> *(5 May 1913, p. 4)*

[181] Missionary Ridge acquired
its name because it was as far
west as Christian missionaries
were allowed into Cherokee Indian territory. Slightly southwest
of Chattanooga, it became the
site of a major Union victory on
25 November 1861. Confederate
General Braxton Bragg had
forces entrenched at the base, on
the slope, and on the crest of the
Ridge, but was nevertheless dis-
lodged and defeated by Ulysses
S. Grant—whose victory won

him promotion as Lieutenant General (Faust, pp. 498–99).

A couple of years later (19–20 September 1863) the Battle of Chickamauga, Georgia, resulted in the greatest victory ever to be enjoyed by Bragg. Unfortunately for his cause, Bragg failed to follow through, and the resulting casualties were enormous. Bragg reported his losses as 2,312 dead, 14,674 wounded, and 1,468 missing, whereas Union Major General William S. Rosecrans reported 1,657 Union dead, 9,756 wounded, and 4,757 missing (Cromie, p. 287; Faust, pp. 136–37).

[182] Chickamauga is now considered the *second* most bloody battle of the Civil War. Worse still, at least in terms of deaths, was the Battle of Antietam, fought near Sharpsburg, Maryland, on 17 September 1862. The Army of the Potomac and the Army of Northern Virginia engaged there in a twelve-hour sort of "fighting madness" that resulted in 4,710 dead, 18,440 wounded, and 3,043 missing (Faust, pp. 18–19).

Fig. 39. A memento of 21 March 1918, taken on Lookout Mountain during the Perrins' return trip from Florida. Bert sits at the center of the rock, and Annie, wearing a white hat, steadies herself by holding his knee. To the right of Bert, in a somewhat lighter suit, is Mr. Aylard. Still farther to the right—hatless, youngest, and boldest—Raym sits with his arms folded and his legs crossed.

Fig. 40. Raym at the inclined railroad, Lookout Mountain, on 21 March, as the Perrins paused on their return from Florida. When traveling far from home, it befit a young farmer to wear his best suit, a white shirt, and a tie, as well as to carry (if not wear) his fedora.

[183] Towering some 1,100 feet, Lookout Mountain, southwest of Chattanooga and spanning the Tennessee-Georgia line, is another Civil War site. The Battle of Lookout Mountain took place on 24 November 1863, and on the following morning members of the Federal 8th Kentucky Infantry hurried to the summit to raise the U.S. flag, signaling victory to the Union troops down in the valley below (Faust, pp. 445–57).

[184] See Figs. 39 and 40.

[185] After touring and traveling for about twenty straight hours and then sleeping for about four and a half hours, Annie apparently wrote this entry some time on Friday, 22 March. Little wonder, then, that she recorded the hotel where she stayed as the Charles (there was no hotel of that name in Cincinnati), when in fact she and Mrs. Aylard stayed at the St. Charles on 341 West Fifth Street.

[186] Though the three men for some reason found it necessary or advisable to check into a different hotel, the Emery and the St. Charles were at least close to each other. Neither was very close to the Central Union Depot, but both were in Cincinnati's central business district. In fact, the Emery was situated on Vine in the so-called Emery "plot" at Fifth, Vine, and Race Streets. An important part of the Emery Arcade, which opened in 1877, it was at one time thought to rank among "the renowned hostelries of the country," but in later years it was neglected. Its demolition was announced in 1929 (*Williams' Cincinnati Directory 1918*, p. 920; *Cincinnati Enquirer*, 25 August 1929, sec. 1, p. 1; sec. 2, p. 2).

Friday, 22 March

Mrs A[ylard] & I got up at 6.30[,] washed & combed[,] then she embroidered & I crocheted until 8 oclock[.] Then Bert & A[ylard] came [and] took us to a restaurant[. We all] had breakfast[,] then went to the Depot to meet a friend of Mr A[ylard]. Went to the rest room and [then] visited until train time. Left Cin[cinnati] at 12.10. [The] Aylards came as far as Galion with us.[187] We got into Cleveland 6.15[,] took a [street]car and went over to Freds.[188] Had supper. Went to bed about 8.30. Bert was sick all night.

[187] From here the Aylards had an easy ride eastward to their home in Medina. Unlike the Perrins, however, for whom Florida would become merely a memory, the Aylards later maintained addresses in both Ohio and Florida. In 1922 they were listed as residents in the section on Pine Castle in the *Orlando, Florida City Directory and Orange County Gazetteer,* and they were also designated there as residents of Medina (p. 368).

[188] Fred Perrin lived at 6811 Kinsman Road. All in all, with its electric lamps, record-player, and thick, American-made oriental rugs, it was a comfortable place to visit.

Saturday, 23 March

Had breakfast about 8 oclock. Mrs Snell had a good breakfast.[189] We done up the work. Then went up to the store [and] got things for dinner. After dinner she played the graphaphone a while[.][190] Then we took a [street]car for 105[th] [Street.] Waited about ½ h[ou]r for train[.] Got into Geneva about 5.10[.] Mr Brown brought us out in an Auto[.][191] Lettie was here. Had every thing aired & clean. Looked done out.[192] Hen came about 6 oclock.[193] So this ends our trip to Florida and back.

[189] Mrs. Snell was Fred's housekeeper. The relationship between them was more cordial than such a term might suggest, however, since later this year (11 August) both Mrs. Snell and her husband, Gerald, accompanied Fred on a visit to Annie and Bert in Geneva.

[190] A Columbia Graphophone (looking very like a Victrola) was advertised in, for instance, the *Star and Beacon* of 1 November 1918 (p. 7). In fact, the Pardon Allens, neighbors of the Perrins in Geneva, owned one (*FPT*, 14 August 1917, p. 2). Various rival products included the Orchestrola, a kind of Graphophone (*S&B*, 8 November 1916, p. 8); the Euphonola (5 January 1917, p. 7); the Aeolina Vocalion (12 January 1917, p. 8); the Lorophone (2 March 1917, p. 8); and the Virtuoso (*Cleveland Plain Dealer*, 27 October 1918, p. 6).

[191] George Brown was a liveryman or, as later times would have it, a taxicab driver. See Annie's entry for 1 August.

[192] Since Lettie could hardly run the farm single-handedly during the past winter, she had had to find living quarters and pay rent down in the village. This weekend, though, she managed to get up to the Ridge to ready the place for the family's return.

Despite the fact that Saturday was a non-teaching day, the timing of the return still posed a problem for Lettie because the teachers in Ashtabula County were supposed to attend the mid-year Christy Institute at Ashtabula Harbor High School (*FPT*, 19 March, p. 1). The chances are not very good that she heard Dr. George D. Strayer of Columbia give his timely address on "Education in War Time."

[193] Traveling up from Akron, Henry made the little family reunion complete.

2

Early Spring to Early Summer

24 March–30 June 1918

Sunday, 24 March

Got up late. We all done as little as possible today. Hen phoned to Barnard [and] had him bring trunks from Depot.[1] Trunk & fruit from 53 Eagle St.[2] Some fruit spoiled but [most] came in fairly good shape. In the after noon Mrs Glover & little daughter [visited]. Lulu & Grace [Lowe] came up.[3] Left about 6 oclock. We visited until about 9.30[.][4] Went to bed[.]

Raym went over to see Bernice.

[1] Though the Perrins had neither electricity nor running water, they did have the convenience of a telephone—which cost $1.50 per month.

Barnard Brothers—recently equipped with a two-ton truck—was a Geneva livery firm doing business at the southwest corner of Railroad and Forest. It handled both moving and general hauling (*FPT*, 11 March, p. 3). Annie's reference here, expressed in the singular, may suggest that the Perrins were better acquainted with one brother or the other—either E. F. or H. G. Barnard (*FPT*, 10 October 1914, p. 5).

[2] That is, the Perrins traveled with a total of at least three trunks.

[3] The "Lowe Girls," as they were always known to the Perrins, were former neighbors on the South Ridge and, more important, easy and lively friends— "real friends," as Henry put it in a letter to Lettie (29 January 1919).

It was sad news, therefore, when the *Free Press-Times* reported that the Misses Lulu and Grace Lowe and their sister, Mrs. P. M. Glover, and her little daughter were all leaving for Bristol, Pennsylvania, because both Mrs. Glover's husband and the widower father of the three young women, William E. Lowe, had found jobs in the shipyard there (6 April, p. 2).

At first it appeared that the Lowes and Glovers would all settle permanently in Bristol, but before long Lulu, Grace, and their father moved on to Trenton, New Jersey (see Fig. 79). Then that same fall, dissatisfied with life in the East, all three returned to live in Geneva.

[4] With the visitors gone, the family members tried to "catch up" with one another.

Monday, 25 March

Cold and clear this morning. Lettie took 8 oclock [Interurban] car for school. Henry went to see the Lowe girls this afternoon. Raym went to store[.] Mr Penney[5] & [Mr.] Allen[6] called on us this afternoon.

After supper Lettie went to a red cross class meeting[.][7] Henry staid with Franklin all night.[8] I dont see why. Pa sure was peeved.

---

[5] Willard M. Penney was a South Ridge neighbor who before long moved with his family to Ashtabula (31 McGovern Avenue). In the 1920 census he appears as the forty-four-year-old manager of Hoover-Bond, an Ashtabula furniture store, and his children as employees—Karl (seventeen), a furniture salesman; Marie (sixteen), a "saleslady"; and young Willis (fourteen), a "helper." Louise (thirty-nine), the wife and mother of the family, was a native of Germany. Though in 1918 the daily press fairly seethed with anti-German sentiment, Annie never wrote a word on Mrs. Penney's origins. Instead, she was glad to borrow her curtain stretchers.

In the spring and summer of 1918, occasional references to the Penney children crop up in the *Free Press-Times*. For instance, both Marie and Willis did well in an arithmetic and spelling contest held at North Geneva (*FPT*, 15 April, p. 4). In fact, Marie's score on a County examination given on 24 May was sufficiently high to win her a certificate "intitling her to attend high school free of tuition" (*FPT*, 12 June, p. 2). And later on, Willis and four other neighbor boys (Charles Seamans, Arthur Swarnick, Arthur Williams, and Lee Woodworth) attracted some local attention for organizing a "Firing Club," their goal being to collect war souvenirs and practice target-firing (*FPT*, 27 December, p. 2).

[6] The Pardon Allens, likewise South Ridge neighbors, lived on a twenty-five-acre farm just a few places to the east, where Myers Road deadends on the Ridge. Neither Pardon's wife, Louisa, nor their daughter, Grace, appears in Annie's diary, but Annie mentions both Pardon and the son of the family, Arthur (or "Art"), who tried to keep in touch with the Perrins.

Though approaching seventy, Pardon, grizzle-bearded and a little bent, was still actively engaged in farming. Unlike Bert, who was no "joiner," Pardon was also active in Geneva's North Star Grange down on East Main and Forest. ("The Order of Patrons of Husbandry, or the Grange . . . was organized in 1867" with the object of helping "the farmers of our country materially and socially" [Willis T. Mann, *FPT*, 6 December 1915, p. 2]. In 1918 there were over eight hundred Granges in Ohio alone, and, according to an estimate in 1919, some eighty-six thousand "Grangers" [*FPT*, 3 December, p. 1].)

Art, in his early thirties at this point, was still living at home but trying to put a little distance between himself and the Allen farm. Willing enough to contribute to the family by working elsewhere, he found employment at the Champion Hardware in Geneva (*FPT*, 5 November 1913, p. 5) and, later, in the New York Central Car Shop in nearby Saybrook (1920 Census).

[7] Ashtabula County was among the first counties in the nation to have a Woman's Auxiliary of the Red Cross. On 25 February, just a month earlier, an item in Geneva's *Free Press-Times* noted that "Fourteen Geneva Ladies with Mrs. T. H. Russell as chairman will constitute a surgical dressing class which will start taking lessons today in the basement of the library building" (p. 2). Since Mr. Thomas Russell was manager of The American Fork and Hoe, one of the main industries in the village, the good work of the Auxiliary began with a certain social éclat.

However, Geneva's own revisionist history soon gave Mrs. A. W. Chamberlin credit about equal to that accorded to Mrs. Russell (*FPT*, 26 May 1919, p. 12). Like Mr. Russell, Mr. Chamberlin was among the most prominent of Genevans—president of The Geneva Metal Wheel, indeed the man chosen to speak on the industrial growth of the village when Geneva held a celebration in 1916 (*FPT*, 15 January 1915, p. 3; 30 March 1916, p. 1).

In any case, beginning in February, Lettie had a chance to sign up for any one of four kinds of Red Cross class: first aid, hygiene and home care of the sick, dietetics, and surgical dressing. She chose the last of these, known colloquially as a Red Cross "S.D.C." This consisted of eight lessons of three hours each. Eventually about 150 local women took the course (*FPT*, 13 August 1917, p. 3; 26 May 1919, p. 12; see also the note to 22 April).

[8] With the family home only one night, Henry chose to spend his third night elsewhere. As the old English proverb has it, "Young cocks love no coops."

Tuesday, 26 March

Snowing & cold[.] Ground is frozen hard. I baked bread and washed a few things [and] nearly froze hanging out clothes. Got the chicken[s] home.[9] Got 8 eggs today. Also got pump to work.[10] Henry took the 2 oclock [Interurban] car for town[.] Has to be examined tonight.[11] Wish the terrible war over.[12]

Mr & Mrs Stowe spent the evening here[.][13]

[9] Annie had "farmed out" her chickens while in Florida.

[10] That is, the pump at the kitchen sink.

[11] Henry was required to take a physical examination to determine his fitness for military service.

[12] This is Annie's first use of the word "war." With Henry likely to go soon, the idea of war was becoming more real for her. Two of the front-page headlines in the Geneva newspaper for this date are "Germans Advancing in Face of Heavy Fire of British Artillery" and "Sixty Four Local Men Go to Camp Next Saturday."

[13] Howard and Martha Stowe and their children (four at this point) were next-door neighbors to the east. Considering their geographical closeness and the general interdependence of neighbors, they play a minimal role in Annie's diary. Even though Howard and Martha were twenty years or so younger than Annie and Bert, the main differences between the families probably related to the fact that Howard worked in town. In the 1920 census he is described as a clerk in a hardware store.

Bright & cold[.] Bert & Raym are cleaning up the cellar. R[aym]. got the fruit home today.[14] Mr Allen gave us some parsnips & horsradish. Took team to town to get coal & groceries[.] I done a big washing [and] have a big one yet to do. Mailed cards to Pine Castle today. Mr & Mrs Wetter spent the evening here.[15] The two Mrs Penny[s] were here this afternoon.[16] Wetters gave us a q[uar]t of syrup[.][17]

[14] A minor puzzle, since presumably Mr. Barnard brought the fruit up on 24 March. Probably Raym picked up the *remainder* of whatever the Perrins had had shipped to themselves from Florida.

[15] J. Frank Wetter and his wife, Freda, had a twenty-acre fruit and poultry farm on nearby Myers Road. Frank was especially interested in chickens. In the 1918 *Farm Journal . . . Directory* he ran an ad that reads: "Grassmere Poultry Farm / J. F. Wetter / Parks Strain Barred Rocks / Hatching Eggs in Season / R.D. No. 2—Geneva, Ohio" (p. 254). In Geneva's *Free Press-Times* about two years earlier, he advertised "B[arred] Rock eggs for hatching, pens headed with males of over 200 egg certified records" (27 March 1916, p. 4).

Altogether a responsible fellow, Frank was also serving in 1918 as one of the Geneva Township trustees (*FPT*, 20 April, p. 2). Long a faithful friend of the Perrins, in the fall of 1954 he signed his name shakily in the guest book provided by the Webster Funeral Home for Lettie's funeral.

The Wetters' daughter Irene, who appears later in the diary, was one of Lettie's best friends. See the notation for Annie's entry of 4 August.

[16] The only two women who were both so named and living in R.F.D. 1, Annie's neighborhood, were Louise Penney (see note to entry for 25 March) and Amanda Penney (wife of the now-retired farmer, James H. Penney) (*Farm Journal . . . Directory,* p. 154).

[17] The Wetters brought fresh maple syrup. Back in February the Federal Food Administration had urged "that every owner of maple trees utilize these trees to

the fullest extent for the production of maple sugar and syrup the coming spring" (*FPT*, 18 February, p. 2). Ten days later the paper noted that "Ashtabula and Geauga counties, the banner counties of the state in the production of maple sugar, have already been tapped and are yielding satisfactory runs" (p. 2). In fact, "As high as 600,000 maples have been tapped in Geauga county." The season always ends when "sunshiny days and hot winds start the maple buds, usually late in March" (*FPT*, 17 March 1917, p. 2).

As the Geneva writer Edith M. Thomas (1854–1925) had asked rhetorically a few years earlier, "Who will read us the idyl of The Sugar Bush? Let us hear no more of the honey of Hybla . . . !" (*The Round Year*, p. 22). Thomas often took up aspects of nature in her verse, but her prose book called *Round Year* has particular pertinence here because she recorded in it some of her observations and reflections on the Geneva countryside. Appreciative Genevans established in her honor The Edith Thomas Garden Club (see, for example, *FPT*, 25 July 1914, p. 2).

Thursday, 28 March

Another bright day[.] Baked a pie and a war cake to-day.[18] Done a big ironing in the afternoon. Got through a little past five oclock. Heard from Henry [and] he has to be examined again. His lung is wrong someway.[19] Raym is burning brush in the orchard.

I think he would like to go to War.

[18] A "war cake" called for substitutes or lesser amounts of scarce ingredients. There were also "Win-the-war Muffins" and "Victory Bread." Bread with more than 25 percent wheat substitutes was considered patriotic bread, and eventually the U.S. Department of Agriculture came up with a recipe for "100 per cent wheat substitute yeast bread" calling for barley (or rolled oats) and corn flour (or rice, sweet potato, or tapioca flour) (*S&B*, 9 July, p. 1).

On the present occasion Annie was probably making prompt use of the previous day's gift from the Wetters, since sugar was also in short supply. Beginning on 15 July, everyone was supposed to be placed on a sugar-card system.

[19] This is Annie's first notice of a problem that manifested itself in various ways over the course of the present year—and for a long time afterwards as well.

Friday, 29 March

I done another big washing today. Mrs Howard brought me some butter milk.[20] Bert has gone to town. Sister Fannie called me up this morning. She is worried about war too. I think every Mother is. Sent Hen a card today. Lettie stayed at Lowes for supper. Raym went down after supper. Tonight is bright moonlight.

So glad to be home.

[20] Mrs. Howard was the wife of Captain I. D. Howard, who had some time since "purchased and taken possession of the former Cummings place on the South Ridge near the George Wood farm" (*FPT*, 25 April 1916, p. 2)—that is, about a mile and a half from Geneva. Three days earlier, in fact, the *Free Press-Times* included in its "Personals" column the information that "Capt. I. D. Howard is home from Cleveland to spend Sunday with his family" (p. 3).

Though Annie mentions Mrs. Howard about a dozen times, therefore, it is not surprising that she never refers to her husband. In any case, Mrs. Howard was another of the kindly neighbors living within easy walking distance of the Perrin farm.

Saturday, 30 March

Had a big day. Lettie washed 8 p[ai]rs of curtains.
Done some up on stretchers,[21] and done Saturdays
work.[22] After dinner Raym went down to see a Dr.[23]
Has head ache so much. Pa was down [in town] all
day[.] Both came home about 7.30 with the Auto.[24]
After supper Raym & Lettie went to town in Auto. Lettie bought me a beautiful red rose plant for Easter.

[21] These stretchers were large
but lightweight and adjustable
wooden frames that could be assembled for use and disassem-
bled for storage. To dry curtains,
one stretched them on the frame,
fixing them in place by impaling
their borders on rows of half-
inch-long pins that lined the
frame and protruded from it. See
entry for 9 October.

[22] That is, Annie had now resumed her pattern of reserving
the more serious housecleaning
for Saturday.

[23] In all likelihood Raym consulted Dr. Edmond A. Childs—
to whom the family turned in
times of illness later this year.
With a newly built home at 125
East Main and a professional
suite over The Geneva Market
on South Broadway, Dr. Childs
was a notable figure in town.
Before the end of the year, moreover, he moved his office to better quarters on the second floor
of the new A. J. Ford block, over
the post office at 11 North Broadway (*FPT*, 22 November, p. 2).
When he first arrived in town
back in 1912 (having purchased
the practice of Dr. Frank C.
Smith), Dr. Childs was quickly
recognized as a "genial dispenser
of powders and pills" (*FPT*, 20
November, p. 2). In 1916 he was
one of the speakers featured in a
newspaper article headlined
"Geneva Citizens Talk Over
Plans for New Hospital" (*S&B*,
25 November 1916, p. 3), and the
hospital he championed would
become the place where Annie's
second grandchild, Lettie's first
child, was born in 1922. Among
other things, Dr. Childs was a

member of the board of education, a faithful member of the local Masonic lodge (in 1916 he assumed the post of Worshipful Master there [*FPT*, 17 November 1915, p. 2]), and an example-setting citizen sufficiently patriotic to raise "Old Glory" in his own front yard (*FPT*, 1 March, p. 2; 12 July, p. 2; 7 November, p. 1; 10 May, p. 2—all in 1917).

24 The family car—an Overland—was in storage during the Perrins' expedition to Florida. Ola Berry and Roy Miller, who ran the Overland-Ashtabula Co. in Ashtabula, specifically advertised themselves as furnishing "Supplies, Storage, Washing" (*Ashtabula Directory, 1918*, p. 7), but penny-wise Bert may have found a way to store the car closer to home.

In any event, the Perrins' automobile was a significant investment and still relatively new: as recently as 4 May 1917 the *Geneva Free Press-Times* took note that "B. H. Perrin has purchased a new Overland Light Six touring car" (p. 2). See Fig. 41.

For an extended period in 1916 the Overlands were by far the most visible cars in the Geneva paper, partly because a specimen Overland was the main prize in a subscription contest. Public interest was further whetted by a handful of news items such as that on 15 May headed "Overland Breaks Record":

> News has just been received by *The Willys-Overland Company of Toledo, [Ohio,]* of another record broken by one of its cars, a 1916 Model Overland setting a new mark in Australia a short time ago by making the run from Albany to Armadale a distance of 238 miles, in 6 hours and 32 minutes, one-third of the running time made by the express trains between the two points. (p. 2)

On 1 April 1918 Henry inquired of Lettie, "Is the machine home yet? Would like to have taken a spin yesterday."

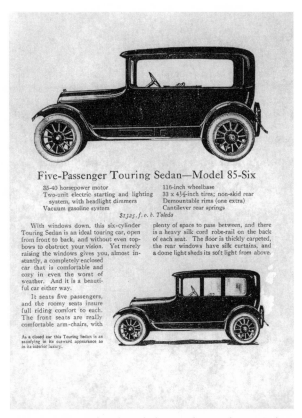

Fig. 41. A source of pride and pleasure, here is the Perrins' "Five-Passenger Touring Sedan" as depicted in the Overland catalogue for 1917 (courtesy of Kim Miller, for the AACA). The small print at the bottom reads: "As a closed car this Touring Sedan is as satisfying in its outward appearance as in its interior luxury."

Sunday, 31 March[25]

[25] Easter Day.

Bright & warmer[.] Pa & Raym went for a drive this morning. Bought some potatoes. After dinner we drove up to Aunt Fannies [and] had a pleasant visit[.][26] We stayed to supper[, and] had a fine supper.

Got home about 7 oclock[,] then Raym took car and went over to see Bernice. Lettie looked sick and I guess felt sicker.

She works too hard[.]

[26] On this first day after the return of the automobile, Annie refers again to her twin sister, Fannie ("Aunt" to Annie's children), and her husband, Walter, who lived a few miles to the west in North Madison (Fig. 42).

Fig. 42. Annie's sister and brother-in-law from Madison, Fannie and Walter R. Keyse.

Monday, 1 April

Cleveland[.]

Looks like rain. Fred called up this morning for Bert to come up.[27] [He] left about 9 oclock. Raym plowed.[28]

I done some ironing. Then ironed kitchen curtains [and] put them up.

Raym went to town after [the] rain. Lettie walked home.[29] Brought her new spring coat.

Every one seemed to have a grouch on after supper. Went to bed at 9 oclock.

Had a poor night.

Fig. 43. Though the nation in general had been assured for a year or so that agricultural work was patriotic, Raym—who had long since registered for the draft—was not altogether comfortable about resuming work on the farm. Carrying the reassuring caption "A Hero of the Trenches," this drawing is reproduced from the *Ashtabula Star and Beacon* of 13 April 1917 (p. 1).

[27] Come up, that is, to Cleveland. This entry recognizes an early stage of the business that would be completed early in May. Very probably these negotiations, like the trip to Florida, may be related at least in part to the death of Bert's and Fred's father, Henry Perrin, on 19 March 1917. At any rate, Fred was an astute businessman who seems to have been able and willing to keep an eye out for Bert. Annie had no hand in working out the details of the business, but see her entries for 9–10 April and 4 June.

[28] Previously the only men's chores mentioned by Annie have been cleaning out the basement (27 March) and burning brush (28 March). The present mention of Raym therefore marks a turning point. As Wheeler McMillen has written in his book *Ohio Farm*, "The hour that finally and definitively marked the beginning of a new farm year came when the first furrow was plowed. From then on until early winter . . . one could expect only occasional respites from work" (65). See Fig. 43.

[29] After teaching school all day Lettie had about a two-mile walk to return to the farm.

Tuesday, 2 April

Quite warm today. Lettie went to school. Raym plowed[.] I done a big ironing. After supper Raym & Lettie went over to Slocums for butter.[30] Thundered quite hard. Had quite a storm after they came home. It seems colder.

Bert isn't home yet.

Wednesday, 3 April

Cold & clear[.]

I done up work[,] then cut out a corset cover for Fannie & made it. Crocheted yoke while in Florida.[31] Hen sent a telegram to meet him coming on [Interurban car] No[.] 44. Raym just got back with Hen when Pa called up to come down and meet him. So all had supper together. Hen passed and expects to soon go into training.

[30] Annie did not return to making her own butter until 17 April.

The Charles B. Slocums were South Ridge neighbors whose household consisted of fifty-eight-year-old Charles himself (a general farmer), his thirty-eight-year-old wife Elizabeth (known as "Lizzie"), and their nine-year-old nephew, Charles Muir (1920 Census and *Farm Journal Illustrated*, p. 177).

As newsmakers, the Slocums appeared in the Geneva paper with some frequency. For example, on 6 July 1915 the *Free Press-Times* reported that during the previous evening the couple "were painfully injured when the buggy in which they were riding was struck by an automobile driven by Claud Buck, one of our local liverymen" (p. 2). "Mrs. Slocum was thrown out through the windshield on the car. Mr. Slocum was thrown to the ground and trampled on by the horse." Then again, perhaps Mr. Slocum found nearly as memorable the time he was trapped and buried up to his shoulders during a gravel pit cave-in on Fred Sprague's place (*FPT*, 27 September 1912, p. 2). And there was also the time he fell from a scaffolding in his barn, broke his left arm, and had to learn to use crutches (*FPT*, 17 December 1915, p. 2; 12 January 1916, p. 2).

[31] While down in Florida, Annie twice referred to her crocheting—21 January and 22 March. The yoke she made there was to be only that part of the finished garment up around the neck and shoulders, front and back. It still had to be sewn to the newly made lower section of the corset cover.

Pictured in the *Sears, Roebuck*

catalogue for 1917 are "many new and pleasing styles" of similar corset covers, some with "strong net lace" comparable to Annie's crocheted yoke (p. 232). The overall effect of most of these catalogue items as well as of Annie's gift is likely to have been that of a garment a cut above a working woman's everyday undergarments.

32 Presumably for the duration of the war.

33 The Perrins drove over to the passenger depot of the Nickel Plate on the corner of Main and East Fisk (*Ashtabula Directory*, 1918, p. 206).

34 Later in the year (1 November) Henry wrote to Lettie about corresponding with Fred Ward.

35 Though Annie seldom knew exactly how the young folks spent their evenings, Fig. 44 shows Raym and Bernice having fun at a friend's house on what, judging from their clothing, may well have been a night following a day that was "Windy & cold."

36 Probably so as to be closer to school the following morning.

Thursday, 4 April

Windy & cold[.] I washed but felt too tired to keep up[.] After dinner I helped put Henrys clothes away[32] [and] ironed some.

We all went to Depot with H[enry].[33] He is going to stay with Wards tonight[.][34] Lettie got home late[,] dident have much supper[.]

Raym went over to see B[ernice.][35]

Lettie went to town for the night.[36]

Fig. 44. Raym and Bernice, sitting comfortably close, share a good time with some friends. Their glee at this particular moment is triggered at least partly by the fact that Raym is trying more or less unsuccessfully to hide (or pretend to hide) an empty drinking glass between his crossed legs. Above the young couple looms a photograph of the Roman Colosseum.

Friday, 5 April

Frosty and cold this morning. Today I felt punk. Dident feel much like work. Bert went to town[.] Got
home just [at] noon [and] brought plants from Lowes.
After dinner [he] went to a sale in Saybrook.[37] Bought
a cow.[38] Henry called me up from Cleveland [and] was
going to leave for Chicago at 4 oclock[.] Goes to training school.[39] Wonder when we will see him again.

[37] Saybrook is the next settlement to the east (population ca.
250), where Bernice Michel lived.
[38] Soon after this purchase
Annie begins to mention her
churning.
[39] Henry was heading toward
the Great Lakes Naval Training
Station at Great Lakes, Illinois.
See Fig. 45.

Fig. 45. Like many other mothers, Annie, after putting
Henry's clothes away and saying goodbye, had to deal somehow with the reality of his absence. The rationalization of
the mother in this cartoon is "Course I hate t'see him go—
but, Pa, he wouldn't be our boy if he didn't." Though the
pump to the right of the sink here is much like the one in
Annie's kitchen, the doorway view of the American flag
flying on the silo is, of course, cartoon hyperbole. Borrowed
here from the *Ashtabula Star and Beacon* of 18 April 1917 (p.
1), the drawing appeared originally in the *Indianapolis News*.

Saturday, 6 April

Sat[urday] morning[,] cold & windy. Bert went to a sale. Vere Smith came on the 9 oclock car[.] Lettie & I done general Saturdays work. I made pie & cake[, and] baked bread[.] About 11 oclock F[red]. Seymour & wife came[,] just home from Florida, [and] ate dinner with us.[40] R[aym].[,] L[ettie]. & V[ere]. went to town after supper, [and] the girls walked home. Pa, Sprague[,] John & I played dominoes.[41] Got a card from War department to hang in window.[42]

[40] A couple of weeks later, on 19 April, Mr. Seymour placed an ad in the *Star and Beacon* (p. 2) announcing that he was opening an office in the new Crosby Block (over Eastman's grocery) in Ashtabula, and that he would now resume the listing and sale of properties. In the coming months and despite some distance between the towns, he seems to have worked fairly extensively in the Geneva area.

[41] Fred B. Sprague was another near neighbor, only two houses to the west on the Ridge. In fact, nineteen acres of land that he held to the south of the Perrin place was eventually purchased by the Perrins. Sprague was significantly older than either Annie or Bert: when his wife, Mary E. Sprague, died in 1917, she was in her early seventies (*FPT*, 5 February, p. 3; *S&B*, 5 February, p. 8). Bert served as one of her pallbearers (*FPT*, 8 February, p. 2).

John was John T. Harley, once a resident to the south on Clay Street (in Harpersfield Township), but now the Perrins' first neighbor to the west. He was an unmarried bachelor ("Mortgage Deed" of 1911, *Ashtabula County Records*, vol. 100, p. 282) who lived with his sister Lyda, and, like Fred Sprague, was somewhat older than Annie and Bert. When he died of heart failure the following year (11 May 1919), his heirs included two brothers, aged sixty-one and seventy-four, and two sisters, aged seventy and sixty-eight (*Ashtabula Record of*

Fig. 46. The depiction of the three service stars here endows them with a quasi-sacred quality: the caption is "A Wayside Shrine." Most such stars, like the one Annie displayed for Henry, were simply hung in a front window of the service-man's home (*S&B*, 23 August, p. 1).

Deeds, vol. 242, p. 8; see also *FPT*, 17 May 1919, p. 3).

Upon hearing of John's death, Henry thought of his own unsettled life and Lettie's and wrote to her facetiously, "You and I will have to live to-gether as John and Lyde only not in quite such filth" (1 May 1919). The sentence provides a quick impression of John and at the same time reveals Henry's sense of closeness to Lettie. The fact is, however, that Lettie had by that time applied for a new teaching post in Warren, and Henry was under quarantine for diphtheria in a hospital in Philadelphia.

[42] "It is your duty and privilege to hang one of these insignias of honor in your window so all may know that a soldier has gone or is on his way to fight for liberty" (*S&B*, 26 September, p. 2). A simple blue star was the essential symbol, but one could buy commercial permutations of it.

The Ashtabula paper of 4 October (p. 6) reprinted a poem on the subject called "The Little Flag on Our House" (from *Leslie's Weekly*), which begins:

> The little flag on our house
> Is floating all the day
> Beside the great big Stars and
>   Stripes;
> You can almost hear it say
> To all the folks in our street,
> As the breezes make it dance:
> "Look up and see my own blue
>   star—
> We've got a boy in France!"

There was even a movie on the subject: Madge Kennedy played the lead in *The Service Star*—"the flag of all mothers" (*S&B*, 14 August, p. 4).

Sunday, 7 April

Very windy,[43] [and I] got up with head ache. We done up the work[,] then got dinner for nine[, including] Fannie & family.[44] Vere Smith and weons[45] had a good dinner and a pleasant visit[.] Every one seemed to enjoy their selves. Got a light lunch for all about 7.30. [Then the] K[eyse].s left for home. L[ettie] & V[ere] went to Ashtabula. L[ettie] stayed all night at Veres.

Monday, 8 April

Cold & windy. Too windy to wash so done up work[,] then sewed[.] Raym was fitting out ground.[46] Pa is about sick with hard cold. Got cards from Henry today. He sent Lettie an Emblem pin.[47] Also a letter from Mrs Fox.[48]

[43] Though this day was simply another in a series of unusually windy ones, it also marked a seasonal turning point. As the *Geneva Free Press-Times* reported, "The southerly wind blew the ice bank away from the lake shore Sunday. It was way out in the lake Sunday afternoon" (8 April, p. 2).

Lake Erie, which is about eighty miles wide off the Geneva shore, had been almost entirely frozen over during the winter—affording unprecedented opportunities for the ice-harvesters but, as usual, slowing the warming of the land.

[44] Besides Annie and Bert, and Raym, Lettie, and Vere, the diners were Fannie, her husband Walter, and two of their sons, probably young Walter (1897–1968) and Melvin (1899–1980).

[45] Use of the plural "weons" is surprising in the context of the Perrin family. Despite its occasional outcropping in rural areas, mainly in Appalachia and the South, it appears to be a fairly rare and largely unstudied word. From *Harper's Magazine* of 16 December 1864, however, Hendrickson cites: "'What for you uns,' said they, in their barbaric dialect, 'come down her to fight we uns?'" (p. 240). Possibly Annie uses the term as a humorous souvenir of the family's trip to Florida. In any case, she uses it only this once.

[46] "Fitting out" means preparing for planting.

[47] The pin consisted of a Navy insignia.

[48] Mrs. Fox, from Indiana, was one of the women Annie met in Florida.

Tuesday, 9 April

Cleveland

Windy & very cold and some snow. Bert went to Cleveland on buisness.[49] Did not feel well enough to go. Raym took him & Lettie down in the auto.[50] Raym has gone for oats for seed, & fertiliser.[51] I made cookies[,] then cleaned up some as Lettie has invited Miss Beaver to supper & stay all night.[52] She did not come[.] L[ettie]. came home all in.

Got a letter from Henry.

Wednesday, 10 April

Very windy and cold. Raym took Lettie down [to Geneva]. I made a p[ai]r of pillow slips [and] finished a piece of under wear for L[ettie]. Had head ache all day. Raym has gone down to drag but [weather] looks stormy.[53] Bert came home [from Cleveland] on the one oclock [Interurban] car [with] nothing settled yet. R[aym]. got a letter from Henry. I got a card[. Raymond] went for L[ettie]. after school[.] Stormy & windy.

[49] Annie does not clarify the nature of Bert's business in Cleveland, but he was in the process of acquiring some rental property on Cleveland's West Side.

[50] That is, down to Geneva. Lettie had to teach.

[51] Less than a year later, the Perrins were able to offer their own "Ellwood seed oats" for sale (*FPT*, 11 February 1919, p. 4).

[52] Eva Beaver, a seventh-grade teacher in Geneva, appears only a few times in Annie's diary, but she was one of Lettie's best friends. Called to Greenville, Pennsylvania, this year by the sickness of her father, she eventually retired in western Pennsylvania. In those later years she and Lettie maintained a Christmas-card friendship, and as late as the 1960s, after Lettie's death, Eva still had a faded but cordial relationship with Lettie's widower, Myron Randall.

[53] A drag is a field or road implement with different forms and uses. The old-fashioned spike-toothed drag and the spring-toothed drag (or harrow) were generally used after plowing in order to break up the loosened clods of soil so as to prepare a seed bed—probably Raym's aim at the moment (see Fig. 47).

Though the same two types of drag could also be used on roads, many a road drag was simply "made of a log, say eight feet long and 12 inches through, split in the middle, or of two pieces of sawed oak or other substantial wood." After fastening these pieces to the doubletree with a chain or rope, "The drag is run at an angle of about 45 degrees, so that dirt can be thrown toward one side" (*FPT*, 9 January 1914, p. 2). Ohio's "dragging act," beginning in January of 1914, required every board of township trustees to name one member as its dragging superintendent, his duty being "to divide the township into dragging districts, . . . and to supervise the dragging of all the earth and gravel roads in such districts" (p. 2).

Whether used for field work or road work, the drag was of greatest use during the spring, before the soil had been baked hard by summer heat.

Fig. 47. A spring-toothed harrow like this one took its name from the fact that each of its "teeth" was a fairly broad steel spur that sprang back and released itself whenever it met a particularly resistant obstruction. The tool was useful for initial breaking up and leveling of soil, or after plowing, or sometimes (for instance, in corn and potato fields) even after a field had been planted—provided the plants had not yet sprouted (from Grim, p. 144).

Thursday, 11 April

Deep snow this morning and still snowing hard. Mrs Holt called me up [and we] had a visit.[54] Raym is oiling up the auto. Went to town this P.M. Mr Stowe came over and visited with Bert.[55] I finished ironing. Done some mending. Raym got a letter from Henry[.] He has been vaccinated.[56]

[54] Annie probably refers here to Anna Holt, a former South Ridge neighbor who was living at 21 Swan Street in the village with her toolmaker husband, Joseph W. Holt.

The call might have come, however, from Anna's daughter-in-law, Edna. Edna and her husband, Luther (privately, always "Lou") Holt, make only a brief appearance in Annie's diary, but they were good friends of the Perrins. Considerably younger than Bert and Annie, Lou, who previously lived with his parents on the Ridge, married Edna May Critzer of Geneva in the fall of 1914 (*FPT*, 21 September 1914, p. 3). Both at that time were already well known locally—and especially Edna, who had been in charge of the music course in Geneva's schools for several years.

Earlier in 1918 the couple suffered the throes of leaving their home at 110 West Main Street in Geneva because Lou, previously employed by The Geneva Metal Wheel Company, had decided to accept a job in Painesville, about seventeen miles to the west. In Painesville he worked as manager of one of the departments in H. F. Byler's store on State Street (*FPT*, 15 January, p. 1).

The experiment did not work well, however, and before long Lou was back at the Metal Wheel (*FPT*, 5 July, p. 3). Happy to be in Geneva again, he was soon elected as an alderman in Lodge No. 294 of the I.O.O.F. (*FPT*, 18 July, p. 2. The Independent Order of Odd Fellows, founded in England in the eighteenth century, was imported to Baltimore in 1819, and in 1918 it was one of the largest fraternal orders in the United States.)

Edna had a special spark. Capable not only of teaching music to schoolchildren and of prepar-

ing music for services at the
Congregational church that she
and Lou attended, she also organized some of the Congregational
ladies into what they decided to
call The Geneva Kitchen Band.
Using a variety of kitchen uten-
sils as instruments, the group
managed to produce "remarkable harmony—with tuneful se-
lections following each other in
rapid succession" (*FPT*, 9 December 1916, p. 1). For herself,
Edna devised a solo version of
"Carry Me Back to Old Virginny."
(See also entries for 4 October
and 10 November.)

55 See note to 26 March.

56 Henry wrote to Lettie
that "About 50 out of our Co.
were taken to the Hospital on
acc[oun]t. of serum. The serum
acts as a light case of typhoid
does. . . . [I] Have had 4 vaccina-
tions but none have taken. I get
two more & if they don't take[,]
they will give me up as a bad
subject" (undated April letter).

57 Mr. and Mrs. Henry *Frizell*,
former neighbors on the South
Ridge, moved to Cleveland in the
latter part of 1913 (*FPT*, 5 November, p. 5). According to an
entry in Annie's address list at
the back of her diary, they lived
at 7405 Detroit Avenue.

58 The front-page headline of
the *Star and Beacon* for 11 April
was "Hindenburg Plans Annihi-
lation of French, British—U.S.
Must Act at Once." For 12 April it
was "British Center Pushed Back
7 Miles in Battle of Flanders" and
"Whole Armies Wiped Out—
Dead Piled High in Race for Victory." Geneva's paper featured
the same lead story (*FPT*, p. 1).

Friday, 12 April

Still stormy. Sleet[,] rain & snow. Raym is drawing
dirt from Spragues[,] filling in the yard.

Lettie went on the [Interurban] car this morning.
I washed some[.] Mrs Howard came in so I visited a
while. Got a letter from Mrs Tyner of Fl[orid]a & Mrs
Firzell.57 Every body is blue. War or weather I dont
know which.58

Saturday, 13 April

Lettie & I done Sat[urday] work. L[ettie]. took 2 oclock car for Ashta[bula]. Raym drew dirt[.][59] Bert went to town. L[ettie] & I got letters from Henry.[60] In evening John[,][61] Bert & I played dominoes[.] Raym went to town. It is quite windy.

Sunday, 14 April

+

A nice bright day. Mrs Smith & Vere came on the 11 oclock car.[62] Was here to dinner. After dinner we visited. Bert went away. Raym took car to Bernices in evening[.] Lettie corrected papers[.] I wrote letters. Then to bed. Bert not home yet.

[59] In other words, Raym was still working to level the yard.

[60] Henry started out at Camp Farragut (Co. 59, Reg. 9, Bar. 1938N). As the Geneva paper informed its readers, Farragut was the "detention or receiving camp. The main building is known as the receiving barracks" (*FPT*, 9 November 1917, p. 1). Hence Henry's address would soon change. Meanwhile, he had been classified as a Hospital Apprentice, 2d Class. He wrote to Lettie that "We have a fine lot of boys in our barracks. Most of them are college men, & farmers, some mechanics but few" (10 April).

[61] Again, the nextdoor neighbor, John Harley.

[62] Vere Smith and her mother, Rose Smith. Mrs. Smith, a seamstress in her later forties, had long been a widow. Back when her children were young and the family was living in Thompson, her husband, Bert Smith, was killed by a horse that kicked him in the head (ALS, John Carlson, 14 February 1997).

Monday, 15 April

This is the first of Annie's several references to the neighbor who for a while helped her with the weekly washing.

William and Ellen Williamson had been joint owners of a farm adjacent to the Perrin orchard on the north side of the South Ridge road. William died in 1910, however, and subsequently Ellen did not have an easy time of it. Finally, in June of 1920 the Perrins bought the Williamson property from Ellen and her daughter and son-in-law, Grace and Bert Rose (*Ashtabula County Records of Deeds*, vol. 243, p. 565). Ellen then moved to a house on Austin Road, a bit to the west. In the 1920 census, aged sixty-seven, she listed herself as the head of a mortgaged farm household of seven, including, besides her daughter and son-in-law, four grandchildren.

[64] That is, the civilian clothes he wore at the time he left Geneva. He warned Lettie that "They will send my clothes home in pretty poor shape" (8 April).

[65] Grace and Lulu Lowe, who had visited the Perrins on their first day back from Florida.

[66] Milton H. Austin, a farm laborer, was described in 1916 as "moving from one of the Walters places on the South Ridge, to the Cook place near the Twin bridges," about a mile south of town (*FPT*, 23 March, p. 2).

Bright & warm[.] Mrs Williamson came.[63] We did a big washing. Dried fine[.] Pa got a letter from Henry. He was feeling good. We received Henrys clothes that he wore away.[64] Lettie & Raym heard from the Lowe girls.[65] Raym is rolling oat ground. Mr Austin burning brush.[66] In the evening Sprague[,] John[,] Bert & I played 3 games dominoes[.] J[ohn] & I beat—3 games. J[ohn] looked pleased.

Tuesday, 16 April

Cloudy & colder[.] I am sore & stiff [and can] hardly get around[.] I guess I took cold. [The men] drilled some oats in but [it] commenced to rain at noon so had to quit.[67] Mr A[ustin] went home at noon. Pa got a letter from Henry.

Had quite a thunder storm in the night.

Wednesday, 17 April

Cloudy and cool[.] Raym is ploughing. Milton[68] taking wire off fence. I done work[,] then churned.[69] In the after noon ironed some. Got a letter from Henry[,] also one from Mrs Aylard.

Lettie stayed down town tonight. Raym has gone somewhere. Bert & I played dominoes.

Thursday, 18 April

Cold and windy[.] Nothing happened today out of usual. Raym & Bert finished drilling oats. Got a letter from Henry.[70] I ironed all the afternoon.

Lettie came home about 5.30.[71]

Spent evening mending[.]

Pa was over to Johns[.]

[67] The men were planting oats with a horse-drawn drill—a device that was supposed to do three things: "(1) it must sow the seed in the proper quantity, (2) it must open up a neat, shallow trench, (3) it must cover the seed at the proper depth" (*FPT*, 17 August 1911, p. 4). Though farmers of the time were still deliberating the relative merits of a four-inch and an eight-inch planting, the latter produced so negligible an increase in yield of both grain and straw that the best solution in effect remained moot (*FPT*, 15 August 1919, p. 4).

In the spring of 1919, at any rate, Bert was able to offer two hundred bushels of oats for sale (*FPT*, 9 April 1919, p. 3).

[68] Once again, Milton Austin.

[69] Bert having bought a cow on 5 April, this is Annie's first reference to churning. After skimming the cream off their fresh milk for several days, she now had enough to work with, so she poured it into her churn and pumped the churn paddle up and down until she could see a good many small pieces of butter floating on the surface. She then had to strain the butter bits from the buttermilk, drain the butter, add some salt, and shape the butter with a small wooden butter paddle.

[70] In a company of nineteen men, Henry was now Assistant Company Clerk Perrin (letter to Lettie, 14 April).

[71] Annie accidentally writes "home" twice in this line.

Friday, 19 April

Raym still working at peach orchard[.] I baked & churned[,] done the rest of ironing[.] Went over to Mrs Howards and Pennys a while in the after noon[.] Lettie bought yarn to make Henry a sweater. I commenced it this evening.[72]

Saturday, 20 April

Lettie & I did the Saturday work.

Raym sowed grass seed[,] then rolled. Bert went to a sale.[73] L[ettie]. took 4 oclock car to Ashtabula[, and is] going to stay all night.

Bert and I spent the evening playing dominoes. Raymond went away after supper.

Sunday, 21 April

Dull & rainy. Nothing to write about today. Lettie is in Ashta[bula.] Raym went to see B[ernice]. about 4 oclock[.] The end of a dreary day.

[72] On 10 April Henry wrote to Lettie, "Who is going to make me a sweater? Sure do wish I had one now."

None other than Secretary of War Newton D. Baker himself issued a statement endorsing sweater-making: "It is true that a sweater is not included in the regular equipment of the army and it is not regarded as an absolutely essential garment. However a knitted sweater is a garment of great serviceability and constitutes a welcome addition to a soldier's equipment" (*S&B*, 11 December 1917, p. 5).

[73] Bert was continuing to stock the farm. Clearly the family had decided to remain in Geneva.

Monday, 22 April

Cloudy so we could not wash today.[74] I knit spare time on Henrys sweater.

Got a letter from Henry today [and] also one from Sister Sarah.[75] <u>Bad news</u> in it[.] Drucy was hurt by a team.[76] And Walter Bently [was] taken to the Asylum.[77] Lettie went to Red cross[.][78] Raym took her down. Sprague [and] John came and played dom[inoes.] Mrs Howard was over too.

[74] In fact, Annie probably could have washed the laundry but not dried it.

[75] Sarah (actually Mary Susanna) Elliott (3 November 1853–27 September 1932) was Annie's elder by about thirteen years. On 3 December 1872 she had married a young Englishman from Somersetshire, Frank (actually Francis) E. Baker (15 October 1848–1 September 1925). Having arrived in the U.S. in 1866, at the age of eighteen, Frank found work in Dover, Ohio, as a hired man, perhaps on the Elliotts' own farm. As the English traveler Griffiths had observed earlier, it was "a common saying among the farmers of the Western Reserve, 'If a man is good enough to work for me, he is good enough to eat with me.' And, accordingly, every hired person, male or female, native or foreigner, whom they employ, 'is treated as one of the family'" (p. 80).

In 1884, after about twelve years of marriage, Sarah and Frank left Ohio for Michigan. In fact, they settled sufficiently early in Lee township, Midland County, to be spoken of in later times as among the oldest pioneers of that area (*Midland Republican,* 3 September 1925, p. 1; and 6 October 1932, p. 6). In 1907, after farming in Michigan for over twenty years, Frank was somehow invalided and subsequently became—and remained—paralyzed.

Nevertheless, Sarah, Frank, and their second-oldest son, Arthur (at that time about forty), and his family were able to visit their Ohio relatives in the summer of 1917. On Sunday, 15 July, that year Annie and Bert entertained some twenty family members, and on Tuesday, 17 July, a similar gathering was held in Madison at the home of Annie's twin, Fannie, and her husband, Walter Keyse (*FPT*, 19 July 1917, p. 3).

76 Drucy was Drucilla, one of Sarah's and Frank's daughters (and Annie's niece). Judging from a snapshot in Lettie's album, she was a pleasant, well-scrubbed, and rather plump woman.

Born in 1883, she had become the second wife of Charles McCreery, a man about eighteen years her senior, in 1905. In the spring of 1918, at the time of the accident reported by Sarah, Drucy had scarcely had time to recuperate from Charles's death in mid-December of 1917. Eventually, however, she took a Mr. DeLine as a second spouse ("Homer Township Cemetery," p. 283).

77 Walter was one of the sons of Lettie Elliott Bentley (3 November 1858–3 June 1943), another of Annie's older sisters—and the one after whom Annie named her own only daughter.

Though born in Dover like her sisters, Lettie married a Massachusetts-born man, Newton Arthur Bentley, in 1881. Some time before 1887—though not before producing two children— Lettie and Newt (as he was known) moved to Michigan, where they settled in Lee township, near to Sarah and Frank Baker and their family.

Walter G. Bentley (1898–1928), apparently the eighth of Lettie's and Newt's children, was the fourth of their sons. Having been born and educated in Midland County, he had been living recently in Detroit, but now, at the age of about twenty, had to be committed. Since Midland itself had only a "poor farm," he was sent to The Northern Michigan

———
Asylum for the Insane, a huge facility in Traverse City (Powers, 1:262). After ten years of confinement there and, as the newspaper put it, "following a lingering illness," he died at the age of thirty (*Midland Republican*, 24 May 1928, p. 6, and notes of Linda Petrak).

78 In April of 1918 the Ashtabula County chapter of the Red Cross made and shipped 13,785 surgical dressings to Lake Division headquarters. Among these, the city of Ashtabula contributed 3,425 and Geneva, with a far smaller population, 2,645 (*S&B*, 22 May, p. 5).

Tuesday, 23 April

Rainy again today. Made oat meal cookies. Sent a box to Henry. Also [sent a] Cleveland paper.[79] L[ettie]. heard from Henry.[80] I have the sweater about ⅓ done.

Dug greens for supper.[81] After supper worked on sweater[.]

Wednesday, 24 April

Cold & clear[.] Mrs Williamson came[.] We washed. Got cleaned up just in time for dinner. The men are plowing the orchard[.] They have the peach trees all out.[82] I hate to see them go.

Lettie was all in tonight[.]

[79] Some days earlier Henry had written to Lettie, "You can send a Cleveland Sun. paper to me anytime. Just the interesting parts" (14 April).

[80] Though still stationed within the Great Lakes naval complex, Henry had now moved on to Camp Boone and, along with his buddies, was undergoing a series of immunization shots. "Ma can send me $5 any time as I need it," he wrote to Lettie. "Have but 80¢ left" (19 April).

Despite some problems, Henry was on the whole doing well: "I have charge of the Y.M.C.A. to-day. Have 10 men here cleaning and etc. I am in the office giving orders." In fact, "have the Vic[trola]. going now." His hopes for the future were high: "By Rayms letter you have learned that if I make good I will be an officer before long. That is a Petty [officer] & if this war lasts will be a gold-braid eventually."

[81] For the Perrins, "greens" usually meant dandelion or pig-weed leaves, which Annie served like spinach. An interesting bit of relevant nomenclature crops up in the *Geneva Free Press-Times* of 1 May: "Dandelion greens and rhubarb are the first spring vegetables available for use" (p. 3).

[82] The 1917 peach crop in Ohio was estimated to be a disastrous 496,000 bushels, as opposed to about 1,350,000 in 1916 (*S&B*, 12 October 1917, p. 7). Furthermore, the extremely cold winter of 1917–18 killed off many of the weaker trees. In the spring of 1918, therefore, many farmers in Ashtabula County were "busy taking out old peach trees, mostly the Elbertas, [because] they do not seem hardy enough for this section" (*S&B*, 23 March, p. 3).

The Perrins' soil and terrain on the north side of the Ridge Road were ideally suited to peaches, however, and Annie certainly does not mean that all of their peach trees were gone—just the targeted ones.

[83] Begun on 19 April, the sweater took only a week to complete.

[84] In an undated April letter, Henry wrote to Lettie, "I have sent dad a book on the [Great Lakes Naval] Training Sta[tion]. here."

[85] Working in a field with heavy clay soil, Raym was probably using a sulky plow—named for its loose resemblance to the light, two-wheeled, one-person carriage known as a sulky. Probably, too, the plow called for three horses because it had not one but two steel moldboards (Raymond Perrin, Jr., 28 August 1997).

[86] A couple of years earlier the Robert C. Clarks had moved to the old Sanderson farm on the South Ridge, about one-quarter mile east of Myers Road (*FPT*, 7 February 1916, p. 2). Though they figure relatively little in Annie's diary, they come into the picture somewhat more strongly during the summer and fall, when Mr. Clark and his son Tom either provided help with haying or needed help with threshing. Moreover, the Clark-Perrin connection had some staying power. On Saturday, 9 April 1927, Myron Randall took Annie and Bert for a drive and recorded the event in his diary thus: "Visited along South Ridge in afternoon. L[ettie]'s father insisted on stopping at Clark's a little too long." Later still one of the daughters of the family, Ruth, would be living on the old Clark farm married to Glenn Cosgrove, and the family's warm relations with the Perrins would be passed on to one final generation: Raym's younger son, Raymond, Jr., was a schoolmate and friend of young Bob Cosgrove.

Thursday, 25 April

Hard frost this morning. Today was windy and quite cold. I churned, ironed some and expect to finish sweater today.[83]

Got a letter from Henry. Also a book.[84] Raym is working over in the south lot. Plowing with 3 horses.[85] Mrs Clark called on me today[.][86]

Fig. 48. Raym on the sulky plow, pulled here by three mules, pauses on the South Ridge road. Left of center in the background is one edge of the Perrins' orchard, and off to the right, beyond the telephone pole, are some of their low-lying fields to the north.

Friday, 26 April

April showers today. Pa took Lettie to school this morning[.] I ironed this afternoon[.] Got a letter from Henry. The sorrel[87] refused to plow. P. S. [Allen] and Bert played dominoes, all the evening.

[87] A light-reddish-brown horse.

Saturday, 27 April

Lettie and I worked all the forenoon[.] Got things quite slick. Pa went to town [and] traded the sorrel for an old white. Vere came on 4 oclock car. We finished work. Had supper[,] then all went to Ashta[bula] in Auto and seen Cleopatra.[88] <u>Very good</u>. Got home 10.30[.] Raymond drove the car. All went to bed quite happy[.][89]

[88] *Cleopatra* was a much-advertised film from 1917, interesting mainly as a vehicle for Theda Bara. "Not content with a mere casual and superficial study of the character, Miss Bara has delved into all the historical records at her command" (*S&B*, 24 April, p. 6; Fig. 49).

To see this movie the Perrins attended Ashtabula's Majestic Theater, at 240–246 Main Street. There they heard for the first time the theater's "new $11,000 orchestral organ unit." Originally designed for a large New York theater, the organ was "said to have over 1000 pipes, not counting the orchestral part of the Vox Humana box" (*S&B*, 16 February, p. 6). A big theater, the Majestic offered 800 seats at 25¢, a few at 35¢, and "loges" at 50¢ (*S&B*, 16 February, p. 6). See also Fig. 14.

[89] The word "happy" occurs in the diary only this once.

Sunday, 28 April

Windy [and] rather dull[.] The girls got up late. We done up work. Lettie played & sang some songs. After dinner L[ettie,] V[ere] & I went to the woods [and] picked wild flowers. After supper L[ettie]. went home with V[ere]. Raym went to see Bernice about 4.30[.] Pa & I spent the evening alone. Had a thunder shower.

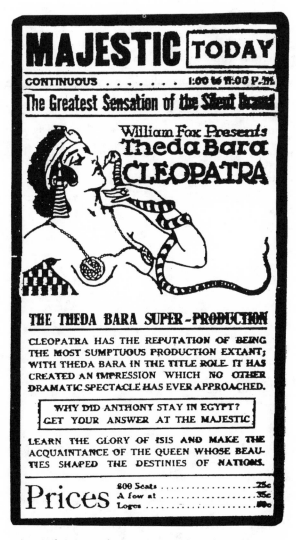

Fig. 49. Showing at the Majestic in Ashtabula, *Cleopatra* was advertised as not merely historically accurate but also "the most sumptuous production extant." Presumably after spending twenty-five cents to see it, one might answer the question "Why did Anthony stay in Egypt?" (*S&B*, 22 April 1918, p. 5).

Monday, 29 April

Terrible windy. Mrs. W[illiamson]. was sick so I done washing alone. Then had all my [everyday] work to do. Got a letter from Mrs Newel & Mrs Fox.[90] Also a card from Henry. He got the letter & box all O.K.[91] Raym is still plowing. Bert brought the little pigs home this morning.[92]

I set 2 hens today.[93] L[ettie] & R[aym] have gone to town[.]

Tuesday, 30 April

Cool & cloudy.

Done up work. Tried to crochet, but rheumatism was too bad in my hand. After dinner I ironed.

Mrs Howard came over about an h[ou]r. Got a letter from Henry. He has changed camps.[94] Does not like it as well there.[95] In the evening Bert and I went over to Wetters a while. She was alone.

[90] Friends Annie saw frequently in Florida.

[91] Apparently the newspaper and oatmeal cookies sent on 23 April.

[92] Bert's restocking of the farm continued. There is no telling where he found these pigs, but his Myers Road neighbor Frank King had an annual sale of "weanling pigs and brood sows" (*FPT*, 14 October 1919, p. 3). Bert himself was not likely to be stirred by patriotic motives, but it was a fact that "As an emergency war measure, Ohio has been asked to increase its pork production 15 per cent" (*S&B*, 2 February, p. 3). In Ashtabula County some two hundred boys and girls were soon raising "Porkers for Prizes" (*FPT*, 14 May, p. 3).

[93] When a hen is ready to "set," she becomes "broody" (that is, crotchety, irritable) and begins to cluck in a new and harsher tone. She is then likely to establish herself in one of the chickens' usual (and usually shared) nests, but the hatching process works best if she is moved to a separate nest in some more or less dark and secluded place—perhaps just a straw-lined wooden box. Once accustomed to her new environment, she will spend most of her time setting on fifteen to twenty fertilized eggs until they hatch.

[94] Though Henry was continuing to move from camp to camp, all of them thus far were part of the huge naval complex at Great Lakes, Illinois.

[95] Nevertheless, Henry realized that as a hospital apprentice he had "a chance to get some fine experience & have it soft, also will see Sea service." Moreover, he was now qualified for "The Officers Material School," which might be still better for him, he thought, if the war were to last a while (letter to Lettie of 21 April).

Wednesday, 1 May

Cold[,] raining and some flakes of snow.

Finished ironing today. All got cards from Henry. The men built [a] fence between [the] pasture & corn field. Bert spent the evening at Allens. Raym went to town. Lettie came home with head ache.

Thursday, 2 May

Pleasant but rather cool. Bert went to Ashtabula[.] Raym fitted corn ground.[96] Mrs Brown called.[97] Also Fred Seymour [and] Mrs Howard.

A letter from Aylards today.

Bert not home. So will go to bed.

[96] With the new fence in place, Raym could begin to prepare the enclosed ground for planting. The Perrins put in their last corn on 25 May.

According to the governor of Ohio and various other state officials, corn had become especially important because of "the almost complete failure of the 1917 crop for reproduction purposes" (*S&B*, 14 February, p. 12).

[97] The Browns best known to Annie are difficult to identify with certainty because more than one local farm family of that name lived on the South Ridge. The most likely Browns, however, about two miles southeast of town, were James W. Brown (like Annie and Bert, in his early fifties), his wife Zella (in her early forties), and their school-age children, a girl and a boy (1920 Census). Running a hundred-acre general farm (unlike W. M. Brown, to the west, who specialized in fruit), James Brown may be glimpsed selling pigs, Jersey cows, hay, corn, and potatoes (*FPT*, 25 July 1916, p. 4; 9 February 1917, p. 4; 20 October 1917, p. 2; 17 December, p. 3; 8 April 1918, p. 4; 23 April 1919, p. 3; see also *Farm Journal . . . Directory*, p. 44).

———

Like the Clarks, the Browns figure most importantly in Annie's diary in late summer and fall, when the local farmers banded together to assist one another with major jobs such as threshing and husking corn.

Friday, 3 May

Set Hen[.][98]

Pleasant & warmer. Mrs Williamson helped me clean up today. Mrs Howard brought us a mess of fish.[99] I got a letter from Henry, [and] he received the sweater and seems very much pleased with it.[100] Bert is working with the mules. Raym with an old team.[101] Expect Miss Beaver here with Lettie tonight.

Saturday, 4 May

Cloudy & warm. Lettie & Miss Beaver went to Ashta[bula].[102] Bert to Geneva. Raym worked with the mules. I went down in the meadow. Got ½ bu[shel] of greens.[103] Raym got a letter from Henry[.] He said he has lost 15 lbs since there. How I wish War was over.[104]

[98] That is, a third hen.

[99] A likely gift, since Mrs. Howard's husband was the captain of a Lake Erie boat.

[100] Five days later Henry wrote to Lettie that "The sweater you & Ma sent me is sure fine. Best I have ever seen. I have had it on ever since I opened the package" (8 May).

[101] Since Raym's team was old, Bert pretty clearly had the better power today. Age aside, "Mules Prove Best for Heavy Farming," according to one newspaper article headline a while back. Good mules eat less than big draft horses, and also do more hard work (*FPT*, 12 December 1914, p. 4).

[102] "You and Eve [*sic*] must be quite chums," Henry wrote to Lettie (8 May). "By your letters I understand you still like theatres and etc. Wish I could have taken you more than I did."

[103] See annotation for entry of 23 April.

[104] Two of the front-page headlines in the day's *Star and Beacon* are "Germany Bombarded All Northern Half of Flanders Front" and "Deserters Face Firing Squad Next."

Fig. 50. Eva Beaver, a friend of Lettie, stands here on the
Barnum Road side of the pasture fence. Sharing the foreground with her are the Perrins' dog Tuff and one of their
mules. In the background are the Perrin barn and silo.

Fig. 51. This picture of Lettie
picking violets down in the
pasture was snapped by Eva
Beaver on 4 May 1918.

Fig. 52. On the morning of Sunday, 5 May, Eva took this snapshot of Lettie, and Lettie took another one of Eva. The day was breezy, yet warm enough for Lettie to lay aside her coat and winged hat. Later she would label this picture "Under the elm."

Sunday, 5 May

A thunder shower this A.M. Cleared off and was a beautiful day. We all took a drive in Auto in the P.M. Went up to Aunt Fannies. Stayed for supper. Had a real pleasant time [and] a lovely ride home.

Done chores, eat & [remained] up about an h[ou]r[,] then went to bed.

Monday, 6 May

Cleveland

Very warm and windy. Mrs W[illiamson]— came. We did a big washing[.] I churned. Bert went to Cleveland[.] Miss Beaver & Lettie went to [catch the Interurban] car about 8 oclock. Raym worked on corn land.[105]

I broke one of my teeth off. B[ert]. got home on ten oclock car. P.M.

[105] The job he began on 2 May.

Tuesday, 7 May

Warm today. Every thing growing fine. Bert went to town [and] got garden seeds & early potatoes.[106]

Wanted me to go but I had no teeth. Mrs Howard came over in the Afternoon. No mail [so I] felt dissapointed. I Dug docks after supper.[107]

Wednesday, 8 May

Cold & windy, [but I] went out and helped put in a few garden seed. Got chilled through. Got a few lines from Henry. He has been in hospital since last Friday.[108]

I ironed all the afternoon. In the evening Lettie wrote letters[.] Raym went away. Bert & I played dominoes. I beat 3 games.

[106] An item in the *Free Press-Times* recommended previously that farmers "plant early potatoes about May 1st. . . . The early seed should be sprouted two weeks, then cut into pieces with two sprouts or eyes to each piece. Sow four inches deep, 1 foot by 2 feet apart" (10 April 1913, p. 4). Ohio standards among early potatoes of the day included "Early Ohio" and "Early Rose" (*S&B*, 27 April 1917, p. 2).

[107] Docks are coarse, tough plants with big leaves and strong taproots. People in the area had long held dock, along with sheep sorrel and mustard, to be good for serving as greens (Ellsworth, p. 22), but Annie—who served plenty of dandelion and pigweed —was probably simply weeding this evening.

[108] On the following Friday (10 May), the Geneva newspaper printed the following brief notice: "Mr. and Mrs. B. H. Perrin have received a letter stating that their son, Henry, is sick, with a severe attack of influenza. He is in the base hospital at the Great Lakes Naval Training Station" (p. 3).

Thursday, 9 May

Very windy but warmer. Done the usual work[.] Ironed all the P.M. Got a letter from Henry[.] He is feeling better. Sarah sent me some rose slips[.][109] Afraid they wont live. Set another Hen today.[110]

Friday, 10 May

Had tooth ache all the morning. Ray is hawling dirt into the yard. Rains part of the time. Bert levels it off. Did not hear from Hen today. Lettie phoned to me she will stay down town tonight. I done up L[ettie']–s pink dress today. Looks nice[.]

Saturday, 11 May

Showers & cooler.

Bert & Raym are still at the dirt buisness. I done up the work, swept clear through, was just doing dishes when L[ettie]. came home[.] She looks done out. Still have face ache. Got a good letter from Henry today[.] He is feeling some better.[111] Vere S[mith]. came up on the 3 oclock car[.] After supper we all went to Geneva[.] L[ettie]. bought me ½ doz[en] roses for Mother's day.

[109] Sister Sarah, in other words, sent cuttings for Annie to root. Now Annie needed to give the stems a fresh, angled cut, set them in the ground, and place over each one an inverted mason jar that would serve as a miniature greenhouse. With luck and a little attention, some might take root.

[110] This makes Annie's fourth broody hen of the season.

[111] Although held back by illness, Henry told Lettie, "They are still at me to transfer. The Store Dept. & Public works are trying to have me transfered but the Hospital Head says no. Don't know how it will come out" (ALS, 8 May).

Sunday, 12 May

Rained nearly all day. The girls had breakfast about 9. A.M. Got dinner.[112] Pretty good. Done up work. Then read and sat around. V[ere] stayed until 9 oclock car.

[I feel] Blue[.] Punk day. Bert ought to be thankful we have enough to eat.[113] I had face ache all night again[.]

[112] It appears that Lettie and Vere joined forces to prepare Sunday dinner as a Mother's Day treat for Annie.

[113] Bert seems to have complained about either the quality of their food or their financial situation or both.

Monday, 13 May

Dull & dreary. I done up work. Then made Lettie a night gown for her birthday. Lettie came home to supper[.] Then Raym took her to Red X. R[aym]. went somewhere.[114] Pa & I played dominoes[.] I beat 2 games. Got a letter from Henry[.] He is some better[.]

I still have face ache[.]

[114] The underlining suggests that Annie shared some of Bert's frustration at not knowing Raymond's whereabouts.

Tuesday, 14 May

Bright today[.] Done up work. Sewed some. Made flower garden & churned.[115] Mary called up, [and I] had a chat with her.[116] Got no mail today.

Wrote letters and played dominoes in the evening.

Raymond and car have gone some where[.][117]

Wednesday, 15 May

Mrs W[illiamson]– came. We did a big washing [and] after dinner [I] done up house work[,] then helped plant garden until supper time. Got supper[,] then made flower garden. Got a letter from Henry[.] He is feeling better.[118] Out of $ again.[119] Sent me the flowers he wore on Mothers day.[120]

[115] Annie names none of her flowering plants other than the rosebush that Lettie gave her (30 March) and the rose slips that Sarah sent (9 May). In later years her yard had a range of everyday flowers such as iris, calendulas, bachelor's buttons, larkspur, and pink rambler roses.

[116] Probably Mary Hartman. See entry for 16 June.

[117] The fact that Raymond took the car again and went out to spend the evening at some place or places unknown may be read as a further sign of ongoing tension in the family.

[118] He had begun to worry, though, about his pharmaceutical studies. On 14 May he wrote to Lettie: "I will have to study like the dickens to catch up with my class."

[119] In a letter to Lettie written on 8 April, Henry reported that he would be paid "$1 per week for 3 mo[nths]."

[120] Though everyone was encouraged to wear flowers on Mother's Day (white if one's mother were dead, otherwise red or "bright" [*FPT,* 12 May 1916, p. 1]), Henry's action here is perhaps the clearest indication relayed by Annie that he was the main sentimentalist in the family. Henry always loved flowers, eventually raised lots of them, and toward the end of his life even worked for a while with a florist in Geneva.

Thursday, 16 May

Warm & pleasant[.] I done up work. Then ironed until 11 oclock[.] Got dinner, then Bert took me down to Mrs Stimpsons to Soldiers Mothers meeting.[121] Got Mrs Fasler on our way.[122] Had a pleasant time[.] Got Lettie from school. After supper ironed some[.] The end of a busy day.

Friday, 17 May

Very warm. Finished ironing. Did sweeping & dusting clear through.[123] Baked a cake[.] Miss [Eva] Beaver came home with L[ettie]. to supper. Then [they] went to a school entertainment.[124] Pa took them down[, and] then he & I went to the <u>new</u> picture show.[125] Saw Sunnybrook farm, by Mary Pickford.[126]

[121] Like Bert, Annie was emphatically no "joiner," but she nevertheless began to attend a few meetings of The Soldiers' Mothers' Club, a new organization whose name would eventually evolve into the somewhat more appropriate War Mothers of America. Later still, the group became The Service Star Legion, an auxiliary of The American Legion (*FPT*, 22 October 1919, p. 1).

In Geneva, The Soldiers' Mothers' Club came into being on 8 April 1918, thanks largely to the initiative of Mrs. B. C. Hodges, who had three sons in service—Ferman, Lynn, and Frank. When a national convention of the group met in September, Mrs. Hodges was chosen to be the delegate from Geneva (*S&B*, 3 October, p. 7).

Mrs. H. Stimson, another early member and the hostess for this Thursday's gathering, was the mother of Floyd A. Stimson, who was serving in the "Engineering Corps" (*FPT*, 2 March 1919, p. 3).

[122] Mrs. Fasler appears only this once in Annie's diary and not at all in the 1918 *Directory* of residents of the village and the outlying districts near Geneva.

[123] Not just the kitchen, that is, but the rest of the house as well.

[124] On Thursday the Geneva paper ran a little notice of the event: "Don't forget the entertainment and box social at North Center School Friday night, May 17th" (p. 2). Though it could take somewhat different forms, a box social was basically a social gathering at which attractive box lunches were sold (Berrey and Van Den Bark, p. 848).

[125] The new movie house in Geneva was the Liberty, which opened only the day before to a

crowd so big that it was necessary to run all three reels of the
feature three separate times
(*S&B*, 17 May, p. 6).

Situated one place west of the
Turner Baking Company in the
Munger block on East Main, the
Liberty was owned by Mr. and
Mrs. H. B. Gregory. It was described somewhat breathlessly by
the *Free Press-Times* as a tasteful
and up-to-the-minute establishment calculated to make a patron "want to forget all these
old-time marks of the small
town show house." (The not-so-
inviting Family Theatre had
gone up in flames on this very
site in December 1917, shortly
before the Perrins left for Florida
[*FPT*, 13 December, pp. 1, 2].)
Now, with an auditorium pan-
eled in old rose and ivory, a ven-
tilating system that changed all
the air every ten minutes, and a
trio of live musicians (piano,
violin, and saxophone), "not a
patron need make apology for
attending its performances"
(*FPT*, 14 May, pp. 4, 6).

Quality aside, the Liberty was
the only theater between
Painesville to the west and
Ashtabula to the east (*FPT*, 20
March, p. 1).

126 That is, *Rebecca of Sunnybrook Farm*. According to *Variety's Film Reviews*, "Superlatives
. . . seem inadequate in properly
approximating the transcendent
merit" of this movie (vol. 1, 14
September 1917).

Saturday, 18 May

Clear & warm[.]

Done up the morning work. Baked 3 kinds of bread.

Dusted clear through. Lettie got home about 1 oclock.

Took the 4 [P.M.]. car for Ashta[bula]. Bert & I spent

the evening alone. Raym went down town.

I am clear tired out.

Sunday, 19 May

Very warm.

Done up the work. Then read about an h[ou]r.[127] Bert & Raym took John and drove around to find some potatoes. Could not find any. After dinner R[aym]. went to see Bernice. Charlotte [Chapman] & her Mother called [and] made a nice little visit.[128] Allen[,] Hellen & Gertrude called just a few minutes[.][129] Mr Johnson called on Bert.[130] Spent the evening alone. L[ettie]– came on 9 oclock car.

[127] At least one nameable book that Annie owned was James Fenimore Cooper's so-so novel called *The Water Witch,* but she herself never cites a book in her diary, and aside from letters she seldom mentions reading. Alone at home on a Sunday morning, she was most likely to pick up a newspaper.

[128] Hattie Myers Chapman's fourteen-acre poultry and fruit farm was the third place north on Myers Road, not far from the Perrins. For a while Charlotte Chapman had taught the second grade in the same building where Lettie was now teaching. Subsequently, however, she found employment in government work with the National Lamp Company at Nela Park in Cleveland. Hence she was said to be a "guest" when coming to see her mother (*FPT*, 1 September 1916, p. 2; 26 February 1917, p. 2; 26 December 1917, p. 3; 3 March 1919, p. 2).

[129] Allen Henry Foster (1886–1969) was the son of Bert's sister Mary Anne—that is, "Mamie" (1861–1907)—and Edward Lewis Foster (1854–1926). Allen lived down in the village of Geneva (at 122 East Main) with his wife, Nina Knapp Foster (1886–1956), and their daughter, Helen (1910–1993) (see Fig. 53).

All in all, the Geneva Fosters were more culturally oriented than the Perrins. Previously in the furniture business with his father-in-law, Edwin A. Knapp (generally known as Ed), and then with E. R. Landon (*FPT*, 3 April 1912, p. 3), Allen in 1918 was earning his living as a truck driver for The Turner Baking Company at 23 East Main (*FPT*, 29 May 1919, p. 3; Geneva section of the *Ashtabula Directory* for 1918, pp. 274, 288). However, it somehow seems more important, more indicative of their nature, that both he and Nina served as pianists for the Park Street Church of Christ and that Allen had been chorister there (*FPT*, 23 January 1917, p. 2; 28 January, p. 2).

Furthermore, Allen was prepared to play either the violin or the cello when some folks tried to get a Geneva Community Symphony Orchestra off the ground in 1917 (*FPT*, 7 May 1917, p. 3). That dream did not materialize, but Allen was at that time already serving as director of Geneva's active, sizeable, and popular I.O.O.F. Band—a post to which he had been elected in 1914 (*FPT*, 18 August, p. 2). Allen had directed this Geneva band ever since it was formed—in fact, ever since its twenty-six members and drum major first began trying to decide what kind of uniforms to wear for their initial public concert in the fall of 1914 (*FPT*, 22 September 1914, p. 2). Eventually the uniforms proved to be dark blue, but mainly they were distinguished by miniature electric lights sewn into all of the men's caps so as to facilitate night-time performances and create a lively visual effect (*FPT*, 30 April 1915, p. 3; see Fig. 54).

A year after the band was organized, according to the local humor columnist, the members began to call Allen "Prof" Foster, presumably because he had "started to call them down for beating time with their feet" ("Phoney Dope," *FPT*, 2 July 1915, p. 2; "Dope" actually was William Sturdevant, the managing editor). The epithet may have been inspired in part, however, by Allen's performance of the role of The Professor in a play presented at the Park Street Church (*FPT*, 8 May 1915, p. 2). His most memorable appearance on the boards, nevertheless, was probably as Captain Hiram Hopper, an old fisherman, in the North Star Grange's 1914 production (directed by Archie McPhail) of Gordon V. May's *Bar Haven*: here he displayed such "natural ability" as "would

Fig. 53. Allen Foster, his wife Nina, and their daughter Helen as photographed by The Broadway Studio in Geneva.

Fig. 54. Allen Foster in his regalia as Director of the I.O.O.F. band.

Monday, 20 May

Hens come off.[131]

Looks like rain. Mrs W[illiamson]– got here late. I fixed the sleeves of L[ettie']–s white waist.[132] Got through washing just 11 A.M. Raym took Bert to train for Cleveland. R[aym]– was going to see a Dr[.] His side pains him.

Clothes [were] dried an[d] in by 3 PM[.] Got a letter from Henry[.] Also Mrs Frizell.[133] Her mother is dead.

L[ettie]– went to R[ed] X tonight. Raym took Auto and brought her home.

win him success with traveling theater companies" (*FPT*, 6 February, p. 2).

Allen also composed various pieces of music, including a waltz, "Thoughts of Thee," dedicated to his mother and published in 1914. When a ten-piece orchestra played his military march called "The Call to Duty," inspired by the "Mexican controversy" that same year, "the players were greeted with a storm of applause" (*FPT*, 15 May 1914, p. 2). Most recently, Allen had composed and directed a piece called "Ohio Boys," which he dedicated to his brother, Lt. Grover Foster of Cleveland (*FPT*, 12 April 1918, p. 2).

As for Nina, she took a role in *Looking for a Wife*, a comedy performed for the Grange (*FPT*, 7 June 1918, p. 1).

A good many years later, Gertrude Louisa Foster (1904–1983), who was Allen's youngest sister and in 1918 living with her widowed father, married Edward Wallace Jensen, the son of Peter Jensen and Rosina MacDonald Jensen. This particular branching of the Perrin clan is pertinent here insofar as three children of Gertrude and Edward—namely, Carol, Edward, and James Jensen—have helped the present editor in tracing the earlier history of the Perrins.

[130] Most likely William Johnson, formerly the Perrins' next-door neighbor to the west. It was he and his wife Rebecca who sold three tracts of their land to John Harley, the Perrins' domino-playing friend to the west ("Mortgage Deed," 29 April 1911, now in the possession of Raymond Perrin, Jr.).

[131] That is, the first three were now through setting. See 22 and 24 May.

[132] That is, "shirtwaist" (or blouse).

[133] This is Annie's second letter from her former neighbor, Mrs. Harry Frizell.

Tuesday, 21 May

Nice cool bright morning. I churned[,] made cookies, done up the work. Had about 10^{min} to rest before getting dinner. Raym dosent feel good this AM. His side still pains him. Has appendicitys[.][134]

Bert called up about 7 PM. for Raym to go down to Geneva & get him. Raym has gone to bed[.] Got pictures from Hen[ry] today[.][135]

[134] Raym put up with intermittent periods of pain in his side for a long while, until at last, early in January of 1920, his appendix was removed at the Ashtabula Hospital (*FPT*, 10 January, p. 2).

[135] In addition to the group picture reproduced here, Henry sent home several snapshots of a band concert he had attended in a large outdoor amphitheater at Great Lakes.

Fig. 55. Henry *(top row, second from the left)* poses here with some of his fellow "bluejackets" at the Great Lakes Naval Training Station in Great Lakes, Illinois.

Wednesday, 22 May

Hot and sultry. Have 18 little chicks from 30 eggs.[136]
R[aym]– is no better. Side pains him all the time. Pa
worked over south on corn ground this AM. Looked
like rain so did not go back after dinner. I ironed part
of the ironing. After supper helped plant squash & cucumbers. The garden seed[s] are coming up fine. Need
rain bad. Showers went all around us.

[136] But see Annie's entry for 5 July.

Thursday, 23 May

Very warm.

I done up work, then ironed. Got dinner and ironed
all the P.M. Got a letter from Henry & 2 pictures. He is
feeling better. Lettie stayed down.[137] Raym is no better.
Bert is working on corn land.

[137] That is, down in the village.

Friday, 24 May

+

Very warm. Bert went down for the potatoes[.] Came home & rolled.[138] Then after dinner I went over with him to tend the drill.[139] Got a little better than half done. Came up all in. Raym was away with Auto. Lettie came home tired out. She got a tie & card from Henry[.][140] 12. nice little chicks[.][141]

Saturday, 25 May

Worked all the morning. Baked[,] cleaned[,] got dinner. Lettie done the Sat[urday] sweeping & dusting in P.M.[142] Went over and helped Bert finish planting corn.[143] Got supper. Then Bert and I went to Geneva & to the picture show.[144]

[138] To smooth the corn ground.

[139] For planting corn. Judging from Bert's sales the previous December, White Cap was the variety he favored (e.g., *FPT*, 4 December, p. 2).

[140] For her coming birthday Henry reported having mailed Lettie a Navy neckerchief. "Probably you won't know how to wear it," he wrote, "but will show you some day" (letter of 23 May).

[141] Presumably making at least a temporary total of thirty (see 22 May).

[142] The timing is of mild interest because these chores were almost always completed in the A.M.

[143] Perhaps Annie means "finish for the day." In any case, Raym planted more on 31 May. The general goal, as Bert often said, was to have corn that was "knee-high by the Fourth of July."

[144] The new Liberty movie house was showing J. Warren Kerrigan in *The Turn of a Card*, which featured genuine gushing oil wells that had been filmed on the LaBrea Ranch in California (adults, 20¢). This was not really Annie's cup of tea, but at least it was a night out for her (*FPT*, p. 2).

Sunday, 26 May

Hot and looks like rain. Got up at 6 oclock[.] Had tooth ache all night. Done up the work, then made an Angle food cake for Lettie's birthday.[145] Raym dont seem to improve very much. Roy Andrews came about 11.45 oclock[.][146] In after noon, R[aymond]. L[ettie]. & R[oy] went down to see Bernice. Brought her home with them to supper. Then they all went to Bernices. Pa & I went to bed about 9 oclock. Wish Hen was here.

[145] Lettie turned twenty-six on 26 May. On 13 May Annie recorded making a nightgown as her gift, and Henry sent the Navy neckerchief.

[146] Roy was clearly part of the birthday celebration. Though Annie has not mentioned him previously, the family would have been pleased had he married Lettie. By all accounts he was a good man from a good farm down in Thompson, but Lettie was not well disposed toward becoming a farmer's wife.

Monday, 27 May

Very warm. Had terrible tooth ache all night[.] Got washing started[,] then Raym took me down to Dr Kelley.[147] Had my tooth out[.] Came out fine. Came home[.] Went right to work. Got washing dried and in by 3 oclock. Looks very much like rain. Raym is still sick. Lettie called up to see if I had my tooth out[.] Got a letter from Henry today. He isn't very well.

[147] Dr. Jay C. Kelley had an office in the village at 18 West Main and lived with his wife, Grace, at 5 Vine Street.

Tuesday, 28 May

Very warm.

I churned in the morning. Done up the work. After dinner helped set 1000 tomato plants.[148] Was all in. Came up [and] had to get supper and tend to little chickens. Got a letter from Florence Elliott. Henry took supper there the 25th.[149]

Wednesday, 29 May

Very close[.] Acts like rain. I done up the work, then ironed until 11 oclock. Got the dinner[.] Done up the dishes. Then set plants until 3.30 oclock.

Bert & I went to picture show.[150] Met Lettie & Vere[.] They came home with us.

Raym is better[.][151] He went down town.

[148] Though the area was known as "The Peach Belt," the local newspaper observed in an item on the Geneva Canning Company that "There is little [q]uestion but that this section of the state is peculiarly adapted to the culture of the tomato" (*FPT*, 23 March 1916, p. 3).

[149] While stationed at Great Lakes, as Annie has recognized earlier, Henry visited some of his relatives in Chicago. On the day after the present visit, he reported to Lettie that "Florence is an Elliott. Very much like Win. Mr. M. is O.K. but sort of a cross between a religious crank & an insurance man." After the death of Florence's father, Thomas Henry Elliott, Florence's mother, Bertie, married a Mr. Maddox— who himself seems not to have lived long (recollections of Doris Weston, 5 October 1997).

Annie's verb "took" here hints of her own English background.

[150] That night the Liberty was showing William Farmer in *The Conqueror*, a drama depicting the career of General Sam Houston (*FPT*, 29 May, p. 2).

[151] After ten days, Raym's appendicitis pain subsided for this time.

Thursday, 30 May

Hen off.[152]

Decoration day.[153] Feel all in. V[ere] & L[ettie] got up about 9 oclock. I did not feel like work, so churned in P.M. V[ere]. spent the day here[.] Raym went to Geneva so she rode down with him[.] Lettie took a ride with a bunch of teachers. Miss [Eva] Beaver came and wished us good bye[.]

Friday, 31 May

Hottest day yet. Done my work. Got dinner[,] then ironed until 6. P.M.[154] Lettie called up that she would not be home. Got a letter from Henry. Bert went to Ashtabula[.] Seymours brought him home and spent evening here. Raym planted corn.

[152] That is, the fourth broody hen, set on 9 May, was now through setting.

[153] Decoration Day was so named because one was supposed to take time out then to decorate graves, especially the graves of members of the armed forces who had been killed in war. Already in 1918, however, the holiday was sometimes known also as Memorial Day. With a great war in progress, Ashtabula marked the occasion with a big parade and what was reputedly the largest public gathering the city had ever seen (*S&B*, 31 May, p. 1).

Though a lesser affair altogether, the celebration in Geneva brought forth eloquent addresses, impressive exercises, a "brilliant" and well-organized parade to Evergreen Cemetery, and, most stunningly of all, the unplanned and unaccounted for appearance of an American eagle, which circled in the air near the Armory, where the procession formed (*FPT*, 31 May, p. 1). As some of the marchers might have recalled from their schooldays, Joseph Rodman Drake had exclaimed stirringly in the last century, "Child of the sun! To thee 'tis given / To guard the banner of the free" ("The American Flag," p. 26).

[154] In other words, Annie ironed the family laundry for about five hours.

Saturday, 1 June

Got up quarter of 5. Had the sweeping done when L[ettie] got home. Did not feel well. L[ettie]. was all in when she got home. B[ert]– has gone to plant corn for Mary.[155] Raym is hoeing. In the evening we all went to the Majestic to see Tarzan of the Apes.[156]

[155] Presumably their friend Mary Hartman. See 16 June.

[156] Based on the writing of Edgar Rice Burroughs, this Tarzan film lasted two hours and ten minutes and starred a ten-year-old boy named Gordon Griffith. During its filming in the jungles of Brazil, "Four lions were killed before the camera and a number of other wild animals slain." Furthermore, "Over 2,000 natives were engaged," and "fifteen serious accidents happened to the players" (*S&B*, 1 June, p. 5). Cost per viewer: 20¢.

Fig. 56. On a Saturday evening in late spring the Perrins drove over to the Majestic and caught the last showing of *Tarzan of the Apes,* "The most stupendous, amazing film production in the world's history." Meanwhile, the rival Dome Theatre ("Home of Good, Clean Photoplays") offered Winifred Allen in *The Man Hater,* but promised mere "Punch and Pep."

Sunday, 2 June

Every one got up tired this A.M. Done up the work.
Planned to all go to Thompson in P.M.[157] About 10.30
Fannie called up to say they were all coming over[.] Got
here 11.30[.] Had a real good visit. The 4 young folks[158]
went for a ride after dinner.

In the evening R[aym] went to see B[ernice]. Allen
& Nina came up a few minutes in the evening.[159]

[157] Roy Andrews lived in
Thompson, and Lettie once
taught school there.

[158] Lettie and Raymond, with
young Walter and Melvin Keyse.

[159] See notes to 19 May and 21
July.

Monday, 3 June[160]

Hot & dry.

We did a big washing[.] Lettie went to school in
A.M. After dinner she commenced cleaning up stairs.[161]
L[ettie]. got a letter from Henry.[162] Austin[163] & R[aym]
are hoeing corn.

In the PM. I got clothes ironed & pressed ready to go
to Cleveland tomorrow.

[160] The *Star and Beacon* headline today records what for
Americans proved to be one of
the most arresting events of the
war: "U-Boats Sink Several Craft
off Coast of New Jersey." The attack took place less than forty
miles from Barnegat, New Jersey,
and enlistments in the U.S. Navy
suddenly zoomed.

[161] Possibly "upstairs," but
cleaning the cluttered stairs
going up *to* the attic may have
been a necessary forerunner of
such a task. In any event, Lettie's
half-day at school indicates that
the term had now ended.

[162] Both Henry's studies and
his financial state continued to
be worrisome. Examinations
were coming up, he wrote, and
"Am afraid I'll flunk as I've
missed so many lectures." As for
money, "I was broke so could not
go to Chi[cago]. So went to
Kenosha, Wis[consin]. . . . Had
3¢ left out of 63" (31 May). See
also the note to the entry for 8
June.

[163] As before, Milton Austin.

Tuesday, 4 June

Cooler today.

Got dinner at 11. AM. Raym took Bert & I to Geneva. We left on the 12.4 for Cleveland. Got there about 1.30. Went to a picture show. Got over to office. Met the crowd there. Got through buisness about 6 oclock.[164] Went home with Bessie.[165] Had supper about 7 oclock. Went to bed at 11.30. Had a bad head ache.

Wednesday, 5 June [166]

Cloudy.

Bessie & I done up work[,] then went over to see Edna[.] She & baby had colds.[167] Had a good visit, [then] went home about 4 oclock. Left square at 5.[168] Got home at 8. Lettie was here alone. Raym over to Johns.

[164] Bert and Annie were concluding the acquisition of some real estate in the Cleveland area. See entries for 9 and 10 April and 1 July.

[165] Bessie Perrin Dobson (21 August 1863–6 June 1938) lived in Brooklyn, south of Cleveland's west side. A square-built woman with steady eyes and a goiter, she had been widowed at this time for nearly twenty years. Her husband, George (born in 1861), was struck by lightning while riding a hay wagon in a sunny field on the fifth of July, 1900.

[166] The startling main headline in the *Star and Beacon* for 5 June is "Yankee Gunners Kill 1000 Germans."

[167] Bessie Dobson's daughter Edna was the wife of Charles Herr. The baby was little Marion Herr, born on 5 January that year.

[168] At the Public Square, in the heart of downtown Cleveland and forty-some miles from Geneva, Annie and Bert were able to catch an interurban trolley heading east.

While they were waiting, they could hardly fail to see, rising from the southeast quadrant of the Square, an imposing, 125-foot-high Soldiers' and Sailors' Monument to the 10,000 residents of Cuyahoga County who served in the Civil War. Inside the raised base of this structure in a forty-foot-square "tablet room" was inscribed the name of Bert's father, Henry Perrin. Born a Wiltshire Englishman, Henry served 111 days in Company G of the 150th Ohio Volunteer Infantry (Van Tassel and Grabowski, p. 942; Johnson, pp. 151–52; and Gleason, pp. 612–13).

Thursday, 6 June

Hot & sultry.

Dident feel good this A.M. Done up the work. Then churned. Got dinner. Lettie left for Cleveland on 3 oclock car.[169] Pa took her down.

Raym cut grass in back yard. Then [used the] lawn mower.[170] I helped rake a little. Feel dissapointed [that I] havent heard from Henry this week. Terrible thunder storm about 8. PM.

[169] Lettie was off on a little "spring fling."

[170] Bert never mowed, and now the grass had grown so tall that it had to be scythed before a lawnmower could be pushed through it.

Friday, 7 June

Cool & clear.

After work was done up I ironed until 11 oclock. Then got dinner. Had Mrs Williamson come & finish ironing so I could get ready for [wall]papering.

Raym and Pa built a bungalo for the pigs.[171] No letter from Henry today.

[171] The pig shed was located out in back, slightly above the beginning of the rather sharp descent on the southern side of the South Ridge.

Because American farmers were being urged to raise more pigs these days, some of the Perrins' young friends and acquaintances—including Arthur Hasenpflug, Charles Seamans, and Lyle Pruden—participated this summer in a pig-raising contest sponsored by Ashtabula County (*S&B*, 3 July, p. 7).

Saturday, 8 June

Cloudy. Mrs Pruden came and papered the two bed rooms.[172] I done the Saturday baking & sweeping. Then cleaned up after papering. Pa wanted me to go to town. I went but was <u>too</u> tired. Lettie came home [from Cleveland] on 8 oclock train. Was pretty cross when I got home. Got a letter from Henry.[173]

Eclipse of the sun this P.M.[174]

[172] The Esley B. Prudens were neighbors a short way down the road to the east, where the southern stretch of Myers Road deadends on the South Ridge. Mrs. Pruden (Addie) was, indeed, formally listed as a "Paper Hanger" in the 1920 census, and her husband as a painter of houses and barns. In later years, however, the family was better known for running The Pruden Hatchery. See also the entry and note for 18 August.

[173] On 1 June Henry informed Lettie that "We had inspection this A.M. Our Co. rated the highest of any Co. in Great Lakes. That means something as there is 40,000 here now. Officer in charge complimented my display." Also: "The boys are leaving here every day for overseas duty. From 100 to 500 every day and some days more." And: "A goodly share of us are dead broke."

[174] Astronomers flocked to Denver, Colorado, to see the sun totally eclipsed. In Geneva only about four-fifths of the sun's surface was covered, but local conditions for observing the phenomenon were ideal, and according to the *Free Press-Times* it was seen by thousands of County people (10 June, p. 1). Beginning at 5:25 P.M. and attaining maximum coverage at 6:25, the whole show concluded by 7:25 (*FPT*, 8 June, p. 1; *S&B*, p. 8). Annie omits the fact that the newspaper for this date lists Raym as one of the many "boys" signed up for the draft in Geneva Township (*S&B*, p. 8).

Sunday, 9 June

All got up late. It is rather cloudy today. Done up the work[,] then baked a cake. Packed a lunch and all went to Thompson. Had dinner at Mr Glines.[175] Brought our lunch in and put with [their] dinner. Left there after 2. P.M[.] Went to Andrews.[176] Found no one there. Came home through Harpersfield. A pleasant ride.

Did not like the Country over that way.[177] Saw the Ledge for the 1st time.[178]

[175] Although B. Glines lived southwest of the Mt. Pleasant Cemetery, down toward Harpersfield, the Glines household that the Perrins visited was still farther from home and harder to identify.

[176] That is, the home of Roy Andrews down in Thompson.

[177] Annie mistakenly wrote this last word as "was."

[178] Thompson Ledges is a pleasant if minor scenic phenomenon.

Monday, 10 June

Raym took Bert down to train for Cleveland. Mrs W[illiamson]– got here about 8. [We] Done a big washing[.] Came on a nasty rain. Had to bring lots of things in and rince over. Lettie cleaned the attic.[179] Raym hoed. Had supper[.] Raym went somewhere. Lettie read[.] I was too tired to do any thing, so went to bed.

[179] With school out, Lettie now began "spring cleaning" in earnest. Henry had written over a month earlier to warn her, "You must not over do when your school is out. You always dig in & try to do it all in a day" (8 May). In the spring of the following year (18 April 1919), when he was seriously ill and hospitalized in Philadelphia, he would look back on their pleasant times tackling the work together. "I too wish I could help you with the cleaning," he wrote then, "and we would have an other good time at it and make things shine." See Fig. 57.

Fig. 57. The annual American ritual of spring housecleaning generally began earlier than June for women who did not work outside the home, but its universality is suggested by this gigantic figure of a woman who in effect sweeps her village clean. The *Geneva Free Press-Times* printed with it the caption "She'll Make a Good Job of It, Too!" (10 May 1917, p. 3).

Fig. 58. Lettie, the reader of the Perrin family.

Tuesday, 11 June

Pleasant.

A.M. I washed out a tub of clothes that got soot on them. Churned. Done up work. Then helped Lettie a little. Lettie painted Hens bed room. I cleaned rugs.[180] Pa came on the 7 oclock car[.] Raym went to bed at 7 oclock. About 9. we had a terrible wind & thunder storm.[181]

I was sick all night.

Wednesday, 12 June

Chilly & windy today. Storm done lots of damage to crops. Bert & Raym built a fence & made a yard for the pigs. Also fenced pigeon yard off for mules.[182] Lettie finished Henrys room and done some to her's. I ironed curtains. Helped a little[.] Havent felt well all day. Got a few lines from Henry & a letter from Mrs Fox.

[180] Though Annie could manage the small rugs of the bedroom, she and Lettie needed Raym's help when it came to the big ones in the sitting room and dining room.

[181] On North Broadway down in the village, the wind was strong enough to cause significant damage to the tent of the Minnelli Brothers stock company, which had been trying to perform *He Fell in Love with His Wife*, a drama by Frank P. Minelli, one of the owners of the company (*FPT*, 11 June, p. 2; *S&B*, 12 June, p. 3).

Out in the countryside the winds—which preceded some rain—"stirred up all the dust to be found in the sandy roads and plowed fields." More particularly, the airborne dust on the unpaved South Ridge was so thick for a while that one driver reported he could see only a few feet ahead of his automobile (*FPT*, p. 3).

[182] This is Annie's only allusion to the matter, but Henry had had a large caged area out in back where he kept pigeons. In later years at Geneva-on-the-Lake he would raise budgerigars.

Thursday, 13 June

Set Hen[.][183]

Bert & Raym have been filling in where the tomatoes were gone.[184] Set in 500. and need about 200 more. Lettie is finishing her room. They look fine[.][185] I ironed in the P.M. After supper L[ettie]– mowed lawn[.][186] I set a few pepper plants[,] thined the turnips. Then Bert & I played dominoes[.] I beat him 3 games. Raym went to see B[ernice]. Lettie wrote letters.

Friday, 14 June

Clear & cool. L[ettie] cleaned my bed room today.[187] Got a letter from Henry. I think he is home sick. Also one from R[oy]. A[ndrews] explaining where he was when we went over there.[188] The soldiers are going by here by train loads today.[189] Mrs Howard was over this evening[.] Was real interesting.

[183] This made a fifth hen.

[184] The "gone" tomatoes were destroyed by the storm on the night of 11 June. Wherever the Perrins found replacement plants, they probably noticed an ad in the Geneva paper for "John Bier tomato plants; 12¢ per doz. . . . 65 Eagle Street" (12 June, p. 4).

[185] "They" probably means both Henry's room and Lettie's, which adjoined each other.

[186] Henry wrote to Lettie: "If I could be there . . . [I] would cut the lawn for you. That used to be my regular job you know" (17 June).

[187] Annie's "my" here is a bit odd. For better or worse, she and Bert shared the same bed.

[188] On Sunday, 9 June.

[189] The second "by" here is conjectural: Annie at this point made a perfectly clear but indecipherable squiggle. From the crest of the Ridge, in any case, though it was hard to see many details concerning the passing trains, Annie obviously could see men in uniform.

Saturday, 15 June

Pleasant & cool. I baked bread [and] cake [and] churned. Then done my work. Lettie did Saturday sweeping & dusting[.] Pa went to Ashtabula. Raym done a big days work. Quit about 8.15 PM[,] then went to town. I picked [a] rooster for Sunday dinner.[190] All in tonight[.] Lettie looks tired out too[.]

Sunday, 16 June

Pleasant[.]

Got work done up. Then made cream pie. Expected Company from Cleveland. Fred Perrin came on 1 oclock car. After dinner we all went to see Mary Hartman.[191] Bought some berries. Came home [and] had lunch[.] Then Raym Ran a race with NY [Central] train to get F[red] there in time.[192]

[190] "Picked" means plucked. A rooster is often the most obvious candidate for the pot because he is a non-laying bird. The duties he performs are important, of course, but only one or two healthy roosters can attend to the needs of a good many hens.

[191] Mary, daughter of the English-born Elmer Joiners (sometime of County Line Road), attended school at Morgan Center, in Ashtabula (U.S. Census, 1910; *FPT*, 18 July 1912, p. 2; 27 December 1913, p. 2). Her husband was William ("Will") Hartman, originally of Rock Creek and apparently a man of some presence. A few years back, at any rate, he was elected to serve as Chief Patriarch and Noble Grand (the presiding officer) in the local lodge of Odd Fellows (*FPT*, 4 December 1913, p. 2). Furthermore, when the Geneva Rebekahs (Mary was a member of this sister organization of the Odd Fellows) celebrated their twenty-fourth anniversary with a play called *The District School*, Will was cast as Deacon Jerome Socrates Kicker (*FPT*, 13 October 1915, p. 2).

In 1917, after Will and Mary had sold their Geneva home at the corner of South Broadway and Union (*FPT*, 7 June, p. 8), they moved to the old Stewart place on the North Ridge. This was a twenty-four-acre farm east of Geneva, far enough east, actually, to be in Saybrook township (*FPT*, 18 July 1917, p. 1).

Perhaps helping to explain why Bert seems to have planted corn specifically for Mary earlier this month (1 June) is the fact that Will was by profession a painter (1918 *Farm Journal . . . Directory*, p. 95). Then, too, Will had some health problems, and he also was older than Bert. In the 1920 census, he is listed as a sixty-five-year-old farmer, and Mary, sixty, as a farmer's wife.

192 Raymond drove to the village fast in order to get Fred to the depot, which was between North Broadway and Eagle.

193 Having finished with Henry's room, her own, and Annie's and Bert's room, Lettie next tackled Raymond's, the fourth, last, and smallest one. On this date Henry wrote to Lettie: "How are you getting on with the cleaning? I'll bet things will look pretty nifty as they always do."

194 According to Public Act 105 of Congress (16 March), commanding officers could grant furloughs without pay to enlisted men to do farm work, especially at seeding and harvest time and so long as the furloughs created minimal interference with military training. Individual applications were to be submitted by the service man's relatives on a form furnished by local draft boards. Hence the "word" sent to Illinois by the local board. As Henry later observed to Lettie, handling the Perrins' request involved "a lot of red-tape" (25 June).

195 To propagate potatoes, choice specimens are first cut into pieces, each with two or more buds or "eyes." See Fig. 59.

196 The *Free Press-Times* took note of the event:

> On Monday the Perrins entertained Mrs William Whale, of Kinsman rd. [Cleveland] and her son and daughter, Leonard Whale, Mrs. Hattie

Monday, 17 June

Clear & cool[.]

Mrs W[illiamson]– came[.] We done a big washing. Lettie cleaned Rayms room.193 [We] Got a letter from [Draft] Board, saying they had sent word to G[reat]. L[akes]. Hope Henry can come.194 I helped cut potatoes[.]195 Just as we got through Whales came[.]196 Were here about 1½ h[ou]r's. Planted potatoes today. Was too tired[.] Went to bed at 8.30[.]

> *Lowe and friend Mrs. Philpot. The party motored there from Cleveland. Leonard Whale is [a] Yeoman . . . stationed at Newport, N.J. and is home on a furlough. (19 June, p. 2)*

Not too long before, a wide-eyed young man, jaunty with his stickpin, fedora, and winter gloves, sent Raym a picture postcard of himself signed "The Original and only 'Spotty' the horse thief alias Fish the Whale alias Silent Pete of Monte Carlo alias Leonard H. Whale" (Raymond's album).

The reference to Kinsman Road—where Bert's brother Fred lived—is a reminder that Fred and Mr. Whale both came together on a visit to the South Ridge Perrins the preceding fall (*FPT*, 6 October 1917, p. 2).

Fig. 59. As is suggested by this cartoon from the *Star and Beacon* (24 June, p. 9), the planting of "spuds" (potatoes) was encouraged because of the shortage of wheat. When fall came, Americans would read that the "Huns" had sunk ships carrying no fewer than eight million bushels of grain. Moreover, American brewers were said to have wasted an additional sixty-eight million bushels in equally execrable ways (26 September 1918, p. 8).

Tuesday, 18 June

Pleasant[.]

I picked wild [straw]berries[,] enough for a short cake[.] We finished up Rayms room, baked bread[.] Got a letter from Henry mailed June 4th. He has heard nothing about coming home.

Wednesday, 19 June

Pleasant day.

Cleaned sitting room.[197] I helped get things out[.] Lettie cleaned. I ironed all the P.M. Bert & Raym hoed corn & potatoes[.] Raym went to see B[ernice]– in evening.

Raym cleaned the [sitting room] rug.[198]

[197] Room no. 5, the sitting (or living) room, was one of the four downstairs rooms facing the road.

[198] Cleaning the rug involved carrying it outside, laying it out on the grass (or, preferably, over a line), and whacking it repeatedly with a wire rug-beater. Success was marked by significant clouds of dust and the surprisingly brighter look of the rug.

For more serious cleaning, one next used a big sponge and a bucket of suds (being careful to use more suds than water so as not to get the fabric too wet). Plain, old-fashioned beating was so ingrained as a way of doing the job, though, that even an early Hoover electric sweeper was offered with the slogan "It actually BEATS OUT the Dirt!" (S&B, 13 June 1918, p. 3).

Thursday, 20 June

Another clear day. Finished up sitting room. Lettie cleaned cupboards & closets in kitchen.[199] I baked bread. Then ironed until 5.30 PM.

Washed sitting room curtains[.] Borrowed Mrs S— stretchers.[200] They looked good.

[199] Room no. 6.

[200] Mrs. Stone seems likely here. See note to 23 June.

Friday, 21 June

Bert went to Ashtabula. Came home on 7 oclock car[.] Lettie cleaned dining room.[201] Raym cleaned carpet. Done a good job[.] Had a terrible thunder storm. Lost 12 of best young chicks[.] After supper L[ettie]. mowed lawn.

[201] Room no. 7.

Saturday, 22 June

Cold[,] only 50%.[202]

Baked bread. Pie & cookies. Made some cushions.[203] Fixed shades. Lettie finished dining room. Cleaned up Kitchen. Bert went to Geneva. After supper Raym went to Geneva.

[202] Obviously a hasty error for the degree sign.

[203] A finishing touch for the sitting room.

Sunday, 23 June

Cold.

Have been uncomfortable all day[.] Really need a fire. Stoves all down.[204] Raym spent AM lying down. Bert went over to Austins.[205]

Irine W[etter]– came up after dinner. I went to bed to keep warm[.] In The PM I went over to Mrs Stones [and] had a pleasant afternoon.[206]

[204] That is, shut down for the summer months. The dining room stove would not be put to use again until 16 September.

[205] See note to 15 April.

[206] For Irene Wetter see the notes to Annie's entries of 27 March and 4 August.

The Eugene ("Gene") C. Stones lived a few doors east on the Ridge, a little this side of Barnum Road, in a home they called Catalpa Place. Lying south of the other properties that intervened between the Perrins and the Stones, the Perrin and Stone pastures touched.

It was Mr. Stone who reported back in January of this year that he had to get his sheep through the winter of 1917–18 without pasturage for three consecutive months (see note to 29 January). That Mrs. Anna K. Stone and Mrs. Annie L. Perrin were very different sorts of farm women— though they could share a pleasant afternoon—is suggested by a small newspaper item the previous year that reported Mrs. Stone's attendance at a style show in Cleveland (*FPT*, 22 March 1917, p. 2). Then again, Mrs. Stone was a professional dressmaker employed at a local dry goods company. In fact, J. B. Stephens and Son Co. ("Not 'Bargain Goods' but Bargain Prices") was the somewhat up-scale sort of establishment that on occasion held its own style show, complete with live models, right in Geneva (*FPT*, 3 April 1916, pp. 2, 3).

Monday, 24 June

Mrs W[illiamson]– dident come over.[207] So I washed [alone]. Lettie done the house work and hung out clothes. Got through 11.30. I got dinner[.] After dinner Bert & I went to Ashtabula. Saw a good show.[208] Got curtains for dining room[.] Lettie had supper about ready when we got home. Bert went to Dr Case again today[.][209] He says, <u>nerves</u>. Raym cultivated tomatoes. Heard from Hen. He dosent know if he can come home or not[.]

Tuesday, 25 June

Cloudy. I feel tired to begin the day. Lettie is sick with head ache this A.M.[210] I churned [and] done up work. After dinner hemmed the dining room curtains and put them up. Mare Penney brought me a boquet of sweet Peas.[211] Spent the evening here. Our new neighbors came to their home tonight.

[207] Without further comment, Mrs. Williamson at this point disappears from the diary.

[208] The Casto was showing May Allison in *Social Hypocrites*, and the Dome currently offered Corrine Griffith in *The Menace*, but since the Perrins usually attended the Majestic (matinee 15¢), they probably saw Dorothy Phillips in *A Soul for Sale*—along with a Mutt and Jeff cartoon (*S&B*, 24 June, p. 4).

[209] Probably the major reason for this trip to Ashtabula, Dr. Clarence E. Case was a physician and surgeon with an office at Center and Main. As early as 8 May 1917 he and some other "prominent" doctors had "made application for enlistment in the medical corps, United States army" (*S&B*, p. 1), but clearly he had not been called.

[210] An example of an entry which Annie began to write in the morning, then finished late in the evening.

[211] Though the form "Mare" here may be a nickname for Marie Penney, Annie in her haste may simply have left out the "i."

Wednesday, 26 June

Cool. Done up work[,] then Lettie & I cleaned the kitchen. Lettie painted the wood work. Got through about 5 oclock[.] L[ettie]. was all in[.] Freddie Hoffman was here all night[.][212] Had a load of wool from Sheffield.[213]

Raym Cultivated corn in s[ou]^th field. Bert felt indisposed. Now all the cleaning is done.[214] Heard from Henry today. He was in Chicago Sunday.

Thursday, 27 June

Cloudy.

Raym is Cultivating in the orchard.[215] I folded clothes [and] done up my work. Mended some. The two Mrs Pennys came so had a visit with them. After they left got supper[.] After supper. We all took a ride down to Mr Seymours[.][216] Took P. S. Allen with us.[217] Had a pleasant time.

Friday, 28 June

Raining[.]

Done up work. Baked cake.[218] Got dinner[.] After dinner I ironed. Lettie ironed some of her clothes. Got a letter from Henry. In the evening B[ert] went over to Slocums. Got home about 11. PM. Raym went to see B[ernice]. I had to fix fence to keep pigs at home.

212 This is Annie's only reference to Freddie. Early in 1919, however, the *Star and Beacon* announced his marriage in Willoughby to Miss Minnie Mauslynwere (19 February, p. 7).

213 Sheffield, just east of Saybrook, was made up mainly of a country store, blacksmith shop, and town hall, with a couple of churches and sawmills. "This was farm country with mud roads and covered bridges" (*Ashtabula County History Then and Now,* p. 121).

214 That is, the special once-a-year spring housecleaning.

215 Cultivating both aerates the soil and helps control the weeds.

216 In other words, to 37 Kingsville Avenue, Ashtabula.

217 Pardon Allen, as noted earlier, lived just a short distance east of the Perrin place.

218 Annie does not mention, however, that today was Henry's birthday. On 29 June he wrote to Lettie, "Ma didn't send a cake did she? Sort of looked for one."

Saturday, 29 June

Bright & warm.

Bert & Raym hoed corn. We done the Sat[urday] work. Lettie clean[e]d to the kitchen[,][219] then washed her hair. After supper we all went to Geneva. I went shopping with Lettie. Then she took me to the show. <u>Good</u>.[220] Came out before it was over. Sat in car waiting for B[ert] & R[aym].[221] Got home about 11 oclock.

[219] In other words, she cleaned the other rooms and stopped at the step leading down into the kitchen.

[220] The Liberty was featuring Wallace Reid in *Nan of Music Mountain*—the story of an adventurous gunman out to avenge his father's death (*FPT*, 29 June, p. 2).

[221] Annie and Lettie matter-of-factly left the movie early in order not to keep Bert waiting. What Bert and Raym were doing during the movie is open to conjecture. One or the other or both, however, may have been shooting pool or billiards at 31 West Main.

Sunday, 30 June

Pleasant.

Done up the work. Then every one rested. I got early dinner. [We] Had a shower. But soon cleared off. Then we all drove up to Fannies. Spent a very pleasant P.M. Had lunch [and] then had a fine ride home. R[aym] went to see B[ernice]. Lettie wrote letters. Pa & I played dominoes[.]

3

From Henry's Furlough to Harvest Time

1 July–30 September 1918

Monday, 1 July

Today is cool.

Bert went to Cleveland to collect rent.[1] Raym hoed. Lettie & I done up work. Then let down and shortened her dresses & sewed some. R[aym]. went to town in evening [and] L[ettie] & I sewed.

Had a terrible wind storm. Got a letter from Henry.[2]

[1] After a handful of indirect references, this is the first explicit sign that the family had now acquired property in Cleveland.

[2] Probably the temper of the latter may be gauged from Henry's letter to Lettie of 29 June: "You don't know how disappointed I am that my furlough has not been granted. Can hardly wait until Mon[day]. [i.e., 1 July] to learn the verdict. Moffet is a very hard man it is said. His word is law with this Sta[tion] & also one other. That means he is over some 100,000 men & holds the highest office here. Will have to be spotless to stand before him at rigid attention." Henry refers to Captain W. A. Moffett, who had been Commander of the Great Lakes Naval Training Station since 17 September 1914.

Tuesday, 2 July

Done a big washing today. And churned. Got a special delivery letter from Henry saying his furlough is granted. Bert came home [from Cleveland] on 8 oclock car. Allen & Nina were up a little while in evening.

Wednesday, 3 July

Pleasant[.]

Baked and done general work. Lettie ironed & looks tired out. Got a telegram to meet Hen. After supper Raym drove [us] to Ashtabula[.] We all went to meet Hen[.] Got home 10.30[.] Every one tired out.

Fig. 60. Still only partly out of his uniform, the soldier here is supposed to be saying, "Guess I can lick the Kaiser this way, too." When the picture appeared about four months earlier, its caption explained that government legislation was being crafted "to allow enlisted men from farms to go home on furloughs for the planting season" (*S&B*, 12 March, p. 1). Some former farm boys, however, were obviously needed during the summer and fall as well.

Thursday, 4 July

Hen off.[3]

The 4th. All got up early. Had an early breakfast. Then left for Brooklyn to attend the Perrin reunion at Bessies.[4] Had a grand dinner and a good time. Every one there. Got home at 12 oclock[.] Every one tired out. A perfect day[.][5]

[3] That is, the fifth and last broody hen of the season was now through setting.

[4] The home of Bessie Perrin Dobson, Bert's sister, was in Brooklyn, south of Cleveland's West Side. Bessie and her home were a focal point for all the Perrins.

[5] This Fourth of July gathering is recorded in a social notice in the *Star and Beacon* of 10 July, along with the news that "Mr. and Mrs. Allen Foster and child [Helen] were also present from Geneva" (p. 8).

Fig. 61. The Fourth of July family reunion at the home of Bert's sister Bessie Perrin Dobson *(seated at center)* enabled Henry *(between Bessie and Annie)* to visit with some of his extended family. Besides Bert *(fourth from the left)*, others who appear in both this picture and Annie's diary include Carl Cappallo *(eighth from the left)*, standing next to his wife, Florence Foster Cappallo. On Florence's other side, wearing a coat and tie, is Bert's and Bessie's brother Fred. Immediately behind Henry, with her hands on his shoulders, is eight-year-old Helen Foster, daughter of Allen H. Foster *(sixth from right)* and his wife, Nina Knapp Foster *(first on the right)*.

Friday, 5 July

Got up at 5.30[,] the rest at 6 oclock. Lettie packed up and got ready to go to Metananga camping[.][6] Pa took her to Geneva to take 8 oclock car. Raym hoed tomatoes[.] Hen walked around to look about a bit[.] After dinner both boys hoed. I picked my first mess of string beans today. Feel all in today. 15 chicks from 15 eggs.[7] Old hen killed one.

[6] With her friend Laura Whittier from Plymouth, Lettie was taking a vacation at Mitiwanga, Ohio, a Lake Erie resort on the far side of Cleveland. Rather than going camping, however (Lettie was not one for roughing it), the young women were staying at a decent resort hotel (Fig. 62). They would go "bathing" in Lake Erie, of course, but it was a time when newspapers ran constant ads for "bleaching lotion" that could fade any unsightly sun-tan a woman might acquire (Fig. 63).

[7] The percentage of hatches here is impressive. Pardon Allen was written up in the Geneva paper later this month for an extraordinary "White Leghorn hen that hatched 18 chicks out of 22 eggs" (*FPT*, 16 July, p. 2).

Fig. 62. Lettie in early July at Heath Cottage, Mitiwanga, Ohio. At her side is a gentleman friend, and in her hands is the box-like Kodak "Brownie" with which she took some of the pictures in the present volume.

Fig. 63. Posing on the Lake Erie beach at Mitiwanga, a good many stair steps below Heath Cottage, Lettie *(at the far right)* sits close to her friend Laura Whittier. The reclining woman is Alma, the man behind Alma is Floyd, and the standing man Royal. Lettie herself has labeled this picture "Sun Bath."

Saturday, 6 July

Done up Sat[urday']s work. Then ironed all the afternoon. In the evening Hen took Marie[, and] Raym & B[ernice] went to Ashta[bula] to a show.[8] Pa & I played dominoes[.] Went to bed at 9.30. I beat 2 games out of 3.[9]

Sunday, 7 July

A clear cold day. I woke up at 20 min of 8. A.M. Got Raym up. We sure had a good sleep. Had breakfast at 9.[10] Frank Seymour [came to visit,] stayed with H[enry] all night and spent the Sabbath with us.[11] In P.M. we all drove over to brother Freds.[12] Took Art Allen.[13]

Henry & Raym took auto after supper.[14]

[8] The only Marie mentioned either previously or later by Annie has been Marie Penney, the bright teenager who lived up the road.

[9] This evening, meanwhile, Lettie attended a wiener roast on the beach at Mitiwanga. In a picture she snapped of the occasion, about fourteen young men and women (the women mainly in white dresses) stand clustered together in the fading twilight.

[10] Meanwhile, Lettie and her friends (somewhat fewer of them, though, than came down to the beach the previous night) gathered for a morning party on the front porch and yard of their hotel.

[11] Frank was the son of the Ashtabula Seymours with whom the Perrins spent so much pleasurable time in Florida.

[12] Only this once does Annie

mention Fred William Elliott (11 August 1855–2 April 1930), one of her two older living brothers, though he and his wife, Ollie Alexander Elliott, had two children and an eight-acre farm (one horse, one cow) over in Plymouth, south of Ashtabula, not far away (*Farm Journal . . . Directory*, p. 72).

13 Art was the somewhat offbeat but pleasant and well-meaning young neighbor who enjoyed being with the younger Perrins.

14 With no other facts to go on, Annie records here only the taking of the family car. Henry later told Lettie, however, that he and Raym picked up Bernice Michel and Vera Westlake and escorted them to a movie in Ashtabula (ALS, 10 July).

Though Annie never mentions her in the diary, Vera was well known to the young folks of the family. The daughter of Thomas and Edith Westlake of Walnut Street, she was, both earlier and later, a teacher in Geneva, in Saybrook, and in Swedetown, Ashtabula (*FPT*, 1 March 1917, p. 4; 30 September 1919, p. 2). Though she was ill when she played the leading role in Steele MacKaye's much-beloved *Hazel Kirke* at the Geneva Armory a few years ago, she nonetheless made effective dramatic use at that time of her own "sweet and winsome manner" (*FPT*, 15 May 1914, p. 2).

In the fall of 1918, wanting to do her bit for the war effort, she left the area in order to take a course of training as a nurse at Camp Jackson, in South Carolina (*S&B*, 15 October, p. 10).

15 Hay is usually a grass of some sort, but it can be any one of a number of crops that are cut and dried for feed—including even cured stalks of corn (Grim, pp. 279–80). Though today the boys bunched clover, the Perrins also raised good timothy (the latter being a grass named for Timothy Hanson, an American farmer who grew it in the early

1800s). The previous December, before departing for Florida, Bert advertised six tons of clover for sale and ten tons of timothy, and come winter of this year, he again had both for sale.

"Bunching" the hay (that is, forming it into clusters) simply made for easier loading on the wagon.

16 When the spring cleaning was proclaimed done, that meant upstairs. The basement was something different, more a man's domain—a place for tools, chopped wood, and coal, for vegetable storage, for fruit needing to be sorted, and so on.

Monday, 8 July

Cool & clear.

I done general work[.] Baked oat meal cookies & bread. After dinner I went to Ashta[bula] with Bert. Saw a show but not very good. The boys were in for supper when we got home. I had it ready in about 20^{min}. Got a card from Lettie today.

Tuesday, 9 July

Cloudy. I done up the work. Then washed[.] Got through 11.45.

Commenced to rain about 3—but clothes were dry enough to take in[.] Then I churned and made a cake.

The boys bunched hay in the A.M.[15] After dinner Bert took a horse down to be shod. Raym. cultivated over s[ou]th. Hen cleaned up the basement.[16]

Looks very rainy. And all the clover cut & bunched.

Fig. 64. This photograph was taken in the summer of 1917, but Henry *(foreground)* and Raym were both lucky enough to be haying together once again in July of 1918.

Wednesday, 10 July

Cloudy & raining a little. Got the work done up[,] peas shelled for dinner & made a cream pie. Picked a chicken. About 11 oclock AM. Mr & Mrs Mailey. [Also] Fred Perrin & Esther came down.[17] We all had dinner[.] Then they went to get lillies[.][18] I done up dinner work[,] then visited until time to get supper. They left about 8. P.M.[19]

Thursday, 11 July

Warm today.

I ironed some [and] baked an apple pie[.] The boys are making hay. In the evening Bert & I went to the picture show. Saw the Cinderella man.[20] Henry would not go. Stayed at home alone.

[17] As the social item in Geneva's *Free Press-Times* puts the case, "Mr. and Mrs. B. H. Perrin entertained on Wednesday a motor party from Cleveland, Mr. and Mrs. Maley, Fred Perrin and friend" (13 July, p. 3).
The only Esther known to figure in Annie's life was her niece Esther Susan Elliott—the daughter of her brother Walter and his wife, Susan Virginia Bailus (always called "Virgie"). In 1918 Esther Elliott was living with Walter and Virgie and "working in Cleveland for the N.Y.C. railroad as a comptometer operator." In the following year she married Charles M. Weston (ALS, Doris Weston, Esther's daughter, 27 February 1997).

[18] A standard entertainment for the Perrins over the years was picking water lilies on Pardon Allen's pond, a short walk to the east on the Ridge. Pardon seems to have enjoyed having people enjoy themselves there. When the young ladies of the "Sunbeam" class at the Park Street Church came up for an outing, Pardon took care that they returned home with "some pond lilies and much useful knowledge of frogs and turtles, also the care and shipping of the lillies" (*FPT*, 17 June 1920, p. 1).

[19] On this same day Henry reported to Lettie at Mittiwanga: "We cut & bunched about 15 loads of hay this week & now it is raining so we can't get it in." Also: "Mother lost 6 little chicks last night. We think a rat killed them."

[20] In this "charming" film, which incidentally offered "the best-trained kittens, dogs and bugs seen on the screen in a long time," "the principal action has to do with the daughter of a rich old grouch and a poor poet who lives in a garret just across a tin roof from the girl's home" (*Variety's Film Reviews*, vol. 1, 21 December 1917).

Friday, 12 July

Clear & hot[.] The boys, Pa & Mr P[enney] are haying. I made caraway cup cakes for lunch. After dinner
Mr Clark & Tom helped.[21] Hen went to Seymours on
7 oclock car[.][22] Bert & Raym went to town. I was
alone[.] They went to picture Show.[23]

Saturday, 13 July

Henry came home on 7 oclock car this A.M.[24] I baked
bread[,] cake & pie. Churned and done some washing.
This P.M. used carpet sweeper clear through[,][25] then
dusted[.] Lettie came on 5 oclock car.[26] After supper we
all went to town & show.[27]

[21] In other words, a total of
six men were haying. This is one
of a number of instances in the
diary where the local farmers de-
pended on one another to get a
major job done.

[22] "Circus in town & Frank
[Seymour] wishes me to go,"
Henry wrote to Lettie (10 July).
Ringling Brothers was featuring
a spectacle of knighthood and
chivalry called "In Days of Old."
It was put on by some 1,200 per-
formers, including the greatest
woman equestrian who ever
lived (May Wirth), a dog that
could catch knives in his mouth
while riding a horse, elephants
dressed like Red Cross nurses
and surgeons, and miscellaneous
trained ponies, seals, cats, and
rabbits (*S&B*, 26 June, p. 6; 5 July,
pp. 2, 6).

[23] The film at the Liberty was
A Branded Soul, which told of a
simple Mexican girl (Conchita)
whose boyfriend (Juan) turns
out to be a German spy (*FPT*,
12 July, p. 3).

[24] In other words, he spent
last night in Ashtabula with the
Seymours.

[25] Annie's Bissell sweeper was
a pre-electric device with two
parallel revolving brushes that
did a good job of picking up surface dirt and then depositing it
into two small, readily emptied
compartments. Because the latter
had a shaping effect on the fuzz
and dirt that had been picked up
and packed in, their emptying
provided the worker with a satisfying sense of accomplishment.
See Figs. 65 and 66.

[26] Lettie now returned from
her nine-day vacation at the
beach.

Somewhere in the U. S. A.

"THE IDEA WHO EVER HEARD TELL OF SUCH A THING- MY CARPET SWEEPER BEING A MACHINE GUN"

"MUCH BOOTY WAS TAKEN"

[27] Douglas Fairbanks was appearing at the Liberty in *Reaching for the Moon*, the story of a poor youth who discovers that he is the heir to a European throne (*FPT*, 13 July, p. 2).

Fig. 65. A hand-pushed sweeper (supplemented here by a newly confiscated mop, broom, and feather duster) might serve children well enough as a pretended machine gun, but it was usually just a weapon against dirt in American homes. It worked best not on bare floors (still the province of the broom and mop) but on rugs. (From the front page of the *FPT* of 14 January 1918.)

Fig. 66. This rather more sober depiction of the ball-bearing Bissell sweeper was printed for a Geneva store in 1915 (*FPT*, 2 November, p. 3), but the device seems not to have changed much over the years. While such a sweeper hardly reduced the labor of sweeping by 95 percent, its performance and durability won it a place in many homes for many years.

Sunday, 14 July

Clear & Hot[.]

Lettie done all the Saturdays work over this A.M.[28]

Fannies folks were here to dinner.[29] Raym has gone to see B[ernice]. Henry & Lettie [have] gone over to Seamans.[30] Bert is writing. 7.30 [and] dishes just washed. Very quiet tonight[.]

Fig. 67. Annie *(left)* and her twin, Fannie, stand on the South Ridge road. Behind them and about even with two of the old sugar maples, a handful of other family members watch the picture-taking. Only slightly farther back is the Perrin farmhouse itself—to the left the dining room, at the center the sitting room (with the attic above it and a bedroom behind it), and at the far right, deep in shadows here, a two-room bedroom wing.

[28] Annie's wording is non-committal, but the unspoken subtext is that Lettie's standards for housekeeping exceeded Annie's, especially when company was expected.

[29] See Fig. 67. Six days later a social item in the *Star and Beacon* recorded that "W. R. Keyse and family were Sunday guests of B. H. Perrin in Geneva" (20 July, p. 7; also, even later, *FPT*, 22 July, p. 4).

[30] Living in the second place up Myers Road, Alanson D. Seamans and his family were fairly close neighbors (Myers Road runs into the South Ridge only a little east of the Perrin place). Mrs. Seamans (Ella) was the daughter of Mr. and Mrs. C. F. Sohn of Dock Road on the western side of the village (*FPT*, 4 April 1916, p. 3). Though she certainly was a farmer's wife, part of her contribution to the household was as a professional dressmaker for the Stephens Company department store down in the village.

Before the close of 1918 Mr. Seamans had helped with the Perrins' oats, tomatoes, corn, and potatoes, and with the butchering of a pig. In fact, the Seamanses considered themselves to be good enough friends of the family to go to Ashtabula later this month to say good-bye to Henry, and when spring came again, the Seamans children sent Henry an Easter basket (ALS, Henry to Lettie, 19 April 1919).

Monday, 15 July

Clear & hot.

Hen carried wash water & bagged potatoes.[31] Raym cultivated corn. Pa mowed and cultivated. [In the] P.M. they bunched timothy and got in 3 loads. Bert P[ruden]– helped them.[32] Lettie is about sick with cold. Sent Winifreds spoon today.[33] Henry got a box of chocolates from Florence E[lliott]. We need rain bad.[34]

Tuesday, 16 July

Little cloudy.

Done up general work. Took it easy until dinner time. Got dinner. Then got ready to go to Mothers meeting[.][35] Met the bunch at [Interurban] stop 59[.][36] Mr King took us down in kid wagon.[37] Had a pleasant time. Bert met me at stop when I came home. Had supper[,] then went to show. Saw four years in Germany.[38] Home at 9.30.

[31] Toting the necessary number of bucketfuls of water was a particular help to Annie.

[32] Bert Pruden (actually, Esley Bert Pruden, Jr.) was a son of the Myers Road neighbors noted here previously. Within a very few weeks he would become one of the local servicemen honored with a star on the big flag sewn by the Soldiers' Mothers' Club (*FPT*, 20 August, p. 1).

[33] Winifred (or "Winnie") was one of Annie's nieces from over in Dover, one of the three children (the other two were twins, Marion and Mildred) of her brother Gilbert and his wife Pearl (see Appendix A). Winifred was very much an "Elliott," as Henry remarked to Lettie (ALS, 26 May 1918), very much a "<u>live-wire</u>," and studying at Oberlin College (ALS, 31 March 1919). Some twenty-five years later she was among those who came to Webster's Funeral Home in Geneva to attend Bert's funeral.

[34] Despite some rain as recently as 10 July, this entry gives the first unmistakable sign in the diary of the serious summer drought on its way.

[35] That is, Annie prepared herself for another meeting of the local Soldiers' Mothers' Club. On Thursday it would be front-page news that Mrs. Francis (Frank) E. King with the assistance of Mrs. William Kirby, both of Myers Road, had entertained nineteen women at Tuesday's meeting (*FPT*, 18 July). According to the article, the mothers "are still engaged in War Relief Work [and] are discussing ways and means whereby it can be arranged to include the wives and sisters of soldiers in their club and so make it a National Institution."

[36] The number indicates that the stop was the next one beyond the Perrins' closest one.

[37] So-called kid wagons were horse-drawn forerunners of school buses. Robishaw describes a typical one thus: "Two horses pulled the wagon along, and the students would run along and climb into the wagon through the one back door. The [front] half-door with the window was closed during bad weather, the reins to guide the team passing through the two notches in the bottom of the door" (caption to Fig. 287). The vehicle was known also as a "school hack" (*FPT*, 16 February 1920, p. 2). On 2 April 1920 the *Free Press-Times* recorded that "Frank King, Myers Road, is nursing a badly sprained left arm, making it difficult to drive the team on the school hack and delaying spring planting" (p. 2). In later years, Raym, too, drove the local hack.

[38] *My Four Years in Germany* was based on a sobering book by Ambassador James W. Gerard. With the personal endorsement of Gerard and with the Kaiser played by Louis Dean, the movie was currently making a considerable splash.

Wednesday, 17 July

No rain yet[.]

Done up work. Then churned. Got things ready for dinner. [At] Mail time got a letter from Sister Sarah. After dinner I went over to Pennys & Mrs Howards. Came home [and] got supper. After supper Lettie worked on dress. The boys went to the lake.[39] Fire down town tonight.[40]

Thursday, 18 July

Very dry & warm.

Every one feels tired today. I done up work[,] then folded clothes for ironing[.] May called up[.][41] She would be up on 10 [o'clock] car, so [I] did not iron. Lettie made pudding for dinner. In the evening word came the Yankies had captured thousands of prisoners[.][42] Such excitement[!] Whistles of shops. Bells ringing and band music[.] Every one excited.[43] Mowed the last of hay today.

Every one all in tonight.

[39] Lake Erie is about five miles due north. If one traveled a short distance east of the farm and turned north on Myers Road, one had a straight run to the lake. Or one could go a short distance west and turn north on Centennial Street—which eventually became Austin Road and led straight to Township Park (the old Battels' woods tract) and the water (*FPT*, 20 February 1917, p. 2). See also the note to 11 August.

[40] Annie did not yet know that one of the oldest landmarks in the village—a large house at 72 South Broadway—had been severely damaged. The home of Mrs. Ellen McMillan (though Charles Hall and his family also lived there in the north wing), the house was not far south of the place where Annie and Bert moved in the 1920s (*FPT*, 18 July, p. 2; *S&B*, 18 July, p. 10).

[41] This is Annie's only reference to May. Conceivably she was May Blakeslee, wife of Carey H. Blakeslee, a farmer living over toward Ashtabula (*Ashtabula Directory*, 1918, p. 113). In any case Annie refers elsewhere to Ashtabula friends named Blakeslee (see 21 September).

[42] The *Star and Beacon's* main headline for this date is "Americans Capture 10 Big Towns." The next day another one reads in part "One American Unit Takes 3,300 Prisoners." See Fig. 68.

[43] A headline in the *Free Press-Times* reports that "Geneva 'Tore the Lid Off' Thursday Night 'For

Fair'" (p. 2). In fact, "Pandemo-
nium reigned in town."

The three main "shops" (factories) with whistles to toot were
The American Fork and Hoe,
The Geneva Metal Wheel, and
The Champion Hardware.
Church bells and school bells
were rung, and the overall din
was swelled at intervals by the
blowing of tin horns and the
banging of kitchen pans. Probably most musical of all, Allen
Foster's I.O.O.F. band somehow
quickly pulled itself together
sufficiently to march around in
the town center playing "Yankee
Doodle," "Marching Through
Georgia," and "The Star-Spangled
Banner."

The newspaper took special
note that the crowd included a
"plentiful sprinkling of patriotic
Italian citizens," some carrying
Italian flags—facts worth reporting because of Geneva's relatively
large Italian-American population and because Americans and
Italians were currently fighting
side by side on the Continent.

The celebrating crescendoed
in two main waves, the first beginning about 8 P.M. and the
second lasting until almost midnight.

Fig. 68. The "turn of the tide" on 18 July 1918 was actually
one of several similar "turns," an earlier one of which was
commemorated by this front-page *Star and Beacon* cartoon
of 5 May 1917.

Friday, 19 July

Got up 5.30[.] Done up work. Lettie commenced to iron about 9 oclock. Ironed until 4.30.[44] Then I finished. Baked bread and churned. Every one tired out. So dry & dusty. The boys went out getting thrift stamps in the evening.[45] Marie went with them.

" YOU COULDN'T PUT IN A STRONGER LINE OF GOODS, MISTER RETAILER!"

GOVERNMENT AGENCY FOR WAR SAVING STAMPS BUY THEM HERE

U.S. WAR SAVINGS STAMPS

THE TORCH OF LIBERTY

ON SALE HERE

ON SALE

Fig. 69. A soberly pleased Uncle Sam, shown here holding a war savings certificate in his left hand, compliments a "patriotic retailer" for doing his part by including patriotic ware among his goods (*S&B*, 27 February, p. 9).

[44] It is easy to read over the fact that Lettie was ironing over a seven-and-a-half-hour period (doubtless with some time out) and that there was still ironing left for Annie to do.

[45] Thrift stamps were one of various means by which the government was trying to raise money for the war effort. Costing twenty-five cents apiece, they were designed to be pasted like postage stamps on the blank spaces of a savings certificate (see Fig. 69). They offered an interest rate of 4 percent and could be purchased from retailers, banks, post offices, postmen, and elsewhere. With their specific buyer ceiling (no one was allowed to buy more than $1,000 in certificates), the stamps were aimed broadly at the general population —including farmers, servicemen, and schoolchildren.

War Savings Stamps (depicted here in Figs. 69 and 70) were more upscale. A leaflet of the day explains that "The price is $4.12 in December, 1917, and January, 1918, and increases 1 cent each month after January, 1918, until in December, 1918, when the price is $4.23" (*U.S. Government War-Savings Stamps*, p. 2). In October, Ohio led the nation in their sale (*S&B*, 6 December 1918, p.12).

Liberty Bonds, at fifty dollars apiece, were designed for those still more affluent—or at least more caught up in the government's pleas. In a letter of 5 October from Henry to Lettie we learn that she has "signed for another bond!"

The main argument for the constant pressure to buy these items was stated succinctly by President Wilson: "The man who buys government securities transfers the purchasing power of his money to the United

Fig. 70. A grimly determined Uncle Sam, shown here empowered by War Savings Stamps, now has the ability to sink German U-boats—a comforting thought to Americans aware of how close the enemy sometimes came to their eastern shore (*S&B*, 5 July, p. 1).

States government until after this war, and to that same degree does not buy in competition with the government" (*S&B*, 11 June, p. 1).

Saturday, 20 July

Still hot & dry[.] Done general work. Then Lettie cleaned to the kitchen. Mr Seymour was here to supper. Then we all went to Geneva[.] Then took Seymour home and all went to the Majestic[.] Saw a good show.[46] Got home 11.30[.] A lovely ride[.]

[46] The Majestic was showing *A Soldier's Sacrifice*, starring William Farnum (Fig. 71). Having been "chosen by exhibitors of the country as one of the six greatest plays produced by William Fox, [it] has been revised, retitled [i.e., provided with new subtitles] and strengthened, until today it stands at the forefront of all photo-dramas which have come out of the war" (*S&B*, 19 July, p. 6; see Fig. 71).

Fig. 71. Once again the Perrins drove over to the Majestic (which was "Cooler than Your Home"), this time to see *A Soldier's Sacrifice* (a revised form of *A Soldier's Oath*), which was said to be "A Tremendous Drama that breathes the heroism of the Western Front." Impressions of William Farnum's stirring performance may have been somewhat attenuated, however, by the evening's added attraction: *Wild Women and Tame Lions* (*S&B*, 20 July, p. 5).

Sunday, 21 July

<u>Hot</u> & dry.

We all got up late. Bert dug new potatoes.[47] We had a chicken dinner. Bernice M[ichel]. & Roy A[ndrews] were here to dinner.[48] In the AM. Art Allen came up, also <u>Pat</u>.[49] We had ice cream & cake.

In the evening, Allen[,] Nina, Florence & Carl, [and] Gertrude were here.[50] Left about 9 oclock.

[47] On 7 May Annie recorded that Bert went to town to purchase new potatoes.

[48] See Figs. 72 and 73.

[49] Annie's underlining of this last name may reflect the fact that Henry was confused and somewhat puzzled as to how he should handle Pat's interest in him. A month or so earlier, when she sent her picture to him, he mailed it back to Lettie (31 May). In later months, after he had returned to duty following his present furlough, the two continued to correspond for a while, but before long Henry lost Pat's address.

[50] The family of Allen Foster, his wife Nina, and their daughter Helen has appeared here previously (19 May, 2 June), and Allen's youngest sister, Gertrude, has been identified in the notes. Today, however, marks the only visit of the year from Allen's sister Florence and her bookkeeper husband, Carl Cappallo, of 2211 E. 95th Street, Cleveland. (Born in 1892, Carl's full name was Carl Anton Christopher Columbus Cappallo.)

Fig. 72. In this photograph taken at the farm by Lettie on 21 July are *(left to right)* Raymond, Bernice, Pat, Henry, Annie (still wearing her apron), Roy (confidently asserting his ease and affection for Annie), and Bert. All are sitting or leaning on the little retaining wall between the milk house *(left)* and the entrance to the lower level of the barn *(off right)*.

Fig. 73. Tuff, the Perrins' three-legged, crop-tailed dog, strolls unconcernedly over his usual chain and in front of Annie and Henry.

Monday, 22 July

Still dry.

Raym took Bert to Geneva to [catch] the 7 oclock car for Cleveland. We did a big washing[.] Got through about 2 oclock A.M.[51] Was about all in. In the evening Raym took us to Seamens.[52] She served two kinds of cake & ice cream. Very nice. Got home a little after 10 oclock[.] Raym cultivated south corn.

[51] Of course, Annie means "P.M."
[52] See note to 14 July.

Tuesday, 23 July

It rained about 3 drops this A.M. Terrible hot. I baked bread, cake & coffee C[ake].[53]

Henry & Lettie met Laura on 3 oclock car.[54] I churned [and] butter very soft. Raym cultivated potatoes. Laura came on 3 oclock car.

[53] Despite the heat of the season, Annie had to keep a fire going in the cookstove for a fairly extended time.
[54] Laura Whittier was the young woman from Plymouth who shared Lettie's vacation at Mitiwanga earlier in the month.

Wednesday, 24 July

Still dry & hotter. I dont feel like work. Ironed a little today.

Pa called up for Raym to meet him in Geneva. Came home on 3 oclock car. In the evening Lettie[,] Henry, Raym & Laura all went for a good time. Thundered but no rain yet.

Thursday, 25 July

Still looking for rain. The boys are hoeing corn. Pa
went to town for Flour. Lettie is ironing[, and] Laura
working on the little dress. Picked my first cucumber
today.

After dinner work was done up <u>we all</u> went up to
Fannies[.] Had a very pleasant time[.] Stayed to supper
[and] had a cool ride home. Stopped & got our pictures. They were all good.

Friday, 26 July

Every one tired[.] We done up the work. Had dinner. Then Pa took Laura to Geneva. Lettie went with
them. [In the] PM. I finished ironing. 90 in the shade
today.[55]

[55] By this time the prolonged
heat and drought were affecting
not just the crops but also the
water supply. At Geneva-on-the-
Lake, several cisterns had run
dry (*FPT*, 26 July, p. 2).

Saturday, 27 July

Very hot[.] Look[s] like rain. They started to cut oats about 10.30[.] Binder would not bind.[56] Made 2 or 3 rounds [and then] came up to dinner[.] In PM. Seamens helped. The binder worked better. Got them about half down. I baked bread & churned. Lettie did Sat[urday] work all but kitchen. R[oy Andrews]– came just as we were through supper. After supper we all went to Ashta[bula]. Henry bought his ticket[57] [and] then we all went to show[.] Saw Jack Packford.[58]

Home 11.30[.] Pa treated all to ice cream & show.

[56] The standing oats were cut by the binder and tied into bundles with hemp twine. The bundles were then dropped on a carrier, and whenever there were a half dozen or so of them, the driver of the binder pressed a foot lever that let them fall to the ground, where they could be stacked together in shocks.

[57] Henry's furlough was fast drawing to a close.

[58] Jack *Pickford* (Mary Pickford's brother) and Robert Gordon were appearing at the Majestic in a film called *Huck and Tom* (matinee, 15¢). Though a Canadian and underage, Jack had made news recently by enlisting in the U.S. Navy (*S&B*, 26 July, p. 11; and 24 July, p. 8).

Sunday, 28 July

The boys had a rough & tumble this morning. Raym & Roy tore the bed to pieces. The 3 boys went to Lake [Erie] & had a bath.[59] [They] Got home & [then] went to Geneva. Boys & Lettie[.] Henry bought a gal[lon] of fine ice cream. I made a cake[.] After dinner we all went to lake. Look[ed] like rain so drove around [and came] home. Managed to rain enough to lay dust. Had supper. Hen & R[aymond]– went for a ride[.] Pa to Pennys. L[ettie] & R[oy] were here.

[59] Going to Lake Erie almost always meant going to Geneva-on-the-Lake (see entry and note for 11 August).

Monday, 29 July

Monday. Cool after the rain. Bert went to town and exchanged twine.[60] Came home and drove binder. Henry & Raym bound oats. In evening Mr Seamans & family, Mr & Mrs Slocum,[61] Charlie M.[,][62] And Seymours all came unexpectedly. Left about 11.30. Had a pleasant evening.[63]

[60] Twine of the wrong sort figured in Saturday's problems with the binder.

[61] Annie mistakenly writes "Mrs & Mrs" Slocum here.

[62] Charlie Muir was the young nephew of the Slocums who lived with them.

[63] Though Annie does not say so, this sudden large clustering of friends on a Monday evening was very probably related to Henry's imminent departure.

Tuesday, 30 July

Dull. But [I] washed. Clothes dried fairly well. Got through a little after 2 oclock P.M. Pa & two boys took Auto to Geneva to fix it up. Phoned about noon [to say] they would not be home to dinner. In PM Bert went to Ashtabula[, then] came home on 6 oclock car. The boys got here about 5 oclock. Allen[,] Nina & Hellen spent the evening here[.][64] Mr & Mrs Stone were here about an h[ou]r.

[64] This is the second time Annie reports that Allen and Nina brought their eight-year-old daughter, Helen, to visit.

Wednesday, 31 July

Cool & pleasant[.]

We just done general work today. Bert & Raym went to Geneva. Henry got every thing ready to pack. Cleaned, brushed[,] & washed. [We all] Took Henry to Ashta[bula] to the train to leave for Camp[.] Went to Seymours.[65] Had ice cream & cake. Left about 945 for Depot. Found Mr & Mrs Seaman waiting there, to see H[enry]. off. They rode home with us. Seymours all went to the train with us.[66]

[65] Before going to the train station, the Perrins stopped on Kingsville Avenue for a last-minute visit.

[66] In other words, there were ten people on the platform to say good-bye to Henry.

Under the headline "Geneva 'Jackie' Helps with Farm Work," the *Star and Beacon* printed the following on its first page: "Henry Perrin, son of Mr. and Mrs. B. H. Perrin, South ridge east, returns tomorrow evening to Chicago, where he is in the Great Lakes Naval Training station. He has been home on a thirty-day agricultural furlough, and has been of immense help with the work at the Perrin farm."

Fig. 74. "Let Me Hear the Songs My Mother Used to Sing" bears the copyright date 1906, but its universal theme of a son leaving home takes on a special poignancy in time of war. As usual, however, Annie's own notations on the subject are restrained and matter-of-fact.

Thursday, 1 August

Bert went to Cleveland this A.M.[67]

Raym Cultivated potatoes A.M. Corn AM.[68] Lettie ironed. I done the work. Ironed about an h[ou]r in P.M. Churned. Picnic today at Cork.[69] I could not go. Raym took Auto [and] went away this evening. Pa called up about 12 oclock, but R[aym] was not home.[70] So had an Auto livery[71] bring him home.

[67] An oddly hybrid item printed in the *Star and Beacon* on 2 August reads: "B. H. Perrin was in Cleveland on business Thursday. His son, Henry Perrin, left Tuesday night for Camp Perry, Ill., a part of the Great Lakes Naval Training station. He expects to be in the service five years" (p. 5). Actually Henry left Wednesday and his plans were still indefinite.

[68] When it comes to the corn, probably Annie means "P.M." here.

[69] Cork is due south of Geneva, on the edge of Harpersfield. A brief notice in the *Free Press-Times* of 3 August explains:

> The Soldier's Mother's Club held an all day session at the home of Mrs. [R. B.] Inscho, [mother of Edwin G. Inscho] of South Harpersfield, on Thursday, August first. Tables were spread on the lawn where a picnic luncheon was served. . . . Interesting clippings, together with several letters from France, which were read, constituted the bulk of the usual program. (p. 2)

Three months or so later the Inschos sold off their horses, cows, hay, grain, and machinery to facilitate their move to Willoughby (*FPT*, 8 November, p. 4). Their hope was that when the war was over and Edwin was back home, they could make a go of the farm again, even if he resumed work in the Geneva Tool Shop (*FPT*, 16 February 1917, p. 4; and 21 November, p. 2). As things turned out, the Inschos were back on their farm in time for planting the following spring (*FPT*, 26 March 1919, p. 3).

[70] When Bert, returning from Cleveland, arrived down in the village at about midnight, Raym was still out with the Overland.

[71] Taxi. The term is an interesting carryover from horse-drawn-vehicle days.

Friday, 2 August

Hot today.

Raym finished corn.[72] Bert went to town[.] Alman Bentley was here to dinner.[73]

Mrs Penney brought me some flowers this evening. Lettie finished ironing while I did the [routine house]-work.

[72] Annie means "finished the cultivating he was doing yester-day."

[73] Almon (or "Al," as he was usually called) was Annie's nephew, the son of her sister Lettie and her husband Newton Bentley. About four years earlier Al had come down from Michigan (where his parents lived) and made many friends—among them Neva Fleming, a local grade school teacher and one of Lettie Perrin's friends.

After their marriage about a year later, Al and Neva at first lived with Neva's widowed mother, Mrs. Mary Fleming, in Geneva (*FPT*, 6 April 1915, p. 2). That same fall, though, the young couple "moved to their newly built bungalow at the corner of Myers rd. and Maple avenue" (*FPT*, 9 September 1915, p. 2). Later on, Al delivered mail in Madison, and later still he, Neva, and their children all moved to Conneaut, about twenty miles east of Geneva (*FPT*, 24 February 1919, p. 3).

Saturday, 3 August

Lettie was invited to spend the day at Mrs Berrises.[74] I done the baking. Cleaned up. Then went to Ashta-[bula] with B[ert]–[.] Got me some <u>garments</u>,[75] & Bert some shirts. Saw Madge N[orris]. Came home. Went down for L[ettie]–. Then Pa[,] L[ettie] & I saw Tom Sawyer.[76]

Sunday, 4 August

Very hot and quiet. Irene [Wetter] called up [and] invited Lettie there to dinner.[77] Raym took her in Auto. Got home at 6 oclock. Art Allen was here to supper. Raym went over to see Bernice. We sat out a while then went to bed.[78]

[74] Though she was a fellow Genevan (55 Eagle Street was her address), Effie Knapp Berris lived in a world quite removed from that of Annie or Lettie. About three years earlier, for example, she and another young lady were entertained overnight in Delaware by the gentlemen of Phi Delta Theta at Ohio Wesleyan (*FPT*, 17 May 1915, p. 4). Making the visit appear even a bit more *outré*, Mrs. Berris had been widowed only the previous month. Her husband, Joseph Berris, who had been born in Spain, worked with the Barnum and Bailey Circus as an animal trainer, but following a serious injury in an accident in May of 1914 he died at the Berrises' home on 23 April 1915 (*FPT*, 24 April, p. 3).

Further clues regarding Mrs. Berris are her membership in The Progressive Literary Circle (where the women made presentations to one another on such topics as "Early English Literature") and The South Broadway Flinch Club, and her sometime presidency of The Merry Matrons' Flinch Club of Geneva. (Flinch was a very popular card game. Copyrighted in 1901, it currently proclaimed itself "The Acme of Parlor Games.") On one occasion back in 1916, when Mrs. Berris entertained the Merry Matrons at her home, the group played its usual games, listened to Victrola music, and enjoyed a 4:30 P.M. luncheon at which jonquils served as the floral decoration (*FPT*, 10 February 1916, p. 3; 23 September 1914, p. 2; 14 February 1916, p. 3).

[75] A euphemism for "underthings."

[76] Another Jack Pickford film, this one was accompanied by Pathé World News and "an extra good comedy" called *Sneakers and Snoozes* (*FPT*, 3 August, p. 2).

77 Irene, the daughter of Frank and Freda Wetter (see note to 27 March) and one of Lettie's good friends, was in Geneva visiting her parents. She was employed these days in Massillon, Ohio, in the offices of The Peerless Drawn Steel Company (*FPT*, 26 December 1917, p. 2). In the fall of the year, however, there would be talk of her returning to Geneva for good (ALS from Henry to Lettie, 20 September 1918).

Irene's one recorded adventure took place in the winter of 1916, when she and a companion became the only women ever to ascend 125 feet above Geneva and remain there for some length of time. (They had ridden to the top of the new smokestack of The Champion Hardware, carried in "one of the buckets in which material is hoisted" [*FPT*, 7 December, p. 1].)

78 If there was any breeze at all in the August heat, it was likely to be in the Perrins' front yard up on the Ridge, especially in the big, white, wooden, two-person platform swing that stood under the maple nearest the drive.

79 Probably because they were helping out. See next entry.

80 Though natural butter is sometimes very pale, the use of artificial food coloring is surprising in so frugal a household as Annie's.

81 The first page of the *Star and Beacon* on this date featured an article headlined "498 Casualties in U.S. Ranks." Many days brought worse news, however. The very next day, in fact, the paper reported an additional 871 casualties and cited, for the current "Big Drive," a death toll of 2,544 (p. 1).

82 In Ashtabula "The scorching heat failed to subside at sundown and far into the night people lay in their yards or in the city parks, trying vainly to get relief" (*S&B*, 7 August, p. 1). Residents of the area were also swarming to the local beaches.

Monday, 5 August

Terrible hot[,] 87° in shade. Done a big washing. Mr Seamans & Broun were here to dinner.[79]

Raym about all in[.] L[ettie] & I took it easy in the after noon. Got a card & letter from Henry. He is at Camp Perry[.]

Tuesday, 6 August

Very warm.

Mr Brown & Seaman are helping with oats[.] Mr B[rown]. here to dinner. Bert took car for Ashta[bula.] Raym went to town. I churned this A.M. Butter very soft. Borrowed some coloring from Mrs Howard.[80] Got a card from Fannie.

War is terrible.[81]

110.° at Ashtabula.[82] 105.° at Geneva.[83] Put in a terrible night[.]

83 According to Geneva's *Free Press-Times*, the "mercury" broke records established over the last two decades (7 August, p. 1). "When Mrs. J. C. Bates of South ridge west, picked up some apples . . . , she found the sun had baked them. A thermometer on the south side of the house registered 122" (reported on the front page of the *Star and Beacon* of 7 August).

Wednesday, 7 August

Some cooler today but it reached the 100° mark by 4. P.M. Raym went to Cleveland today. It rained about two min[utes] this A.M. We took things pretty easy after having such a time last night. With the heat. Got a letter from Henry. Says it isn't very clean where they are now. R[aym]– got a card from J.J.E.[84] He is in New York State.

Raym did not come home tonight.

Thursday, 8 August

Some cooler.

Showers went around us. Ironed some this A.M. Got dinner[,] then Bert took Lettie & I up to Fannies. Got there [and] the two boys were in Cleveland with a load.[85] F[annie]. looked about all in. The boys came about 4. P.M. [and] brought Water M[elon] home. So we were invited to stay to lunch. Had a pleasant ride home. Done chores. Raym came about 8. oclock[,] just before the storm[.] Had quite a shower.

[84] Since 1882, Annie's brother James John Elliott (18 January 1851–5 June 1931) had been operating a big farm three or so miles north of LeMars, Iowa. Raym was hearing now from James's son, known as J.J., who had been drafted. Earlier this summer Henry commented to Lettie that it "Seems queer J.J. was taken from the farm at such a busy season" (ALS, 29 June).

[85] Apparently young Walter Keyse and his brother Melvin had gone to the city to sell some of the family produce.

Friday, 9 August

Very close this morning. Raym is drawing out manure.[86] Bert went to town. Got flour and substitutes[.][87] Paid $3.41. Lettie finished ironing this A.M. I ironed a few pieces[,] then done up work[.] Got dinner. Made an apple pie. Sweetened with syrup. In the P.M. we rested[.] Every one seems all in with the heat.

Saturday, 10 August

Still warm.

Lettie done Sat[urday] work to the kitchen. I baked bread [and] cookies & churned.

Got through about 4. PM. After supper, Pa took us all to Ashta[bula] to the Majestic[.] Saw a <u>good</u> show.[88] Had a pleasant & cool ride home.

All had a good nights rest.

[86] That is, he was cleaning the barn.

[87] Bert bought substitutes for scarce foods such as wheat flour and sugar. Though the rationing of sugar was already in effect, the state food administration would soon reaffirm its somewhat conflicted position by declaring that "We are facing a sugar shortage in the midst of the canning season[,] and the great scarcity of fruit throughout the state makes it imperative that every particle of the supply be preserved" (S&B, 12 August, p. 1).

[88] The Majestic was featuring Wallace Reid and Ann Little in *Believe Me, Xantippe*, directed by Donald Crisp.

Fig. 75. On yet another summer Saturday evening, the Perrins motored over to Ashtabula and the Majestic, this time to see "one of the most enthralling screen romances shown here in a long time," a Jesse L. Lasky drama called *Believe Me, Xantippe*. Also showing was a two-reel Mack Sennett comedy, *His Smothered Love*. (From S&B, 10 August 1918, p. 5).

Sunday, 11 August

Very dry & hot.

Fred Perrin, Mr & Mrs Snell came on 11 [o'clock] car. Bert drove down & got them. We had a chicken dinner. After dinner[, we] did up the work[, and] then Raym drove us all to Geneva on the Lake[.][89] Fred treated to ice cream. Came home [and] had lunch[.] They took 7 oclock car home. Vere came about 6 oclock.[90] Had a thunder storm in evening but very little rain.

Monday, 12 August

Another scorcher.

I got up with head ache, done up dishes[.] Then Bert & I went to Geneva[.] I got some things to send to Henry. Came home [and] had dinner. Then I hemmed a dress for L[ettie]–. Raym wormed tomatoes. Picked a peck of tomatoes[,] fine ones.

Mrs Pruden called in P.M. L[ettie] & R[aym] got letter from Henry.

[89] This is Annie's only specific reference to the nearest and oldest summer resort on Lake Erie. Also one of the biggest, Geneva-on-the-Lake could boast in early 1917 that it had "151 cottages, business places and boarding houses. . . , with a population of over 2,000 during the height of the season" (*S&B*, 20 January 1917, p. 7). As Large described it a few years later (1924), it had "all the attractions of a typical resort, and in the height of the season its transitory population runs into thousands" (1:146).

In the early 1950s the editor of this diary worked in Geneva-on-the-Lake as a short-order cook at an outdoor stand called Eddie's Grill (foot-long hotdogs and Lake Erie blue pike were the specialties), and then as a yard-boy and handyman for Hotel Colonial. The latter was founded in 1887 by Charles Warner, the largest landowner in the area and a civilized fellow who during the winter delighted in taking friends ice-yachting on Lake Erie (*FPT*, 24 February 1917, p. 1). In the 1950s Charles Warner's wife, Myrtle, was still living, but the hotel was managed by his son, the lawyer (later a judge) Howard T. Warner—one of whose teachers had been Lettie Perrin.

[90] The social notice in Thursday's newspaper is therefore not altogether correct in reporting that "Miss Vere Smith of Akron, was the Guest over Sunday of Miss Lettie Perrin" (*FPT*, p. 2).

Tuesday, 13 August

+

Terrible hot[.] 100° at 3. P.M.[91]

We did a big washing. I got dinner [and] made a pie. Calla G[uenther with her] husband & child were here a while in P.M.[92] After dinner B[ert] & R[aym] went down to vote.[93] Vere called up to have us come down for her. She is filling Helens place.[94]

After supper Raym took Auto [and] went somewhere.

Things very unpleasant at home.[95] I sent Henry a box today.

[91] This is the third time this summer that, even up on the Ridge, the thermometer reached 100° or more.

[92] Calla and William ("Will") Guenther—now of Cleveland—were accustomed to come up to the South Ridge to visit Calla's parents, Mr. and Mrs. William Beeman (e.g., *FPT*, 27 October 1914, p.3; 18 August 1917, p. 2). This time the young couple brought along either William, Jr., or Melvin.

[93] For days the papers had been filled with names and pictures of candidates running in the primary. The Republicans' choice for the governorship of Ohio was of particular interest, partly because the incumbent Democrat, James M. Cox, had no opposition. Women, of course, had no vote, though there were major stirrings to suggest that that would not long remain the case.

[94] Vere's sister Helen (11 August 1893–23 April 1978) was the wife of Oscar Carlson, a young man from Sweden. Though she had a desk job down in the village at the grocery of A. J. Ford and Sons (see entry for 26 August), Helen was now pregnant with a daughter who would be born on 30 November. Named Helen Jean, the child died of diphtheria in the early 1920s (*FPT*, 6 December, p. 2; ALS, John W. Carlson, 14 February 1997).

[95] Annie's "very" is worth noticing. Whatever else was transpiring besides stressful heat, Bert was probably irritated by both Vere's request and Raymond's departure with the Overland for "somewhere."

Wednesday, 14 August

A little cooler.

I ironed a few things [and] picked 4 bushels of tomatoes. No sale for them. [In the] PM. made a little Catsup. Baked bread & a crum cake.

No letters today. Raym Cultivated corn. Picked the last green corn. Too old to be good.[96] Bert went up to Clarks in evening[.] Raym was out late. Vere & Lettie visited[,] then to bed.[97]

Thursday, 15 August

Much cooler.

Lettie ironed while I done work & churned. Bert went to Ashtabula. Raym dug the early potatoes. Bert, Lettie, Vere & I went over to Mrs Hartners a while in evening[.][98] She played several pieces on piano for us. Raym went away. Got in late. Mrs Howard came over a while this P.M.

Friday, 16 August

Some cooler.

I done the work. While Lettie ironed. Bert & Raym took the Auto to Ashta[bula] to have something fixed. R[aym]. got home at 11 oclock[.] Bert went on to the City[.] Got home on 6 [o'clock] car P.M.

Baked bread & cake. Bert brought [a] side of Bacon & a ham from G—s.

[96] Annie refers to sweet corn for the table.

[97] Annie's realities here are far removed from the previous day's primary elections, which drew some 391 local men to the polls. As reported by Geneva's *Free Press-Times*, the main election news was that Frank B. Willis had emerged as the Republican candidate for the governorship (14 August, p. 1).

[98] Alzada Hartner was the wife of W. J. Hartner, a cook on the *W. P. Murphy*, a Lake Erie freighter (*FPT*, 1 June, p. 4; *Farm Journal Illustrated*, p. 95). When his boat was docked and unloading, her husband was said to come "visit" her down in Cork (*FPT*, 13 November 1917, p. 3). Fortunately Mrs. Hartner was unusually self-reliant. According to the newspaper, "We have a woman in this village who is re-modelling her house, putting on a porch, building on a dining-room and laying the wall under the house, while her husband, W. J. Hartner, is steward on the lake. She is also farming" (*FPT*, 15 June, p. 2). Mr. Hartner's recurring absences explain why his wife stayed overnight with the Perrins on several occasions. When he himself was nearby, he brought them a pan of white

grapes and a half bushel of fine pears, and when it looked as though the couple would be moving to Cleveland, Annie wrote that she would miss them (7 October).

[99] Provided the Perrins went as usual to the Majestic, not the Dome or the Casto, they saw Harriet Beecher Stowe's "immortal" *Uncle Tom's Cabin*, in which Marguerite Clark played both Little Eva and Topsy. The best part of the evening probably was Ben Turpin in an added attraction (*S&B*, 15 August, p. 4).

[100] Annie's colloquial use of "great" here is striking.

[101] That is, the *Cleveland Plain Dealer*.

[102] As before, from Pardon Allen's pond down the road.

Saturday, 17 August

Much cooler.

Lettie done work to the kitchen. I done baking[.] Vere is still here.

Mended some in P.M.[,] then took a short rest. After supper Bert took us <u>all</u> to Ashtabula & a show.[99] Not very good but ride was great.[100] A beautiful night.

Sunday, 18 August

Pleasant & cool[. Got] up rather late. Done up work. Sat around a while[.] Ray, Vere, & Lettie went to Geneva [and] got the Sun[day] paper.[101] After dinner V[ere] & L[ettie]. got water lilies.[102] Then we all went

Fig. 76. After dinner on a pleasant Sunday in August, Art Allen takes Lettie and Vere punting on the Allens' water lily pond.

to Vernies grave[.][103] Art Allen went with us. Came home about 3.30[.] R[aym]– went over to B[ernice's house]–. In the evening Harriet Pruden was here. Played several pieces for us.[104]

[103] Vernon Elliott Perrin (1889–1899). See also Introduction (pp. 70–71) and Appendix A (note 8).

[104] Miss Pruden played well. She was the current best pupil of the best piano teacher in town, Miss Harriet Webster—who herself had fairly recently received an honorary degree from her *alma mater*, Knox College, in Illinois (*FPT*, 18 May 1917, p. 1). In March of 1917 Miss Webster chose to play a duet with Miss Pruden (Saint-Saëns's "Danse Macabre") in a recital at the former's residence and studio at 97 East Main Street (*S&B*, 3 March, p. 3). The following month, in another two-piano performance, Miss Pruden took the main part, Miss Webster the secondary one, in a rendition of Mendelssohn's "Capriccio in B Flat Minor" that occasioned "a storm of applause" (*FPT*, 11 April 1917, p. 1; *S&B*, 18 April, p. 5). More recently, as a prelude at the funeral service for Wade L. Holden, Geneva's first serviceman to die in France (5 May 1918), a victim of "pleuro-pneumonia," she played Grieg's "Ase's Death" (*FPT*, 1 July, p. 1).
Moreover, Miss Pruden was no cultural prude. At a meeting of the North Star Grange she played the piano accompaniment for Howard McNutt's performance on both the tubaphone and the zelaphone (*FPT*, 11 September, p. 1).

Fig. 77. On the same August Sunday, Raym and Art pose here with the water lilies that Lettie and Vere have gathered, some to be taken to Vernie's grave.

Monday, 19 August

Bert took 7 oclock car for Cleveland. Raym & I picked 110 crates of tomatoes[.] Coming up[,] Tuff had a fight [that] made me about sick.[105] I rested a while. Then churned & got the dinner. Raym is feeling sick again. Lettie done up work[.] I went and fixed grain sacks[.] Worked until 5. P.M.

After supper we went to Geneva to the picture show. Pretty good.[106] Bert did not come home tonight[.]

[105] Tuff was the dog that appears in some of the family photographs taken this year (see Figs. 50 and 73)—and in Annie's diary only one other time (30 August). Probably he was a so-called "tramp dog," the sort who adopted the family rather than the other way around.

Though the Perrins were not canine fanciers, they did keep a dog now and again over the years. Early in 1913, when a rabid dog bit a couple of local children and a number of farm animals (including one of Eugene Stone's cows), Justice C. D. Adams and Constable A. W. Loveland had to kill half a dozen South Ridge dogs. Bert, who was the one to kill the mad dog, had to kill his own dog, too (*FPT*, 6 February 1913, p. 2). Later that same year, when another rabid dog on the Ridge attacked Eliza Harley, "her brother, John Harley, drove the dog away and Rob Harley, with a gun borrowed from Bert Perrin, pursued and killed the animal near the home of Pardon Allen" (*FPT*, 12 May 1913, p. 2).

For long stretches the Perrins went dogless, but at some level Bert probably felt that a country dog has its uses. When he built his retirement bungalow, he took advantage of the south slope of the Ridge and tucked a secure and cozy kennel inside a brick retaining wall near the back of the house.

[106] Playing in Geneva was George Beban in *Jules of the Strong Heart*, a story of "virile manhood" in the great North Woods ("The smell of the pine and the breath of love mingle into a plot that brings a lump to your throat" [*FPT*, 19 April, p. 2]). Presumably more thought-provoking was the supplementary "Allied Official War Review," consisting of footage filmed at various fronts.

Tuesday, 20 August

Cool. Done a big washing. Got through 11.30. Raym
is feeling some better. I made a sugarless cake & frosting. Corn <u>syrup</u>. Bert came home on 10 oclock car. [In
the] P.M. Lettie cut ruffles for waist.[107]

In the evening I wrote to Henry. Got a letter from
Bessie.

[107] As before, Annie means
"shirtwaist."

Wednesday, 21 August

Some cooler[.]

Lettie got up when Vere did. Went to town on 8
[o'clock] car. Came home all in. [But then she] Ironed
some. I ironed some[,] went to garden[, and] baked
bread. After dinner we drove up to Fannies [and] wished
Walter good bye.[108] Then went to Madison Park to the
Harvest picnic.[109] Got home at 6 oclock. Lettie went
right to bed [with a] <u>head ache</u>. Mrs Hartner was here
all night.[110] No rain yet.

[108] Twenty-one-year-old Walter James Keyse now joined the
U.S. Army, where he remained in
service for about two years—all
of the time at Fort Campbell,
Kentucky (ALS, Richard B.
Keyse, 13 May 1997).

[109] Organized by Frank R.
Latham, held at Madison's own
Township Park, and previewed
in Geneva's *Free Press-Times* of
12 August (p. 1), this Madison
affair featured a ball game (with
a $50 prize), a variety of conces-
sions, and Mr. L. J. Taber, Master
of the Ohio State Grange, as a
speaker. ("Perhaps his biggest
point was to emphasize the conservation of coal power, food
power and man power of the
country" [24 August, p. 1].) Truth
to tell, even the locals could acknowledge this event to be, so to
speak, "small potatoes."

[110] Apparently her husband
was off on another of his lake
trips.

Thursday, 22 August

Hot[,] dry & dusty.

Raym wants to go to Fair [and I] decided to go.[111]
Called up Harriet [Pruden]. She went with us. Drove to
Geneva[.] Got lunch to take with us. Went to Ash-
ta[bula,] then to Jefferson.[112] Did not see many I knew.
So hot I sat in Auto most of the time. The ride home
was fine & cool. Got supper. Then I ironed some[.] The
evening was clear and bright. Raym went away[.] Vere
& Lettie went to bed.

Friday, 23 August

Still dry & hot.

I done up work. Then ironed 1½ h[ou]r before dinner[.] Got the dinner[.] Lettie ironed this P.M. Raym
picked tomatoes [until he] had 21 crates. Bert went over
on Clay St.[113] Lettie still feels all in. After supper we all
went over to Prudens. Harriet played. Lisle sang for
us.[114] Left about 10 oclock.

[111] For three days, beginning on 21 August, Ashtabula County's seventy-second annual fair in Jefferson was offering "Ball Games, Two Brass Bands, Special Attractions, Fast Races. A Big Time"—all for 25¢ (S&B, 14 August, p. 7). The midway there "presents the usual appearance of noise and bustle and the merry-go-round and ferris wheel are doing a rushing business" (FPT, 23 August, p. 1). Despite the noise, confusion, and heat of the place—all distressing to Annie—she probably took at least a brief look into the long hall, which was temporarily teeming with Grange exhibits of fancy needlework, canning, bak-ing, and flowers.

[112] The fair-goers drove first north, then east, then south. Their destination, the seat of Ashtabula County, acquired the name Jefferson because its first major shaper was Gideon Granger, Jr., a member of Thomas Jefferson's cabinet (Williams [1878], p. 146).

[113] Clay Street, running more or less east and west, was the first road south of the South Ridge. Bert knew a number of farmers down that way.

[114] Previously Lyle has been glimpsed here entering the Ashtabula County pig-raising contest, and later we will find him buying a Liberty Bond. Altogether, he was a bright and enterprising young fellow—just the sort to have been chosen to serve as a juvenile officer of the North Star Grange (FPT, 10 Jan-uary, p. 1).

Saturday, 24 August

+

Lettie done Sat[urday] cleaning[.] I baked &
churned[.] Done general work.

After dinner, Bert went to Ashta[bula,] Raym to
Jefferson to see about <u>war</u> papers.[115]

B[ert]– got home 7 oclock[,] Raym 10.15. Lettie &
Vere went to Ashta[bula] after supper.

War is H. and makes H.[116]

Sunday, 25 August

Hotter & dry.

Pa went away with Auto [and] got home at dinner
time. Roy [Andrews] came over about 11 A.M[.] After
dinner the young folks all went to Ashta[bula].[117]

Bert and I were alone all P.M.

[115] According to the conscription act of 1917.

[116] Whatever triggered them, Annie's characteristically muted words here (she abbreviates) were in the air at the time. In the *Star and Beacon* a big ad for the Ashtabula War Chest headed "WAR IS HELL!" continues thus: "What if the Germans invaded your street and chopped off YOUR baby's arm?" (22 May, p. 5).

With Raym concerned about "<u>war</u> papers," a couple of more immediately hellish questions for Annie had to do with what might happen to him and what might become of the Perrin family and farm if he had to leave.

In January of 1919, Homer Michel, the brother of Raym's girl, Bernice, was featured in a long newspaper article headlined "Is War Hell?" The piece is affirmatively subtitled "Saybrook Boy Relates Experiences Going over the Top and Under Terrific Shell Fire" (*S&B*, 11 January, p. 9). Described as an infantryman "who is 24 years of age, 6 feet tall and husky of stature," Homer was gassed and shell-shocked in September fighting near St. Mihiel, France. "We had to push right in to the middle of a field," he reported. "We were attacked by three fires, a low fire, a high fire, and a middle fire. One bullet hit my helmet; another hit my coat. I kept going."

[117] When it comes to entertainment, Annie records most about movies, but there were a good many other ways to have

fun on a summer evening in Ashtabula and Ashtabula Harbor. At Woodland Park in the Harbor, for instance, there were a roller coaster, merry-go-round, shooting-gallery, pool hall, and baseball field, as well as food stands and facilities for bowling, bathing, and boating. Probably most appealing to these young folks, there also was dancing to a live orchestra.

[118] Annie's mention of Lettie's attendance signals that school was soon to open for the fall term. In fact, both Lettie's name and that of Bernice Michel appeared on the front pages of the *Geneva Free Press-Times* and the *Ashtabula Star and Beacon* because they were among the ten Geneva registrants for the fall session of the Ashtabula County Christy Institute, meeting that week at Ashtabula Harbor High School.

The first speaker (and one of the main ones) on the first day of the event was Miss Jessie Lee Newlin, an instructor in English from The University of Chicago. Her topic was "The Reading Lesson: A Lost Opportunity."

[119] Vere was once again substituting for her sister down at Ford and Sons.

[120] That is, he helped his mother by carrying the water.

[121] From this point until about the end of September, peaches are a major theme in Annie's diary (see especially 4, 8, and 10 September).

This being the peach season in the so-called "Peach Belt" of the state, the C.P. & A. added to its usual rail service "a special peach car, a trailer, on the regular package car west each afternoon shortly after 3 o'clock" (*FPT*, 13 August, p. 4).

[122] Since threshing required a dozen or so hands, it was necessarily a neighborhood project. In these years before the combine, a steam traction engine, generally fueled with wood, was belted to the threshing machine in order to run both the grain separator and the wind-stacker. Usually the

Monday, 26 August

Dry & hot. Lettie went to Institute.[118] Vere to Fords.[119] Raym got wash water[120] & picked peaches[.] Sold 9 baskets[.] 1.50 per Basket[.][121] I done a big washing. [At] 10 A.M[.] Bert & Raym went to Clarks threshing.[122] [In the] P.M. I done up work, ironed curtains, [and] picked a bu[shel] of peaches. Every one tired tonight.

Got a letter from Henry.[123]

----

water to make the steam had to be hauled to the field by a team of horses.

A month or so earlier (23 July), the *Free Press-Times* published a long front-page article by Earl C. Sleeth, the Jefferson-based Ashtabula County Agricultural Agent, who offered extensive advice on threshing. For example, he suggested that $5.00 per hour was about right for use of the threshing equipment. He also advised that "Proper care should be taken on the part of both farmers and threshermen to see that the right man is in the right place. A good feeder or bundle pitcher should not have to work on the straw pile or grain measure."

[123] Probably Henry reiterated a request that he had expressed in a letter of 21 August to Lettie: "I want Ma to send me $10 as soon as she can as we may get a furlough and I will not have eno. to get home."

In this same letter he explained to Lettie how he should be addressed now that his rank had changed: "The HA1 [Hospital Apprentice, 1st Class] is my rating & should follow my name. Before I was HA2 and the next exam. will make me P.M.3. [Pharmacist's Mate, 3rd Class] and so on."

Tuesday, 27 August

Up early. Went to lot[.] Got tomatoes & peaches[.] Packed a box and sent to Henry. Then made pies. Vere helped me today. Had threshers[, making a total of] 11 to dinner.[124] Raym got his card [and] goes tomorrow to be examined. Also [received a] letter from Henry. Expects to soon go. Lettie came on 5 [o'clock] car[.] All in & quite peeved[.][125] B[ert] & R[aym] got home about 7.30[.] Threshed six places.[126]

[124] A further sign of the farmers' interdependence. Bucking common custom, Mr. Sleeth advised the farmer's wife to "Avoid the 'big dinner' idea. Serve simple meals. Often the meals served are too elaborate" (*FPT*, 23 July, p. 1).

An historian of Ashtabula County writes "that just as the [threshers'] steam engine could burn any fuel, coal, old fence posts or barn siding, straw, or elm chunks, so the stomaches [*sic*] of the threshers could handle any item served and in huge quantities" (Ellsworth, p. 23).

[125] There is no telling why Lettie was peeved, but after a long morning session devoted to temperance (Mrs. Edith Peck, president of the Ashtabula County W.C.T.U., was the speaker), and afternoon sessions devoted to music, arithmetic, and reading (*S&B*, 27 August, p.

Fig. 78. Threshers posing on a late summer day in 1918 over in Thompson—the home of Roy Andrews. Raymond Perrin, Jr., writes: "The thresher looks similar to an Agitator model made by the J. I. Case Co. with an elevator straw stacker, and the steam engine looks similar to a 1910 J. I. Case 40 horsepower tractor" (ALS, 17 September 1997).

6), she may have thought there were better ways to spend a summer day. A good teacher and role model herself, Lettie was never much impressed by theorizing about the classroom.

126 The logistics of moving the threshers and threshing equipment into and out of six different places on a single day is impressive, even though all of the workers came from farms in the area.

127 The teachers' Christy Institute continued, and Miss Newlin from Chicago was again one of the day's featured speakers (S&B, 28 August, p. 2).

128 "M. Hasenflug" probably refers to "Mr." rather than to "Mildred" Hasenpflug. In any case, the Hasenpflugs were a prominent Geneva family. Mr. John Hasenpflug—deemed by the *Free Press-Times* to be "a cultivated and thoroly up-to-date man" (28 November 1911, p. 2)— was the current president of the Geneva School Board, sometime president and one of the directors of The People's Telephone Company (the Hasenpflug number was No. 1; *FPT*, 20 July 1915, p. 3; 16 September 1915, p. 4), a director of The Geneva Savings Bank (re-elected as of 11 January 1917; S&B, p. 10), treasurer of the board of directors of Geneva Canning (S&B, 24 January 1917, p. 8), and a Sunday School teacher known for his generosity to his young charges at the First Methodist Church. As for his own children, they were delighted a few years back when he surprised them with a beautiful Shetland pony and a cart big enough to carry them all (*FPT*, 22 July 1911, p. 2).

Mildred, the Hasenpflug daughter, was a spring 1918 graduate of Lake Erie College in Painesville, and this summer, as Geneva's newspaper put the case, she was "doing graduating work" at Columbia University (*FPT*, 15 July, p. 2). Toward the end of the year, she was employed as a hospital laboratory technician at

Wednesday, 28 August

Looks like rain[.]

Bert & Raym went to Jefferson. The Dr's passed R[aym]. The girls Lettie & Vere took 8 oclock car this A.M.127 I ironed some. Picked tomatoes and done my general house work.

Raym picked tomatoes [and] had [enough to fill] 41 crates. Got a letter from Mrs Newel. Lettie came home by Auto with M. Hasenflug.128 Had a little shower this evening.

Could not go to show with the [Soldiers' Mothers'] Club.129

Camp Dodge, Iowa (*FPT*, 23 January, p. 2).

A suggestive glimpse of the family automobile was provided in 1917, unfortunately, because of an accident that befell the oldest of the Hasenpflug sons, Leroy. Returning from Lake Erie via Austin Road one night in June, he was stopped, beaten, and left unconscious by four thugs who, finding themselves unable to start it, had to leave behind the Hasenpflug "Cadillac eight" (*FPT*, 18 June 1917, p. 2). Nevertheless, the most immediate connection between the Hasenpflugs and the Perrins was that young George Hasenpflug was currently one of Lettie's eighth graders (*FPT*, 12 May, p. 1).

129 Tuesday's newspaper explains what Annie missed: "The Soldiers' Mothers club heartily enjoyed the production of 'The Unbeliever' at the Liberty Theatre Wednesday afternoon, and the members are very grateful to Manager [H. B.] Gregory for the courtesy. Twenty-five members of the club attend[ed] in a body" (*FPT*, 29 August, p. 3).

Thursday, 29 August

Today Bert went to Ashtabula.

Raym picked peaches[,] then went to Jefferson.[130]
Vere came [to our] home at noon [and] took 2 oclock
car for [her own] home. Bert came on 7 oclock car. Lettie got home on six [o'clock] car.[131]

I finished ironing, then washed 3 dresses for Lettie.[132]

[130] The reason for Raym's trip
to Jefferson the day after passing
his physical examination must
be surmised. On 30 August, however, the Geneva newspaper announced that the Draft Board for
District No. 2 had designated
thirty-one men for departure to
Camp Sherman on Wednesday,
4 September, and included in
the list was "Raymond Perrin,
Geneva" (p. 2). Since Annie
records nothing of the matter,
and since Raym worked straight
through 4 September and beyond
—indeed, worked very hard—he
must have made the trip to Jefferson to request a postpone-
ment based on agricultural need.
In any case, the spectre of his
possibly imminent departure
was very real.

[131] Highlights of today's session at the teachers' Christy Institute included an orchestral
concert and the awarding of various prizes to various children
(*S&B*, 28 August, p. 2).

[132] Life was too full of demands for Annie to bother noting
that she was missing a meeting
of the Soldiers' Mothers' Club at
the home of Mrs. Ray Foster
down on East Main in the village.
Mrs. Foster was the mother of
First Lieutenant Neil J. Foster,
who only one year later would
already be working in the office
of the New York Central in
Cleveland, in fact using some of
his spare time to organize a
chapter of the American Legion
(*FPT,* 18 August 1919, p. 3).
Meanwhile, and despite
Annie's absence, a star for Henry
was sewn on the big Community
Service Flag that the Soldiers'
Mothers' Club was preparing for
display on Labor Day (*FPT,* 28
August, p. 1; 31 August, p. 2).

Friday, 30 August

Has been a blue day. Raym picked peaches. Some men came from Youngstown. Bought peaches & the dog.[133] In P.M. Bert sold the Auto[.][134] Raym felt pretty bad about it [and] so did I. Bert went to Ashta[bula] on 4 oclock car[,] Raym on the 5. L[ettie] & I had supper in Silence.[135] I ironed dresses this P.M.

Saturday, 31 August

I Done general house work. Lettie did Saturday Cleaning. Got a few lines from Henery.[136] Saying he expects to be sent to Key West[,] Florida.

Busy with peaches and tomatoes. Bert & Raym threshed over to Slocums[.] Raym came home sick[.][137] Went to bed. Got up about 8 oclock & went to town.

[133] Thus ends the story of the three-legged mutt the family called Tuff (see 19 August). Since Annie mentions him in only one other place, it is clear that he was never the focus of much sentiment in the household. His likeness is nevertheless preserved for posterity here in Figs. 50 and 73.

[134] Whatever motivated Bert, loss of the Overland, which was not yet a year and a half old, fell heavily on the family. The auto had been not only a major pleasure and convenience, but also a source of unspoken pride, the nearest thing to a status symbol that the family owned. As recently as 1917 only about one Ohio man in fourteen owned any sort of automobile (*S&B*, 5 February, p. 7).

[135] Beyond the sobering threat of Raym's departure and the loss of the family automobile and the family stress over both, Lettie had had to endure yet a fifth day of programming at the Christy Institute in Ashtabula (*S&B*, 28 August, p. 2).

[136] An odd slip of Annie's hand or mind produced here an English variant of her son's name. To her and the rest of the family, however, he was always either "Henry" or "Hen."

[137] Aside from the hot, hard work involved, there seems to have been something about threshing that made many farmers feel ill. (See entry for 9 September.)

Sunday, 1 September

Pleasant day. Very quiet. No Autos allowed to run today.[138] Got chicken dinner for Company. They did not come. P Cook Spent the P.M. here [and] stayed to supper.[139] R[aym] went away right after dinner. A[rt] Allen called to see R[aym].

Harriet Pruden spent the evening here. Was glad to see her come.

Monday, 2 September

Bert left on six oclock car for Cleveland.[140] Jim[,] Nellie[,] Jane & family came about 9. AM [and] left about 8 P.M.[141] Had a good visit[.] Gave them tomatoes & Peaches. We all went to field after dinner and picked T & P.s. Left light all night for Bert, but he came not.

Raym picked peaches A.M. Threshed [in the] P.M.[142]

[138] In order to conserve fuel needed by the armed forces, the Federal Fuel Administration on Tuesday, 27 August, banned the Sunday use of gasoline-powered vehicles for pleasure purposes (*S&B*, 27 August, p. 10; 28 August, p. 1; see also *FPT*, 10 September, p. 1).

[139] With a large farm just east of the place where Myers Road dead-ends on the South Ridge, Pliny N. Cook was at one time a fairly near neighbor of the Perrins. For the last eight years or so, however, he had been living at 28 Blaine Street in the village. After his wife died in April 1915 (Edna Holt sang "Beautiful Isle of Somewhere" at the funeral), Cook remained on Blaine (*FPT*, 16 April 1915, p. 1) and eventually began sharing his home there with his daughter Nellie Wood, his son-in-law Edward Wood (a cashier in one of the local factories), and an infant grandson, Robert (1920 Census).

[140] It was rent-collecting time again.

[141] The visitors were Bert's sister Nellie Alice (1875–1920), her husband (whom she had married in 1894), James C. Hudgeon (a butcher by trade), and their daughter Jane (actually Nellie Jane), the wife of Alvin Jackson. On 15 July 1920, slightly less than two years after this visit, Geneva's *Free Press-Times* reported that Nellie Alice Hudgeon had died from "cancers" (p. 1). In many ways the opposite of her sister Bessie, she would be remembered as being "very pretty but almost consumed with self," a woman referred to by her own grandchildren as "The Lady" (Carol Jensen, "Henry Perrin and Jane G. Ody Family," p. 1).

[142] For Annie and her family it was of no great consequence that Monday, Labor Day, had been

set aside by the nation as a legal holiday. In the village, however, some of Annie's friends were participating in what the newspaper claimed was "the hugest affair witnessed here in many a year" (*FPT*, 27 August, p. 1). The major part of it was a grand parade in which members of the Soldiers' Mothers' Club figured prominently—preceded in line only by the marshal (Roy Woodworth on a handsome horse), a bugler (Miss Mary Maltbie, also suitably mounted), the I.O.O.F. band (directed by Bert's nephew, Allen Foster), and the G.A.R. (Formed in 1866 by veterans of the Civil War who had served in the Union forces, the Grand Army of the Republic was a social, patriotic, and political organization that attained its greatest strength in the 1890s. Though much weakened in 1918, it continued to make notable appearances on the public scene until 1949, when its "83d and final encampment was attended by 6 of its 16 surviving members" [Faust, pp. 317–18].) Prominently in evidence, too, on this Labor Day was Geneva's own Service Flag, which bore stars like those Annie's friends had sewn to represent each of the local men in the armed forces—now over 150 of them (*FPT*, 30 August, p. 1).

Also making an impression were fifty-one S.D.C. ladies from the Geneva Red Cross (all garbed in white with red crosses), the Goddess of Liberty (as portrayed by Miss Adna Hanson), and Uncle Sam (George Baily) (*FPT*, 3 September, p. 1).

143 Like everyone else, Annie saved canning paraphernalia from year to year. When Mr. and Mrs. E. A. Knapp (Allen Foster's parents-in-law) moved to Alabama, one of the household items auctioned off was a barrel of their "fruit jars" (*FPT*, 10 October 1911, p. 2).

If Annie needed some new things this year, though, McClure's in Ashtabula was selling a dozen mason quart jars for

Tuesday, 3 September

Rainy. I helped Raym pick peaches in the forenoon. Then he took 13 baskets to town. [In the] P.M. he picked tomatoes. I canned 12 q[uar]ts peaches.143

Lettie came home at noon.144 [In] P.M. ironed her pink [shirt]waist. Bert came home on 8 oclock car.

Art Allen was her[e] in evening.

———

$1.00. Mason pint jars were 90¢ a dozen, and jelly glasses 50¢ (*S&B*, 13 August, p. 2).

Whether or not Annie had the time or inclination to comply, she saw many notices this fall urging housewives to save peach stones, plum stones, and nutshells for turning over to the Red Cross. Both stones and shells were then to be converted into charcoal for use in gas masks. As of 21 October, Ashtabula County had supplied 325 bushels of stones—enough to make 9,750 masks (see, e.g., *S&B*, 26 September, p. 1, and *FPT*, 21 October, p. 1).

In December, looking back on the situation, Secretary of War Newton D. Baker reported that "The serious shortage of carbon for gas-mask canisters in the summer of 1918, due to the scarcity of cocoanut shells, was relieved in a large measure by the cooperation of the American Red Cross in the vigorous campaign throughout the country for the saving of fruit pits and nut shells" (*War Department Annual Reports 1918*, 1:64).

144 The Geneva schools opened for the fall term on 3 September, but remained in session only until noon (*FPT*, 5 September, p. 1).

Wednesday, 4 September

Cool & cloudy.

Bert went to town[.] Raym picked peaches. I sorted
and packed 55 baskets[.] Melvin[145] came with truck
about 3. PM. Raym went with him [and] will go to Cleveland tomorrow.[146] Commenced to rain about 5.30 [and]
rained all night. Mrs Hartner stayed here all night.

Thursday, 5 September

Rainy all day[.] Raym was in Cleveland market with
peaches. [Selling] Went slow. Got home on 6 [o'clock]
car.[147] I done a big washing [but] left it in rince.[148]
[In] P.M. sorted peaches and done up the house work.
Baked cup cakes. Mrs Hartner stayed all night. Got a
few lines from Henry.[149]

Friday, 6 September

Clear & cool. Hung out clothes, done up house
work. Sorted peaches. Got dinner. Took dry clothes in
[and] folded them[,] then ironed until 5 PM. Raym &
Seaman finished picking tomatoes. 1½ tons. Had a very
unpleasant evening.[150]

[145] Annie's nephew, Melvin E. Keyse.

[146] Apparently after loading the truck, Melvin took Raym home to Madison, which was on the way to Cleveland.
Meanwhile, the Geneva news-paper described in some detail the sendoff given in the village to the men in Raymond's group who left that day for Camp Sher-man, down in Chillicothe (*FPT*, p. 3).

[147] Raym's return home via trolley indicates that he managed somehow to dispose of all the peaches—though not as quickly or profitably as the Perrins had hoped.

[148] Because the wash could not be hung out to dry on a rainy day, it remained soaking overnight.

[149] Not until later did the family learn that this was the day Henry finally left the Great Lakes Naval Training Station and began his journey to Key West, Florida (*FPT*, 19 September, p. 1).

[150] Perhaps the fact that Bert was not doing much to help with the work was increasing what-ever tension already existed be-tween him and Raym.

Saturday, 7 September

Today I churned [and] done General work.

Raym picked peaches in A.M. Bert went to town. Got flour. Lettie done work [up] to the kitchen. [In] P.M. I finished ironing. Baked cup cakes. Alvin[,] Jane & family [came to visit].[151] Mrs Marshall [and] Wisel wood were here to supper & Vere Smith[.][152] Went to bed tired.

Sunday, 8 September

Cool today[.]

All got up late [and] had breakfast about 8 oclock. Done up work. Lettie[,] Vere[,] Wisel & Raym picked peaches. I got dinner. After dinner sorted 44 baskets peaches. Raym took 3 oclock car to B[ernice']–s. Bert picked peaches. L[ettie] has gone to [Interurban] car with V[ere]. B[ert] is somewhere. I am alone[.][153]

Monday, 9 September

Cool & pleasant.

I done a big washing[,] then sorted peaches. [In] PM done general house work. Raym went over to Browns threshing [and] came home sick. Bert went to town with peaches.

Got cards from Henry[.] He is on his way to Key West[,] Florida.

Lettie came home with head ache.

151 Jane (Nellie Jane Jackson) was Bert's niece from Cleveland.

152 The only Mrs. Marshall in the Geneva area appears to have been Anna, the wife of William Marshall, who lived down in the village on 17 Burrows. Young Wisel Wood, a sometime neighbor and particular friend of Raym's, was now living in Madison. His visit may have been timed so that he could lend a hand with the peaches.

153 With everyone else in the family gone, Annie's sense of aloneness probably was intensified not only because there were five peach-pickers there earlier in the day, but also because this was another "gasless Sunday."

Be this as it may, one Geneva resident, Elmer Bates, enjoyed what he called a "beautiful, quiet, autoless day, just like a Sabbath of twenty-five years ago." Bates was struck particularly by "the number of pretty fair looking nags and perfectly good top buggies that can still be scared up when the occasion, or the country requires" (*S&B*, 10 September, p. 6).

Tuesday, 10 September

Cold.

Bert and Raymond are picking peaches[.] I sorted 25 baskets. Done my work. Ironed a few pieces. Then churned. Got a card from Henry. Still on his way. Lettie walked home.[154] Looks all in. B[ert] & R[aym] went to picture show tonight [and] saw Beast of Berlin[.][155] Irene [Wetter] was here to see Lettie[.]

Wednesday, 11 September

Cloudy & cool. Got my work done up [and] baked a peach pie.[156] Bert went to stop 59 & met Mrs Newel[157] on 10 oclock car. Had dinner. Then after dinner, we visited a while[.] Then I sorted peaches. It commenced to rain about 4.30[.] Lettie came home wet.[158] We got a card from Henry [and] he was at Jacksonville[,] Fl[orid]a–[.][159]

[154] From school, a distance of perhaps two miles.

[155] The fact that Bert and Raym went to a movie together is conceivably to be explained by the additional and otherwise unnoted fact that today was Bert's fifty-first birthday. In any case, it was a man's film that they saw. *The Beast of Berlin* was described in the Geneva newspaper as "The most amazing Picture of the century, showing the kaiser to be a war maniac, drunk with power and possessing an insane desire to place the world under German rule" (*FPT*, 10 September, p. 3).

[156] The peaches were coming on fast now. After sorting forty-four baskets on Sunday, an unstated number on Monday, then twenty-five more on Tuesday, Annie merely baked a peach pie Wednesday. It was probably also on Wednesday that the Perrins submitted the following ad for Thursday's *Free Press-Times*: "For Sale.— Peaches, Alberta [*sic*] and Crosby. B. H. Perrin. Phone, 723" (p. 3). It would run eleven days.

For all their efforts, the Perrins could not match their Myers Road neighbors William and Mary Kirby. Under the heading "A Bumper Peach Crop for Geneva," the *Free Press-Times* reported that from his 1200 trees Mr. Kirby "has picked over 900 bushels and will have a thousand altogether" (*FPT*, 1 October, p. 2). Kirby had been farming in this part of the "Peach Belt" for nearly a decade, but unfortunately he was a tenant, and less than a year later a new owner would himself take possession of the farm (*FPT*, 5 August 1919, p. 4).

In any case, other fruit-growers at a somewhat greater distance but still in the area raised more peaches than the Perrins and Kirbys combined. As long ago as 1912 the *Free Press-Times* reported that the peach committee of the Boosters' Club had compiled "a list of seventy-five growers with 500 to 5,000 trees each, a total of 94,450 trees and over 700 acres of land . . . in the vicinity of Geneva" (13 March, p. 3).

157 The friendly widow from Ashtabula who hired Raym to help with her orange grove in Florida.

158 Apparently after walking home.

159 Passing through northern Florida, Henry was still on his way to Key West.

160 Though Annie was "canning," of course she was really using glass jars. The previous day's *Star and Beacon* had a full-page reminder of the importance of such canning. Despite the scarcity of sugar, "It is very necessary that the request of the United States Food Administration be complied with and as much home canning be done this fall as possible so that the large canning factories may devote their time to war orders" (p. 5).

161 With her hands full on her own home front, Annie did not record that the Soldiers' Mothers' Club met this Thursday down on Prospect Street in the village at the home of Mrs. B. C. Hodges. No casual member of the group, Mrs. Hodges would soon be named as Geneva's delegate to the War Mothers of America convention in Evansville, Indiana—Evansville presumably being the hometown of the first American soldier to fall in France (*FPT*, 17 October, p. 1; and 3 October, p. 2).

Thursday, 12 September

+

Still raining. Mrs. Newel stayed over night. I done up work. Then washed Letties waist. Ironed it. Then pressed white skirt. Then pealed peaches for five cans.160 Got dinner. Bert went to Ashtabula with Mrs N[ewell]. Got home on 6 oclock car.

Every one cross today. L[ettie]– came home with head ache. Had no supper. Mrs H[artner] stayed all night[.]161

Friday, 13 September

Got work done up at 9.30 AM[,] then ironed till 11.30. Got dinner. Washed dishes[,] then went to Ashtabula to get L[ettie']–s dress. Came home on 4 oclock car. Raym went to town. From there to see Bernice. Lettie went to a teachers doing at Hasenflugs.[162] Bert took her down. Mrs Hartner was here all night.[163]

Saturday, 14 September

Cool & cloudy.

I got breakfast[,] then done sweeping to dining room. Then Lettie came. [She] Finished sweeping to kitchen & dusted. I done general house work [and] got the dinner. [In] PM done up dinner work. Cleaned up the kitchen[,] then finished weeks ironing. Got a few lines from Henry[.] He is settled at Key West[,] Florida.[164] Lettie went to Ashta[bula] [and] got a hat[.][165] Raym went to town. Bert & I were alone.[166]

[162] The Hasenpflugs entered the Perrins' life again because the Geneva Board of Education was entertaining the teachers of both Geneva High School and the grade schools, the goal being to get acquainted with the new teachers. After Mr. Hasenpflug and others completed the formal welcoming, the evening turned mainly to music, particularly the singing of patriotic airs. It closed with conversation and light refreshments (*FPT*, 20 September, p. 2).

[163] Annie says nothing of the day's main headline, "Americans Take 9,500 Prisoners" (*S&B*, p. 1).

[164] Henry was now detailed in the main Naval laboratory there (ALS to Lettie, 12 September).

[165] In a letter to Lettie of 11 October Henry comments, "You don't care what you pay for a hat do you? Would like to see it. It must be a beauty."

Quite unusually, a handful of Ashtabula stores had all published Friday ads announcing hat sales for Saturday. Wherever Lettie made her purchase, she had the opportunity to consider the wares of—for example—White Wholesale Millinery (featuring "Beautiful Exclusive Styles" at $3.95, $4.95, and $5.95) and Donnelly's, which was pricing all hats at $5.00 in order "To further demonstrate the value as well as the style our millinery department is capable of producing" (*S&B*, 13 September, pp. 5, 8).

[166] In Ashtabula's newspaper the main headline for the day reads "Yanks Take 15,000 Prisoners; French Advance 11 Miles Front" (*S&B*, p. 1).

Sunday, 15 September

Cool & cloudy [and] in P.M. rained. We had no company. Lettie went to Irenes, Raym to Art Allens a while. I went out[,] got mushrooms enough for supper.[167] Put up 2 q[uar]ts of peaches. So lonesome I dident know <u>what</u> to do. Bert went away in evening[,] also Raym[.] Lettie read.[168] I went to bed at 8 oclock.

[167] Annie usually fried her mushrooms, preferably in butter but sometimes in bacon drippings.

[168] Lettie may have had to prepare for teaching during the coming week. In any case, she was the "reader" in the family.

Monday, 16 September

Rained all day. I done the work [and] canned some peaches. Got cucumbers ready for [making] pickle[s.] Bert & I went for mushrooms. Raym went to Ashtabula on 10 [A.M.] car. Got home about 10 oclock P.M. We all got cards from Henry. Views of Key West[,] very pretty.[169] Lettie came home soaked through. We put the dining room stove up today. Bert says this is our line storm.[170]

[169] The two that Lettie received, however (Figs. 109 and 110), were more informative than pretty.

[170] A "line storm" was popularly thought to be an especially violent storm that occurred during one of the equinoxes.

Tuesday, 17 September

Cool & clear. I think the rain has gone for a while[.] I done up work [and] churned. Then got dinner[.] Grace Lowe called up in P.M. Said she & Lulu were coming out[.] They just returned from Trenton N.J.[171] So I baked cup cakes and got supper. They were here all night. We all got cards from Henry.

[171] As the *Free Press-Times* explained, "W. Lowe and his daughters, the Misses Lulu and Grace Lowe, . . . returned to Geneva Tuesday to make their home here" (21 September 1918, p. 2).

Fig. 79. On this postcard of themselves mailed to Lettie in August from Trenton, New Jersey, one of the Lowe sisters has written, "There are some of the prettiest places around this town. The Delaware [glimpsed in the background here] is truly beautiful, but not any prettier than Lake Erie." Geneva, after all, was where their hearts lay.

Wednesday, 18 September

Raining this A.M. Grace has a bad cold[.] Lulu has gone to town to see about rooms. Bert and Raym are culling corn.[172] Mr Martin came up to see G[race] about working for him.[173] I got dinner. After dinner canned peaches. Mr L[owe]. spent the evening here. Bert was over to Allens. Got up 10 oclock. Grace & I fixed Letties plaid skirt.

[172] That is, they were sorting the ears and setting aside the poorer ones.

[173] With no evidence but Annie's comment here, one might wonder if this Martin was Mr. Frank W. Martin of A. B. Martin's Sons, the company that appears to have been Geneva's busiest dealer in real estate. If so, the job did not pan out. On 21 November, Henry wrote to Lettie inquiring whether Grace was working at Harley Brothers Hardware. A lively, companionable young woman, Grace was previously "in charge of the soda fountain department" at F. J. Hoffner's drugstore in the village (*FPT*, 29 April 1915, p. 4; 25 September 1916, p. 4).

Thursday, 19 September

Still raining.

Every one is as blue as the weather. Lulu has gone to find rooms. [She] Called G[race] up to come down to Andrews and spend the night there. Raym went to get Lettie.[174] G[race] rode down with Raym [and] took every thing so guess she dosent expect to come back. Lettie went [back] to town with Irene [Wetter] after supper[,] then stayed with I[rene]. all night.

[174] Apparently with the horse and buggy.

Friday, 20 September

Nasty[,] rainy & cold.

Bert & Raymond filled silo at Clarks. Mrs Howard came over [and is] excited about War.[175] I got a lunch[,] then canned peaches. Got a telephone message from Mr Aylard [who] said he & wife would be here in about 2 h[ou]rs. They were here in time for supper. Spent a pleasant evening. Got a letter from Henry[.] He hasent received any mail yet[.]

Saturday, 21 September

Raining & cold.

Raym has gone to Akron[.][176] I done up dishes and then got ready and went to Ashtabula with Bert & [the two] Aylards[.] We called on Mrs Newel[,] Seymours & Blakesly.[177] Bert staid to [go to a] show and I got home about 4 oclock[.][178] Lettie done Sat[urday] work[.] I got supper. Went to bed early. Got a card from Henry[.]

[175] Whatever triggered Mrs. Howard's excitement, the main headline of the day in the *Star and Beacon* was less scary than usual: "Moeuvres, 7 Miles West of Cambria [i.e., Cambrai] Taken by British."

Probably few in the country paid much attention to the newspaper's notice that influenza—rumored to have been planted by German U-boats—was spreading along the coasts of Spain (p. 1). Therefore called "Spanish" influenza in 1918 and long afterwards, the disease would be discovered about seventy-nine years later to be a mutation that had evolved in American pigs. Basing their findings on lung tissue from a twenty-one-year-old Army private who died at Fort Jackson, South Carolina, on 26 September 1918, a research team at the Armed Forces Institute of Pathology in Washington, D.C., announced their findings in March 1997 (Jeffery K. Taubenberger et al., pp. 1793–95).

[176] Though Raym eventually took a job in Akron, this overnight trip on a weekend was probably merely social.

[177] Annie may refer here to Carey and May Blakeslee, a farming family living out on Fargo Avenue. Or perhaps B. C. Blakeslee of Tyler Avenue, a dealer in real estate. Blakeslees were fairly numerous in Ashtabula, however, and positive identification of this friend seems unlikely.

[178] None of the movies in town seem to have been much to Bert's taste. The Majestic, which the Perrins generally frequented, was featuring Norma Talmadge in *The Safety Curtain*, a film billed as "another emotional triumph" (*S&B*, 21 September, p. 5). Maybe Bert went elsewhere.

Sunday, 22 September

Bert[,] Lettie and I were here to dinner. Seems very quiet, no Autoes running.[179] Irene came in P.M. L[ettie] & she went to Ashta[bula]. Bert and I went mushrooming. Got enough for supper. After supper B[ert] & I took a little walk[, then] came home[.] Wrote to Henry. Raym came about 10 oclock[.]

[179] The ban on Sunday driving was continuing.

Monday, 23 September

I done my washing, but seemed so tired I could hardly finish. Bert & Raym picked tomatoes. Raym has a terrible cold. Bert complains of his back all the time.[180] Another letter from Henry[.] He hasent heard from home yet.

Mr Hartner gave me a pan of white grapes.

[180] The collective view here of a farm family at harvest time contrasts tellingly with the romantic nostalgia of Lettie's sheet music on the subject, "When the Harvest Moon Is Shining."

Fig. 80. Though many farm families find harvest time the most difficult period in the year, the so-called harvest moon (the full moon that shines nearest the autumnal equinox) supposedly inspired Arthur Lamb and S. R. Henry to write their sentimental "When the Harvest Moon Is Shining on the River." Copyrighted in 1904, the song proved to be a durable favorite with farm-dwellers and town-dwellers alike.

Tuesday, 24 September

Raining in the morning. Raym & I finished picking tomatoes[.] R[aym] hauled them to factory.[181] Bert took 8 oclock car to Ashta[bula]. I got the dinner[,] then ironed some, and made some tomato preserve. Got a letter from Henry[.] He has heard from home. Seems quite contented there.[182] Aylards were here tonight.

Wednesday, 25 September

Raining this[183] A.M. Had breakfast. Then Mr Aylard & Bert went to Seamans [and] got peaches & onions. I picked a <u>rooster</u> for dinner. Had dinner at just 12 oclock. Then Aylards left for home. Raymond went to the dentist. Mrs Hartner was here all night. Lulu L[owe] was here about an h[ou]r this P.M.[184]

[181] With a team and wagon, Raym took the tomatoes down to The Geneva Canning Company on North Eagle Street. Back in the spring, the company had run a series of ads appealing both to the farmers' patriotism (the government must have canned tomatoes for the boys in service) and to their financial hopes ("There will be big money this year for the grower at $18 a ton"). The immediate point back then was that farmers should "get a contract at once" with the company (*FPT*, 19 April, p. 2; 23 April, p. 4). Though modest by some measures, clearly the G.C.C. was a thriving concern: the preceding year it had approximately 90,000 tin cans shipped in by rail in order to handle the local tomato crop (*S&B*, 5 June 1917, p. 8). See also Annie's entry for 2 October.

[182] A letter of 20 September from Henry to Lettie reveals an artistic appreciation of the Florida setting that in later years and other places manifested itself in watercolors, colored pencils, pen and ink, oils, and pastels. Henry writes, "The ocean is as calm as can be today. Sure is pretty. At sun set it is beautiful to watch the many changes in the hew of the water. The cloud effects are wonderful."

The same letter, however, also has Henry's observation that "This life is more or less like prison. There is a high steel fence around the grounds and Marines on guard." Also, "You have no idea how hot the sun is here."

[183] Annie mistakenly wrote "thins" here.

[184] Ashtabula's *Star and Beacon* for this date printed what might be called its first serious item on Spanish influenza. Headlined "Influenza Is Sort of Virulent Grip," it reported that

the disease was now "seemingly about to break out seriously in this country." Though the flu itself was sometimes fatal, the newspaper goes on to observe that the main danger was that it often led to pneumonia, tuberculosis, and other respiratory diseases. Normally "the individual case extends over three or four days, or sometimes a week" (p. 1).

[185] Focused on work as Annie was, her entry omits any mention of the afternoon's meeting of the War Mothers down in the village. Other mothers did, nevertheless, gather at 31 Woodlawn, the home of Mrs. A. Tanner, whose son Albert (of the Rainbow Division, 117th Engineers) was one of the servicemen honored with a star on that flag sewn by the members of the Club (*FPT*, 24 September, p. 2; 28 August, p. 1).

[186] Whether or not the Perrins realized it, the influenza epidemic as of this day affected Raym's position regarding the draft. The flu scholar Crosby writes:

The unthinkable was happening: something had appeared of greater priority than the war. On September 26 . . . the Provost Marshal General of the United States Army cancelled an October draft call for 142,000. Practically all the camps to which they had been ordered were quarantined. The call-up of 78,000 additional men in October had to be postponed, and the war ended before most of them ever put on a uniform. (p. 49)

Having reported on 28 August that Raym was "passed" by the doctors in Jefferson, Annie does not record until 6 November that he was "to be ready by the 15th." By the latter date, however, the Armistice was four days old.

Thursday, 26 September

Cloudy, but does not rain. Bert and Raymond picked 20 baskets of peaches. I sorted them. Then done my work. Made some catsup [and] canned 5 q[uar]ts fruit.[185] Got a card from Henry. Bert went to town.[186]

Friday, 27 September

Bert and Raym cut corn,[187] and Bert went to town [and] got a little coal. R[aym] finished picking peaches. Got a letter from Aylards[.] They made good time going home. The sun is shining today. I ironed all the P.M. Lettie & Raym went to show in the evening.[188]

Saturday, 28 September

Finished sorting peaches. Then done up morning work. Lettie done Sat[urday] work to dining room [and] took 1 oclock car for Ashta[bula]. Vere came on 3 [o'clock] car. Raym went to the dentist. After supper Bert went to town. B[ert] & R[aym] came home about 12.15 [A.M].[189] Got 3 letters from Henry.

[187] The double aim of cutting corn is to clear the field and produce fodder. Done by hand, the job is both difficult and unpleasant because the corn stalks are tough, their dry leaves are sharp and dusty, and corn fields tend to be big. Though farms of the day were beginning to be somewhat more mechanized, the Perrins still used individual corn knives—simple hand tools consisting of a wooden handle attached to a sharp and slightly curved steel blade (Raymond Perrin, Jr., 28 August 1997).

An article in the *Free Press-Times* discussed the timing of the job thus:

To be of greatest value as a feed for livestock corn fodder should not be cut too green. The best time to harvest corn is after the kernels have become well dented and hard and the husks are partly or entirely dried. After reaching this condition there is ordinarily a period of about two weeks in which the feeding value in both the stalks and ears is at its best. If cutting is delayed until the ears are mature enough to husk and crib [i.e., store in a corn crib], the stalks have lost considerable of their feeding value. (FPT, 16 October 1912, p. 4)

[188] The Liberty (assuming that was where they went) was showing not only Emily Stevens in *A Man's World*, but also the eighteenth chapter of *The House of Hate* and a short comedy called *Bullies and Bullets* (FPT, 27 September, p. 2).

As for the world outside, the main *Star and Beacon* headline was "Greatest Battle Now Being Fought," with smaller type adding "Longest Battle Front in History Nearly 300 Miles," and the lead reading "The greatest series of battles in the history of the world is being fought today." U.S. and British forces were currently operating in the area between Rheims and Verdun.

On its eighth page the same issue of the newspaper recorded also that the cases of Spanish influenza in the army and at home had reached a total of 29,002, and that "The epidemic has now spread into 26 states."

189 A late night for both father and son.

190 An afternoon nap for Bert was unusual, but so was his bedtime the previous night.

191 With or without an automobile, Raym felt no need to account for his comings and goings.

192 Henry wrote on this date to Lettie: "We are filled to full capacity and besides have the drill field covered with large tents all filled with new cases. Expect to receive 50 more patients from the training camp to-day." He also passed on a scrap of news from the naval station at Great Lakes: "They are using the drill halls for hospitals there."

Sunday, 29 September

Had a chicken dinner today. After dinner V[ere] & L[ettie]. went to church[.] I done up the work. B[ert]– slept all P.M.190 Raym took horse & buggy [and] went some where.191 I churned [and] baked bread. Got through about 4 P.M.192

Monday, 30 September

Raym cut corn until 10 oclock. Then went to the dentist on 11 car. Commenced to rain about 10.30. Pa took peaches to town[.] Sold 8 baskets [and] left 6 at Tylers[.][193] I done my work up [and] got dinner[.] Bert took 2 oclock car for Cleveland.[194] I canned a basket of Peaches in P.M. Sweet run over a young rooster.[195] So I picked that.[196] After supper Lettie marked Papers. Raym went to town. I wrote three letters. Went to bed at 9.30.

[193] Tyler's was the grocery run by Azro M. Tyler at 10 North Broadway down in the village.

[194] Bert was off on his monthly rent-collecting and city-visiting trip.

[195] Possibly C. J. ("Chet") Sweet, one of those Genevans who in the winter of 1916–17 preceded the Perrins in their exploration of Florida (*FPT*, 28 March, p. 3). In fact, back in the fall of 1917 Sweet was considering selling his Geneva home (17 Maiden Lane) and his new Dodge in order to go south again. Apparently interested in experimenting with potato-growing, he observed at that time that "One beauty of raising potatoes in Florida is the lack of potato bugs there" (*FPT*, 19 October 1917, p. 1). Now, after dealing in local real estate for a while, he and L. C. Kelsey were in the process of establishing a new realty firm (*FPT*, 5 October, p. 2).

[196] No longer were hawks and foxes the main foes of chickens (*FPT*, 29 May 1918, p. 2). With the advent of the automobile, chicken mortality in the U.S. jumped dramatically. Only a month before, the *Star and Beacon* ran an article headed "Farmers Want Autoists to Save Dead Chickens" (27 August, p. 1). It opens: "Say, Mr. Autoist, when you run over a chicken, Hooverize—that is, save the dead chicken." (Herbert C. Hoover, currently the U.S. national food administrator, was in charge of both conserving food supplies and stimulating food production.) Local farmers who were losing chickens (a particular problem on the North Ridge, where the traffic was now heavier than on the South Ridge) thought that a motorist who hit a chicken should be kind enough to stop and take it to the farmhouse so it might be cooked.

From First Frost to Year's End

1 October–31 December 1918

Tuesday, 1 October

Had our first frost last night. Every thing white this A.M. I done a big washing [and] clothes all got dry. Then went down [and] picked 5 crates of tomatoes.

We got a card from Henry[.] The influenza is bad down there.[1]

Rained tonight.

Wednesday, 2 October

Bert is still in Cleveland. I done up house work [and] then picked tomatoes. Came up [from field at] 11.30 [and] got dinner for Raym & I. Was back at 1.15. Got through and load[ed them for taking] to [canning] factory just as it commenced to rain. We had a hard rain[.] Lettie called up for R[aym] to come and get her. Got home[.] We had supper[.] Then I washed dishes and went to bed all in.

L[ettie] & I got a letter from Henry[.][2]

B[ert] came 11.30 PM.[3]

[1] This is Annie's first mention of a subject that was to become increasingly worrisome in the coming days and weeks.

[2] Henry's letter to Lettie of 27 September indicates that people were confused because the new and more deadly strain of flu differed from what they had seen previously. He writes: "Have you heard about the plague? It acts somewhat like Influenza." Crosby observes that some medical men really thought they were dealing with "pneumonic plague, that form of the Black Death of medieval history which is transmitted by breath, just like influenza" (p. 9). Henry continues: "We are filled up and are now putting beds in tents outside. All the wards are full, the porches and all. Nine new cases just brought in from the USS Dorthea." Here Henry refers to the *Dorothea*,

one of the most powerful armed yachts of its time, in fact a vessel valued as a "minor warship." Provided it set out with its full complement of sixty-nine, a whopping 13 percent of its men were flu-stricken when it docked in Key West (Gardiner, pp. 168–69).

3 As Annie focused on immediate domestic details, the good news conveyed in the main headline of the *Star and Beacon* today was that "St. Quentin, Cambrai in Allied Hands, Huns Face Total Collapse."

4 So-called "stoop labor" is difficult, and Annie had just had two days of it.

5 The home-drying of fruit was encouraged because it helped conserve sugar. However, since the year was too advanced for sun-drying (cf. last note to entry of 6 August), Annie now had to dry the peeled peach slices on one of her stoves. Then during the next few days, according to the *Star and Beacon,* she needed to transfer the fruit several times from container to container (14 September 1917, p. 8).

6 For the week ending 28 September the Navy recorded 880 ashore deaths from influenza and pneumonia (Crosby, p. 58).

7 The six-feature course of the Lyceum this fall included three lectures, one dramatic reading (by Edwin Whitney, the "peer of dramatic readers"), and two musical events (one presented by a Kentucky mountaineer and the other by The Lilioukalani Hawaiians).

Opening the course at the Congregational Church, the first of the lecturers was Dr. Arthur W. Evans, a nephew of British Prime Minister David Lloyd George, who delivered a talk entitled "What America Means to Me" (*FPT,* 2 October, p. 3).

Since the Lyceum was sponsored by the seniors of Geneva High School, a four-minute introductory sales-talk for Liberty

Thursday, 3 October

Cloudy. I am so lame from picking tomatoes[.][4] I done my house work and ironed a few pieces. Pealed peaches for drying.[5] Bert is home but not feeling like work. Got a card from Henry[.] Influenza is very bad at K[ey]. West.[6]

Mrs Brown visited a while this A.M.

Friday, 4 October

Warm & clear. Today finished ironing[,] done general house work[,] canned some peaches. Lettie came home to supper[.] She & Irene took 7 oclock car for Geneva [and] went to the first number of the Lecture course.[7] Stayed at Mrs Holts all night[.][8] Raym went to Bernices.

———
Bonds was made by John Hasenpflug, president of the school board. The speaker himself was introduced by Superintendent Cleon E. Webb.

8 Annie refers here to Mrs. Anna Holt, of Swan Street.

Saturday, 5 October[9]

Lettie came on 8 oclock car. Looked all in. We done Sat[urday] work. Bert got me peppers & onions for pickling & chili sauce. Raym cut corn over to Browns[.] Got letters from Henry[,] a card from Sister Sarah. Mr Hartner brought me ½ bu[shel] of fine pears.

Sunday, 6 October

Got up late[,] done up work[,] then pulped grapes.[10] Raym went to Seymours for the day. Lettie & Irene went to church. Bert and I went to garden[.] I got potatoes and tomatoes. L[ettie] got home in time for dinner.

After dinner she & Irene went to Ashty.[11] Mr & Mrs Hartner were over for an h[ou]r or two in P.M.[12]

Monday, 7 October

Rainy. Did not wash. Made chili sauce & grape jam. Knit on Rayms sweater. Mr & Mrs Hartner went to Cleveland to live this A.M. Will miss them. Raym & B[ert]. cut corn. Got a letter from Henry[.] He got the apples all O.K.

[9] The *Ashtabula Star and Beacon* for this date reported that in relatively near Erie, Pennsylvania, the Spanish influenza had occasioned the closing of all churches, schools, and amusements—in fact, the banning of all public gatherings (p. 1).

[10] For making jam (see next entry).

[11] That is, Ashtabula.

[12] Down at the North Star Grange another friend, Pardon Allen, led "an interesting discussion on 'Renewing Old Pastures'" (*FPT*, 8 October, p. 1).

Tuesday, 8 October

Clear & cool today[.] Done my washing. Baked bread. Seaman helped cut corn. Was here to dinner[.] Finished up ours[,] then went over and helped Brown.

The schools closed today on account of the Influenza.[13]

"FLU" MASKS READY TO CHECK EPIDEMIC

[13] As the school closing was viewed in the *Free Press-Times* for this date, "Geneva is not going to have an epidemic of the Spanish influenza, if the precautions instituted in the schools by John Hasenpflug, president of the board of education, are supplemented by the co-operation of the entire community" (8 October, p. 3).

Though it is true that the flu had not yet hit Geneva hard, the newspaper reported on the same page that currently there were between 15,000 and 20,000 cases in Ohio, and that at Camp Sherman in Chillicothe, where many local servicemen had been sent, the influenza-pneumonia combination had now caused 104 deaths in a single twenty-four-hour period.

In nearby Ashtabula, on the other hand, there was thought to be "no cause whatever for alarm" (*S&B*, 9 October, p. 1).

Fig. 81. A typical flu mask of 1918, as depicted in the *Star and Beacon* of 11 October (p. 12). Alfred Crosby, with the advantage of scholarly hindsight, writes that

> to be even slightly effective . . . masks must be worn at all times when people are together, at home and at work and in between, must be of a proper and probably uncomfortable thickness, must be tied firmly, and must be washed and dried at least once daily. Enforcement of such conditions is impossible and so the communities where masking was compulsory during the Spanish influenza pandemic almost always had health records the same as those of adjacent communities without masking. (p. 101)

Wednesday, 9 October

Went over and borrowed Pennys curtain stretchers[.][14] Got nicely to work. Aunt Fannie[,] Walter & Melvin came [and] were here for dinner[.] Bert took 8 oclock car to Ashty, came home on 6 oclock car.[15]

Raym husked corn[.]

Lettie washed curtains & windows.[16]

Thursday, 10 October

I churned[,] baked bread[,] and ironed some. Got dinner. Then helped Raym gather apples[.] Went to Prudens to [War] Mothers meeting in PM[.][17] 9 there. Scared of the Influenza.[18]

Spent a very unpleasant evening.

[14] See entry and note for 30 March.

[15] In other words, Annie entertained her sister and her family without Bert.

[16] With school out, Lettie could help more at home.

Whether he was following Mr. Hasenpflug's example of closing all schools or perhaps planning with him, the newspaper reported that day that Mayor J. H. Copp on Tuesday afternoon had "issued a drastic order closing all the public places until further notice." It was he who took action, moreover, because Geneva's Health Officer, Dr. Frank C. Smith, was himself ill and confined at home. Thus not only Geneva's schools closed but also its churches, pool and billiard rooms, dance halls, and picture show (*FPT*, 9 October, p. 1).

Though Geneva at this point still had only four or five cases of flu, Mr. Charles D. Adams (one of the village's two justices of peace) was quickly appointed as a substitute for Dr. Smith. Because Adams had held this post previously (in more cheerful days, the newspaper occasionally referred to him as "Healther Adams" [e.g., 18 July 1914, p. 3]), he was a logical choice. Now, "Some placards having been hastily printed," he was already placing them on those houses where the disease had struck (*FPT*, 9 October, pp. 1, 3; also *Ashtabula Directory* for 1918, p. 267).

[17] The Prudens' oldest son, Esley B. Pruden ("Bert," a brother of Harriet and Lyle), was drafted in July and departed for camp in August (*S&B*, 20 July, p. 1; 16 August, p. 1). In September he sent home a print of what was said to

be the largest picture ever taken at Camp Zachary Taylor, the country's biggest military training camp, six miles south of Louisville, Kentucky: it depicted ten thousand soldiers of the 159th Depot Brigade (*FPT*, 16 September, p. 1). Before his release in early 1919 Bert had served in both the infantry and the hospital corps, and thence returned to his former job in the handle mill of J. B. Smith and Son (*FPT*, 12 March 1919, p. 3).

Though young men continued to be drafted, the war news of the day was encouraging. Three of the front-page headlines of the *Star and Beacon* were "Half of German Line Is Broken," "Greatest Victory in Military History Being Won by Allies," and "Kaiser Abdicates, Report Says."

[18] This closing four-word comment provides perspective on the one that immediately precedes it. Only the previous week no fewer than twenty-three women turned out for a meeting of the War Mothers at the Tanner home on Woodlawn Street (*FPT*, 4 October, p. 3).

There were now twelve cases of flu in the village and one in the adjacent area (*FPT*, 10 October, p. 1).

[19] Raym was suffering a recurrence of the trouble with his appendix.

[20] On this same day Henry, now fully engaged in naval hospital work, wrote to Lettie "Am all in Sis. Too many sick men. Another went 'West' about 15 min[utes] ago." It was becoming increasingly clear that the pneumonia that typically followed a flu case was increasing the seriousness of the situation.

In much of Ohio the epidemic had now reached alarming proportions. As of this date, "In every Ohio community where there are cases of Spanish influenza, the doors of theaters, moving picture houses, schools and churches will be closed and all

Friday, 11 October

Done up general work. Then ironed[.] Lettie cleaned windows. Raym was sick [with] pain in side.[19] Bert went to town.

Got a card from Henry. The influenza is still very bad there.[20]

public indoor meetings prohibited by an order of the state department of health" (*Cleveland Plain Dealer*, 11 October, p. 1).

In Geneva there were sixteen cases (*FPT*, 11 October, p. 3).

Saturday, 12 October

Brighter today[.] Lettie helped with work. Done cleaning[.] After dinner I finished ironing. Raym got two red squirrels.[21] Pa went to town. I have Rayms sweater about ⅔ done. No word from Henry today. Got a phone call from Fred [Perrin] tonight[. The two] Snells & F[red]. will be down tomorrow[.][22]

[21] The squirrel season opened officially on 16 September and extended to 20 October (*S&B*, 14 September, p. 1; 25 September, p. 2). There were far fewer hunters this year, however, because of the war.

[22] Though Annie's mind was focused on doings at home, the national news warranted an "extra" edition of the *Star and Beacon*. In mammoth type it proclaimed on the front page that "Germany Wants Peace" and "Accepts All Terms of President Wilson."

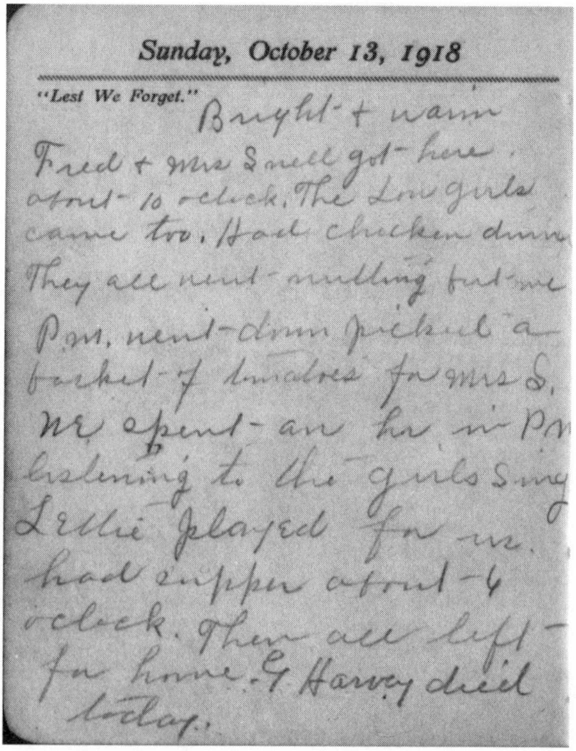

Fig. 82. Annie's diary, 13 and 14 October 1918. Actual size.

Sunday, 13 October

[23] On different occasions the family went out to gather chestnuts, walnuts, butternuts, and pignuts. Years later, Annie's son-in-law, Myron, made note of one such expedition on which the family handily garnered a bushel of them (7 October 1934).

[24] Despite the troubling times, everyone was attempting to live as normally as possible. One of Lettie's liveliest pick-me-up songs was "Put Your Arms Around Me, Honey" (Fig. 83).

[25] George Charles Harvey, age fifty-three, died that morning at his residence on Park Street. Having been thrown from a buggy back in May 1914, at Geneva's

Bright & warm[.] Fred & Mrs Snell got here about 10 oclock. The Low girls came too. Had chicken dinner. They all went nutting but me[.][23] [In the] P.M. went down [and] picked a basket of tomatos for Mrs S[nell]. We spent an h[ou]r in PM listening to the girls sing[.] Lettie played for us[.][24] Had supper about 6 oclock. Then all left for home. G Harvey died today.[25]

Monday, October 14, 1918

"Lest We Forget."

School is closed on account of Flue. had no srap. so I canned 17 cans of Tomatoes. Lettie done the work. Vere came on 4 oclock car. Bert went to town Raym picked the last picking of tomatoes Tone of green ones left —

Fig. 83. Lettie's "Put Your Arms Around Me, Honey" from *Madame Sherry* was introduced in 1910. After quoting the title, the chorus of the song continues: "hold me tight, / Huddle up and cuddle up with all your might." Despite this invitational mode and despite the publisher's attempt to hitch the song to the star Elizabeth Murray, the picture at the lower right features a rather severe Anna Boyd.

Monday, 14 October

School is closed on account of Flue.[26] Had no soap.[27] So I canned 17 cans of Tomatoes. Lettie done the [general house]work. Vere came on 4 oclock car.

Bert went to town[.] Raym picked the last picking of tomatoes[.] Tons of green ones left[.]

dangerous "diagonal crossing" (where his horse was frightened by a streetcar), Harvey broke a leg and badly injured his neck. A couple of years later the *Free Press-Times* reported that he had won his damage case against the C.P. & A. and been awarded $1,000 (23 November 1916, p. 1), but he spent the remaining years of his life as a near-total invalid.

Well known to local residents, Harvey was admired both as a naturalist and as an inventor, his principal invention being a method and machine for reinforcing concrete silo blocks (*FPT*, 14 October, p. 1; *S&B*, 14 October, p. 8).

[26] The closing of schools was noteworthy to Annie because Lettie was a teacher, but this time all schools, churches, and theaters were ordered closed not just locally but throughout the state. In fact, all public gatherings were banned.

This Monday also brought Geneva's first death from flu. Fourteen-year-old Ross D. Maltbie died in the morning and was buried in Evergreen Cemetery that afternoon (*FPT*, 14 October, p. 3; *S&B*, 15 October, p. 9). For Ross's parents, Mr. and Mrs. James W. Maltbie, the death was a tragic sequel to the loss of their twenty-year-old son, Curtis, who had committed suicide that spring (*FPT*, 16 April, p. 1).

[27] Evidently Annie's thought here is that Monday was normally a washday.

Fig. 84. In this advertisement from Ashtabula's *Star and Beacon* of 14 October (p. 7), a local doctor smilingly offers his skills to anyone who may be worried about the threat of Spanish influenza. (The abbreviations following his name stand for "Doctor of Chiropraxis" [Bonk, 1:797] and "Philosopher of Chiropractic" [Rogers, p. 150].)

Spanish Influenza

No occasion for panic. Chiropractic Adjustments are more effective and more permanent than any medicine that you can take; and you won't suffer from any effects of it in the future.

O. W. BUGBEE, D. C. Ph. C.

Office Hours 9 to 11:30 A. M., 1:30 to 4:30, 6:30 to 8 P. M.
Outside Calls Made by Appointment

206 ½ Main St.   Phone 2618

Tuesday, 15 October

We Done a big washing. Then got dinner. After dinner L[ettie] & V[ere] went to Geneva. Got cloth for pillow slips. All spent the evening reading. I knit on Rayms sweater.

Got a letter from Henry[.] Flue very bad down there.[28] This is the day R[aym]– was to go.

[28] On this same day, ironically, the Geneva newspaper printed on its first page a short article headlined "Epidemic Mild Key West, Fla., Writes Perrin." Though "Boat loads of patients are being sent in there for treatment almost continually," the reporter paraphrased, the flu cases in Key West "are comparatively mild, due to the warm climate," and Henry himself was keeping well at least in part because "Every four hours he takes a preventative for the disease."

In Geneva Mr. Adams closed the barbershops (*FPT*, 15 October, p. 2).

[29] Annie first wrote "& Raym" here, but then crossed out "Raym."

Wednesday, 16 October

Pleasant[.]

Bert[29] husked corn. Lettie is about sick today. Vere ironed a few pieces while I knit. [She] Went home on 4 oclock car. [In the] P.M. I ironed. Got a letter from Aylards today. Also card from Henry. Raym hauled onions for Seamans[.]

Thursday, 17 October

Every one busy. Has been a grand day. Lettie cleaned pantry. I done the [usual] work. Made catsup. Low girls came up in the evening. I finished knitting R[aym]–s sweater today.[30]

Friday, 18 October

The men husk[ed] corn. We done up work. I got some pears of Stones. Then churned[.] Lettie finished ironing[.] I made two p[ai]r pillow slips.[31] Band broke on machine.[32] So could not sew any more. Bert went to town [and] got groceries.

[30] Also on 17 October, Bert placed an ad in the local paper: "For Sale Corn stalks, . . . no delivery also large work horse. B. H. Perrin, Phone 723" (*FPT*, p. 3).

[31] From the material purchased Tuesday.
[32] Annie had a foot-powered treadle sewing machine.

Fig. 85. Annie's sewing machine was not unlike the one shown here in the lower tier of bargains available in 1917 at Hoover-Bond in Ashtabula. It had a strong belt or band (dimly discernible on the right) that connected a foot-treadle to the mechanism inside the wooden cabinet above it. In the two front-facing sets of drawers at the sides, a woman could keep threads, thimbles, pins, and tape measures, and still have room for a few scraps of cloth for mending. (From an advertisement in the *S&B* of 2 April, p. 6.)

Saturday, 19 October

Another busy day. Had a hard frost last night. Lettie got a letter from Henry. He is about tired out. Harriet Pruden called this P.M. Tonight R[aym] has gone away[,] also Bert[.] Lettie is reading and I am going to bed. Rained all night[.][33]

[33] This last comment is an example of information recorded the next day.

Whether Annie mentions it or not, the flu was now an ongoing factor in the life of every community. Nearby Ashtabula, with a hundred authenticated cases, may have seemed to be faring better than Geneva proportionally, but the fact that almost all of these cases developed during the past week was quite alarming. Much harder hit was Madison, where Fannie lived. Though a good deal smaller than Geneva, Madison had close to seventy cases of flu—and three deaths (S&B, 18 October, pp. 1, 10; 19 October, p. 1).

[34] Though the fact had little impact on the autoless Perrins, Gasless Sundays were revoked as of this date. Washington officials estimated that at least a million barrels of fuel had been saved (S&B, 18 October, p. 1).

[35] Annie has said earlier (7 October) that the Hartners were moving to Cleveland, but they continue to crop up in her accounts.

Clearly the Perrins and their friends were not taking to heart Health Officer Adams's admonition of 18 October that "If people want to stamp this epidemic out soon, they must keep out of other people's houses" (p. 3; a misprint has been corrected). Though Geneva now had had a total of fifty-seven cases of Spanish influenza, people generally seemed to agree that the "slight epidemic here is abating" (FPT, 17 October, p. 1).

Sunday, 20 October[34]

Still raining[.] Raym went over to B[ernice]. M[ichel]s to dinner. Irene Wetter had dinner with us [and] spent the PM here[.] We all went over to Hartners a while in PM[.][35] Lettie played on their Piano. Hartners spent the evening here. We have been married 31 y[ea]rs today.

Monday, 21 October

Bright & clear this A.M. We done the washing. After work was done up Lettie went to Lows for supper. I picked [a] crate of tomatoes[.] Ray brought them up.

Berts arm is some better.[36] Heard from Henry today.[37]

Tuesday, 22 October

One beautiful day. I made chilli sauce & catsup.

Lettie helped with work. Bert & Raym worked at fodder & corn. Finished the corn job[.] In orchard every thing cleaned up. Viola Hanson died of Influenza today.[38]

[36] Annie refers to this problem only here.

[37] Annie might have noted also that a member of the family was named in that day's paper. In its continuing effort to press for sales of U.S. Liberty Bonds (Geneva's goal was a whopping $200,000), the *Free Press-Times* printed the names of those who had signed up to buy them in installments. The list for Monday includes, among others, the piano teacher Harriet Webster, from the village; the talented young neighbor Lyle Pruden; and that hard-working sixth-grade teacher "Lettis" Perrin (p. 3).

[38] Having been ill about ten days, Viola Hanson, of 50 Eastwood Street, died that morning (*S&B*, 23 October, p. 10). Survived by her husband and two small daughters (Viola herself was only about twenty-five), she probably was known to the Perrins through Lettie, and especially through their mutual connection with the Park Street Church of Christ. Quickly—though not so quickly as young Ross Maltbie, who was buried the same day he died—Viola was buried at Mt. Pleasant Cemetery, on the South Ridge, on the day following her death.

Wednesday, 23 October

In the AM I churned. Picked up a bu[shel] of nice apples.[39] Lettie ironed all the starched clothes. [In] PM baked bread.

Then went down and gathered our crop of cabbage in a half bu[shel] basket. Bert and Raym are husking over in s[ou]th lot.[40]

Got word from Henry he has the Flue[.][41]

Thursday, 24 October

A beautiful day. Bert & Raym hauled the corn in H.s corn crib.[42] Raym split Chunks.[43] Then B[ert] & R[aym]. sawed some wood. Roy [Andrews] came in for a few minutes [but] would not stay for dinner. Lettie finished ironing in P.M. I made 3 q[uar]ts of chow chow.[44] Got a few lines from Henry[.] He is some better[.]

[39] Such windfalls or "fallings" are likely to be fully ripe, but birds and bees often get at them, so Annie was lucky that hers were still "nice."

[40] Continuing to run his cornstalks-and-horse ad (this time appearing on p. 4), Bert now began to advertise also "For Sale —Good hard corn. $1.50 for 72 lbs. B. H. Perrin, Phone 723" (*FPT*, p. 2).

[41] On 19 October Henry wrote to Lettie that he had been in the Navy hospital for six days. "The skin," he reported, "is coming off of my hands & feet and my hair is falling out." Odd as it may seem, such symptoms may, indeed, be associated with acute viral illness.

For the week ending this same day, the Navy officially recorded 332 ashore deaths from influenza and pneumonia (Crosby, p. 58). As of 23 October, Ohio had some 200,000 cases of influenza (*FPT*, 23 October, p. 1). And locally, according to Mr. Adams's count, there had now been a total of 87 cases within Geneva village (*FPT*, 24 October, p. 1).

Nationally, the total number of deaths from flu and pneumonia between September 1918 and June 1919 climbed to approximately 675,000. Crosby compares this figure with the total of 423,000 battle deaths of U.S. Armed Forces personnel in World War I, World War II, and the Korean and Vietnamese conflicts (p. 207).

[42] Probably the Howards' crib.

[43] "Chunks" are fairly uniform pieces of firewood. One spoke, for example, of a "chunk wood stove" (*FPT*, 2 October 1916, p. 4).

[44] Chow-chow is a relish made of vegetables that have been chopped and pickled with mustard. Bert was especially fond of mustard.

Friday, 25 October

Rather cloudy today. No special work on hand to day. Got a card from Henry[.] He sat up a few min[utes] the day he wrote. [In] P.M. I mended quilts[.] Lettie darned stockings.[45] Mrs Seamans came over a while[.] Was knitting Charles a sweater. Bert & Raym husked corn.

[In the] Evening L[ettie]. went over to Irenes.[46]

Saturday, 26 October

Sat[urday] morning got up dragging my foot again.[47] Every one seems cross about it[.] Lettie done Saturday cleaning[.] Bert went to town. Got the groceries. Still more cases of Flu.[48] Raym got a load of coal. [In] P.M. Bert went to Ashtabula. Raym went to Ashta[bula] in evening to get a hair cut.[49] Henry is still on the gain.

[45] In her haste, Annie wrote "stickings." For all but the smallest holes, Lettie used a wooden darning "egg," over which she first stretched the stocking and then interwove her stitches until the thread filled in the opening. The trick was to do the job so that the mended place did not feel lumpy underfoot.

[46] The *Free Press-Times* for this date had a first-page story on the soldier brother of Raym's girlfriend, Bernice: "Homer Michel over the Top Three Times." Though Homer had seen considerable action in the war, the news at the moment was that he had been assigned the job of buying horses in France for the U.S. Army. (See also the notes to Annie's entries for 24 August and 18 December 1918.)

[47] A letter of 3 November from Henry to Lettie reinforces the impression that Annie's "again" here refers to at least one very serious prior episode.

[48] Geneva now had forty-six active cases (*FPT*, 26 October, p. 2).

[49] The minor luxury of an evening haircut ended that day. As the *Star and Beacon* explained on Friday, "groceries, meat markets, restaurants, barber shops and news stands are allowed to keep open tomorrow evening, October 26, until 9 p.m., but after tomorrow evening they must close at 6 p.m. with the other places of business." In other words, officials had established a simple hierarchy of closings. "Last night all pool rooms and shooting galleries were closed until further notice" (25 October, p. 1). See Fig. 86.

Flu cases in Ashtabula now totaled 319; deaths, 8 (*S&B*, 26 October, p. 1).

Fig. 86. When the movie theaters were closed either locally or throughout the state, a wide range of viewers was disappointed. The caption accompanying this drawing "By Temple" (published on 26 October in the *Cleveland Plain Dealer*, p. 8) is "Aintcha never goin t' have 'ny more pi'chers?" On the other hand, the drawing suggests that the downtime at least gave theater owners a chance to make some minor repairs.

"Aintcha never goin' t' have 'ny more pi'chers!"

Sunday, 27 October

Warm and windy[.] After work was done up Lettie went over to Irenes for the day. Roy A[ndrews]. was here to dinner[.] After dinner Raym & R[oy]. went over to Wetters.[50] Bert and I were here all P.M. and evening alone. Wind gets worse[.] Think it will rain[.] Mr & Mrs Miller from Ashta[bula] came for potatoes.[51] Had none dug. The end of a lonesome day[.]

[50] That is, to Irene's house, thus forming a young foursome.

[51] Possibly a reference to Elmer S. Miller, a retail grocer in Ashtabula, and his wife, Belle (1920 Census).

Monday, 28 October

Raining hard[,] a regular thundershower. A beautiful Rainbow in A.M. Cleared up in P.M. I mended quilts
[and] Lettie stamped and cut out a cuff & collar set.
Very pritty. Raym & Bert sorted corn. And got crates
ready for potatoes.[52]

In evening Mr Allen & Arthur came up and had 4
domino games with B[ert]. & R[aym].[53]

Tuesday, 29 October

Some cooler & the sun dips like more rain. Lettie
done up the house work. I started washing[.] We got
through about 11. A.M.[54] Then I got the dinner. Baked a
pie. Seamans & C.[55] helped dig potatoes but went
home to dinner. [In the] P.M. I sorted apples. Evening[,]
Bert went over to Spragues. Raym went Auto riding
with Bernace[.][56] Lettie imbroidered.[57] I sewed.

[52] The crates were for the
potatoes to be dug on Tuesday.
In dry weather, potatoes may be
left on the ground to dry for a
day or so, but they generally last
best if stored fairly promptly in
crates that are kept in a cool and
reasonably dry place such as the
Perrin cellar. A few such crates
appear in the background of
Figs. 11 and 100.

[53] Short notices in that day's
Free Press-Times (p. 1) and *Star
and Beacon* (p. 8) report that
Henry Perrin, now in Key West,
"finally succumbed to the influenza, after getting tired out working over hundreds of boys ill with
the disease." The journalist's word
"succumbed" is used loosely,
however, for Henry's own letter
is also said to have "stated that he
was getting along nicely."

[54] Because of the rain yesterday, the women were a little off
schedule.

[55] Probably Charles, the Seamanses' son.

[56] Though not, of course, in
the Perrin auto. In her haste,
Annie misspelled "Bernice."

[57] Probably on that cuff and
collar set (28 October).

Wednesday, 30 October

This morning looks rainy. Hope it dont rain as there are five in potato field ready for a good days work. Commenced to rain at noon [and] men went home. Bert went to town. I canned 16 q[uar]ts apples in P.M. Got a card from Henry[.] He is feeling some better.[58]

Thursday, 31 October

Cloudy today. We done up work. In P.M. Lettie went to town [and] stayed to supper at Lowe's[.] The girls [Grace and Lulu] came home with her. Stormed so they stayed all night[.] Sang some songs.[59] I ironed in P.M. Raym cleaned up cellar [and] I put canned fruit away.[60]

[58] In the village of Geneva there had now been a total of 113 cases of flu but, so far, only four deaths (*S&B*, 30 October, p. 6). Ashtabula, however, had had fourteen flu-related deaths (*S&B*, p. 1). Though the spread of the disease may have been slowing, the current number of sick people there was so great that the city was converting one of its buildings to a makeshift hospital (*S&B*, 29 October, p. 1).

[59] On a cold and rainy night the girls were likely to riffle through Lettie's collection of sheet music and sing any one of many songs—for instance, "Silver Bell" (Fig. 87).

[60] Annie takes no notice of Halloween (which was of no consequence) or, more surprisingly, of one of the main front-page headlines in the day's *Free Press-Times*: "Stories Such as These Are only Propaganda." The opening sentences of the story go thus:

> B. H. Perrin received a letter Tuesday from his son, Henry Perrin, at Key West, Fla., stating that he is convalescing from an attack of influenza.
>
> Several persons called up Mr. Perrin Tuesday to ask him whether the influenza had proven fatal with his son. If any such thing had happened, naturally Mr. Perrin would have been the first to have heard of it.
>
> This only goes to show how people take up with idle rumors and spread stories which are not true. Such actions,

whether intentional or not, are only part of the propaganda that the Germans delight in.

Probably the best one can say for such a skewed piece is that it is a fairly good sign of its time.

Fig. 87. Edward Madden, a prolific lyricist known for "By the Light of the Silvery Moon," "Moonlight Bay," and "Your Eyes Say No But Your Lips Say Yes," collaborated with Percy Wenrich to produce "Silver Bell." Though almost forgotten in later years (Cohen-Stratyner's guide omits it), this song is another one known well enough in the Perrin household to warrant Lettie's sewing-machine stitchery.

Friday, 1 November

Bert went to Cleveland this AM on 6 oclock car. [Lettie and] The [Lowe] girls got up at 8. [The two Lowes] walked home after breakfast[.] Lettie finished ironing in P.M.[61] Raymond picked up potatoes till noon[.][62] Then Milt.[63] came and helped in P.M. Bert got home about 12 oclock P.M. I commenced Letties sweater.[64]

[61] Though the flu seemed to be abating, the Geneva newspaper observes that local "School teachers are beginning to think there will be no school before Thanksgiving day" (*FPT*, 1 November, p. 1).

[62] Picking up potatoes is a particularly tiring form of stoop labor.

[63] Milton Austin.

[64] In her spare time this year Annie knit sweaters for each of her children.

Saturday, 2 November

We done up the general work. Lettie done Sat[urday] cleaning.

Raym sorted potatoes for Millers.[65]

In evening Raym went to town. I knit on sweater. Got a letter from Henry[.] He is on the gain. Sounds as if War will soon end.[66]

Sunday, 3 November

Quite pleasant[.]

Charlotte Chapman and Vere Smith were here to dinner in P.M.[67] The young folks took some pictures. Sang & played.[68] Harriet P[ruden] came over [and] was here to supper[.] V[ere]. stayed all night. Bert traded the old Grey off.[69] We had chicken dinner[.][70]

[65] A follow-up job relating to the entry for 27 October.

[66] Annie was right. The headline for the day's lead story in the Geneva paper reads "Allies Start Three Big Drives on Western Front." The main headline of Cleveland's *Plain Dealer* is "Vienna Revolts, Karl Flees; Americans Take 3,000 Huns." On 31 October the allies captured some 108,343 prisoners and 2,064 guns.

Though the main story in the *Star and Beacon* concerns waste and graft in a Dayton, Ohio, aircraft plant, a small item on the front page quotes an unidentified allied diplomat as saying that the time has come when the "Huns will Accept Any Kind of Terms."

[67] Concerning Charlotte, see the notes for 19 May and 1 December.

[68] Though of course there is no telling for sure, it is quite possible that the afternoon's all-girl chorus assayed Jacobs-Bond's "I Love You Truly," which was already associated with weddings. Lettie played the piano at least well enough to provide the music for the wedding of her "chum in High School and Sunday School," Lyda Lyman (Lettie to Myron William Randall, 25 September 1945).

Given the focus on France at the time, another reasonable choice for singing this afternoon might have been "When It's Apple Blossom Time in Normandie." See Figs. 88 and 89.

[69] Thus Bert disposed of another horse (cf. 27 April), probably the work horse he had been advertising lately.

[70] Henry, meanwhile, was by no means out of the woods yet. In a letter written to Lettie on this date he says that the doctors have told him he has "the Flu., malaria and pleural trouble"— for which they have prescribed iron, quinine, and strychine three times a day. Still plagued with fever, he has sold a pair of shoes in order to pay someone else to do his washing. Also making him feel bad is the fact that during his illness most of his old unit shipped out.

In the same letter he says wryly, "So you and I both were reported among the flu. victims, eh? We fooled 'em this time." At this point Lettie had not yet become ill.

Fig. 88. Published not only in the U.S. but also in Canada and England, "I Love You Truly" is one of a series of seven art songs by Carrie Jacobs-Bond. Though Lettie generally sang soprano, she for some reason purchased this time a version pitched "Low."

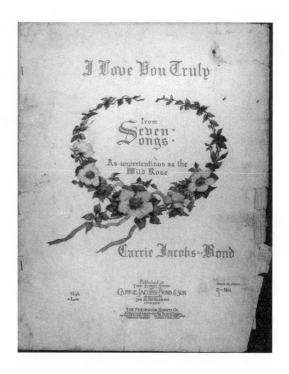

Fig. 89. Put forth by Jerome H. Remick and Co., "When It's Apple Blossom Time in Normandie" is a catchy song that was copyrighted back in 1912, well before the outbreak of war, and only minimally concerned with France. Lyrical though it is, Remick's own list of hits places it after "What D'ye Mean, Ye Lost Your Dog" and "Oh You Lovable Chile." On this copy Lettie signed her name hastily at the upper right of the white frame.

Monday, 4 November

Too stormy to wash. Raym did not feel well today. Bert went to town.

Lettie is learning to knit.[71] Vere went home on 3 oclock car.

Got a letter from Henry[.] He is sitting up.

Flu is still bad in town.

Tuesday, 5 November

Done a big washing today. Raym feels some better today. Did not hear from Henry today. Lettie is knitting on her sweater today.[72] This is Election day. Pa & Raym have gone down to vote[.][73]

[71] The fact is that Lettie never enjoyed or became proficient at either knitting or embroidery. In later years she faithfully mended her family's clothes so as to prolong their usefulness, but that was about as much sewing as she cared to do.

[72] Though Lettie was still not back to teaching, the *Free Press-Times* announced on this Tuesday that Sunday probably would see the lifting of the ban on church attendance and that "On Monday the Geneva village schools will open and the pool and billiard rooms will resume business. Dance halls may open next week too" (p. 3).

[73] Some political leaders were privately saying—in some cases, hoping—that everyone's preoccupation with military victories and an armistice might make voting seem less important. Ohioans trooped out, though, to express their stand on prohibition (see Fig. 90) as well as to cast a variety of other votes on a fully slated ticket. Particular attention was focused on the question of who was to be the next governor of Ohio, mainly because the race between James M. Cox (Democrat) and Frank B. Willis (Republican) promised to be close.

Women, of course, had no vote. In fact, the suffrage bill had been recently defeated in the U.S. Senate by a vote of 54 to 30. Presumably a two-thirds approval would be necessary if ever the resolution was to be handed on to the individual states for voting.

On the matter of suffrage, it turned out, Ohio was slow to see the handwriting on the wall. Unlike certain other states, Ohio refrained from granting women suffrage until passage of the Nineteenth Amendment in 1920.

Geneva, on the other hand, had had its own first equal suffrage meeting in the spring of 1912 (*FPT*, 17 May, p. 2), and that same fall the voters of Geneva favored giving women the vote (*FPT*, 4 September, p. 3). A couple of years later the *Free Press-Times* even attempted to launch a suffrage column by Mrs. Henry Hill (2 December 1914, p. 2).

The Ohio Saloon is Playing the Kaiser's Game

Fig. 90. The caption of this *Star and Beacon* cartoon of 17
October (p. 6), sponsored by the Ohio Dry Federation (J. A.
White, manager), argues that "If the Kaiser could he would
reach out his bloody hand and pat the man on the back who
is boosting the Hun game by voting wet." In other words,
readers should "Vote 'Yes' for Prohibition November 5th."

Wednesday, 6 November

Good & clear today[.] Raym & Seaman finished the
potatoes today. Neeley was here to dinner.[74]

Mrs Seaman came over in the evening. Raym got his
card today saying to be ready by the 15th[.][75] Got a card
from Henry[.] He is feeling better.

[74] "Neeley" may have been
Ford Neely, a farmer from
nearby Rock Creek (*Farm Journal Illustrated*, p. 144).

[75] On 10 October an article in
Cleveland's *Plain Dealer* headed
"Flu May Delay Draft" was one
of numerous sources stating that
"Ohio's local health boards have
been given authority by Provost
Marshal General Crowder to decide whether registrants will be
examined now to fill up the state's
quota of 4,000 men" (p. 2). In
Ashtabula County, the ban on
calls had been lifted.

Thursday, 7 November

A beautiful day. Lettie got house ready for the [War] Mothers meeting.[76] They came on 2 oclock car. 14 came[.] Had a pleasant time.[77] Also got word <u>War</u> is over.[78] Ohio went dry.[79] Bert went to Ashty in PM. [In] Evening Pa & Raym went to the Celebration in Geneva. Lettie & I stayed at home[, and] listened to the whistles.[80] The end of a pleasant day[.]

---

[76] Fig. 91 provides pictorial evidence of Lettie's determination when it came to house-cleaning.

[77] On 11 November, on the same front page that announces "War Ends" in huge type, a *Free Press-Times* item headed "War Mothers" refers also to Annie's hostessing—but gets her name wrong. It reads:

The War Mothers Club resumed its bi monthly gatherings at the home of Mrs. B. H. Price South Ridge on Thursday afternoon, November the seventh.

The meeting which was exceptionally well attended, was given over to a ceremonial celebration, apropos to the recent peace cable.

Attractive refreshments were served by the hostess, assisted by Mrs. Foster and Mrs. Starkey. . . .

At the time of this meeting, Mrs. Ray Foster had not yet heard that her son, 1st Lt. Neil J. Foster, an infantryman in Belgium, had been wounded in the leg, foot, and shoulder by enemy machine gun fire (*FPT*, 2 December, p. 1; 11 January 1919, p. 2).

Furthermore, Mrs. Homer Starkey had yet to learn that one of her sons, Ben E. Starkey, who was serving in the Marine Corps, had been hit in the mouth by a machine gun bullet while fighting in the Argonne (*FPT*, 6 December, p. 3). Mrs. Starkey also had three other sons in the service: Herbert (like Ben, a Marine), Harold (136th Field Artillery), and Floyd (Hospital Corps) (*FPT*, 31 March 1919, p. 1).

[78] All America was electrified by the fact that the Germans had radioed to Marshal Foch the names of their armistice envoys (7 November). Besides the outsized headline in the *Star and*

Beacon (a bold "Germany Surrenders"), the lead article proclaimed that "The war is over. Germany and the Allies signed the armistice at 11 a.m. today, and hostilities stopped three hours later."

Actually, Field Marshal Haig had ordered that on 8 November the 4th, 3rd, and 1st Armies were to continue their present operations, and the 5th and 2d armies were on 11 November supposed to drive the enemy back over the river Dencre (Gray, 2:242).

All across the nation the premature announcement of Germany's surrender triggered strong and emotional public reaction. In the village of Geneva, according to the *Free Press-Times*,

The most appropriate of all was the little ceremonial conducted under the service flag on the square by the War Mother's Club, which arrived on the 5 o'clock car from a meeting at the Perrin home in the south Ridge. Underneath the flag they sang "Praise God, From Whom All Blessings Flow" and repeated the Lord's Prayer.

[79] For weeks Geneva's *Free Press-Times* and Ashtabula's *Star and Beacon* had been championing prohibition in stories, cartoons, and ads. Among the more

Fig. 91. Dressed for some serious housecleaning, Lettie poses here on the back porch with a broom. She not only wears a dust hat and a cotton work-dress but also has taken the extra precaution today of donning rubber gloves. Moreover, judging from the rolled rugs to the right, some of the more portable floor coverings of the household have been carried outside for special attention.

interesting of the latter was one sponsored by the Ashtabula County Dry Federation, which quoted General John J. Pershing, Commander in Chief of the American Expeditionary Forces:

> Banish the entire liquor indus-
> try from the United States,
> close every saloon, every brew-
> ery, suppress drinking by severe
> punishment to the drinker and
> if necessary, death to the sellers
> or makers, or both, as traitors,
> and the nation will suddenly
> find itself amazed at its effi-
> ciency and startled at the in-
> crease of its labor supply. (4
> November, p. 4)

On 6 November the same paper observed that "Geneva village and township not only rolled up a huge dry majority, but also carried the Republican ticket better than two to one" (p. 12). Both houses of the U.S. Congress were won by the Republicans—bad news for President Wilson. Closer to home, however, the Democrat Cox narrowly won the governorship over Willis, the Republican.

[80] According to the *Free Press-Times* of 8 November, "Promptly at 7 o'clock, the time announced for the evening celebration, the whistles of the Champion Hardware Co. and the American Fork and Hoe Co. began to blow, and shortly afterward the church and school bells rang. Again at 7:30 the whistles and bells started another prolonged chorus" (p. 1). On this occasion, too, Annie's friends and acquaintances among the War Mothers were much in evidence: "The I.O.O.F. Band, War Mothers Club, part of the Martial band, Boy Scouts, Italian citizens, together with Geneva's stand of colors, carried by Victor Wright and Boy Scouts, started in East Main street, opposite the I.O.O.F. hall, and paraded the business portions of Main and Broadway several times, like a rolling snowball, gathering size as it advanced" (p. 1).

Friday, 8 November

This A.M. we hear War is not over. So all dissapointed. I hope it will soon end.

Lettie ironed today, while I hemmed her brown dress and done some fixing to it. Bert and Raym husked corn.

Did not hear from Henry.[81] Raym got his notice to appear at Jefferson next Thursday.[82]

Saturday, 9 November

Cloudy today. We done up the work [and] then I finished the ironing. Got dinner[.] Lettie & I took 2 oclock car to Ashty. Came home on the 5. Raym was gone. Pa was peeved[.] Hartners spent the evening here[.] Mrs H[artner]. told our fortunes.[83]

Got a card from Henry.

Sunday, 10 November

Colder but pleasant. Fannie[,] Walter and Howard[84] were here to dinner. [In] P.M. Seymours came up[, and] also Lou & Edna Holt.[85] In the evening we went over to Hartners.

[81] This Friday, however, was Henry's final day in Key West. Soon he would be writing from St. Helena Station, Berkeley, Virginia. Equally important, his new "rate" went into effect that day. He was now a Pharmacist's Mate, 3rd Class, and proudly anticipating wearing a crow and chevron. "You know I'm a non-com. now so rate a shirt" (letters to Lettie of 3, 8, and 23 November).

[82] Thursday was one day earlier than noted previously.

[83] How Mrs. Hartner happened to acquire this particular parlor skill is probably beyond anyone's saying. Women of the day did occasionally play at the game, however. At a Halloween wedding shower in Geneva in 1912, for instance, Miss Mildred Spring, dressed "as a witch, told fortunes" (*FPT*, 2 November, p. 2). Indeed, real gypsies had come through Geneva in this autumn of 1918, "endeavoring to tell fortunes and relieve the citizens of spare pieces of silver" (*FPT*, 16 September, p. 2). Precedents aside, in any case, Mrs. Hartner displayed other and clear indications of being a many-talented woman (see notes to entry for 15 August).

[84] Howard W. Keyse (27 December 1891–3 April 1947) was the oldest son of Fannie and Walter.

[85] This is Annie's last reference to the Seymours. On 17 February of the new year, after an illness of only one week, forty-eight-year-old Fred Seymour died of pneumonia at his home in Ashtabula

(*S&B*, 17 February 1919, p. 3; *FPT*, 18 February, p. 1).

Monday, 11 November

Good news. <u>War is over</u>.[86] They are celebrating today.[87] All the stores closed. Bert[,] Lettie & Raym went to town. I stayed at home. No mail but [news]papers today. L[ettie] did not come home tonight. Rather lonesome day.

Satan Dances on Coffin of Kaiser in Holiday Parade

SATAN ORATES ON KAISER'S COFFIN

Fig. 92. The caption below this newspaper photograph from Cleveland reads "Satan Orates on Kaiser's Coffin." Below, in smaller print, is a further description: "One of the trucks in an impromptu parade Monday carried an antiquated coffin bearing the announcement 'William Hohenzollern's remains lie within.' On top of the coffin an impersonator of Lucifer danced with glee that was hardly simulated" (*Cleveland Plain Dealer*, 13 November, p. 12).

[86] Annie's underlined words are the same as those of the huge headline in the day's *Star and Beacon*. The Armistice had at last really been signed in the Compiègne Forest at 5:05 A.M. and had come into force at 11:00 A.M., French time. The Germans were to evacuate France and the Low Countries in fourteen days (Gray, 2:246–47).

[87] "Geneva simply tore off the lid from the cup of joy Monday morning" (*FPT*, 12 November, p. 1). Already "by 9 o'clock it had gained full headway." Tin pans and horns made a din. B. M. Murphy beat his bass drum. Some high school boys "hitched up a goat" and labeled it "The Kaiser's goat." "Harry Randall rode a sorrel colored mule." And Barnard's truck, which back in March had carried trunks for the Perrins, now carried a coffin-like box bearing the sign "the Kaisers last ride" (cf. Fig. 92). "Oh, yes," the article concludes, "it was a big day for Geneva."

In Ashtabula, thousands marched that night in a victory parade. The Kaiser was hanged in effigy on many floats, and "Miss Eva Reebel, representing the Goddess of Liberty," headed a parade, her float being driven by M. E. Miller dressed as Uncle Sam (*S&B*, 12 November, p. 6).

Tuesday, 12 November

War over.[88] The Hay bailers came today[.] There were 7 men here to dinner. Raym took Mr Bro[w]ns Auto[.] Got things down town for me.[89] Got card from Henry today. He left Key West for Norfolk V[irgini]a–.[90] Raym went to Ashta[bula] for the men[.][91]

Fig. 93. This drawing from Cleveland's *Plain Dealer* of 12 November (p. 12) expresses the great outburst of joy felt everywhere at the dawning of peace. It is captioned simply "Victory!"

[88] The *Cleveland Plain Dealer* headline reads "Surrender of Germany Is Complete; Joy Fills Land." One story begins: "A raving, hysterical mob, members hugging and kissing each other, shouting and laughing, singing and crying, swept convention and the city's normal activities aside from dawn till midnight yesterday in the wildest, noisiest celebration the city has ever seen" (p. 1).

In Geneva, moreover, citizens who had been disappointed by the lack of an evening demonstration on Monday ("as in other towns") mounted a second celebration (*FPT*, 13 November, p. 1). Leading this Tuesday parade were the Allied colors and the I.O.O.F. band, and prominent once again were the War Mothers, this time riding a float and wearing their service stars. A particular "hit" was the devil himself (played by William LaMarsh, a local baker and former actor, at one time associated with the Minnelli Brothers traveling show), "in a red suit mounted on a lame mule." One of his devilish messages, delivered with the aid of a megaphone, was "Don't send the kaiser to hell I don't want him," and another concerned "two benefit dances to help the War Mother's Club raise funds for a celebration for the boys whenever they come back home."

[89] Annie needed extra groceries for the next day or so.

[90] In a letter to Lettie of 6 November Henry told the family that he might be leaving soon for Norfolk to "stand by for overseas duty." His last day in Key West proved to be 8 November. Now for a while his letters would be dated from St. Helena Station, Norfolk.

[91] So much else was going on that it is little wonder Annie neglected to record that the Geneva village schools reopened on this

Wednesday, 13 November

Hay bailers still here[.] 10 men to dinner today. [The bailer] Keep[s] breaking down[.] Raym got a phone message[.] They do not want him to answer his <u>call</u>.[92]

No washing done yet. Henry thinks he will go over seas.

Mrs Hartner is no better[.][93]

Thursday, 14 November

Bailers Here yet[.] Lettie called up to have Raym come and get her. Dr Childs says it is Flu.[94] [I] Had 9 men to dinner.[95]

Feel about tired out.

Was up with Lettie[.] Gave her medicine every h[ou]r.

Tuesday after a five-week hiatus occasioned by the flu. To make up for lost time, Lettie had to begin teaching fifteen minutes earlier each morning and then try to hold her pupils' attention fifteen minutes later in the afternoon. In addition, fifteen minutes were clipped off everyone's "nooning" (*FPT*, 13 November, p. 2).

[92] As recently as 8 November Raym had been instructed to appear on 14 November. On 12 November, however, America's draft boards were told to cancel "all army calls" (*S&B*, p. 1).

[93] Too busy to do even the weekly wash, Annie took no notice of the dance sponsored that night on behalf of the War Mothers. Held in Gray's Hall and managed by the Hustler's Club (with music by Harley's Four Piece Orchestra), the event attracted "Close to 200 people, old and young" (*FPT*, 16 November, p. 3).

[94] Less than a month before, Dr. Childs himself had been "very ill with pneumonia" (*FPT*, 17 October, p. 2). He was first "able to sit up at the breakfast table" on 20 October (*FPT*, 21 October, p. 2).

More recently, in an article headed "Old Man Flu Is in Full Retreat," the Geneva paper reported that there were a mere nine cases of flu in the village—and seven of them were in one household (*FPT*, 9 November, p. 2). On 13 November, nevertheless, in a story date-lined Columbus, Ohio, the *Star and Beacon* reported that "state officials strongly advise extreme caution in lifting bans" (p. 3).

[95] Judging from the figures of these last three days (seven, ten, nine), the number of noontime diners was not exactly predictable.

Friday, 15 November

Card put on house today.[96] I done a big washing.

Bert & Raym husked corn. Lettie & Raym got cards from Henry. Slocums brought out meat & groceries for us.[97] Had lots of phone calls today inquireing for Lettie.

Saturday, 16 November

Looks stormy. Lettie rested pretty good. B[ert] & R[aym] are still working at corn[.] Seaman is helping. Got two letters from Henry today[.] He is going on a big ship.[98] Expected to start the day he wrote[.] Am too tired to stand up.[99]

Sunday, 17 November

Lettie seems better today. It is raining. A pretty gloomy Sunday. Raym went to Ashta[bula] in the evening. Saw a show.[100] In evening Bert and I wrote to Aylards and to Henry. Dont have to stay up tonight[.][101]

[96] A quarantine card had to be displayed to indicate that there was a case of flu within. Health Officer Charles Adams held the ten-dollar-a-day job of first quarantining houses and then fumigating them when the quarantine was lifted (*FPT*, 5 November, p. 1). Previously kept very busy during the height of the flu outbreak (he had to have one assistant for fourteen days and another for eight), Mr. Adams could now attend to his duties without help.

[97] Opinions varied as to the obligations of a quarantined family, but it was just as well that the Perrins did not go shopping for themselves.

[98] In about a month and a half, Henry sailed for France on the S.S. *Louisiana*.

[99] Annie's concerns were far removed from the evening's second War Mothers' dance, this one at Gregory's Hall. The *Free Press-Times* of 20 November reported on its front page, however, that Mrs. Pancost "donated the piano music and the use of the hall and August Alberts donated the cornet music. There was also violin music and trap drum." The admission fee was 40¢ per couple, and the War Mothers cleared over $50.

[100] Whether Raym was breaking the quarantine is hard to say. Dr. Zalmon O. Sherwood, who in December replaced Mr. Adams as local Health Officer, explained then that "The reason for putting cards on the house [was] to keep out persons who might enter and get near to a patient" (*FPT*, 12 December, p. 2). Family members who were well did not need to be quarantined.

Over in Ashtabula, meanwhile, after being closed for four weeks on account of the flu, the movie houses had been allowed to re-open on Monday, 11 November. Hence Raym could take in a show

there this evening. Later this same month, however, Ashtabula suffered another major flare-up of the disease: on 29–30 November alone, ninety-six new cases in the city (*S&B*, 30 November, p. 1).

[101] That is, Annie did not need to look after Lettie.

Monday, 18 November

Was too tired to wash today[.] Knit on L[ettie]'s sweater what time I got. Lettie's feaver is gone. Raym hauled manure & sorted potatoes.[102]

102 On this Monday, another of Bert's ads began to appear in the *Free Press-Times*: "For Sale—Corn stalks, ear corn, and potatoes" (p. 3).

Tuesday, 19 November

Bert went to Ashta[bula] and got shaved today. I have Neuralgia[.] Dr left medicine for it.[103] Got a few lines from Henry. He is still at Norfok V[irgini]a–. Lettie sat up one h[ou]r today.

[Corn] Too wet to husk.

103 Almost every day for about a week, Annie mentions her pain.

Wednesday, 20 November

Lettie had a good night. Is feeling better. Dressed and sat up nearly all day. Raym is slicking up hen park & [our] cellar. Sorting potatoes. Got a letter from Henry[.] Still in V[irgini]a–. Dr made his last call [on Lettie] today.

Thursday, 21 November

Sleet & rain. Lettie sat up all day[.] Raym sorted potatoes [and] got them nearly all done. Slicked the basement up fine. My face is worse today. Lettie got a letter from Henry. Raym went to town[.] Got boots and trousers[.][104]

[104] Annie does not bother to say that her War Mothers Club met in the village at 203 West Main, the home of Mrs. James Connell, mother of James Connell, Jr. (*FPT*, 20 November, p. 3).

Friday, 22 November

Rain & sleet and growing colder.

Raym husked corn over to Browns this A.M[.] [In the] P.M. Bert & Raym got potatoes in the cellar. Dr Childs came and gave me something to ease my face. Lettie is cleaning up.[105] Dr says it is nerves of my face.

[105] In other words, Lettie's bout with flu lasted about eight days.

Saturday, 23 November

Snowing some[.] Raym husked over to Browns. Pa went to town. Lettie is cleaning out the pantry. I done Sat[urday] sweeping at a fashion.[106] Mrs Hartner is better. Letters from Henry today.

Lettie and I both all in.

[106] That is, Annie did only a so-so job.

Sunday, 24 November

Raining.

Every thing very quiet[.] Raym went over to B[er-nice]'s[.] No one came[.] Has been a long lonesome day. My face still aches [and] eye swollen badly. Got a Sunday Plain Dealer[.][107] Saw Some Dover folks pictures in it[.][108] Lettie is much better[.]

Monday, 25 November

Colder today[.]

Bert[,] Raym & Seaman butchered one of our pigs.[109] Dressed 234^{lbs}. My face is worse. Seems I cant stand it. Fannie called up today. Are not going to have our [Elliott family] Reunion this year. Too much sadness I guess.

[107] Buying a copy of Cleveland's major newspaper was worth mentioning because the Perrins generally read only the local papers.

[108] Having been born and raised in Dover, Annie was interested to see an article featuring it in *The Sunday Magazine:* "Cuyahoga Men Show How Scientific Farming Pays" (p. 4). The Cuyahoga County Farm Bureau had "conducted spraying demonstrations, particularly in the Dover section and introduced improved spraying machinery." The point of the article (by Frank C. Dean of Ohio State University) is that both savings and improvement were now apparent in a large variety of crops.

[109] Apparently one of the pigs purchased last spring (29 April). Now that the season had turned cold, much of the meat could be cut up in sections and hung in an unheated building for ongoing table use. The bacon and ham were salted and smoked, however, the pig's feet were pickled in salt brine, and some cuts were made into sausages (Raymond Perrin, Jr., 28 August 1997). The fat (or at least some of it) was rendered (melted so as to be useful for cooking) as of 27 November, and the smoking was completed by 21 December.

Tuesday, 26 November

My face is still bad. I got up as usual this A.M. Turned dizzy [and] fell down[.] Bruised my hip pretty bad. Dr Childs came[.] Said I should not sit up any. Bert took care of me[.] Raym got meals and done the work.

Lettie stayed down to [Grace and Lulu] Lowes all night.[110]

[110] Apparently Lettie had now resumed teaching.

Wednesday, 27 November

Raym husked corn over to Browns today. I have crawled around. Tried out some lard.[111] Got a letter from Henry[.] He is still in Norfolk V[irgini]a.

Dr came this A M[.] Said I must not try my eyes any.

[111] Annie's use of the verb "try" here is ambiguous. Thinking of the recently butchered pig, she may have written "tried" to mean either "To extract . . . from . . . fat by heat; to melt down; to render" (*OED*, "try," 4.a) or simply "to test" (*OED*, "try," 5.d) lard that already had been rendered. Either reading is reasonable, though the first seems more likely in view of both Annie's shaky condition on 26 and 27 November and her entry of 29 November regarding further "trying."

[112] A couple of days earlier Henry asked, "What are you going to do Thanksgiving day? Have a big feed and a good time I suppose" (letter to Lettie, 12 November). See Fig. 94.

Thursday, 28 November

Thanksgiving day.[112] Have much to be thankful for but every one seems to be peeved.

Had a good dinner. Raym went away. Lettie read[.] Was lonesome all day. I called on Mrs Hartner[.] She is better. [In the] Evening Bert and I played dominoes [and] Lettie read. Not a very cheerful day.

Fig. 94. This drawing suggests a medley of memories of home such as Thanksgiving or Christmas might be expected to arouse in the mind of a serviceman like Henry (*S&B*, 4 April 1919, p. 1).

Friday, 29 November

Today I washed out a few pieces[.] Rained so hard Raym took them in[.] I dried them around the stove. Bert & Raym put up 16 bu[shels] of potatoes. Lettie got a letter from Henry. I tried out the lard and salted the meat.

Saturday, 30 November

+

Lettie did the Sat[urday] work to the kitchen[.] I made pies [and] done the work. [In the] P.M. ironed what I washed Friday. Raym took potatoes to town [and] brought home coal[.] Bert stayed down until 5 oclock [and] brought home groceries[. In the] Evening R[aym] went to town.

Sunday, 1 December

Pleasant outside[.] Lettie went to church[.] I done up work [and] got the dinner. After dinner Raym went away. Bert cleaned up the cellar.

Charlotte Chapman & Mr Honnaman were here to supper.[113] L[ettie] & I called on Mrs Hartner[.]

[113] Charlotte, though currently working in Cleveland, was essentially a Genevan, the daughter of Hattie Chapman of nearby Myers Road, just north of the railroad tracks. In fact, she worked for a while in the office of Geneva's *Free Press-Times* (*FPT,* 3 March 1919, p. 2). Her friend Mr. Edward (later always "Ed") J. Hanneman, who was originally from Austinburg, had been away in military service since September 1917. Sent to France in June 1918, he was now back in the U.S., and the couple was able to marry in early 1919. For a while they lived in Ashtabula because Ed had a job there with the New York Central Railroad (*FPT,* 3 March, p. 2). Eventually, however, they returned to Geneva and settled on Myers Road. Many years later (1944), a friend to the end, Ed served as one of Bert's pallbearers.

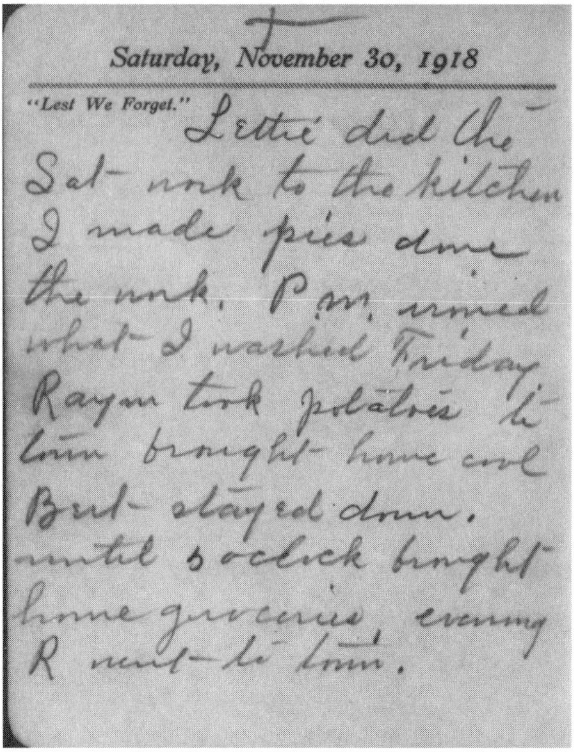

Fig. 95. Annie's diary, 30 November and 1 December. Actual size.

Monday, 2 December

Monday[.] I done a two weeks washing[.] The wind blew a perfect gale all day. I got up at 5. A.M[.] Bert took 6 oclock car for Cleveland. Came home on 5 oclock car. Raym helped me hang out some of the clothes. Took one basket in wet as I did not want to leave them out over night.

Sunday, December 1, 1918

"Lest We Forget."

Pleasant - outside Lettie went - to church I done up work got - the dinner. after dinner Rayme went - away. Bert cleaned up the cellar. Charlotte Chapman + Mr. Honnaman were here to supper. L + I called on Mrs Harbin

Tuesday, 3 December

[114] As of 2 December the card system for rationing sugar was ordered stopped, effective 1 December. Nevertheless, people were asked to limit themselves reasonably and voluntarily (*S&B*, 2 December, p. 3).

[115] Without electricity, Annie found it hard to do close work on a dark winter day. The family's nickel-plated kerosene Rayo burned brighter than most lamps, but prolonged detailed work with it was still difficult. See Fig. 96.

Today is quite wintery. I got 7 lbs sugar today so now I can bake[.][114] Raym is down town today. Lettie stayed to Lowes all night. I ripped trimming off of L[ettie']s green dress[.] Got dark so early[,] did not do much.[115]

RAYO
LAMPS *and* LANTERNS

Scientific investigation has shown that the light of a good kerosene lamp is the softest and least tiring of any light. The Rayo is the best oil lamp made. The Rayo is a low priced lamp, but you cannot get better light at any price. Can be lighted without removing chimney or shade. Easy to clean and rewick.

The Rayo Lantern assures you a steady, flickerless light in the stormiest weather. Solidly built and neat in appearance, it combines durability with real efficiency.

RAYOLIGHT OIL
is the best oil for lamp or lantern.

THE STANDARD OIL CO.
(OHIO)

Rayo

Lamps and Lanterns

Fig. 96. Depicted at the left here is a "low priced" but efficient Rayo lamp like Annie's. The major secret of its superiority over other lamps of the day is that it has a circular wick and therefore provides a greater surface for the flame (*S&B*, 3 January 1917, p. 7).

Wednesday, 4 December

Raym has made up his mind to go to Warren and get work.[116] I wish things were different here.[117] Lettie came home tired out. Bert went to town[.] I was here alone.[118] Got a letter from Henry[.] He is still in Norfolk V[irgini]a.

[116] Warren, Ohio, is about forty-five miles south (and a bit east) of Geneva—in 1918, a ride on the Interurban of two hours and forty-five minutes.

[117] At least in part, Annie's comment is a guarded reference to father-son difficulties. See her next entry.

[118] A world or so away from the Perrin farm, the local War Mothers had planned for this date a special meeting to entertain their husbands, the War Fathers, at the Prospect Street

home of Captain and Mrs. B. C. Hodges (*FPT*, 25 November, p. 1). The meeting was canceled, however, because belated word had just come of the death on 30 September of Private George H. Call of the 145th Machine Gun Company. The first Genevan to fall in action in France (*FPT*, 2 December, p. 3), Call would have been twenty-four in March.

Thursday, 5 December

Today I tried to fix L[ettie']–s dress but can not get along with it.

Raym is down town again. Pa feels peeved at him being out every night. Lettie did not come home tonight. R[aym] did not feel well this evening [and] went to bed early[.] Sister S[arah] sent a card[.] She was operated on last Sat[urday.]

Friday, 6 December

This A.M. I baked pies and a fruit cake[. In the] P.M. I ironed until 5 oclock. Raym has been down town all day. Came home to supper[,] then went over to see B[ernice]–. I helped Lettie get ready to go to Cleveland[.][119]

Bert spent evening at Slocums. My B.H. order came today[.][120]

[119] In a letter to Lettie of 12 December, Henry says he "Would like to have been with you and Irene on your lark."

[120] A puzzling entry, unless Annie is using here a transparent, Christmassy reference to Bert, who was often known as "B. H. Perrin."

Saturday, 7 December

I got up at 5. A M[.] Got Lettie off for Cleveland[.][121] It was terrible windy.

[In the] P.M. Raym went over to help Seamans butcher his pig[.] Bert has head ache today. I done Sat[urday] work but felt all in all day[.] It is warmer again. Raym went to town tonight[.] I got a nice long letter from Henry.

[121] The village newspaper reported on Tuesday, 10 December, that "The Misses Lettie Perrin and Irene Wetter have been guests of Miss Perrin's uncle F. W. Perrin of Cleveland" (p. 3). Though Henry in a letter of 18 December refers to the trip as a "spree," it was not a long one, for Annie says on 10 December that both Irene and her mother have come visiting at the Perrin farm that evening.

Sunday, 8 December

Got up late this A.M. It has been a beautiful day[,] 50° in the shade at noon. We had breakfast about 9 oclock[.] Poached eggs[,] toast[,] coffee & [pan]cakes[.] Then at 10 I got Raym a lunch[.][122] He left on 11 oclock car for Warren O[hio]. Expects to get work. Bert and I were alone to dinner. Pretty lonesome day.[123]

[122] As Raym prepared to go seek his fortune, Annie went all out to make sure he was well fed.

[123] All three of Annie's children were now gone: Henry in Norfolk, Lettie in Cleveland, and Raymond in Warren.

Monday, 9 December

Warmer and bright. Got up [and] done up work. Bert said lets go up to Fannies[.] SO went [and] found Walter & Fannie washing. They seemed pleased to have us come[.] B[ert] & W[alter] got a rabbit[.][124] We brought it home[.] Got home 5. PM [and] found the cow sick.[125] Had a letter from Sarah.

[124] If the shooter had a license, the men were on the sunny side of the law: the rabbit season opened on 14 November and extended to 1 January 1919 (*S&B*, 14 November, p. 5; see Fig. 97).

[125] Annie's wording suggests that the Perrins still had only a single cow. Both previously and later on, they had a good many more.

Fig. 97. This drawing of Uncle Si Sureshot appeared on the front page of Ashtabula's *Star and Beacon* on 22 October, some while before the rabbit season opened on 14 November. Uncle Si is supposed to be saying, "That fool rabbit's got 'bout as much chance of reachin' that bresh pile alive as th' Kaiser has of winnin' th' war!" It turns out that possible parallels between hunters at home and hunters abroad provided many folks with food for thought.

Tuesday, 10 December

Today I done a big washing.[126]

Bert is not feeling well. Tom Clark came back to day. Raym stayed down there[.][127] No mail from Henry today. Mrs Wetter and Irene were here this evening.

[126] Bert's sudden suggestion to go visiting the day before threw Annie a little off her accustomed Monday work schedule. Fannie, however, whom Walter had been helping, may have been able to complete the Keyse family's laundry more or less at its usual time.

[127] That is, Tom and Raym, two good friends, had both been down in Warren.

Wednesday, 11 December

Cloudy[,] rainy & dreary. Got a long letter from Henry. Also letter & card from Raym[.] Card from Sister Lettie.[128] I ironed all PM. [In the] AM I done up work [and] baked sugar cookies[.] Lettie staid with Grace L[owe] tonight so Bert and I are alone.

Fig. 98. Annie's sister Lettie and her husband, Newton (Uncle "Newt") Bentley. The picture probably was taken when the Perrins visited Michigan in 1916.

[128] Annie named her daughter after this sister, Lettie Louisa Bentley, the wife of Newton Alfred Bentley (Fig. 98).

Having spent almost all of her married life—about forty years—on a farm near Midland, Michigan, Lettie moved to Detroit fairly soon after Newt's death in June, 1922. Newt had had his fatal disease, cirrhosis, for a long while, but when the end came, he had been confined at home for only about a week (*Midland Republican*, 29 June 1922, p. 1; *Midland Sun*, 29 June 1922, p. 1).

Less than a full three years later, Lettie's and Newt's thirty-five-year-old son, Alfred, a prominent Mt. Haley farmer (and husband and father) shot himself in the right temple with a .32 caliber pistol (*Midland Republican*, 1 January 1925, p. 1; *Midland Sun*, 1 January 1925, p. 1). In the news items relating details of the tragedy, Lettie is already said to be living in Detroit.

As Lettie grew older, moving to Detroit probably seemed advisable partly because three of her daughters (Mabel, Virginia, and Frances) had homes there. Settling down may have proved problematic, however. Even before Annie's death in 1938, Lettie had at least three different Detroit addresses. When she died at the age of eighty-five in 1943, nevertheless, Lettie Bentley had survived her husband by over twenty years (*Midland Daily News*, 4 June 1943, p. 5; 5 June 1943, p. 1).

Thursday, 12 December

Rainy & cooler[.]

I done up work[,] then ironed. Flu cases are increasing in Geneva.[129] Mr Brown just brought children home[.] Said schools have closed again.[130] Mrs Penny came in. Rode down town with Bert.

Bert[,] Lettie and I spent the evening at Allens. They seemed pleased to have us come.

Friday, 13 December

Dark & dreary. We got up late. I done up kitchen work.

[In the] P.M. I finished ironing what I had folded. Too dark to iron starched clothes.[131] Got a letter from Henry. He seems dissatisfied.

[129] As of the preceding Monday there were thought to be forty-eight cases in Geneva—workers at The American Fork and Hoe shop being hit especially hard (S&B, 9 December, p. 7).

Despite the heavy work load of the village health officer, Charles Adams (who personally had to carry some of the patients in their homes and otherwise put himself at risk), the Village Council recently offered to pay him only two dollars a day for the period from 6 to 31 December—a far smaller amount than they paid during the previous outbreak (FPT, 10 December, p. 2; cf. note to 15 November). Adams declined the offer and as of the evening of 11 December a new health officer, Dr. Zalmon O. Sherwood (formerly a lieutenant in the Medical Corps), was on the job (pay: $200 for 11 December 1918 to 31 December 1919). Whether or not Adams was treated fairly, Dr. Sherwood, a 1911 graduate of the Medical Department of Western Reserve University, was "considered one of the best physicians and surgeons in the county" (Tom Steman, Case-Western Reserve University Archives; FPT, 8 July 1914, p. 2). With a professional office at 40 West Main, he made an appropriate replacement.

[130] Dr. Sherwood's first action was to close the village schools (FPT, 12 December, p. 2). As best he could estimate, there were currently at least seventy cases of flu in the village (FPT, 13 December, p. 2). Soon, in fact, the town would find itself considering renting the former Cowden Hotel on Depot Street so as to convert it to a temporary hospital, supplementing the newly remodeled

facility on South Broadway (14 December, p. 5).

The schools did not reopen until January of 1919.

[131] Another reminder that the house lacked electricity (see Fig. 99). In fact, there was no electricity in this section of the South Ridge until 1927, when Raym mobilized the neighbors. According to a receipt for The South Ridge Electric Club from The Illuminating Company of Painesville, $775 was the cost of fifty poles and fifty sections of wire on Myers Road and the South Ridge road—mainly on the latter, extending 535 feet eastward of Myers Road and 4,815 feet westward (4 October 1927).

Fig. 99. This advertisement from the *Star and Beacon* specifies some of the conveniences—electric washers, flatirons, vacuum cleaners—that were denied a housewife without access to electricity (13 December, p. 9). Other ads of the day picture other groups of newfangled electric items, including fans and—most frequently of all—lamps.

Saturday, 14 December

Still raining. Lettie done Sat[urday] work to kitchen. I baked bread and fussed around.

Grace Lowe came up on 8 oclock car[. She was here in the] P.M. [and] stayed all night with Lettie[.] Bert and I played six games dominoes[.] He beat four of the six.[132]

Sunday, 15 December

Bright and cooler. Lulu L[owe]. came up to dinner[.] Also Vere. So the three girls were here all day with Lettie[.] Had chicken dinner[.] Bert went over to Slocums [and] bought 12 Ancona hens.[133] Vere stayed all night[.] [The Lowe] Girls left on 10 oclock car.

Monday, 16 December

Brighter today. We done up morning work. Then got dinner[.] After dinner I went to Geneva with Bert[.]

Got a little xmas[.][134] Met Lulu [Lowe] down there. Also got my first glasses[.] They were $4⁰⁰[.][135]

[132] On this Saturday Bert began to run a new ad in the *Free Press-Times*: "For Sale— Timothy or clover hay by the bale or ton. Corn $1.50 for 72 lbs., Potatoes $1.50 a bu." (p. 4).

[133] The hardiness, good laying habits, and black plumage with white tips of Anconas make these attractive chickens. At the time it was even claimed by some that Anconas "hatch the largest per cent of all breeds." Imported from Europe fairly recently, at any rate, they had rapidly "gained much prestige" in the U.S. (*FPT*, 1 March 1912, p. 3).

[134] That is, Annie did a little Christmas shopping.

[135] Though the *Free Press-Times* for this date reports that the number of Spanish influenza cases was peaking a second time (there were now over a hundred cases in the village [p. 3]), Annie apparently had no trouble in shopping for an off-the-counter pair of glasses.

Tuesday, 17 December

Windy and not very bright. We done a big washing. Most of the clothes dried. Got a letter from Henry[.] He expects to sail soon.[136] Raym is still in Warren.[137] Got a card from Sister Lettie. One year ago today we left for Florida[.] Today the thermo[meter] is 50°.

Wednesday, 18 December

Today is pleasant[.] We did up house work. After dinner Lettie went to town to do xmas shopping.[138] Grace [Lowe] invited her to stay all night with her. Bert and I were alone.

Got a letter from Henry saying that he would sail the 24th for France[.][139]

[136] As always, Annie had more information than she recorded. Writing from temporary quarters on the U.S.S. *Richmond*, Henry had informed Lettie that his next ship, the U.S.S. *Louisiana*, a second-class battleship in the Atlantic Fleet, was rumored to have been fitted out for troop transport duty. "We think it quite possible as there are 14 Ph[armacist's]. M[ate]s on this draft. [Normally] A ship only rates about that many hospital men in all" (12 December). As Henry put it later, their mission was "to bring back Doughboys" (5 January 1919).

Considered to be one of the Navy's "good sea boats," the 456-foot *Louisiana* was launched in 1904, normally sailed with a complement of 827, and was sold in 1923 (Bauer, p. 97).

[137] On this, his tenth day away from the farm, the Geneva paper printed a tiny item stating that "Raymond Perrin has gone to Warren where he is employed" (p. 3).

[138] School now seemed farther than ever from reopening. Because of the fresh upsurge in influenza, an emergency hospital had been created in the graded school where Lettie taught, but the somewhat dubious arrangements there were so new that no patients had been admitted yet (*FPT*, 18 December, p. 2).

[139] Annie and Bert probably read also the day's prominent *Free Press-Times* article on Bernice's soldier brother, Homer, and his recent involvement on the Verdun front. Its secondary headline summarizes thus: "Homer Michel, of Saybrook, Gassed and Shell-Shocked, Bullets in Clothing But Never Once Hit" (p. 1).

About two weeks later, on

New Year's Eve, after the elder Michels had retired and before the young people (including Bernice and Raym) had returned from dancing, Homer arrived home at the family farm in Saybrook (*FPT*, 2 January 1919, p. 2). Thus he succeeded in astounding "the members of his father's family by coming down stairs to breakfast on New Year's morning."

[140] He did. On 26 December Henry wrote Lettie: "I couldn't resist the temptation of eating ma's good cookies and the apples as soon as I opened the boxes." Three days later "The life-savers taste pretty good after our Navy chow." Then on New Year's Day, 1919: "I had the tomato preserves today. They were sure great. . . . My Xmas is nearly gone. Am leaving the bottle of candy till last. Tell Lou [i.e., Lulu] the nuts & grapes were fine and the box of candy Grace sent was great."

[141] This acquisition was an especially happy one because presumably there was "a great national shortage of Victrolas and Victor Records" (*FPT*, 24 December, p. 2). The Victor Talking Machine Company was said to be heavily involved in war work, including the manufacture of "thousands upon thousands of a secret war device of which the War Department has made no mention." More obviously, the company also "manufactured thousands of Victrolas and tens of thousands of Victor Records, which have been shipped to our boys—in camps, aboard ships, in the trenches, and, last but not least, in hospitals."
    Knowing of Lettie's hope that the family might acquire a Victrola, Henry wrote from the *Louisiana* on 16 December—his "first day of watch"—that "We have quite a few Vics. aboard. The music comes to us thru the blowers that supply us with fresh air. The blowers are not for musical purposes but they serve as such." About four months later (18 April 1919), when he was a patient in the Protestant Episcopal Hospital in Philadelphia, he wrote: "I think you have done well having paid for your share of the Vic."

Thursday, 19 December

Bright and cooler[.] I called up Lettie to tell her about Henry. She & Lulu bought things and got here on 11 oclock car. Then we packed two boxes for Henry [and] sent them out by mail this P.M. Hope he gets them all O.K.[140] Did no ironing[.] Too excited with boxes.

Friday, 20 December

Cloudy.

We done up work [and] then Lettie ironed nearly all day. I bought a xmas tree from a little boy. Had a load of them. Wanted the money for xmas. Got 14 eggs today. Our Vic[trola] came today.[141]

Saturday, 21 December

We done the Sat[urday] work. Got dinner[.] Lettie too[k] two oclock car for Ashty. Bert and I went to town for <u>our</u> smoked meat.[142] Got home about 4 oclock. Found Raym here.[143] He played the Vic [and] thought it fine. Raym looks sick.

Sunday, 22 December

Got up late[.] Done up work. Lettie and Vere came on 12 oclock car. I made pumpkin pie. We had a chicken dinner. Raym thought every thing fine[.] V[ere] went home on 7 oclock car. Bert and I played 3 games of dominoes.

Raym went over to see B[ernice]–[.]

Monday, 23 December

Rainy & nasty[.] Raym took a Ton of hay to N[or]th Center.[144] Lettie washed curtains[.] We put two p[ai]r on frames[.][145] They dried through the night.

[In the] Evening I made candy for xmas. Bert went to Allens. Raym to town[.] Lettie played the Vic. Got Henrys pictures by mail today.

[142] Apparently some of the pig butchered on 25 November.

[143] Raym was back from his two weeks in Warren.

[144] With the team and wagon, Raym delivered some of the timothy or clover that Bert had advertised in the *Free Press-Times* (16 December, p. 4).

[145] These "frames" were the same as the "stretchers" that Annie mentioned previously. She refers to them again on Tuesday.

Tuesday, 24 December

Today I made my xmas pies[,] cake & plum pudding.[146] We put the rest of curtains on stretchers. L[ettie] & I were both tired out[.] Rained all day. Raym went to sale [and] then to B[ernice']–s[.] Did not come home till late[.] Mr A[llen] & Arthur brought over[147] some of their records. We played them all through and our bunch too.[148]

Wednesday, 25 December

Xmas day.

We had a late breakfast[.] Then had music and our presents from the tree. All fared fine. We done up work[,] then got dinner[.] Grace & Lulu came on one oclock car.[149] Bernice & Effie came over.[150] So the 4 girls were here to supper[.] Raym went home with B[ernice] and to a dance.

All got xmas cards from Henry[.][151]

[146] The plum pudding provides a glimpse of English tradition surviving in the Perrin household.

[147] Annie mistakenly wrote "of" here for "over."

[148] On this Christmas Eve Henry was aboard the *Louisiana* near Hampton Roads, writing to Lettie and preparing to depart for Brest, France. Even as he wrote, the ship's crew was "hauling in lines, making fast chains, closing port holes and hatches, taking on stores." At 10 A.M. came the order "up-anchor."

[149] Looking forward to Christmas about a month earlier, Henry wrote to Lettie, "I suppose you will have a tree as usual, and perhaps have the Lowe girls up" (21 November).

[150] Annie refers here for the first time to Bernice's sister Effie. She also records what was only Bernice's second visit to the Perrins in 1918. Though it has long since been obvious that the only really significant contact between the Michels and the Perrins was that of Bernice and Raym, it is still noteworthy that Annie never had any occasion at all to mention Bernice's brothers, Homer and Jay.

[151] On this same day Henry wrote to Lettie: "Beans for breakfast and I can truthfully say I like them yet."

Thursday, 26 December

To day washed and butchered. Clothes did not dry [so] had to hang them around the stove[.] Mrs Slocum was here while he[152] helped butcher. [In the] Evening Raym went to bed. I knit[.] Lettie wrote. Bert played [the] Vic.

[152] Mr. Slocum.

Friday, 27 December

+

Done up the work. Got dinner. Lettie took 2 oclock car for Ashty.[153] Raym got up about 11. a.m [and] felt some better. Spent the evening over to Bernices. Pa bought a cow up to Clarks.

I knit a while[,] then went to bed with a bad headache[.]

[153] Because she was not teaching, Lettie was able to go visiting in Ashtabula on a weekday afternoon. Dr. Sherwood announced, however, that the Geneva village schools would be reopening the following Monday (30 December). There was now so much back work to be made up that classes were instructed to meet even on New Year's Day (*FPT*, 27 December, p. 2). So much time had been lost during the fall, in fact, that "The Geneva village and township schools will have no spring vacation" (*FPT*, 9 April 1919, p. 3).

Saturday, 28 December

I done up Sat[urday] work. Baked bread & pies [and] got dinner. Then ironed a few pieces. Raym went to town. Then down to B[ernice'].s. Lettie is at Smiths.[154] Some colder today. Bert and I played dominoes this evening[.]

[154] Vere was living these days with her mother, Rose Smith, in the Alpha Apartments in Ashtabula.

Sunday, 29 December

A lonesome dreary day. Bert[,] Raymond and I were here to dinner. Raym took 3 oclock car for Ashty[,] then to Warren.[155] Lettie came home on 7 oclock car[.] Saw Raym in Ashty[.] His train was late. Looks like rain. Spent evening reading. Another day has gone.

Monday, 30 December[156]

Today I salted the meat.[157] Done some ironing. Bert hauled some hay to town.

Raym isn't feeling very well. Got a card from Fannie[.] They are all quite well.

[155] Whether Raym's base was to be Geneva or somewhere else was a problem that remained to be solved. There may even have been some thought that Raym might work in town during the winter months and return to the farm for the rest of the year. According to the *Free Press-Times*, in any case, "Raymond Perrin returned Sunday to Warren after a week's visit with his parents, Mr. and Mrs. B. H. Perrin" (31 December, p. 2).

[156] Not even on this Monday did Lettie return to school as planned, since it had proved "impossible to move the [flu] patients from the emergency hospital in the graded school building" (*FPT*, 30 December, p. 3).
[157] Even in December, it was just as well to do the salting fairly quickly because of the lack of refrigeration.

Tuesday, 31 December

Lettie went down to Lowes [and] stayed all night. I boiled meat for head cheese.[158] Then done some work for New Years day. Raining some today[.][159]

[158] Head cheese is a seasoned jellied loaf made from the chopped and boiled head meat of an animal—in this case, the recently slaughtered pig.

[159] Henry, meanwhile, was still off on the adventure of his life. On this eve of 1919 he wrote to Lettie: "Well sis I'm nearer France than I am the U.S.... During the picture show to-night 'collision' sounded. All tho[ugh]t it was drill but it was not. The storm had wrecked our steering gear." However, "In side of an hour all was well and we were on our own way again.... Am going to turn in as we all have to get up at midnight to see the old year out and welcome the new year in. I would surely like to be at home to-night with all of you. Am having a wonderful trip tho[ugh] so suppose I should be satisfied." On 3 January 1919 he wrote to Lettie, "I dream of home nearly every night."

Henry made two round trips to France, both devoted to evacuating soldiers. From the first trip he returned on 24 January 1919; the second extended from 18 February to 17 March.

All told, between 1 January and 30 July 1919, some 112,131 sick and wounded servicemen were returned from abroad, and Henry's ship, the *Louisiana*, carried 4,714 of them (*Annual Reports of the Navy Department ... 1919*, pp. 111 and 21).

Postscript
Annie's Later Years

IN THE YEARS THAT immediately followed 1918, life at first became still more difficult for both Annie and Bert. Most importantly, Raym, the hardest-working farmer on the farm, found a job in Akron.[1] From his parents' perspective the move was devastating. Probably the major public sign of their distress was an advertisement Bert placed in the *Geneva Free Press-Times*: "For Rent— House and ten acres at [Interurban] stop 58. Will rent house. Give more than enough work to pay rent. Inquire Bert Perrin, Phone 723."[2]

Fortunately the situation was resolved fairly soon when Raym decided to return home. But the resolution itself entailed new problems, for Raym married Bernice Michel on 23 June 1920 and naturally brought his bride home to live with him.[3] Easy for none of the Perrins, the new two-family living arrangement may have been hardest on the women, not least because Bernice herself was a strong-minded and outspoken individual whose place in the household, notwithstanding Annie's gentle nature, was inevitably ambiguous. Creating still more tension was the birth of Raym and Bernice's first son, Grant (4 July 1921), and even, for a while, Lettie's move

[1] In the city that came to be known as "The Rubber Center of the World," Raym was employed by Firestone Tire and Rubber— where Henry had worked before going into the Navy.

[2] Newspaper of 1 December 1919, p. 2. The ad refers to the old William Williamson place that Bert purchased from Williamson's widow, Ellen, and their daughter, Grace (see note to diary entry for 15 April).

[3] See Fig. 100.

Fig. 100. Bernice Michel, Raym's bride-to-be, stands here with Bert at the back of the farmhouse on a day in late February 1920. At the top of the picture are two kitchen windows, and, off to the right, the back-and-side porch that overlooks the driveway and the barn.

back to the farm with her newborn son, Myron, Jr.[4] Never one to contain himself, Bert reacted badly, and Raym took to sleeping in the attic.

Even after Lettie and her baby left for Cleveland, the Perrins' most perplexing problem remained. If it was in some sense not ever to be totally solved, time at least brought some stumbling steps toward resolution. The first one that is now recordable took over two years in coming. In May of 1923, however, after opening a letter from her mother, Lettie told Myron that Annie and Bert were "to leave Bernice in control."[5]

[4] Lettie's return was occasioned by the hospitalization of Myron, Sr., in the fall of 1922. On 10 October, three days after Myron, Jr., was born, Myron, Sr., had to leave for Dawson's Springs, Kentucky, where he signed in as a patient at the U.S. Naval Hospital. With a three-day-old baby in hand, Lettie had little choice but to stay at the farm until Myron's return to Geneva on 6 December.

[5] Myron Randall, Diary, 24 May 1923.

Fig. 101. On Sunday, 27 May 1923, a breezy and beautiful day up on the Ridge, Lettie took this picture of her mother and father at the rear of their home, with the milk house serving as a backdrop. This was the elder Perrins' final full year on the farm.

The second step was even more drastic. However obvious or difficult the right decision may have been at the time, Bert and Annie eventually set about finding a house for themselves in the village. On 30 April 1924 Myron recorded in his diary that they were "looking at houses." On 16 June he wrote that he and Lettie "Drove [the] folks down to see [a] couple pieces of property." And on 1 July he wrote that they had bought a place on South Broadway.

Psychological stress and strain aside, business matters were going better for the family by this time, and the elder Perrins' new home was a comparatively grand yellow-and-turquoise place on a major, brick-paved street.[6] Situated on the south side of town, nearest to the farm, it was also just one door north of the old nineteen-room white house that had been renovated in 1917 to serve as Geneva's hospital—where Lettie's baby had been born. After a lapse of many years, the Perrins again had an urban street address: No. 63 at the time and, in later years, No. 370 (see Fig. 102). Built in 1900[7] and recently owned by a Lake Erie ship captain,[8] its frame was constructed of sturdy two-by-fourteen timbers. It had a large, wrap-around porch, and, inside, downstairs woodwork made of quarter-sawed golden oak. (Upstairs, the woodwork lapsed into mere pine.) It had two high-ceilinged parlors and two stairways to the second floor, as well as running water and even electricity. Equally major changes for the Perrins, moreover, were the slim, forty-foot-wide lot on which the house stood and the fact that now they were within easy walking distance of Geneva's town center. Only about four blocks to the north, South Broadway and North Broadway met each other and intersected with Main Street.

Convenient in some ways as this new home undoubtedly was, the tracks of the Nickel Plate at the south end of town proved to be too close. Though the Perrins had been comfortably south of those same tracks on the farm, they now lived only slightly north of them. "Hear that, Ann?" Bert would say when he heard the shriek and rumble of a passing train. "It's coming right through the living room!" A still bigger disadvantage of

[6] In the latter part of 1911, South Broadway from Walnut southward to the Nickel Plate became the second street in Geneva to be paved (*FPT*, 2 September, p. 3). A section of North Broadway was first.

[7] When the wallpaper was steamed off the walls of an upstairs bedroom in 1950, the date "1900" was found scrawled on the original plaster.

[8] Four years before Annie wrote her diary, the *Geneva Free Press-Times* noted that "Capt. [James] Birmingham and others have purchased the steamer St. Joseph of Buffalo, and will operate her on Lake Ontario and the St. Lawrence river" (2 April 1914, p. 2). Two years later it noted that Birmingham was in Toronto for a while in order "to fit out his boat, the steamer, St. Joseph" (23 March 1916, p. 2). And in early November of the diary year itself, the same paper reported that he had just purchased 63 South Broadway (*FPT*, 1 November, p. 2).

Fig. 102. The Perrin home at 63 South Broadway as it looked in 1924. In later years, after Bert and Annie returned to the South Ridge, and even after Annie's death, Bert rented this house to a long and constantly shifting succession of nurses who worked at the house-turned-hospital next door, out of view to the left.

the new place was the mile or so that now separated the couple from the farm, especially since Bert was constantly going up to the Ridge to help Raym. Myron remarked at one point that Bert was "playing the part of a hired man all week—roofing making hay etc." (3 September 1925). Sometimes Bert stayed at the farm overnight. Sometimes he actually moved back to the farm in order to help Raym—and naturally that created a difficult situation for Annie. Eventually, whatever they had gained or lost by moving to town, Bert and Annie began to contemplate a move back up to the Ridge.

Since they had learned the hard way that living in the same house as a grown son, a daughter-in-law, and an infant grandson was unworkable, the elder Perrins thought for a while about buying a five-acre tract on the South Ridge in nearby Saybrook, across from Allen's nursery.[9] Finally, however, they simply decided to build for themselves a red-brick-and-brown-shingle bungalow on Perrin ground some two hundred or so feet to the east of their old house.[10] Raym excavated for the

[9] Diary of Myron Randall, 10 April 1927. W. A. Allen and Sons had been in business on the Ridge since the latter part of 1913 (*FPT,* 21 November 1913, p. 2).

[10] See Fig. 103.

basement of the new structure with a horse and team, and another Genevan, Roscoe ("Ross") Casselman, a young man in his twenties, did the carpentry. On 2 June 1929, in his earliest diary notation on the project, Myron wrote of driving the family up to the farm "to see what had been accomplished toward [the] new house." Constructing it was not a fast process. On 17 June 1929 Myron recorded that Bert "always rushes to [the] farm to supervise his building and then works for Raym all day." On 19 October of that year, however, there was a completed house for Lettie and Myron to visit on those occasions, usually weekends, when they could drive out from their own new home in Cleveland Heights.[11] From the front porch of the bungalow—and also from its front sunroom windows—Annie and Bert could now once again look out over the South Ridge road and beyond to the Perrin orchard and the comfortably distant tracks of the Nickel Plate Railroad. And from the west-facing window at the foot of the stairs leading to the second floor, Bert could—and often did—stand and look out toward the old homeplace. If Raym's car or, later on, his mud-spattered blue truck went dashing out the drive, Bert would like as not call out, "There they go again, Ann!"[12]

Throughout the time that Annie and Bert lived in their new house, Bert continued to lend a hand next door. It was still his farm, after all, and would remain so until he deeded it to Raym in 1939. In 1930 Lettie wrote of his driving the mowing machine and seeming "quite proud of it."[13] The whole arrangement would not have

[11] After living in rented quarters for several years, the Randalls had managed to buy a plain but capacious two-story house on Beechwood (a name later changed to Colonial Drive). Myron was now teaching Spanish at Cleveland Heights High School, one of the newest and best high schools in Ohio. After he received his J.D. from the Lake Erie School of Law (1932), however, his interest in Spanish waned a little, and commercial law became and remained his favorite class at Heights right through to 1951, when he retired. At that point, having remodeled the old Birmingham-Perrin house, which Lettie had inherited, he and Lettie moved to Geneva. Myron then began practicing law at 30 East Main, where Robert R. Marsh and he rented an upstairs office suite from Jennie Gregory.

[12] Situating Bert's and Annie's house next to Raym's and Bernice's might be viewed as an interesting echo of the fact that Bert's father and brother, Henry and Fred, are said to have lived next to each other on a single lot in Cleveland (Carol Jensen, notes, 20 May 1997).

[13] Letter to Myron Randall, 24 June.

Fig. 103. The west side of the new bungalow on the South Ridge as it looked in late April of 1930. On the first floor at the right is Annie's kitchen window; on the left, the window where Bert stood to look out toward the old farmhouse; at the far right, a pile of stones for the retaining wall that was yet to be built on this side of the house; at the far left, a glimpse of Myron's and Lettie's Ford "Lizzie"; and, in the left background, the Stowe residence. In the foreground are four of Bert's cherry trees, three sour and one sweet.

worked, of course, had Raym and Bernice not both been hard workers.

Somewhere along the line they also took on a full-time hired man—making space for him in the small bedroom at the northeast corner of the house. As the years slipped by, there were a number of these men, but Frank Cook was the sturdy, red-faced, taciturn fellow who settled in and made the place home for the longest stretch. At the time Annie wrote her diary Frank was working in Painesville, more or less midway between Geneva and Cleveland. Apparently his job there of "oiling at the C.P. & A. Power house" had less to recommend it than did the hard but healthy work in the fields and orchards of the South Ridge.[14] In any case, Myron records that Frank was sharing the Perrins' Christmas celebrations as early as 1921 and attending a family reunion as early as 1922.[15] With Frank as with a real family member, moreover, there were ups and downs. In the fall of 1922 he suddenly departed, "bag and baggage."[16] The family had to replace him and then had to replace the replacement, and eventually they were glad to welcome Frank back home again.

Even before there were two sons to help out (Raymond, Jr., was born in 1926), the Perrin place was on its way to becoming one of the best fruit and dairy farms in Ashtabula County. Peaches always remained important, but in any given season Raym also drove truckload after truckload of grapes in to Cleveland—both to Little Italy and to one or another of the big downtown markets. Everyone helped pack the truck after supper, and at about two in the morning Raym would get up and head for the city. Some of the Perrin apples got special treatment: they were wrapped individually in pieces of colored tissue for selling as "fancy." And the old homeplace itself was constantly looking better, too. After one visit in 1927, Myron wrote in his diary that the Perrin farm looked "almost a picture" (29 May).[17]

In still later years Bert retained a vital interest in

[14] Notice of Frank's Painesville job was printed in the *Geneva Free Press-Times* on 22 January 1918, p. 2.

At various times previously he had tried both marriage and barbering—the latter being the more durable of these interests. When he was part owner with DeWitt Thomas of the Massena shop in Ashtabula, the two men were known to customers as Mutt (DeWitt was tall) and Jeff (Frank was short) (*FPT*, 4 September 1912, p. 2). In Geneva, Frank barbered for a while in Joseph Lowrie's shop called The Marble Palace, which boasted blue-veined Italian marble (*FPT*, 25 March 1913, p. 2; 13 December 1912, p. 2), but later that same year he moved on to "the tonsorial room of R. B. Morey" (*FPT*, 14 October, p. 2). In 1914 he bought out Morey and refurbished the shop with two-toned oatmeal wallpaper, gas lights, and "bathroom equipment" (*FPT*, 26 January, p. 2; 2 April, p. 2).

A well-known citizen in the village, in other words (his lowest ebb came when the newspaper reported his arrest and sentencing for stealing a bicycle [*FPT*, 9 June 1913, p. 2]), Frank at one point rented a farm on the South Ridge with his mother, Nora (*FPT*, 7 April 1914, p. 2). Things never ran smoothly with him for long, however. In July that same year the paper reported that both mother and son, "who have been helping at the George Carter farm on the South Ridge, have moved back to Geneva"—at which time they moved in with Frank's brother, Ernest (p. 3).

Many years later, after Annie's

death, Frank returned to the Ridge yet again and moved in with Bert for a while. Raymond Perrin, Jr., recalls him during this period as becoming a sort of "Man Friday" for Bert. "He cooked, cleaned house, made errands and provided his car to chauffeur Grandpa around" (ALS, 24 March 1996).

[15] Diary, 21–23 December 1921; 4 September 1922.

[16] Diary, 28 September 1922.

[17] Later still, in 1941, after Raym and Bernice found the old farm too much to care for, they moved to a much smaller one a few doors east on the Ridge. It was the first land that Raym had ever purchased. Traumatic as such a move was for him and Bernice, it was in some ways also minimal because the new little farm was so close to the old one. In fact, its two acres stretched southward to meet part of the old Perrin pasture.

Still working on the Ridge, then, but now altogether on its southern slope, Raym planted 125 fruit trees and 14 grape vines. Though working alone, he maintained his old standards, perhaps even raised them a bit. When the *Geneva Free Press* featured him in a series entitled "Men of Accomplishment," it would note among other things that "The Perrin farm was the highest producing farm in the county soil conservation organization, a fact that testifies to Mr. Perrin's continued work and care" (9 July 1960).

By that time Raym had sold the old farm. It had belonged to others, in fact, ever since the spring of 1946, about two years after Bert's death. Strange though it might seem to one familiar with how much living and work had been involved, it was Perrin property for only forty-two years.

the old place, toward the end helping simply by tending the family's roadside produce stand—a sturdy, white, wooden structure with a top that slanted down toward the now-paved South Ridge road. As Myron saw it, "Raym has quite a store at [his] front door" (31 August 1929). On his own new turf, however, Bert wisely succeeded in not over-committing himself. Between the old clapboard farmhouse, painted a glistening white now, and the new bungalow there were some sweet and sour cherry trees (it was prime fruit country, after all), and eventually, beneath the cherries, a rustic bench where Bert or anyone else might sit, catch a summer breeze, and watch the traffic on the road. Now that the road had become Route 84, there certainly was more to see. A short distance farther south down the slope, Bert also planted a little vineyard and a garden, and at various times, as the spirit moved him, he raised a few sheep or rabbits or pigs or ducks. With some tobacco to chew and some wine in the cellar (wine made from Perrin grapes), Bert had a reasonably good life.

As part of that life, he had Cleveland. To make a visit there, in fact, Bert had the regularly recurring excuse of collecting monthly rents. There he could also visit the homes of Lettie or Henry or both on the east side of the city, as well as a whole slew of relatives on the west side. And when he felt like it, he could see a show downtown. Of course, being a landlord was not all peaches and cream. For example, Myron recorded a time when one of Bert's "tenants fell down stairs & had a baby & [was]

Fig. 104. Annie on a summer Sunday in 1932, a worn and gentle old woman of sixty-six, seated on one of the dark green porch rockers that has been carried out for her and placed on the lawn in front of the bungalow. At the far left one can glimpse the South Ridge road, now paved with cement and bordered by a protective cable strung between white posts.

Fig. 105. A study in contrasts, Annie and Bert stand together in their still-new front yard on the Ridge in the summer of 1935. After Annie's death in 1938, the dress she wears here (navy and white, with some wavering red and yellow stripes) was for some reason the only article of her clothing that Lettie saved.

suing him."[18] On the whole, though, coming to the city to collect money was not a bad way for Bert to occupy himself.

[18] Diary, 16 January 1926.

As for Annie, she returned to keeping a few chickens out in back, and in the sandy loam near the side door she made a small rectangular flower garden. She was able to "do" more flowers these days—orangey-yellow calendulas, pink and blue larkspur, and a creamy yellow strain of iris. Somewhere along the years she acquired an old moss rose that was thick with thorns, but delicately pink and pungently fragrant. Shrubs in the yard were easier than flowers, of course, and the site was good for lilacs—which she was glad to share. Before long, a flourishing row of cascading white spiraea bushes lined the front of the house, and alongside the drive the new shoots of the flowering locust could scarcely be controlled.

Mainly, though, Annie kept the household running. It was she who washed and hung out the sheets, ironed the shirts, stewed the rhubarb, and pared the apples and pitted the cherries for pies. It was she who made the plain, good, light, crusty white bread that somehow embodied the continuity and warmth of the place.

Annie and Bert spent the remainder of their lives in this bungalow on the Ridge. Between 1921 and 1929 their three children (Raym, Lettie, and Henry) together with their spouses (Bernice, Myron, and Vere) presented them with seven grandchildren—six of whom survived into maturity.[19] Thus in the 1920s and 1930s, there were

[19] A seventh child, Vernon (known as "Buddy"), one of Henry's and Vere's twins, born on 10 December 1925, died on 12 January 1930. (For a partial family tree, see Appendix C.)

Fig. 106. Annie's and Bert's grandchildren as photographed on the South Ridge in 1935. In the back row (left to right) are Myron William Randall (1922–), son of Lettie and Myron, and Grant Michel Perrin (1921–1959), son of Raymond and Bernice. In the front row are Dale Bertrand Jonas Randall (1929–), son of Lettie and Myron; Raymond Austin Perrin, Jr. (1926–), son of Raymond and Bernice; and Vere Estelle Perrin (1925–1999) and Robert Henry Perrin (1923–1975), the two surviving children of Henry and Vere.

plenty of fresh young sprouts to be variously fussed over, cooked for, entertained, and loved.

Fifty-one and fifty-two at the time of writing her diary, Annie lived to celebrate her fiftieth wedding anniversary with Bert in 1937 and then her seventy-second birthday in 1938. By this time, however, she had had a couple of heart attacks, and varicose veins were a more or less constant source of pain and worry. Though her health was obviously growing worse, Annie continued to work as much as she could. In March, one of her last major chores was helping to trim and tie Bert's grapevines on their wires. Then for about nine weeks in the late summer and early fall of 1938 her condition grew ominously worse. Her legs swelled badly and needed to be salved and bandaged, then unwrapped and rewrapped, with the soreness growing ever greater. Toward the end she flickered into and out of consciousness. And, finally, at 9:30 A.M. on Sunday, 16 October 1938, Annie died at home of a coronary thrombosis.

From down in the basement of the bungalow Henry commenced an unabashed wailing that filled the house with his pain. Lettie, though a person with uncommon self-control, nevertheless needed a doctor. Raym was deathly pale and mainly still. As for Bert, damp-eyed and stunned at his unimaginable loss, the choice of a costly copper casket conveyed a meaning that for a good many years he had seldom managed to express.

For this woman to whom family had meant so much, the family arranged a home funeral. She was to have a new pink dress and wear the fiftieth-anniversary brooch —a gold bow—that Henry and Vere had given her, and on Tuesday the front sunroom where she lay would be filled to overflowing with flowers. Though he scarcely knew her, the Reverend G. A. Parsons came up from the First Methodist Church of Geneva and spoke about her exemplary life to the relatives and friends who had crowded together in her house to remember her. A woman sang "Beautiful Isle of Somewhere" and "Abide with Me."

> Abide with me: fast falls the eventide;
> The darkness deepens; Lord, with me abide!
> When other helpers fail, and comforts flee,
> Help of the helpless, oh, abide with me!

Surrounded by those who loved her, then, Annie was driven a short distance westward down the South Ridge and, near the top of a large and grassy hill, bright in the October sun, she was laid to rest in the Geneva cemetery called Mount Pleasant.

A Letter from Annie to Her Sister-in-Law Pearl[1]

[1] Annie's brother Gilbert Wilson Elliott (5 July 1863–21 May 1946), born in Dover Center, Ohio, married Pearl Hall on 12 June 1895, only two years before this letter. Annie therefore sent it to Dover Center, since, as Doris Weston recalls, "They lived on a goodsized farm at the corner of Dover Center and Detroit Roads all their lives" (ALS, 24 February 1997).

In later years Gilbert still kept a sea biscuit that his father, William, had brought with him on the *Cosmo* in 1849 (Fannie Keyse, "Brief History," p. 2). A tall, thin old man with a mustache and straw hat, and wearing garters on his shirtsleeves, he would now and again come visiting and help Bert at the Perrins' roadside produce stand.

[2] With a pioneer history dating back to 1799, Austinburg—the earliest permanent settlement in Ashtabula County—was at one time envisioned as an American Land of Ophir. At the time of this letter, however, it was already a shrinking village, far smaller than Geneva and about four miles southeast of it.

[3] Annie's and Gilbert's mother was Louisa Parfitt Elliott, the wife of William Elliott (see Introduction, pp. 7–15, and Figs. 6 and 107).

Austinburg, Ohio[2]

July 21st 1897

Dear Pearl,

I received your few lines. And was very much pleased to get a word from you again[.] You said I have owed you a letter a long time, and I have said all the time, why dont Pearl write. I wrote a letter to you & Mother a month ago, but never mind[.][3] We will try and do better after this, wont we?

Fig. 107. Louisa Parfitt Elliott (1824–1900), Annie's mother, in her later years.

Fig. 108. William Elliott (1824–1897), Annie's father, in his later years.

You are way ahead of me with your canning. You always put up a nice lot. It is such a help too.

How sorry I do feel for poor Father.[4] I know he suffers. I so often wish it was so I could see Father and Mother and do something for them. I am so thankful Mother is with you again[.] I always feel <u>sure</u> she has the best of care while there. And she will do nothing to hurt or tire herself[.] That is such a comfort to me, for the poor soul has done enough. I know it is hard for Father to stop calling on her but if he can not use reason someone must for him. Mother must rest.

Well Pearl it is nearly a year ago we were taken sick. And how kind you and Gilbert was to me and mine[!]

[4] Annie's and Gilbert's father (Fig. 108), who was not quite seventy-three at this time, had been lame for a number of years. A great walker in his early days, he now used a cane and moved haltingly, blaming what he called his rheumatism on having worked so often and so long on damp roofs. When Annie wrote this letter, he had only about three and a half more months to live.

[5] Lettie Jane Perrin was then five years old.

[6] The number seven here is striking because, according to all official accounts, Annie and Bert had four, not five, children. One can only guess who the seventh individual could have been (a hired hand is one possibility), but this probably is the place to record the shadowy old family story of a fifth Perrin child who died in early infancy yet lived long enough to be called Willie. Such things sometimes occurred in earlier days, and the name sounds plausible inasmuch as Annie's father was named William.

[7] A Children's Day program of the time typically consisted of songs, recitations, and prayers by the "little ones." Lettie many years later recalled that her first church was the Church of Christ. In Austinburg the First United Church of Christ, said to be the first congregation in the Western Reserve, was founded in a log cabin in 1803.

[8] Vernon at this point was about eight years old. Very likely Bert's favorite child, he died of diphtheria about two years later. Many years later still, one of Annie's and Bert's grandsons, Henry's and Vere's Vernon, named after his uncle, also died young. Hence Myron's diary notation of 4 July 1930: "Took L[ettie]'s folks to the Vernons' graves in PM."

[9] Unlike the similar +'s in Annie's 1917–18 diary, these crosses are obviously conventional signs for kisses.

[10] With the foregoing letter to her sister-in-law, Annie enclosed the following note to her mother.

Dont think I have forgotten it. I never shall. Lettie speaks of you both very often.[5] I have been so miserable all summer sometimes I feel like giving up. You see there are 7 for me to do for.[6] Wash, bake, sew[,] scrub and every thing else.

The children took part in the exercises on Childrens day.[7] I felt proud of them[.] They did splendid, especially Lettie[.] I worked so hard to get Vernons blouse and her a dress made but I felt well paid for my work.[8]

Have you any heavy storms there[?] The old people here say they are the most severe they ever saw.

I expect I have made lots of mistakes but I am writing and baking at the same time. With love I will close. Write soon[.]

As ever Annie

+ + +[9]

My Dear Mother,[10]

I was so pleased to get your letter[.] I have felt so anxious to hear how you are and I am so glad you are back to Gilberts again. I know they are kind and thoughtful of you. I have been there.

Mother I know you feel for Father, but you must not do for him. And any one dont expect you to. And he knows you ought not but he has always called on you and always will if you are near[.]

I know the weather has been very trying but I am in hopes the worst is over. I do not think I could of stood it many more days. I guess I am getting lazy[.] It cant be old age makes me so—what?[11] Not want to work. Call it anything[.]

[11] Annie was thirty-one years old.

I am glad you had a good visit at Mrs S—. I know she was kind to you. And that is what you need. I wrote you a few lines. I expect you have them by now.

Yes Mother my hands are full[.] As you say 7 to do for is quite enough.

Lots of love

++++++

Annie

APPENDIX B

Four Letters from Henry B. Perrin to Lettie Perrin

1

∞

Great Lakes, Ill.

4-20-18

My Dear Sis,[1]

I rec'd. my first mail to day since I have been at school[.][2] It surely made me feel more content.

The weather here is the worse thing of all. It has rained almost steadily for two weeks & is cold enough to snow. Will have to tell you of the great event of the week. MacAdoo was here yesterday to see the boys.[3] It was an awful day so 20,000 of us marched to the drill hall to maneuver & to hear his speach. He is a very plain man but a very good speaker.

We also drew more clothes. I was lucky enough to get a very good serge. Have my leggings now so look quite slick.

Sun[day]. at 12:30 P.M. 42 of us received our first liberty. We were a happy bunch. Left here at 12:30 on the "Jackies Special" for Chi[cago].[4] On our arrival we got a milk chocolate. Sure tasted good. Then we saw the town. Went thru the Art Museum.[5] Surely wish you could have too. It is a most wonderful & interesting

[1] A sufficient address at this time was a mere "Miss L. J. Perrin, Geneva, Ohio." Henry's feelings for Lettie are suggested by his naming of her as the beneficiary of his new life insurance. "If I happen to see the bottom of the ocean," he told her, "you won't have to work so hard teaching" (undated letter from April, 1918).

[2] Henry was now at Camp Boone in Great Lakes, training as a naval Hospital Apprentice.

[3] Secretary of the Treasury William Gibbs McAdoo was also Director General of Railroads and (since 7 May 1914) the husband of President Woodrow Wilson's daughter Eleanor. Almost immediately after the armistice in November, however, he returned to private business, accompanied by such headlines as "Resigns Because Salary Isn't Big Enough" (*FPT*, 23 November 1918, p. 1).

[4] Even officers used variants of the term "bluejacket." Later this year Henry wrote to Lettie that "One time when two of us recognized Adm. Fletcher he said 'How do you do Jacks' and smiled very friendly" (29 September). Soldiers, on the other hand, were "doughboys" and "Sammies" (as in "Sammies Go

337

sight. There are several Egyptian Mummies on exhibition. Also every renouned Statue we read of in History.

From there we saw Douglas Fairbanks in "Reginald."[6] It was good. Then we hiked to the Sailors Club & Rec'd invitations out to dinner. There were 100 of the boys in blue, all clothes in ship shape. Had to be to pass inspection at the gate.

Well we were entertained by Mr. & Mrs. Carter[,] many times a millionaire.[7] There were girls for all of us. The finest Chi[cago]. society can produce. We danced, listened to talented singers, musicians & etc. The rooms were dreams. Floors of polished oak & some of marble. The ball room was decorated as a garden.[8] It looked like a stage setting to see so many boys in blue & girls in their frills. At 6:30 we dined & believe me we had some chow.

I met Mr. & Mrs. Carter & had a nice chat with them. They are very sociable.

A sailor can get anything he wants in Chi[cago]. There are girls stationed around to invite them to their homes. Theatres free[,] & all is a smile & Hello Sailor or Jackie. That all seems like a dream to us.

We got back at 11:45 & were not due 'til 1 A.M. but played safety first.

I called up Grace A. but she was not in.[9] Had a nice visit with her sister. She wanted to know how the folks were[,] especially that beautiful sister of mine. They want me to come every time I can. Also called up Bertha.[10] They also want me to come & they are coming out to see me.

Over Top to Hun Trench" [S&B, 13 March 1918, p. 1]).

[5] The Art Institute of Chicago is on Michigan Avenue at Adams Street.

[6] Since Fairbanks seems never to have made a film called Reginald, perhaps Henry was misremembering that actor's Reggie Mixes In ("For who but Mr. Fairbanks could mix in with the name of Reggie and get away with it?" [New York Times Film Reviews, 1:17, for 29 May 1916]). Currently playing in Chicago's public theaters, in any case—for example, at the Julian on Belmont at Clark—was Fairbanks's latest picture, Headin' South (Chicago Daily Tribune, 13 April, p. 15).

[7] Henry refers to Ford Rodman Carter and his wife, Fay Thompson Carter, of 1411 North State Street. Carter had been in the stock and bond business for over twenty years and recently served as president of the Chicago Stock Exchange (Marquis, p. 121). (Archie Motley of the Chicago Historical Society has provided the editor with this identification and described the Carter residence as being "very near Chicago's 'Gold Coast' on the near North side about two miles north of downtown Chicago" [ALS, 29 May 1996]).

[8] Henry's description is suggestive of the later work of his hostess, for Mrs. Carter not only was socially prominent but also became known as a fashion stylist and floral director who supervised arrangements for posh weddings.

[9] Mrs. Grace P. Andress appears twice in Annie's address list, both times with a Chicago address. Apparently she was the wife of Charles Andress of Chicago, who came to visit his sister, Miss Margaret Andress of North Broadway, Geneva, in June of 1917 (FPT, 27 June, p. 2). During a still earlier visit in 1914, Margaret and the Chicago Andresses went over to Madison,

where they "visited the old-time Andress home, now the Tom Nolan farm" (*FPT*, 16 September 1914, p. 2).

Many years earlier still, the Reverend Lucius Andress built a home on the South Ridge on the site of the residence and cooper shop of Lemuel Wiard, one of the area's first settlers (*FPT*, 25 January 1916, p. 3; a cooper shop or cooperage is the place where a cooper makes and repairs casks, pails, and tubs). It is therefore of interest that some of the property bordering the Perrin farm was owned for a time by F. R. and M. "Andruss" ("Deed to Henry Perrin," *Ashtabula County Records*, vol. 172, p. 303).

10 Henry may write "Bertha" here in an effort to give the correct form of the nickname "Bertie." In any case, chances are that he refers to his Aunt Alberta Coffman Elliott. Whoever he had in mind by writing "they," however, he could not have meant to include Bertie's husband (Annie's brother), Thomas Henry Elliott, who died of pneumonia back in 1905.

11 In recording for Lettie the following list of his studies Henry is even less concerned than usual about regular punctuation.

12 Like most of Henry's letters, this one is written on stationery provided by the "Y." At the top of each sheet is a red, white, and blue American flag, the motto "WITH THE COLORS," and the logo (letters inside a red triangle) of the Young Men's Christian Association.

13 Lulu Lowe. See note to Annie's entry for 24 March.

Well there are other things besides pleasures here. I do a little washing nearly every night. Have an awful time of it too. Can hardly get my heavy underwear clean.

I will name the studies I am taking [and] then you may judge as to how busy we are.[11] 1. Anatomy. 2. Physiology. 3. First Aid. 4 Emergency Surgery. 5 Bandaging 6 Operating Room & Surgical Technic. 7 Nursing 8 Hospital duties 9. Ward Management 10–Naval Hospital work 11–Hygiene & Sanitation 12 Pharmacy 13–Materia Medica 14–Pathology 15 Chemistry– 16 Toxicology 17– Clerical Duties and Rules of the Hospital Corps. Our books are furnished—free while we are schooling. I think my head will ache when I get it all learned.

While going to the Y. Sat[urday].[12] I met an officer that had spoken to me about transfering to the Public works. He wants me to take it up. I can't decide yet.

Your letters are surely interesting but [I] have so much to tell you that I can't touch much on things you say. But even so I read & reread them all.

My first mail consisted of your letters & card— Rayms[,] Mothers & one from Lulu.[13] Was sure glad to get them[.] One of my Ohio mates received a big box of cookies & candy to-day from his mother. We always share with each other. We are four. That is[,] we four stick around pretty closely.

We don't get many liberties while at school. Our com[mander]. is very rough but good.

Some chow we get. For breakfast we had grape fruit, rice, oat meal—coffee cake, cocoa—bread & butter. Sure do get some feeds. Plenty for me. Some of the boys ask for seconds & some 3rd's. It is a sight for sore eyes to see us all eating. When we get eggs they are generally hard boiled & we get 2 each.

Was surprised to hear of little Hazel[,][14] also Steve Allen.[15] Queer how things turn out.

Am going to have a picture taken as soon as I get some meat on.[16] Have lost awfully this last week. Think I've had too much work & being all new it got on my nerves.

Ed Burwell enlisted as a seaman.[17] Hasn't even a rate.[18] Should [have] tho[ugh]t he would have tried for something else. He doesn't look very well. Says he likes the Navy fine so far.[19]

Well sis I must cut this short.

Am feeling fine and trying to be content. Glad to hear Mother has sent my sweater. I thank you both for it.[20]

Tell everyone hello & write often to me.

Will close with lots of love.

from your bro. in blue.

xxxxx[21]

You can make me some candy any time you wish. You don't know how good things taste from home.

Yours

Hen.

[14] Perhaps Lettie's friend Hazel E. Pierce (daughter of the Byron Pierces), who had been boarding on Vine Street for several years and currently was working as a stenographer (*FPT*, 11 November 1913, p. 3; *Ashtabula Directory 1918*, p. 283).

[15] Stephen Allen (originally from Saybrook) and his wife (a daughter of the James Maltbies) lived on the South Ridge (*FPT*, 10 December 1918, p. 3). Back home he had worked for a while at the Adams Express in Ashtabula (*FPT*, 23 November 1915, p. 3). Now in 1918, like Henry, he was to become one of those local servicemen who fell victim to but then survived the epidemic of Spanish influenza and pneumonia (*FPT*, 1 November 1918, p. 6).

[16] That is, gain some weight.

[17] In his haste, Henry writes "seamen" here.

[18] A rating is "an enlisted classification according to a certain specialty or proficiency" (Tomajczyk, p. 459). Henry, in contrast, had been rated very quickly at Great Lakes (see notes to Annie's diary entry of 13 April).

[19] An old friend from Geneva days, Edwin Burwell was at one time part of the "office force" at The American Fork and Hoe (*FPT*, 16 August 1913, p. 2). Over six months after this letter he was still at Great Lakes. His mother, when she happened to hear of the death of another Ed Burwell, wrote from Cleveland to assure Genevans who knew him that her own son—Henry's friend—was "alive and well" (*FPT*, 8 November, p. 1).

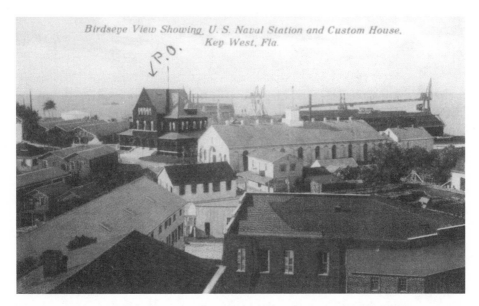

Fig. 109. The caption on this postcard sent by Henry to Lettie in the fall of 1918 reads "Birdseye View Showing U.S. Naval Station and Custom House, Key West, Fla." The red-brick Customs House at Front and Greene Streets doubled as a post office and dominated the waterfront. To its right here is the Naval Depot (the long, low, white building), and seeming to loom up between the two like part of a giant erector set is some of the major hardware of the Navy's coaling plant (Malone and Strunk, pp. 29, 56).

[20] Annie finished the sweater about 25 April. Henry thanked Lettie, too, because she bought the yarn.

[21] Immediately following these five Xs (representing five kisses) Henry placed an underlined superscript "100"—confusing and difficult to set in type here, but apparently denoting "to the hundredth power."

2

[22] Henry was now stationed in Key West at the naval hospital, a new facility which had been in commission only since 4 June that year. It was designed to handle 156 patients and had a total of 264 beds (including beds for medical officers, nurses, corpsmen, ma-rines, guards, and others) (*Annual Reports of the Navy Department . . . 1919*, p. 2265).

Key West, Fla.[22]

9-12-18.

My Dearest Sis,

I tho[ugh]t surely I would hear from home to-day but did not.

Sure is hot here during the day, especially in the morning from 7 to 12. The evenings are nice and cool but very short as it is dark by 6:30.

Fig. 110. This second postcard from Henry to Lettie is labeled "Duval Street, Looking West, Key West, Fla.," and Henry has written toward the bottom (on the tracks running along Greene Street) that this is "Practically the center of town." On a choice site at the left here is the dry goods and clothing store of Abraham Wolkowsky, and just beyond is Frank Johnson's jewelry store. In the distance, the building with the view-commanding cupola is The Jefferson Hotel (Malone and Strunk, pp. 31, 43).

I am detailed in the main laboratory. Yesterday I made 17 urinalysis tests for bacteria, urea, albumin, sugar, acid and etc. Also blood test and several others of which I will not relate. Did a lot of recording in the P.M. & microscopic work. It is very interesting work. Have a fine Dr. & pharmacists' mate to work with. Did not have quite as much to do to-day as we had school this P.M. I also prepared specimens of blood and sent them to Wash. D.C. for test. We are supposed to go to school from 1:30 to 2:30 every P.M. but if we are busy we don't go.

Have to wear rubber gloves & white robes in Lab.

23 See Figs. 109 and 110 for postcard images of Key West.

Last night 4 of us went to explore the city.[23] Every thing is so queer. The only white folks here are Gov[ern]ment]. men & men in the service. The houses are mostly one story and all pretty much alike. They are all nicely painted with well kept yards around them. Nearly all have bannana trees or cocoa nut palms in their yards.

We went thru the Naval Training camp. There are about 1000 boys there. Also have the naval aviation camp & marines here. I haven't been there as yet. While at the station last night we saw quite a few torpedo boats & sub. chasers, also a ferry with 30 loaded cars leaving for Cuba. It is all so strange to me.

This P.M. while at school we saw 8 men of war in fleet formation westward bound. Some said they were troop ships with the fleet to guard them.

Am sitting on our front porch (I am on the 2nd floor)[.] From here I can see the Gulf of Mex[ico]. & the Atlantic. The Golf [sic] on the N[orth]. and East & the Atlantic on the West.[24] From the Hospital we can see over the entire island.[25] We could from here if we could see out the back way but there are'nt any windows. Every where we look we can see nothing but blue water. The sunsets are beautiful here. The clouds look so different here. Nearly at all times we can see a storm at sea but they say they seldom come here. Glad of that. You can't make us think we are in USA. Never hear the natives speak English at least.

[24] It appears that Henry has carelessly reversed "East" and "West" here.

[25] The outstanding architectural feature of the hospital was its large screened verandas, which alone could accommodate fifty beds (*Annual Reports of the Navy Department . . . 1919*, p. 2265). Key West is about one mile wide and four and a half miles long.

I have had liberty from 3 P.M. to 6 A.M. while here but we get in at about 10 as I would hate to stay out all night. We get up at 6:30 and have morning exercises[,] then chow at 7. And it is some chow. The best Uncle Sam can produce and put up in style. Have black sailors to serve us. I like the iced fruit drinks we get here. Can have all we want. Also have sugar & butter. Had okra for chow this noon. Never heard of it before but it was good.

The sky is full of air craft to-night. They fly day & night. Have to guard against submarines. They also have the big observation baloons here. They look fine, have a pretty speedy motor in them.[26]

The water for showers & washing is salt water right from the old Sea.[27] Our clothes sure are white after using such water & then leaving them in the sun all day. I washed this P.M. Have to be _real_ clean here.[28] Our clothes don't soil very fast tho. No dust or soot to soil them.

There is a section in this place that we are not allowed in. It is guarded day & night. Used to be worse than it is now as they sold drinks there.

They call the Cuban girls Spicks.[29] They sure have some eyes. Like Lula's.[30]

I feel about 90 y[ea]rs. old. Can hardly put one foot before the other to walk. The boys say we will feel that way for several weeks. A goodly share of the boys have the itch.[31] I hope I don't get it.

The four that came with me are eaten up with mosquitoes. I haven't had even a nibble. Some mosquitoes here too. Truthfully sis they are ¾ of an inch long and all covered with fur. Also [there] are little frogs here

26 "Ballooning," which had made possible "a system of ever-watchful sentries," provided a vital supplement to Air Service reconnaissance. An observer stationed in a balloon at an altitude of a mile was said to have about an eight-mile range of vision in every direction (_War Department, Annual Reports, 1918_, 1:1389).

27 Water supply clearly posed a problem. Henry later told Lettie of seeing "tank trains" hauling "about a hundred large tanks of fresh water from Miami daily" (1 November), and an official report stated that "Water for drinking and galley use and for the sterilizer, laboratory, and dispensary is collected from the roofs of various buildings and stored in cisterns" (_Annual Reports of the Navy Department . . . 1919_, p. 2265).

28 Henry refers particularly to the hospital and laboratory where he worked.

29 "Spick" (or "spic") is actually non-gendered but offensive slang for any hispanic person.

30 Lulu Lowe. See, e.g., the entry and note for 25 December 1918.

31 Probably scabies—either a homegrown variety or perhaps the "French itch," so called because it seemed to have been brought back to Paris from the front (_FPT_, 3 February 1919, p. 1).

that make more noise than our big bull frogs. They sit on the bannana trees around the yard here and nearly drive us mad with their noise. They aren't any larger than a cricket.

On the way from [the] Fl[orid]a mainland, crossing over the overseas R.R. we saw sharks, pelicans, and lots of funny creatures.[32] Passing thru the Everglades all we saw was swamps, bannana groves & once in a while a native shack. Would hate to live there. The prettiest scenery was thru the Tenn[essee]. hills. We passed thru 2 tunnels. The gas almost put me under. Made me awfully sick. I still feel it in my lungs. Think that started my cold.

We are fenced in here just like a prison with Marines guarding the gates. They are the Navy's police.

Am going to get some white canvas shoes. These I have are too heavy for here.

Don't know how long we will be here. Some of the boys have been here 6 mo[nths]. and are just preparing to leave with the Marines for France. Hope we are not here that long.

I suppose your school has started. You must write & tell me about it.

We are only 45 so you see you must write often so I won't get lonely.[33]

Will try to write a more interesting letter next time. Lots of love to all.

Your loving bro.

Henry

[32] Henry is backtracking here, recalling his journey via the Overseas Railway from Florida City to Key West.

[33] Henry miswrites this word as "lonley."

Fig. 111. A deadly serious Uncle Sam here pours from a cornucopia of arms made possible by the current Liberty Loan. Caught in the deluge and very angry is Wilhelm von Hohenzollern, his identity made clear by the initials on his shoe soles. Complicating the simple message ("Lend To Uncle Sam!"), however, the artist has for some reason given Wilhelm three hands and three feet. (From the *FPT*, 10 October, p. 1.)

3

∽

Key West, Fla.

10-11-'18

My Dear Sis,

I haven't heard from home for three days but hope to hear from you to-day.[34]

It is cool to-day. Had several storms during the night and another one is on it's way over-seas. The clouds are very low and brown in color. Look pretty wild to me. This is the hurricane season but we haven't been notified to prepare for one as yet.

There is a storm-bell here. A guard rings it when a bad storm is due or in sight. The ocean is awfully rough to-day, [or I] should say "a heavy sea on."

[34] Evidence abounds that frequent communication was one of Henry's goals.

[35] This nickname for Kaiser Wilhelm Hohenzollern may be found in many places. For example, a bit of newspaper doggerel entitled "Yanks Will Make It Hotter'n Hell for Kaiser Bill" runs thus:

> The Devil said "Hello" to Bill
> And Bill said, "How are you?
> I'm running here a hell on earth,
> So tell me what to do."
> (S&B, 2 May, p. 6)

[36] Lettie had bought another Liberty Bond. A series of huge campaigns had been mounted to sell so-called Liberty Loans in order to finance the nation's war effort, and the fourth such campaign was currently underway. (Fig. 111. See also note to Annie's diary entry for 19 July, and Figs. 69 and 70.)

[37] Like many teachers, Lettie was managing the classroom collection of money for War Savings Stamps. Back in May a nationwide "Army of School Sammies" had been created so as to constitute a buying pool for the stamps. At that time, every child was automatically made a "private." Each one might then become a "corporal" by selling $100 worth of stamps. Near the top of the ladder were the "Generals" (with sales of $5,000 each), and, at the very top, some extraordinary schoolchild "Commanders-in-Chief" ($50,000) (FPT, 12 August, p. 1).

[38] One of the ongoing problems in the school where Lettie taught was overenrollment. On 29 October 1917 the Free Press-Times published an article discussing "the crowded condition of the graded school building"— and, strikingly, on the same page there was a social item with the news that "Miss Lettie Perrin visited the schools at Warren on Thursday and spent Friday at the Northeastern Ohio Teachers' meeting" (29 October 1917, p. 2).

The good news just before school opened in 1918 was that officials had agreed to hire "an

We received word last night that Bill had been abdicated.[35] I hope it is true. It caused quite a lot of excitement here when we heard of it.

So you have signed for another bond![36] You surely are doing more than your bit.

I suppose you'll have oodles of money now you are a treasurer. Don't skip the country. It must mean a lot of extra work for you.[37] Glad to hear your class has been divided.[38]

I have the blues to-day. Every thing is gloomy here. Nothing but sick boys to look at.

Yesterday I went over to see the pneumonia patients. I never want to see them again. Will not discribe what I saw because it is too awful. The Dr's all tho[ugh]t that pneumonia would not set in here but it has.[39] One good thing, they don't suffer long.

Would hate like heck to die down here. But even at that it is not as bad as "over-there."

One thing we know, we are saving lives instead of taking them. Aunt Ella wrote that she tho[ugh]t it was such grand and noble work of God that I was sent here to save instead of kill.[40] Quite a nice letter but sort of "dizzy."

You don't care what you pay for a hat do you? Would like to see it. It must be a beauty.[41]

How is the weather these days? Colder I suppose. We feel quite a change here. Sure hope it stays cooler.

Fall oranges are in market here. They are green as grass on the outside but real sweet and seem ripe inside. I wish you could see some of the cocoa nuts that grow here. They are giants. If I can get one am going to send it home. Don't know how you will open it, but try an axe. Apples are 5¢ each and are not as good as those that ma sent to me. Every thing is higher than a kite, hardly see how they have a right to charge so much. Suppose it is on account of being so far away from god's country.

Have you seen Pat lately.[42] I lost my little address book so can't write to her. Do you think we'll be home by Xmas? I hope so. When we have the Grand Review at Washington I want you to be there.[43] Sure will be some sight.

Well sis it is time for medications again so will have to start the ball.

Will not mail this until P.M. mail arrives as I may hear from home. Here's hoping.

bye bye—Hen.

7 P.M.

Well Ma's letter arrived[,] also one from Mrs. S.[44] Was sure glad to hear from home. Does Raym go the 15th?[45] Let me know. Am all in Sis. Too many sick men. Another went "West" about 15 min[utes] ago.[46] Write often[.]

xxx Lovingly Hen.

extra teacher for the overflow from the fifth and sixth grades" (*FPT*, 21 August, p. 1). The bad news as late as 6 September was that the sixth grade still had forty-seven students (*FPT*, p. 1). Worst of all, however, judging from a front-page item in the *Free Press-Times* on 12 May of the following spring, Lettie was simultaneously teaching the sixth and eighth grades (George Hasenpflug was one of her pupils in the latter). Little wonder that she moved that fall to Warren—which town, according to the Geneva paper, had "some of the best schools in the state" (23 May 1919, p. 1).

[39] Spanish influenza, unlike any other kind, was generally succeeded by pneumonia, and the latter was the actual cause of many deaths attributed to "flu."

[40] Ella Spicer Elliott was the wife of Annie's brother James John Elliott. They lived in a large house on a large farm near LeMars, Iowa.

[41] See Annie's diary entry for 14 September.

[42] Pat was the young woman who visited the Perrins on the South Ridge on 21 July. Henry had some difficulty trying to determine how to handle her interest in him.

[43] As it turned out, New York welcomed the returning U.S. Naval fleet on the day Henry sailed for France (Tuesday, 24 December). All was done on a "tremendous scale": "thousands of incandescent light bulbs" were strung so as to outline the vessels, and thousands of sailors marched through the streets (*S&B*, 24 December, p. 1).

[44] Probably Rose Smith.

[45] Raym's date with the draft board was canceled on account of the flu. Later it was rescheduled for 15 November—and then, once again, canceled.

[46] Though few servicemen were likely to be aware of the fact, their euphemistic slang for "died" may be traced back to the ancient Egyptians.

4

~

Key West, Fla.

11-8-'18

Dear Lettie,

Your nice long letter rec'd. yesterday with "Flu. clippings" enclosed.[47] They seem to be having quite a time of it.

I am feeling better than I have felt for some time. Weigh 155, eating like a pig and sleeping good. I have never had better care. All the Dr's. and nurses were very good to me. Three of the Dr's. are new here but are regular pals to us. The old unit is about cleaned out now.[48] Most of them were sent to Base Hospital No. 1 in France.[49] I wish I could have gone.

Well sis this is my last day in Key West. Would have left last night but yesterday was a day of celebration here so our records could not be made out for us.

Dr. Donaldson[,] our new Exec. Larson,[50] Bocock, Mrs. Gardner (nurse) two pharmacist's mates and myself leave to-night at 6:30 for Norfolk, Va. where we will stand by for orders. We are in hopes we will board a Transport and go over but we may be detailed there until peace papers have been signed and then be discharged. We never know what to expect and as our orders are sealed we do not know what they are.

The Admiral of this 7th Naval Dist[rict]. gave us the town last night.[51] I think all of the Fleet were in the harbor. There were so many sailors here that it was al-

[47] These clippings probably included the news that Geneva had now had a total of 113 cases of flu, that currently it had thirty-three cases, that Viola Hanson had died of the disease, and that Henry himself had come down with it (*S&B*, 28 October, p. 8; 30 October, p. 6; and *FPT*, 31 October, p. 1). In the interval between this letter and that of 11 October Henry himself had been seriously ill.

[48] Most of Henry's friends shipped out during his illness.

[49] Base Hospital No. 1 was situated at Brest. As of 6 February 1919, "a Regular Army officer of high rank" blew the whistle on the American operation there, declaring it "the vilest hole in France" (*FPT*, 11 March, p. 1). Over 3,000 American servicemen who had been reported killed in action were now said to have died in Brest because of inadequate housing and sanitation. Another informant went so far as to "charge that Brest has been a scandal from the very day it was selected as a rest camp and debarkation point; that an incompetent officer was sent there to organize and made a miserable failure." Nevertheless, Brest soon became also the official port (colloquially, the "Bride Port") where French brides had to go in order to depart for America (*FPT*, 2 September 1919, p. 1).

[50] Arthur J. Larson, a pharmacist, was Henry's executive officer (U.S. Navy, *Register of the Commissioned and Warrant Officers . . . 1918*, p. 244).

most impossible to walk. The sidewalks & streets were crowded.

About 7ᴾᴹ a snake dance was started. There were thousands of sailors, marines and soldiers in it. It reached for miles it seemed. Officers & all joined in. I guess the ten cent store was cleaned out as for whistles, horns and all kinds of noise makers. The "line" went thru all the stores, restaurants, hotels, theatres and every place of business. We went down the isles of the theatres, on to the stages, right while the show was going on. The orchestra played our National song until we left. Hard to tell how long it took to go thru as I was about the center of the line and could not see the end. I never took part in such an exciting affair before. All the church bells were ringing, factory whistles blowing, the boats in the harbor and out were ringing their bells and blowing the[ir] sirens. Believe me it made the chills run up our spines.

Can imagine what it would be like in a regular town.

As I told you my new rating was to take effect the 15ᵗʰ.[52] Well, as I am to leave[,] Dr. Orvis our Com'der. made it effective at once.[53] I surely appreciated it. Of course I would only had to have waited 8 da[ys]. if I had have stayed here[,] but would had to have left here an Ha1 as the rating would have been void if I left this 7ᵗʰ Dist[rict]. before it took effect.[54] Pretty nice of him, eh?

This is going to be a long day for me. Nothing to do but wait around for 6:30 to come. I wish you could take the trip with me. Surely am seeing some country.

[51] Rear Admiral William B. Fletcher of Vermont had been commandant of the 7th Naval District since 15 January this year (*Register of the Commissioned and Warrant Officers . . . 1919*, p. 10). In a previous letter Henry told Lettie that "Fletcher . . . was commander of the whole Atlantic Fleet at the beginning of the war but he lost a ship so was dropped to Com. [of] the anchor fleet" (29 September).

[52] On 3 November Henry wrote that he was looking forward to putting a crow and chevron on his arm as a Pharmacist's Mate, 3rd Class. This meant that he was to become a petty officer, third class. "Would be a Sargt," he wrote, "if I had the same rate in the army."

[53] Dr. Ralph Thompson Orvis of Illinois received his assignment as a commander in the Medical Corps on 27 November 1917 (*Register . . . 1918*, pp. 128, 472).

[54] As a Hospital Apprentice, 1st Class, Henry had been a seaman, first class.

I hope any of you haven't sent me a box as it would sure be delayed. Haven't rec'd the box you sent yet.

I have every thing clean, heavy underwear and all. Think I will need it up there.

Am going to drop some more cards on the way to Va. so you'll know I'm getting there. Will telegram also when I get to Jacksonville.

How about the Vic?[55] I hope dad will help you get it. Sure hope all are well and smiling.

Don't dream such <u>orful</u> dreams about me, sis. When I get humps on my back I'll take to the desert.

All for now[.]

Lots of love to all

Hen.

[55] The arrival of the family's new Victrola is noted in Annie's diary entry of 20 December 1918.

A Partial Family Tree
of the Elliotts and Perrins

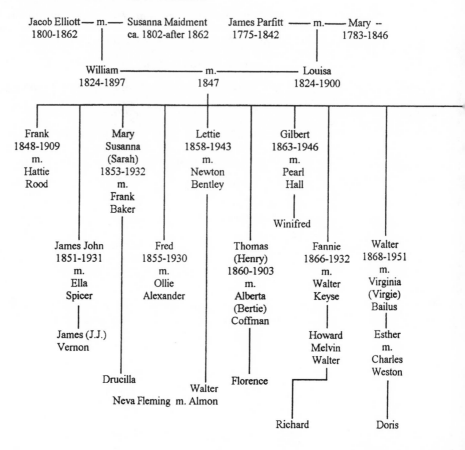

Jacob Elliott — m. — Susanna Maidment
1800-1862   ca. 1802-after 1862

James Parfitt ——— m. ——— Mary --
1775-1842   1783-1846

William ————————— m. ————————— Louisa
1824-1897   1847   1824-1900

Frank
1848-1909
m.
Hattie
Rood

Mary
Susanna
(Sarah)
1853-1932
m.
Frank
Baker

Lettie
1858-1943
m.
Newton
Bentley

Gilbert
1863-1946
m.
Pearl
Hall

Winifred

James John
1851-1931
m.
Ella
Spicer

Fred
1855-1930
m.
Ollie
Alexander

Thomas
(Henry)
1860-1903
m.
Alberta
(Bertie)
Coffman

Fannie
1866-1932
m.
Walter
Keyse

Walter
1868-1951
m.
Virginia
(Virgie)
Bailus

James (J.J.)
Vernon

Howard
Melvin
Walter

Esther
m.
Charles
Weston

Drucilla

Walter
Neva Fleming m. Almon

Florence

Richard

Doris

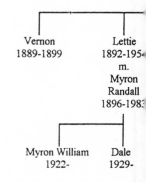

Vernon
1889-1899

Lettie
1892-195◄
m.
Myron
Randall
1896-198⁀

Myron William
1922-

Dale
1929-

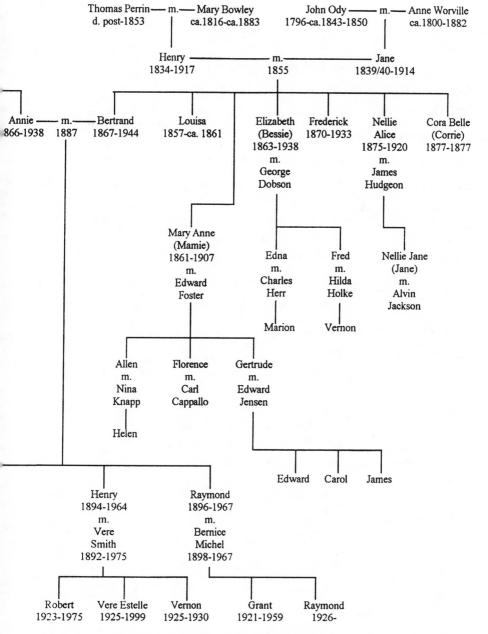

"Soliloquy of a Farmer's Wife"

The poem presented in this final appendix appeared anonymously in Geneva's *Free Press-Times* of 6 June 1918.[1] Though the verses themselves are hopeless doggerel, they and the three-sentence headnote that introduces them in the newspaper provide a thought-provoking sounding board for the exactly contemporaneous diary of Annie Perrin.

The newspaper headnote reads as follows: "From somewhere out in the rural district come these little verses. The writer calls her offering 'The Soliloquy of a Farmer's Wife.' It is quite probable that there are other women who will appreciate this 'Soliloquy.'"

The poem itself goes thus:

> *There was a man,*
> *A man of deeds,*
> *He sowed his garden full of seeds,*
> *And when the seeds began to grow*
> *His worthy wife went out to hoe.*
> *And hoe she did,*
> *From day to day,*
> *This faithful wife*
> *Without her pay.*
> *She washed and baked*
> *On the rainy day*
> *To be ready to hoe*

[1] P. 2. A few minor editorial corrections have been made in this transcription.

In the sun's bright ray.
When harvest came
This farmer bold
Gathered his crops
And kept the gold.
But the faithful wife said,
"Oh! Where is my share,
For the work I have done
In the sun's fierce glare?"
The farmer sees nothing
But the needs of the farm,
And in robbing his wife
He sees no harm.
As the years roll by,
With toil and strife,
This good wife tires
Of this sort of life.
As she sees the women
With nice pretty clothes
She, too, wants a dress
With the furbelows.
And who can blame
This worthy wife,
Who had pretty things
In her single life?
Now a farmer should recall
The Golden Rule,
And not treat his wife
Like a useful tool.
Old age will come on,
And hairs will turn gray,
But both will be happier
If both receive pay.

Research Sources

Individuals

(For space reasons, this listing omits a good many librarians—mainly at Duke University, but elsewhere as well—who have helped to provide material without which this book could not have been completed.)

Baker, Candace S. Deputy Clerk (Probate Court), Ashtabula County Common Pleas Court. Jefferson, Ohio.

Baker, Elizabeth. Halifax Historical Society. Daytona Beach, Florida.

Barta, Judith A. Ashtabula County Recorder. Jefferson, Ohio.

Behm, Ford. Behm Funeral Home. Geneva, Ohio.

Blackburn, John O. Maitland, Florida.

Brockway, Jerome R. County Superintendent, Ashtabula County Schools. Jefferson, Ohio.

Carlson, John H. ("Jack"). Cuyahoga Falls, Ohio.

Colling, May. Ashtabula County Genealogical Society. Geneva, Ohio.

Family History Center. Chapel Hill, North Carolina.

Follett, Steve. Geneva, Ohio.

Haskin, June. Rocky River, Ohio.

Hocking, Philip J. Somerset Record Office. Taunton, Somersetshire, England.

Humphreys, Margaret. Department of History and Department of Medicine, Duke University. Durham, North Carolina.

Jensen, Carol A. Parma, Ohio.

Jensen, Edward W. Chester, Virginia.

Jensen, James L. Palm Beach, Florida.

Larimore, Virginia Cappallo. Cambridge, Ohio.

Keyse, Richard B. Southern Pines, North Carolina.

Miller, Kim M. Antique Auto Club of America. Hershey, Pennsylvania.

Motley, Archie. Curator of Archives and Manuscripts, Chicago Historical Society. Chicago, Illinois.

Nizen, Kathy. Deputy Recorder, Ashtabula County. Jefferson, Ohio.

O'Brien, Sandra. Ashtabula County Auditor. Jefferson, Ohio.

Pepin, June S. Geneva, Ohio.

Perrin, Raymond A., Jr., and Eileen Pfeiffer Perrin. Hendersonville, North Carolina.

Petrak, Linda. Midland Genealogical Society. Midland, Michigan.

Sferra, Jane J. Ohio Historical Society. Columbus, Ohio.

Steman, Thomas. Case-Western Reserve University Archives. Cleveland, Ohio.

Sumners, Bill. Director, Southern Baptist Historical Library and Archives. Nashville, Tennessee.

Thrift, Nell. Florida Conference Archives, United Methodist Church. Lakeland, Florida.

Tingley, Charles A. St. Augustine Historical Society. St. Augustine, Florida.

Wade, Larry R. Pastor, Park Street Christian Church. Geneva, Ohio.

Weston, Doris E. Westlake, Ohio.

Published Sources
(Including Photocopies and Microforms)

Abbot, Willis J. *Bluejackets of 1918, Being the Story of the Work of the American Navy in the World War.* New York: Dodd, Mead, 1921.

Ainslie, Ricardo C. *The Psychology of Twinship.* Lincoln: University of Nebraska Press, 1985.

Annual of the Florida Baptist Convention 1917–1918. Tallahassee, 1918.

Ashtabula County History Then and Now. Comp. and ed., Ashtabula County Genealogical Society. Dallas: Taylor Publishing Co., 1985.

Ashtabula, Geneva, Jefferson, Kingsville and North Kingsville Directory 1918. Erie, Pa.: Atkinson Erie Directory Co., 1918.

Ashtabula Star and Beacon. Ashtabula, Ohio. 31 October 1916–18 April 1919.

Aytoun, William Edmondstoune. "Edinburgh after Flodden." In *Lays of the Scottish Cavaliers*, pp. 13–31. Chicago: Donohue, Henneberry and Co., 1900.

Bauer, Karl Jack. *Ships of the Navy 1775–1969.* Troy, N.Y.: Rensselaer Polytechnic Institute, 1970.

Begos, Jane DuPree. *A Women's Diaries Miscellany.* Weston, Conn.: Magic Circle Press, 1989.

Berrey, Lester V., and Melvin Van Den Bark. *The American Thesaurus of Slang.* New York: Thomas Y. Crowell, 1960.

Bonk, Mary Rose, and Regie A. Carlton, eds. *Acronyms, Initialisms and Abbreviations Dictionary.* Vol. 1 of 3 vols. Detroit: Gale Research, 1998.

Bright, Charles D., and Robin Higham, eds. *Historical Directory of the U.S. Air Force.* New York: Greenwood Press, 1992.

Burke's Genealogical and Heraldic History of the Landed Gentry. London: Burke's Peerage, Ltd., 1939.

Caird, James. *English Agriculture in 1850–51.* London: Longman, Brown, Green, and Longmans, 1852; reprint ed., Farnborough, Hants., England: Gregg International Publishers, 1968.

Campbell, Charles A. R. "My Observations on Bedbugs" [1903]. In Campbell, *Bats, Mosquitoes and Dollars*, pp. 219–27. Boston: Stratford Company, 1925.

Campbell, Edward C. *Geneva, Ohio: The Building of an American City 1866–1966.* Geneva: Lions Club of Geneva, 1966.

Carleton, Will. *Farm Legends.* New York: Harper and Brothers, 1875.

Cary, Alice, and Phoebe Cary. *The Poetical Works of Alice and Phoebe Cary.* Boston: Houghton, Mifflin, 1888.

Chapman, Sydney. "The Aurora in Middle and Low Latitudes." *Nature* 179 (5 January 1957): 7–11.

Chicago Daily Tribune. 13 April 1918.

Cincinnati Enquirer. 25 August 1929.

Clark, Rufus. *Early History of the South Ridge.* Index comp. by Mildred Thompson Scott. Jefferson, Ohio: Ashtabula County Genealogical Society, 1981.

Cleveland Plain Dealer. 11 October 1918; 26 October 1918; 27 October 1918; 12 November 1918; 13 November 1918; 24 November 1918.

Coe, Marianne E. *Westlake United Methodist, 1825–1975.* Westlake, Ohio: Westlake United Methodist Church, 1975.

Cohen-Stratyner, Barbara, ed. *Popular Music, 1900–1919.* Detroit: Gale Research, 1988.

Crittall, Elizabeth, ed. *A History of Wiltshire.* Vol. 4 of *The Victoria History of the Counties of England.* London: Oxford University Press, 1959.

Cromie, Alice Hamilton. *A Tour Guide of the Civil War.* Chicago: Quadrangle Books, 1965.

Crosby, Alfred W. *America's Forgotten Pandemic: The Influenza of 1918.* Cambridge: Cambridge University Press, 1989.

Davis, Thomas. *General View of the Agriculture of Wiltshire.* London: Sherwood, Neely, and Jones, 1813.

Daytona City Directory . . . 1914. Jacksonville: R. L. Polk and Co., 1914.

Dean, Frank C. "Cuyahoga Men Show How Scientific Farming Pays." *The Sunday Magazine* (p. 4), *Cleveland Plain Dealer,* 24 November 1918.

Dodwell, Edward, and James Miles (East India Army Agents), comp. and ed. *Alphabetical List of the Honourable East India Company's Bengal Civil Servants, from the Year 1780, to the Year 1838.* London: Longman, Orme, Brown, and Co., 1839.

Dorland, W. A. Newman. *Dorland's Illustrated Medical Dictionary.* Philadelphia: Saunders, 1994.

Dovell, James Elmore. *History of Banking in Florida, 1828–1954.* Orlando: Florida Bankers Association, 1955.

Drake, Joseph Rodman. "The American Flag." In *One Hundred Best American Poems,* selected by John R. Howard, pp. 25–28. New York: Thomas Y. Crowell and Co., 1905.

Eaton, Emma Florence. *Dramatic Studies from the Bible.* Boston: Pilgrim Press, 1906.

Ellis, William D., and Mary Ellen Wobbecke. *A History of Westlake, Ohio 1811 to 1961.* Westlake: s.n., 1961.

Ellsworth, Catherine T. *Ellsworths Historical Sketches of Ashtabula Co., Ohio as First Published by the Star-Beacon, Ashtabula, Ohio 1975–1976[,] 1986–1988.* Ashtabula: Great Lakes Printing, Inc., 1988.

Fales, E. N. *Learning to Fly in the U.S. Army.* New York: McGraw-Hill Book Co., 1917.

The Farm Journal Illustrated Rural Directory of Ashtabula County 1918. Philadelphia: Wilmer Atkinson Co., 1918.

Farmer, John S. *Americanisms—Old and New.* London: Thomas Poulter and Sons, 1888.

———, and W. E. Henley. *A Dictionary of Slang and Colloquial English.* London: George Routledge and Sons, 1912.

Farr, Grahame E., ed. *Records of Bristol Ships 1800–1838 (Vessels over 150 Tons).* Bristol Record Society's Publications, vol. 15. Bristol: Bristol Record Society, 1950.

Faust, Patricia L. *Historical Times Illustrated Encyclopedia of the Civil War.* New York: Harper and Row, 1986.

Felt, Ephraim Porter. "Household and Camp Insects." *New York State Museum Bulletin* 194 (1917): 1–84.

Fielding, Henry. *Joseph Andrews.* Ed. Martin C. Battestin. Oxford: Clarendon Press, 1967.

Florida: "The East Coast": Its Builders, Resources, Industries, Town and City Developments. Miami: *Miami Herald,* ca. 1924.

Florida: "The Playground of the Nation." Jacksonville: R. L. Polk and Co., 1925.

Florida Times-Union. Jacksonville, Florida. 13 December 1951.

Foster, Allen H. "Thoughts of Thee" (waltz). Washington, D.C.: Kirkus Dugdale Co., 1914.

Gardiner, Robert, "Editorial Director." *Conway's All the World's Fighting Ships 1860–1905.* New York: Mayflower Books, 1979.

Geneva Free Press. Geneva, Ohio. 9 July 1960.

Geneva Free Press-Times. Geneva, Ohio. 1 September 1914–31 July 1920.

Gerard, James W. *My Four Years in Germany.* New York: George H. Doran Co., 1917.

Gifford, Harry, Tom Mellor, and Huntley Trevor. "When It's Apple Blossom Time in Normandie" (song). New York: Jerome H. Remick and Co., 1912.

Gilmore, J. R. "Malmesbury and Its International Links." In *Malmesbury: 1100 Years a Borough,* pp. 18–28. N.p.: 1980.

Gleason, William J. *History of the Cuyahoga County Soldiers' and Sailors' Monument.* Cleveland: The Monument Commissioners, 1894.

Gordon, Janet, and Edward Gabriel. "Let Me Hear the Songs My Mother Used to Sing" (song). Chicago: Frank K. Root and Co., 1906.

Grant, H. Roger. *Railroad Postcards in the Age of Steam.* Iowa City: University of Iowa Press, 1994.

Grant's Tourist Guide of Orlando, Florida. DeLand: E. O. Painter, 1919.

Gray, Frank A. *Gray's New Map of Cincinnati.* Philadelphia: O. W. Gray, [1880].

Gray, Randal, with Christopher Argyle. *Chronicles of the First World War.* Vol. 2: *1917–1921.* London: Butler and Tanner, 1991.

Greenwood, C. and J. *Somerset Delineated: Being a Topographical Description of Each Town, Parish, Chapelry, &c. in the County.* London: C. and J. Greenwood, 1822.

Griffiths, D., Jr. *Two Years' Residence in the New Settlements of Ohio, North America, with Directions to Emigrants.* London: Westley and Davis, 1835; Readex Microprint Corp., 1966.

Grim, James S. *Elementary Agriculture.* Boston: Allyn and Bacon, 1916.

Hadsell, R. S., and Hazel Rutherford. *A History and Civics of Dover Village.* Ed. William M. Robishaw. Dover, Ohio: Dover Village Boad of Education, 1981; 2d ed., 1986.

Hafner, Arthur W., ed. *Directory of Deceased American Physicians, 1804–1929.* 2 vols. Chicago: American Medical Association, 1993.

Hagedorn, Judy W., and Janet W. Kizziar. *Gemini: The Psychology and Phenomena of Twins.* Droke House: Anderson, S.C., 1974.

A Happy Message to Northerners from the Land of Year-long Spring. Moore Haven: South Florida Farms, 1918.

Hatcher, Harlan. *Lake Erie.* Indianapolis: Bobbs-Merrill Co., 1945.

Hendrickson, Robert. *Whistlin' Dixie: A Dictionary of Southern Expressions.* New York: Facts on File, 1993.

Hilton, George W., and John F. Due. *The Electric Interurban Railways in America.* Stanford, Calif.: Stanford University Press, 1960.

Hodge, Bernulf. *A History of Malmesbury.* Minety, Wiltshire: The Friends of Malmesbury Abbey, 1986.

Holbrook, Stewart H. *Down on the Farm.* New York: Crown Publishers, 1954.

Hubbard, Freeman. *Encyclopedia of North American Railroading.* New York: McGraw Hill, 1981.

Jacksonville and South Jacksonville City Directory 1926, Polk's. Jacksonville: R. L. Polk and Co., 1926.

Jacobs-Bond, Carrie. "I Love You Truly" (song). Chicago: Carrie Jacobs-Bond and Son, 1906.

Jenkins, Isaac C., ed. *Florida Annual Conference in Barlow December 4–9, 1918.* Lakeland: Florida Methodist Publishing Co., [1919].

Johnson, Crisfield, comp. *History of Cuyahoga County, Ohio.* Cleveland: D. W. Ensign and Co., 1879.

Kipling, Rudyard. *Recessional: A Victorian Ode.* New York: M. F. Mansfield, 1897.

Lamb, Arthur J., and S. R. Henry. "When the Harvest Moon Is Shining on the River" (song). New York: Joseph W. Stern and Co., 1904.

Large, Moina W. *History of Ashtabula County Ohio.* 2 vols. Topeka-Indianapolis: Historical Publishing Co., 1924.

Linton, Ruth Barber. *Pine Castle: A Walk Down Memory Lane.* Orlando: Benn Books, 1993.

McCree, Junie, and Albert Von Tilzer. "Put Your Arms Around Me, Honey: I Never Knew Any Girl Like You" (song). New York: York Music Co., 1910.

Macdonald, Ballard, and Mary Earl. "Beautiful Ohio: Song." New York: Shapiro, Bernstein and Co., 1910.

McFell, B. G. *Miss Topsy Turvy, or, The Courtship of the Deacon.* Clyde, Ohio: Ames Publishing Co., 1899.

McMillen, Wheeler. *Ohio Farm.* Columbus, Ohio: Ohio State University Press, 1974.

Madden, Edward, and Percy Wenrich. "Silver Bell" (song). New York: Jerome H. Remick and Co., 1910.

Malone, Shelley Boyd, and Phyllis Bostrom Strunk. *Postcards of Old Key West.* Key West: Malone and Strunk, Inc., 1989.

Marlatt, C. L. "The Bedbug." *United Sates Department of Agriculture Farmer's Bulletin* 754 (14 October 1916): 1–12.

Marquis, Albert Nelson, ed. *The Book of Chicagoans.* Chicago: A. N. Marquis and Co., 1917.

Mathews, Mitford M., ed. *A Dictionary of Americanisms.* Vol. 2 of 2 vols. Chicago: University of Chicago Press, 1951.

Midland Daily News. Midland, Michigan. 4 and 5 June 1943.

Midland Republican. Midland, Michigan. 29 July 1922; 1 January 1925; 3 September 1925; 24 May 1928; 6 October 1932.

Midland Sun. Midland, Michigan. 29 June 1922; 1 January 1925.

Miner, Jack. *Jack Miner: His Life and Religion.* Kingsville, Ont.: Jack Miner Migratory Bird Foundation, 1969.

———. *Jack Miner and the Birds.* Toronto: Ryerson Press, 1923.

Mittler, Peter. *The Study of Twins.* Middlesex, England: Penguin Books Ltd., 1971.

More, Hannah. *The Shepherd of Salisbury-Plain.* Bath: "Sold by S. Hazard," 1795.

Mountain Makin's in the Smokies. Gatlinburg, Tenn.: The Great Smoky Mountains Natural History Association, 1957.

Munich, Adrienne. *Queen Victoria's Secrets.* New York: Columbia University Press, 1996.

The National Cyclopaedia of American Biography. Vol. 8. New York: James T. White and Co., 1924.

Navy, U.S. *Annual Report of the Secretary of the Navy for the Fiscal Year (Including Operations and Recommendations to December 1, 1918).* Washington: Government Printing Office, 1918.

———. *Annual Reports of the Navy Department for the Fiscal Year 1919.* Washington: Government Printing Office, 1920.

———. *Register of the Commissioned and Warrant Officers of the United States Navy and U.S. Naval Volunteers Marine Corps Medical Reserve Corps and Dental Reserve Corps 1918.* Washington: Government Printing Office, 1918.

———. *Register of the Commissioned and Warrant Officers of the United States Navy U.S. Naval Reserve Force and Marine Corps 1919.* Washington: Government Printing Office, 1919.

New York Times Film Reviews 1913–1968. Vol. 1 of 6 vols. New York: New York Times and Arno Press, 1970.

Norton, Charles Ledyard. *A Handbook of Florida.* 3d ed. New York: Longmans, Green, and Co., 1894.

Opie, Iona, and Peter Opie. *The Lore and Language of Schoolchildren.* Oxford: Clarendon, 1960.

Orlando, Florida City Directory 1915–1916. Vol. 4. Asheville, N.C.: Florida-Piedmont Directory Co., 1916.

Orlando, Florida City Directory and Orange County Gazetteer 1917. Vol. 5. Asheville, N.C.: Florida-Piedmont Directory Co., 1917.

———. *1919–1920.* Vol. 6. Asheville, N.C.: Florida-Piedmont Directory Co., 1920.

———. *1921.* Vol. 7. Asheville, N.C.: Florida-Piedmont Directory Co., 1921.

———. *1922.* Vol. 8. Asheville, N.C.: Florida-Piedmont Directory Co., 1922.

———. *1923.* Vol. 9. Asheville, N.C.: Florida-Piedmont Directory Co., 1923.

Orlando Morning Sentinel. Orlando, Florida. 9 March 1918.

Packard, Winthrop. *Florida Trails.* London: Frank Palmer, 1912.

Petrie, William. *Keoeeit: The Story of Aurora Borealis.* London: Pergamon Press, 1963.

Post Route Map of the State of Ohio Showing Post Offices with the Intermediate Distances on Mail Routes in Operation on the 1st of July, 1918. Published by order of Postmaster General A. S. Burleson, 1918.

Powers, Perry F. *History of Northern Michigan.* Vol. 1 of 3 vols. Chicago: Lewis Publishing Co., 1912.

The Rand McNally Banker's Directory . . . : The

Original "Bankers' Blue Book." Chicago: Rand McNally and Co., 1915.

Reese, J. H. *Florida Flashlights*. Miami: Hefty Press, 1917.

Reports of Special Assistant Poor Law Commissioners on the Employment of Women and Children in Agriculture. London: W. Clowes and Sons, 1843. Rptd. in *British Parliamentary Papers*. Shannon: Irish University Press, 1968.

Rhodes, L. M. "The Material Progress of Florida." In *Florida: "The East Coast,"* pp. 65–69. Miami: *Miami Herald*, ca. 1924.

Rice, Harvey. *Pioneers of the Western Reserve*. Boston: Lee and Shepard, 1883.

Rice, Marjorie B. *Poems of Worth*. Cleveland: Buehler Printcraft Co., 1921.

Riley, James Whitcomb. "Griggsby's Station." In *Riley Farm-Rhymes*, pp. 83–88. New York: Grosset and Dunlap, 1905.

Roberts, Robert B. *Encyclopedia of Historic Facts*. New York: Macmillan Publishing, 1988.

Robishaw, William M. *You've Come a Long Way, Westlake*. Westlake, Ohio: Westlake Historical Society, 1993.

Roe, George Mortimer, ed. *Cincinnati: The Queen City of the West*. Cincinnati: Cincinnati Times-Star Co., 1895.

Rogers, Walter T., ed. *Directory of Abbreviations*. London: George Allen and Co., 1913.

Rose, William Ganson. *Cleveland: The Making of a City*. Cleveland: World Publishing Co., 1950.

Ross, Theodore A. *Odd Fellowship: Its History and Manual*. New York: M. S. Hazen Co., 1888.

Sears, Roebuck and Co. Chicago: Catalogue No. 155. Chicago: Sears, Roebuck and Co., 1917.

The Seminole[:] Winter Park Florida. Pamphlet, 1889.

Simmons, Amelia. *American Cooking 1796*. Ed. Gail Weesner. Boston: Rowan Tree Press, 1982.

"Soliloquy of a Farmer's Wife." *Geneva Free Press-Times*, 6 June 1918, p. 2.

St. Augustine Evening Record. St. Augustine, Florida. 21 December 1917.

Standard Guide, Florida. St. Augustine: Foster and Reynolds, 1916.

Stockbridge, Frank P., and John Holliday Perry. *Florida in the Making*. Jacksonville: DeBower Publishing, 1926.

Sturdevant, William. "Phoney Dope." *Geneva Free Press-Times*. Geneva, Ohio. 2 July 1915, p. 2.

Sutliff, Veda Ritter. *The Loveliness of Love*. Berea, Ohio: Veda Ritter Sutliff, 1995.

Taubenberger, Jeffery K., Ann H. Reid, Amy E. Krafft, Karen E. Bijwaard, and Thomas Fanning. "Initial Genetic Characterization of the 1918 'Spanish' Influenza Virus." *Science* 275 (21 March 1997): 1793–95.

Taylor, Tell. "Down by the Old Mill Stream" (song). Chicago: Tell Taylor, 1910.

Thomas, Edith M. *The Round Year*. Boston: Houghton, Mifflin, 1886.

Thornton, Richard H. *An American Glossary*. Vol. 2 of 2 vols. Philadelphia: J. B. Lippincott Co., 1912.

Tomajczyk, S. F. *Dictionary of the Modern United States Military*. Jefferson, N.C.: McFarland and Co., 1996.

Upton, Harriet Taylor. *History of the Western Reserve*. Vol. 1 of 3 vols. Chicago: Lewis Publishing Co., 1910.

U.S. Government War-Savings Stamps: What They Are and Why You Should Buy Them. Washington: Government Printing Office, 1918.

Van Tassel, David D., and John J. Grabowski, eds. *The Encyclopedia of Cleveland History*. Bloomington: Indiana University Press, 1996.

Vander Veer, Norman R. *The Bluejacket's Manual: United States Navy*. Baltimore: Franklin Printing, 1917.

Variety's Film Reviews 1907–1920. Vol. 1 of ongoing series. New York: R. R. Bowker, 1983.

Veith, Ilza. *Hysteria: The History of a Disease.* Chicago: University of Chicago Press, 1965.

Voight, Ellen Bryant. *Kyrie.* New York: W. W. Norton, 1995.

Wallace, W. Stewart, ed. *The Macmillan Dictionary of Canadian Biography.* 4th ed. Toronto: Macmillan of Canada, 1978.

War Department Annual Reports, 1918. Vol. 1 of 3 vols. Washington: Government Printing Office, 1919.

Watson, Peter. *Twins.* New York: Viking Press, 1981.

Wekiwa Baptist Association. *Annual.* Wekiwa, Fla.: 1918.

Weston, May E. *The First 100 Years of Dover Schools.* Westlake, Ohio: Westlake Historical Society, 1969.

Williams, William W. *History of Ashtabula County, Ohio.* Philadelphia: Williams Brothers, 1878. Reproduced for The Ashtabula County, Ohio, Genealogical Society by Unigraphic, Inc., 1975.

Williams' Cincinnati Directory. Cincinnati: Cincinnati Directory Office, 1918.

Williams' Cincinnati Directory 1931–32. Cincinnati: Williams Directory Co., 1932.

Wilson, Charles Reagan, and William Ferris, eds. *Encyclopedia of Southern Culture.* Chapel Hill: University of North Carolina Press, 1989.

Manuscript and Typescript Sources

(This listing includes photocopies and microforms. Items within some entries are listed chronologically.)

"Abiding Memories." Funeral register for Lettie Perrin Randall from Webster Funeral Home (Geneva, Ohio). September 1954.

Ashtabula County Records and Deeds. *See* Perrin, Bertrand Henry; Perrin Family Farm.

Carlson, John. ALS to Dale Randall, 14 February 1997.

Census, U.S. Bureau of the. Twelfth U.S. Census of Population, 1900; Thirteenth Census, 1910; Fourteenth Census, 1920.

Deeds. *See* Perrin, Bertrand Henry; Perrin Family Farm.

Elliott, James J. ALS to Dale Randall, 13 June 1948.

Elliott, William. Typescript excerpt transcribed from a letter to Jacob Elliott, 1849.

Ernst Family Documents. Introductory note by Tom Mayberry. Somerset Record Office (Taunton, Somersetshire). DD/SWD.

———. Journal of T. H. Ernst of a Tour in Switzerland, Germany, Belgium and the Netherlands, 11 April–8 July 1815[?]. DD/SWD/4.

Hocking, Philip J. ALS to Dale Randall, 7 May 1998.

"Homer Township Cemetery." Midland County Michigan Cemetery Records. N.d.

Jensen, Carol A. ALS to Dale Randall, 17 October 1991.

———. "Henry Perrin and Jane G. Ody Family: A Brief Sketch." N.d.

———. Miscellaneous notes and photocopies, 1991–98.

Jensen, James L. Miscellaneous notes and photocopies, 16 September 1997.

Keyse, Fannie Elliott. "A Brief History of the Elliott Family by the Historian Written for the Annual Reunion, Sept. 15, 1923." Typescript.

Keyse, Richard B. ALS to Dale Randall, 27 January 1997.

———. ALS to Dale Randall, 13 May 1997.

Motley, Archie. ALS to Dale Randall, 29 May 1996.

[Parfitt]. "To the Memory of James Parfitt." An anonymous one-paragraph tribute [1842].

Pepin, June S. ALS to Dale Randall, 20 October 1997.

Perrin, Annie Elliott. ALS to Pearl Elliott, 21 July 1897.

———. ALS to Louisa Parfitt Elliott, 21 July 1897.

———. "Lest We Forget." Diary, 17 December 1917–31 December 1918.

Perrin, Bertrand Henry. "Warranty Deed." From Ellen Williamson and Bert and Grace Rose to Bertrand Perrin. *Ashtabula County Records of Deeds.* Vol. 243, p. 565, 10 June 1920.

———. "Last Will and Testament." Probate Court, No. 26298. Ashtabula County, Ohio, 16 September 1942.

———. Mrs. B.H.P. (Agnes). "Exceptions by the Widow to the Inventory." Probate Court, No. 26298. Ashtabula County, Ohio, 13 October 1944.

———. Mrs. B.H.P. (Agnes). "Exceptions Overruled." Probate Court, No. 26298. Ashtabula County, Ohio, 20 March 1945.

Perrin, Henry. AL (with ALS from Jane Ody Perrin) to all his children, 23 July 1883.

———. "Claim for Pension of Henry Perrin." Pension Certificate No. 887898. Cuyahoga County, Ohio, 27 June 1894.

———. "Deed to Henry Perrin." Probate Court. *Ashtabula County Records.* Vol. 172, p. 303, 9 May 1904.

———. "Warranty Deed." From Henry and Jane Perrin to Bertrand Perrin. Ashtabula County, Ohio. Vol. 296, p. 350, 13 July 1910.

———. Heirs of H.P. "Application for Letters of Administration." Probate Court of Cuyahoga County, Ohio, 29 March 1917.

Perrin, Henry B. ALS to Lettie Perrin, 1 April 1918.

———. ALS to Lettie Perrin, [?] April 1918.

———. ALS to Lettie Perrin, 8 April 1918.

———. ALS to Lettie Perrin, 10 April 1918.

———. ALS to Lettie Perrin, 14 April 1918.

———. ALS to Lettie Perrin, 19 April 1918.

———. ALS to Lettie Perrin, 20 April 1918.

———. ALS to Lettie Perrin, 21 April 1918.

———. ALS to Lettie Perrin, 8 May 1918.

———. ALS to Lettie Perrin, 14 May 1918.

———. ALS to Lettie Perrin, 23 May 1918.

———. ALS to Lettie Perrin, 26 May 1918.

———. ALS to Lettie Perrin, 31 May 1918.

———. ALS to Lettie Perrin, 1 June 1918.

———. ALS to Lettie Perrin, 29 June 1918.

———. ALS to Lettie Perrin, 10 July 1918.

———. ALS to Lettie Perrin, 21 August 1918.

———. ALS to Lettie Perrin, 12 September 1918.

———. ALS to Lettie Perrin, 20 September 1918.

———. ALS to Lettie Perrin, 27 September 1918.

———. ALS to Lettie Perrin, 29 September 1918.

———. ALS to Lettie Perrin, 5 October, 1918.

———. ALS to Lettie Perrin, 11 October 1918.

———. ALS to Lettie Perrin, 19 October 1918.

———. ALS to Lettie Perrin, 1 November 1918.

———. ALS to Lettie Perrin, 3 November 1918.

———. ALS to Lettie Perrin, 8 November 1918.

———. ALS to Lettie Perrin, 12 November 1918.

———. ALS to Lettie Perrin, 21 November 1918.

———. ALS to Lettie Perrin, 23 November 1918.

———. ALS to Lettie Perrin, 9 December 1918.

———. ALS to Lettie Perrin, 12 December 1918.

———. ALS to Lettie Perrin, 16 December 1918.

———. ALS to Lettie Perrin, 24 December 1918.

———. ALS to Lettie Perrin, 25 December 1918.

———. ALS to Lettie Perrin, 26 December 1918.

———. ALS to Lettie Perrin, 31 December 1918.

———. ALS to Lettie Perrin, 3 January 1919.

———. ALS to Lettie Perrin, 5 January 1919.

———. ALS to Lettie Perrin, 29 January 1919.

———. ALS to Lettie Perrin, 31 March 1919.

———. ALS to Lettie Perrin, 18 April 1919.

———. ALS to Lettie Perrin, 19 April 1919.

———. ALS to Lettie Perrin, 1 May 1919.

———. ALS to Lettie Perrin, 22 May 1919.

Perrin, Raymond A. Photograph album, ca. 1914–19.

———. "Application for Erecting 50 Poles and Stringing 50 Sections of Wire" (with receipt from The Illuminating Co., Painesville, Ohio), 4 October 1927.

Perrin, Raymond A., Jr. ALS to Dale Randall, 18 December 1978.

———. ALS to Dale Randall, 24 March 1996.

———. Miscellaneous notes, 28 August 1997.

———. ALS to Dale Randall, 17 September 1997.

Perrin Family Farm. Transfer of fifty-five acres on South Ridge, Geneva, Ohio, from Enoch Barnum (grantor) to Truman Watkins (grantee). *Ashtabula County Records*. Deed Vol. K, p. 240, 4 March 1831.

———. Transfer of three and 12/160 acres from Truman Watkins (grantor) to Lemuel Wiard (grantee). *Ashtabula County Records*. Deed Vol. 30, p. 9, 7 March 1844.

———. Transfer of three and 12/160 acres from Lemuel and Anna Wiard (grantors) to Erastus Carmer (grantee). *Ashtabula County Records*. Deed Vol. 37, p. 766, 29 April 1850.

———. "Mortgage Deed." From John Harley to William and Rebecca Johnson. *Ashtabula County Records*. Vol. 100, p. 282, 29 April 1911.

———. "Affidavit for Transfer." From William Williamson to Ellen Williamson and Grace Rose. *Ashtabula Record of Deeds*. Vol. 236, p. 15, 23 April 1919.

———. "Affidavit for Transfer." From John Harley to Robert Harley et al. *Ashtabula Record of Deeds*. Vol. 242, p. 8, 12 January 1920.

Randall, Lettie Perrin. Photograph album, ca. 1912–19.

———. ALS to Myron Welcome Randall, 1 November 1922.

———. ALS to Myron Welcome Randall, 6 December 1922.

———. ALS to Myron Welcome Randall, 24 June 1930.

———. ALS to Myron William Randall, 22 November 1944.

———. ALS to Myron William Randall, 25 September 1945.

———. ALS to Myron William Randall, 16 October 1945.

Randall, Myron Welcome. Diary, 7 June 1918–30 September 1920.

———. ALS to Lettie Perrin Randall, 13 October 1922.

———. Diary, 1 October 1920–11 February 1923.

———. Diary, 11 February 1923–30 September 1924.

———. Diary, 1 October 1924–19 August 1925.

———. Diary, 20 August 1925–9 July 1926.

———. Diary, 10 July 1926–31 December 1935.

———. Diary, 1 January 1936–3 December 1940.

Weston, Doris. ALS to Eileen Perrin, 10 February 1974.

———. ALS to Dale Randall, 24 February 1997.

———. ALS to Dale Randall, 27 February 1997.

Index

Dawson's Springs, Ky., 318n
Dayton, Ohio, 51, 283n
Daytona and Daytona Beach, Fla., 2,104, **105**, 108
Dean, Frank C., 296n
Dean, Louis, 213n
Decoration Day, 182
DeLand, Fla., 105
Delaware, Ohio, 228n
Delaware River, 254
DeLine, Drucilla Baker McCreery ("Drucy"), 157, 352
Denver, Colo., 187n
Detroit, Mich., 157n, 306n
diary, xvi–xvii, xxv–**xxvi**–xxviii, 1, 17, **110**–11, **270–71, 300–301**
Dickey Avenue School (Warren), 51n
diphtheria, 70, 233n, 335n
District School, The (drama), 192
Dixie Highway, 91, **92**, 96
Dobson, Edna. *See* Herr
Dobson, Elizabeth Perrin ("Bessie"), 43n, 44, 98n, 108, 185, 204, 238, 246n, 353
Dobson, Fred, 98, 99, 100, **101**, 353
Dobson, George, 185n, 353
Dobson, Hilda Holke, 99n, 353
Dobson, Vernon, 99n, 353
Dodwell, Edward, 9n
dogs, **165**, 210n, **220**, 237, 245
Dome Theatre (Ashtabula), 183, 198n, 235n
dominoes, 55, 145, 152, 153, 154, 155, 156, 160, 168, 170, 171, 191, 200, 206, 280, 297, 309, 312, 314
Donaldson, Dr. (Key West), 349
Donnelly's store (Ashtabula), 252n
Dorothea (ship), 264n–265n
Dovell, James Elmore, 3n
Dover and Dover Center, Ohio, 11, 63, 102n, 156n, 213n, 296, 333n
Dover Center South (school), **17**, 18
Dover High School, 18
Dover Methodist Episcopal Church, 11, **12**
Dovid, Mr. and Mrs., 108
"Down by the Old Mill Stream" (song), 65, **66**
draft, military, 21, 240, 244n, 259n, 286, 292n
drag (farm tool), 148, **149**
Drake, Sir Francis, 77n
Drake, Joseph Rodman, 182n
drill (farm tool), 154, 179
drought, 58, 213, 214, 218, 219, 221, 222, 223, 229, 230, 232, 233
ducks, 80, 325
Due, John F., 33n
Dunkirk, N.Y., 45n
Durrance, Charles L., 87, 109

eagle, 182
Eagle Hill, 26n

Earle, Thomas, 10
Earlham College, 50
East Knoyle, England, 8n
Easter, 138, 140
Eastman's grocery (Ashtabula), 145n
Eaton, Emma Florence, 26n
eclipse, 187
Eddie's Grill (Geneva-on-the-Lake), 232n
Edith Thomas Garden Club (Geneva), 135n
elections, 233, 234n, 285
electricity, 5, 129n, 132n, 301, **308**, 320
Elliott, Alberta Coffman ("Bertie"), 117n, 181n, 338, 352
Elliott, Annie Luella. *See* Perrin
Elliott, Drucilla. *See* DeLine
Elliott, Eliza, 8n
Elliott, Ella Spicer, 157n, 348, 352
Elliott, Esther Susan. *See* Weston
Elliott, Fannie Idella. *See* Keyse
Elliott, Florence, 116, 181, 213, 352
Elliott, Frank Riddle, 11, 13, 157n, 352
Elliott, Fred William, 206, 352
Elliott, Gilbert Wilson, 213n, 333n, 334, 352
Elliott, Hattie Rood, 352
Elliott, Jacob, 8, 352
Elliott, James John, 9n, 230n, 340n, 352
Elliott, James Vernon ("J.J."), 230, 352
Elliott, John, 8n
Elliott, Lettie Louisa. *See* Bentley
Elliott, Louisa Parfitt, xxix, 8, 9–10, 11, 12–**15**, 18, **333**, 334, 335, 336, 352
Elliott, Marion, 213n
Elliott, Mary Susanna (Sarah). *See* Baker
Elliott, Mildred, 213n
Elliott, Ollie Alexander, 207n, 352
Elliott, Pearl Hall, xxix, 213n, 333–35, 352
Elliott, Susan Virginia Bailus, 209n, 352
Elliott, Susanna Maidment, 8, 352
Elliott, Thomas Henry, 117n, 181n, 339n, 352
Elliott, Walter, 14, 209n, 352
Elliott, William, 7–8, 10–13, 18, 333n, **334**, 335, 352
Elliott, Winifred, 181n, 213, 352
Elliott family reunions, 157n, 296
Ellis, William D., 11n
Ellsworth, Catherine T., 30n, 33n, 45n, 242n
Emery Arcade (Cincinnati), 128n
Emery Hotel (Cincinnati), 126
Erie, Pa., 266n
Erie Canal, 11n
Ernst, Elizabeth Strachey, 8, 9n
Ernst, Harriet Ann, 9
Ernst, Henry, 9
Ernst, Thomas Henry, 8–9
Etty, Horace, 93n
Etty, Jane, 93n, 123
Etty, Pearly, 93n

Geneva Market, 138
Geneva Metal Wheel Company, 133n, 150n, 215n
Geneva-on-the-Lake, Ohio, 44, 45, 113n, 190n, 222n, 223n, 232
Geneva Savings Bank, 243n
Geneva State Park, 34n
Geneva Tool Shop, 226n
Geneva Township Park, 45, 214
"Georgie Morgan Played the Organ" (song), 54
Gerard, James W., 69, 213n
Gilmore, J. R., 5n
Gleason, William J., 185n
Glenn Hotel (Chattanooga), 126
Glines, Mr. (of Thompson), 188
Glines, B., 188n
Glover, P. M., 132n
Glover, Mrs. P. M. (*née* Lowe), 132
gloves, 42, 101
goats, 17n, 290n
Godwin, David, 4n
Gollin, Pearl Malle, 17
Gordan, Robert, 223n
Grabowski, John J., 11n, 185n
Grand Hotel (Cincinnati), 74
Grand River, 26
Granger, Gideon, Jr., 239n
granges, 133n, 238n. *See also* North Star Grange
Grant, H. Roger, 74n
Grant, Ulysses S., 126n–127n
grapefruit, 79, 80, 84, 107, 108, 116, 339
grapes, 11, 32, 40, 235n, 257, 266, 324, 325
Graphaphone, 130
Grassmere Poultry Farm (Geneva), 135n
Gray, Arthur, 78n
Gray, C. W., 77n
Gray, Frank, 78n
Gray, Ralph, 76n
Gray, Randal, 287n, 290n
Gray's Hall (Geneva), 292n
Great Lakes, xxi. *See also* Lake Erie; Lake Ontario
Great Lakes, Ill., 144, 337
Great Lakes Naval Training Station, 22, 23, 61, 144, 158n, 159n, 162n, 168n, 177, 193, 202n, 225n, 226n, 248n, 337, 340n
Green, Delma Ford, 87n
greens (vegetables), 41, 158, 164, 168n
Greenville, Pa., 148n
Greenwood, C. and J., 8n
Gregory, H. B., 173n, 243n
Gregory, Jennie, 173n, 322n
Gregory's Hall (Geneva), 293n
Grieg, Edvard, 236n
Griffith, Corrine, 198n
Griffith, Gordon, 69, 183n
Griffiths, D., 10n–11n, 156n

Grim, James S., 149, 207n
grippe, 94
Guenther, Calla Beeman, 233
Guenther, Melvin, 233n
Guenther, William, 233
Guenther, William, Jr., 233n
Guernsey (Channel Isle), 9
gypsies, 289n

Hadsell, R. S., 17, 19n
Hagedorn, Judy W., 16n
Haig, Douglas, 287n
Halifax River (Florida), 104
Hall, Charles, 214n
Hall, Clinton C., 116.
Hall, Pearl. *See* Elliott
Hall, Sarah M. K., 116n
ham, 234, 296n
Hamilton, Ont., 66n
Hampton Roads, Va., 313n
Hanneman, Charlotte Chapman, 174, 283, 299
Hanneman, Edward J., 299
Hanson, Adna, 247n
Hanson, Timothy, 207n
Hanson, Viola, 276, 349n
Happy Message to Northerners, A (pamphlet), 3
Harley, Eliza, 237n
Harley, John T., 145, 152, 153, 154, 156, 174, 176n, 185, 237n
Harley, Lyda, 145n
Harley, Rob, 237n
Harley Brothers Hardware (Geneva), 255
Harley's Four Piece Orchestra, 292n
Harpersfield Township, Ohio, 145n, 188, 226n
Harris, W. J., Co. (St. Augustine), 77
harrow (farm tool), 148n, **149**
Harte, Bret, xxii
Hartman, Mary Joiners, 171, 183, 192
Hartman, William, 192n–193n
Hartner, Alzada, 43, 234, 238, 248, 251, 252, 258, 266, 275, 289, 292, 295, 297, 299
Hartner, W. J., 43, 234n, 238n, 257, 266, 275, 289
Hartsgrove, Ohio, 47
Harvey, George Charles, 271
Harvey, Will, 26
Harvey, Will Wallace, 6n
Hasenpflug, Arthur, 186n
Hasenpflug, George, 243n, 348n
Hasenpflug, John, 243, 265, 267n, 268n
Hasenpflug, Leroy, 243n
Hasenpflug, Mildred, 243n
Hasenpflug family, 243n, 252
Haskin, June, 18n
Hastings, Fla., 76
Hatcher, Harlan, 45n

Lowe, William E., 132n, 254n, 255
Lowe family, 43, 137, 144, 276, 281, 297, 301, 316
Lowrie, Joseph, 324n
Lyceum lectures, 265
Lyman, Lyda, 283n

MacAdoo, William Gibbs, 337
macaroni, xxi
McClure's (Ashtabula store), 247n
McCormack, John, 68
McCreery, Charles, 157n
MacDonald, Rosina. *See* Jensen
McFell, B. G., 124n
MacKaye, Steele, 207n
McMillan, Ellen, 214n
McMillen, Wheeler, 141n
McNutt, Howard, 236n
Macon, Ga., 125
McPhail, Archie, 175n
Madame Sherry (musical), 272
Madden, Edward, 282
Maddox, Mr. (later husband of Bertie Elliott), 181n
Madison, Ohio, 102n, 140n, 227n, 238, 248n, 249n, 275n, 338n
Mailey (Maley), Mr. and Mrs., 209
Maitland, Fla., 96n
Majestic Theater (Ashtabula), **28**, 69, 160n, 161, 183, 198n, 218, 223n, 231, 235, 256n
Mallone, Shelley Boyd, 341, 342
Malmesbury, England, 4n–5n
Maltbie, Curtis, 272n
Maltbie, Mr. and Mrs. James W., 272n, 340n
Maltbie, Mary, 247n
Maltbie, Ross D., 272n, 276n
Man Hater, The (film), 183
Manhattan Restaurant (Cincinnati), 74
Mann, Willis T., 133n
Man's World, A (film), 260n
manure, 231, 294
Map of the State of Ohio . . . 1918, xxx–xxxi
maple trees, 4, 79n, 135n, 212
Marble Palace (Geneva barber shop), 324n
"Marching through Georgia" (song), 215n
Marden, Frank L., 103n
Marden, Melissa, 100, 103
Marion, Francis, 77n
Marks, Louis T., 115n
Marlatt, C. L., 91n
Marquis, Albert Nelson, 338n
Marsh, Mae, 69
Marsh, Robert R., 322n
Marshall, Anna, 249
Marshall, William S., 74n, 249n
Martin, Mrs. (Elliotts' friend), 13
Martin, A. B., Sons (Geneva realtor), 255n
Martin, Frank W., 255

Martins Ferry, xxi
Marvin (family friend), xx, 118
Masons (Freemasons), 139n
Massena (Ashtabula barber shop), 324n
Massillon, Ohio, 229n
Matchett, Charity H., 109n
Matchett, J. W., 96n
Mathews, Mitford M., 87n
Mauslynwere, Minnie. *See* Hoffman
May (visitor), xx, 214
May, Gordon V., 175n
Maytime (musical), 68
meat, 107, 293, 296, 298, 312, 315, 316. *See also* bacon; chicken dinners; ham
Medina, Ohio, 90, 129n
Memorial Day, 182
Menace, The (film), 198n
Mendelssohn, Felix, 236n
Menéndez, Pedro, 77n
menopause, 54n
Merry Matrons' Flinch Club (Geneva), 228n
Methodists, 63, 87n, 88n, 90, 96n
Michel, Bernice Jane. *See* Perrin
Michel, Effie, 45, 313
Michel, George, 45n
Michel, Homer, 240n, 278n, 310n–311n, 313n
Michel, Jay, 313n
Michel, Rose Carter, 45n
Midland County, Mich., 156n, 157n, 306n
Milan, Ohio, 115, 122n
Miles, James Samuel, 9n
milk house, 35, **219**, **319**
milking, 29
Miller, Belle, 279
Miller, Elmer S., 279, 283
Miller, Kim, 139
Miller, M. E., 290n
Miller, Roy, 139n
Milwaukee, Wis., 11
Minelli, Frank P., 190n
Minelli Brothers (stock company), 190n, 291n
Miner, Jack, 18n
Miss Topsy Turvy (comedy), 124n
Missionary Alliance (Pine Castle), 96n
Missionary Ridge Battlefield, 126
mistletoe, 114
Mitiwanga, Ohio, **205**, 206, 221n
Mittler, Peter, 13n
Moffett, W. A., 202n
Montville, Ohio, 46n
Mooney family, 115, 122
"Moonlight Bay" (song), 282
More, Hannah, 42
Morey, R. B., 324n
Morgan, George, 54n
Morgan, Jenny, 54n–55n

Morgan Center School (Ashtabula), 192n
mosquitoes, 344
Mothers' Day, 169, 171
Motley, Archie, 338n
Mt. Haley, Mich., 306n
Mt. Pleasant Cemetery (Geneva), 34n, 188n, 276n, 331
movies. *See* picture shows
mowing. *See* hay; lawn mowing
Muir, Charles, 142n, 224
mulberries, 122, 123
mules, 5, 36, **159**, 164, **165**, 190, 290n, 291n
Mumaw, Agnes. *See* Perrin
Munger Block (Geneva), 173n
Munich, Adrienne, 57n
Murphy, B. M., 290n
Murray, Elizabeth, 272
mushrooms, 41, 253, 257
music, 6, 64–68, 86, 150n–151n, 160, 173n, 175n, 176n, 214, 234, 236, 239, 252n, 265n, 271, 275, 281, 283, 292n, 293n, 311n, 313. *See also* bands; piano
Mutt and Jeff (cartoon), 198n
"My Blue Heaven" (song), 65
My Four Years in Germany (book and film), 69, 213
"My Isle of Golden Dreams" (song), 68
Myers, Hattie. *See* Chapman
Myers, W. A., 26n

Nan of Music Mountain (film), 200n
National Lamp Company, 174n
Naval Reserve Corps (Akron), 22
Navy, U.S., 40n, 184n, 223n, 265n, 277n, 311n. *See also* Great Lakes Naval Training Station; Perrin, Henry, military service
Neely, Ford, 286
New Cambridge, Conn., 31n
New Jersey, 184
New Smyrna, Fla., 104
New Year's Day, 70, 84n, 314n, 316
New York (state), 230
New York, N.Y., 10, 348n
New York Central Railroad, 22, 74, 133n, 209n, 244n, 299n
New York, Chicago, and St. Louis Railroad Co. *See* Nickel Plate Railroad
Newell, Ellen, 2, 94n, 108, 111, 116, 122, 123, 124, 162, 243, 250, 251, 256
Newell, Lester C., 94n
Newell orange grove, 94, 97, 113, 116, 122
Newlin, Jessie Lee, 241n, 243n
Nickel Plate Railroad, 33, 45n, 143, 320, 322
"nigger" (word), 82
Noel, Mrs. John, 93, 95, 119, 120
Nolan, Tom, farm, 339n
Norfolk, Va., 62, 291, 294, 297, 302, 349

Norris, Emma, 53, 76, 80, 81, 82, 84, 85, 87, 88, 89, 123
Norris, Lee L., 76, 80, 81, 84, 87, 88, 89
Norris, Madge, 76, 81, 85, 86, 88, 228
Norris family, 74, 89, 90
North Olmsted, Ohio, 102n
North Ridge, described, 32
North Star Grange, 22, 26, 133n, 175n, 176n, 236n, 239n, 266n
Northeastern Ohio Teachers Association, 23, 347n
Northern lights (aurora borealis), 119
Northern Michigan Asylum for the Insane, 157n
Norton, Charles Ledyard, 77n, 84n, 100n
Nova Scotia, 88
nuts and nutting, 271, 347–48

oats, 5, 30n, 136n, 148, 154, 212n, 223, 224, 229
Oberlin College, 213n
Odd Fellows, 12n, 150n, 192n; band, 175, 176, 215n, 247n, 288n, 291n
Ody, Anne Worville, 5n, 353
Ody, Jane Gertrude. *See* Perrin
Ody, John, 5n, 353
Offenbach, Jacques, 68
"Oh You Lovable Chile" (song), 284
Ohio, 6–7, 216n, 269n, 277n, 286n, 287
Ohio, map of northeastern (1918), xxx–xxxi
"Ohio Boys" (march), 176n
Ohio Dry Federation, 286
Ohio River, 66
Ohio State University, 296n
Ohio Wesleyan, 228n
okra, 344
onions, 23, 258, 266, 273
Opie, Iona, 55n
Opie, Peter, 55n
Orange County, Fla., 3n, 79n, 80n, 91n
oranges, 6, 39, 79, 80, 82, 84, 88, 89, 94, 99, 103, 104, 107, 112, 115, 116, 347
organ, 116, 160n
Orlando, Fla., 3n, 78, 79, 80, 84, 87, 88, 89, 91n, 94, 95, 97, 98, 99, 100, 101, 104, 107, 108, 110, 116, 117, 119, 120, 122, 124
Orvis, Ralph Thompson, 350
Outerbridge, William, 10n
outhouse, 36–37
"Over There" (song), 66
Overland. *See* automobiles
Overland-Ashtabula Co., 139n
Overseas Railway, 125n, 345

Packard, Winthrop, 82n
Painesville, Ohio, 33n, 150n, 243n, 324
painting, 37, 190, 191, 193n, 199
Paisley, Elisabeth Mary, 30n
Palatka, Fla., 78

Soliloquy of a Farmer's Wife

Mrs B. H. Perrin
B. H. Perrin